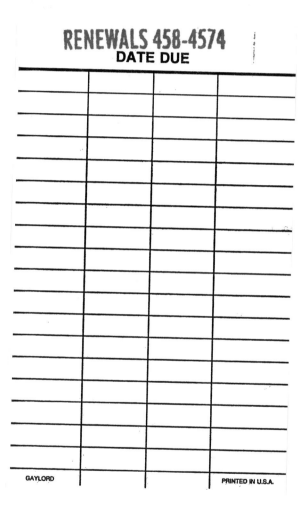

RENEWALS 458-4574
DATE DUE

GAYLORD			PRINTED IN U.S.A.

Yevgeny Mravinsky

The Noble Conductor

Gregor Tassie

THE SCARECROW PRESS, INC.
Lanham, Maryland • Toronto • Oxford
2005

SCARECROW PRESS, INC.

Published in the United States of America
by Scarecrow Press, Inc.
A wholly owned subsidiary of
The Rowman & Littlefield Publishing Group, Inc.
4501 Forbes Boulevard, Suite 200, Lanham, Maryland 20706
www.scarecrowpress.com

PO Box 317
Oxford
OX2 9RU, UK

British Library Cataloguing in Publication Information Available

Library of Congress Cataloging-in-Publication Data

Tassie, Gregor, 1953–
  Yevgeny Mravinsky : the noble conductor / Gregor Tassie.
      p. cm.
  Includes bibliographical references (p.   ), discography, and index.
  ISBN 0-8108-5427-9 (hardcover : alk. paper)
   1. Mravinsky, Yevgeny, 1903–. 2. Conductors (Music)—Soviet Union—Biography. I.
Title.
ML422.M75T37 2005
784.2'092—dc22   2004026377

∞™ The paper used in this publication meets the minimum requirements of American
National Standard for Information Sciences—Permanence of Paper for Printed Library
Materials, ANSI/NISO Z39.48-1992.
Manufactured in the United States of America.

Contents

Chronology   v

1   The Mrovinskys   1

2   "Zhenya"   14

3   The Conservatoire   26

4   "A Future Conductor of World Class"   41

5   The Leningrad Philharmonic   52

6   The Year 1937   64

7   The Chief Conductor   77

8   Evacuation   97

9   The Great War   106

10   The Great Victory   125

11   The Year 1953   150

12   Inna   162

13   The Unfortunate Thirteenth   194

14   The Years of Crisis   203

15   The Patriarch   225

16   The Last Concerts   246

Appendix A: Andrey Zolotov Interview of Yevgeny Mravinsky 257

Appendix B: Selected Discography 261

Bibliography 263

Index 272

About the Author 280

Chronology

1903 **22 May (4 June new style)**: Birth of Yevgeny to Alexander Konstantinovich (1869–1918) and Yelizaveta Nikolayevna Mravinsky, née Filkova (1871–1957), in St. Petersburg.

1909 Yevgeny is taken to a performance of *Sleeping Beauty* at the Mariinsky Theatre under the direction of Albert Coates and begins piano lessons.

1914 Begins studies at the Alexander 11 Gymnasium.

1918 **30 October**: Alexander Mravinsky dies; the family is evicted from its home by Red Guards and moves to 12 Theatre Square. Yevgeny begins work as a mime at the Mariinsky Theatre.

1920 **1 September**: Yevgeny enrolls in the Biology Faculty of Petrograd University.

1921 Begins work as a *répétiteur* at the Vaganova Dance School.

1922 Mravinsky marries Marianna Schwalck (1888–1979).

1923 Mravinsky's application to enter the double-bass class of the Petrograd Conservatoire is rejected.

1924 **1 September**: Following an appeal by his aunt, Mravinsky enters the composition class of Professor Chernov at the Petrograd Conservatoire. His first and only child, Yelena, is born.

1927 Mravinsky graduates from the composition class of Vladimir Shcherbachyov and begins his studies in the conducting class of Nikolay Malko.

1929 **4 March**: Mravinsky's compositions are performed in public for the first time. Transfers to Alexander Gauk's conducting class. **July 19**: First public concert as a conductor.

1931   Mravinsky completes his studies at the Conservatoire and begins employment as a junior conductor at the State Ballet Theatre. **June 30**: Makes his debut with the Leningrad Philharmonic Orchestra.

1932   **20 September**: Makes his debut at the ballet conducting *The Sleeping Beauty.*

1935   **May**: Makes his debut at the Bolshoi Theatre on tour with the Kirov Ballet.

1937   **21 November**: Directs the world premiere of Shostakovich's Fifth Symphony in D minor.

1938   **March**: Makes his first recording in Moscow with the Philharmonic, recording the Fifth Symphony. Marries his second wife, Olga Alexeyevna Karpova (1903–1990). **1 October**: Wins the All-Union Conducting Competition in Moscow and is appointed chief conductor of the Leningrad Philharmonic Orchestra.

1939   **21 November**: Gives world premiere of Shostakovich's Sixth Symphony in B major.

1940   **20 May:** Conducts the first concerts by the Leningrad Philharmonic in Moscow and makes a TV recording with the Kirov Ballet.

1941   **4 October**: Opens season of concerts by the Philharmonic at Novosibirsk in Siberia following evacuation after the outbreak of war with Germany.

1943   **3 November**: Mravinsky directs the world premiere of Shostakovich's Eighth Symphony in Moscow. He turns down the conductorship of the USSR State Symphony.

1944   **21 October**: Mravinsky opens new season of concerts in Leningrad following the lifting of the siege of the city.

1945   **3 November**: Mravinsky conducts the premiere of Shostakovich's Ninth Symphony.

1946   **March**: Makes his first foreign concert tour, to Helsinki, and in May conducts at the Prague Spring Festival. Awarded the Stalin Prize First Class.

1947   **11 October**: Mravinsky conducts the world premiere of Prokofiev's Sixth Symphony in Leningrad.

1948   **3–5 March**: Mravinsky defends the symphonies of Shostakovich at the Composers Union.

1949   **15 November**: Mravinsky gives the world premiere of *Song of the Forests* by Shostakovich in Leningrad. Mravinsky is criticized for his repertoire policy.

1952   **March**: Death of Alexandra Kollontay and his teacher, Vladimir Shcherbachyov. Meeting with Inna Serikova.

1953   **17 December**: Mravinsky directs the world premiere of Shostakovich's Tenth Symphony.

1954 **1 January**: Awarded title of peoples artist.

1955 **29 October**: Conducts the premiere of Shostakovich's Violin Concerto (with David Oistrakh). Conducts at Prague Spring Festival.

1956 **May–June**: Major tour of Western Europe and records Tchaikovsky symphonies for Deutsche Grammophon.

1957 **3 November**: Leningrad premiere of Shostakovich's Eleventh Symphony. Death of Mravinsky's mother.

1959 **4 October**: Directs the premiere of Shostakovich's Cello Concerto (with Rostropovich).

1960 **September–November**: Major European tour beginning at Edinburgh International Festival and records Tchaikovsky symphonies for DGG. Marries his third wife, Inna Mikhailovna Serikova (1923–1964).

1961 **25 September**: World premiere of Shostakovich's Twelfth Symphony. Mravinsky is awarded the Lenin Prize.

1962 Final studio recording. Major tour of North America. Ban on foreign touring by Philharmonic. First symptoms of Serikova's leukemia.

1963 **26 October**: Directs the USSR premiere of Sibelius's Third Symphony.

1964 **1 July**: Death of Inna Serikova. Directs the USSR premiere of Hindemith's *Harmony of the World*.

1965 **29 October**: Directs the USSR premiere of Stravinsky's *Agon*. Major tour of Moscow at Festival of Leningrad Music.

1966 Celebrates Shostakovich's sixtieth birthday. Major tour of Italy and Austria.

1967 Marries his fourth wife, Alexandra Mikhailovna Vavilina (1928–). Tour of Prague, France, and Switzerland.

1970 Mravinsky leads a major tour of the German Democratic Republic marking the Beethoven Bicentenary.

1972 **5 May**: Leningrad premiere of Shostakovich's Fifteenth Symphony. Ban is revoked for major tour of West Germany.

1973 **3 June**: Awarded the Hero of Socialist Labour on seventieth birthday. Beginning of series of TV films. First tour of Japan.

1975 **9 August**: Death of Shostakovich. Dedication of season of concerts to his music.

1977 Award of Arthur Nikisch prize, making him the first non-German to be awarded.

1978 Award of honorary membership of the Society of Friends of Music in Vienna.

1982 **18 November**: Centenary of Philharmonic is marked by concerts in Moscow.

1983   **19 March**: Mravinsky directs a centenary concert for the Philhar-
            monic. Final film by Andrey Zolotov, of Shostakovich's Eighth
            Symphony.
1984   **16 September**: Directs opening concert of Shostakovich Festival
            in Duisburg, Germany. Final concert recording of Shostakovich's
            Twelfth Symphony.
1986   **20 November**: Penultimate concert at the Leningrad Philharmonic,
            of Wagner preludes and overtures.
1987   **6 March**: Final concert, of Schubert's *Unfinished Symphony* and
            Brahms's Fourth Symphony, at the Philharmonic. **November**:
            Heart attack and hospitalization in Vienna.
1988   **19 January**: Following return to Leningrad, Yevgeny Mravinsky
            dies at home.

Chapter One

The Mrovinskys

"To Serve the Emperor"

Founded in 1703 on the Neva delta, St. Petersburg was built as a citadel against attacks from Russia's historical enemies: Sweden, Finland, Poland, and Germany. The fortress on the wind-swept, barren mudflats was fashioned as a modern conurbation within several short decades, the finest architects of Italy, France, and Germany designing ornate palaces for the new aristocracy. The squares, wide avenues, and buildings of the city followed an ornate Italian design, classical and severe in style, the canals and river embankments giving the city the name of "Venice of the North." As a nucleus for business and commerce, Russia's window on the West was the most opulent, precocious, and enlightened metropolis in the empire.

It was here that the aristocracy flourished amid the smoky chimneys of industrialization. It was in St. Petersburg that the giant European entrepreneurs Siemens and Hals, Thornton and Laferme, Grapp and Beck, Maxwell and Frank, Singer and McCormick advanced their métier. Here the Academy of Sciences was founded under Peter in 1717 and great scholars, including Lomonosov, Mendeleyev, and Pavlov, lived and worked. On the stage of the Imperial Theatre, Mikhail Glinka produced the first nationalist operas, *A Life for the Tsar* and *Ruslan and Lyudmila*, founding the school of Russian classical music. During the reign of Alexander II, Anton Rubinstein opened the first Conservatoire, Tchaikovsky being among its first students, and the "mighty handful" of Balakirev, Borodin, Cuì, Musorgsky, and Rimsky-Korsakov opened a fresh, colorful page in Russian music based on Western technique and yet using ethnic music of the Russian, Central Asian, and Caucasian peoples.

The Mrovinsky family tree (as the name was originally spelled) reveals blood from Germany and Sweden, and the earliest known members took part in Alexander's campaigns against Napoleon Bonaparte.[1] The Mrovinsky

1

credo of "serving the emperor" was a proud and glorious one bonding refined young men, a tradition carried down through the family. The career of Konstantin Iosifovich Mrovinsky, born in 1829, was one of remarkably contrasting fortune; following in his father's footsteps, he enrolled at the Mikhailovsky military engineering school, where among his fellow students was the young Fyodor Dostoyevsky. During the Anglo-French campaigns, Lieutenant-Engineer Mrovinsky was appointed chief military engineer of the Petropavlovsk fortress at Kamchatka in the Russian Far East. Arriving at the citadel on 24 July 1854, Mrovinsky had only three weeks to fortify the defenses of the military base before the opponents attacked. He was seriously wounded in the ensuing melee and is mentioned in dispatches as displaying great courage and adherence to duty.[2] Following his recovery, he was promoted to captain-engineer and returned to St. Petersburg in 1858.[3]

Mrovinsky's war wounds exempted him from further active service, and he decided to settle down in the capital, in 1859 marrying the Finnish girl Alexandra Massalina. Their early years together bore all the signs of a prosperous and happy marriage; the first child, Alexander, was born within a year and was followed by two daughters, Adéle and Yevgeniya. Despite the couple's ostentatiously prosperous match, Alexandra began to tire of her husband, and the harmony in the marriage gradually dissolved.[4] To gain an understanding of the consequences of this affair, we must turn back to the period before Mrovinsky's wedding.

Alexandra Massalina's father was a serf who had bought his freedom and at the age of eighteen, to make his fortune, walked all the way to St. Petersburg.[5] Massalin established his trading enterprise there and, for a spouse, found a young Russian aristocrat, Krylovaya, taking the vows of marriage in a Russian Orthodox ceremony. Massalin, having acquired respectability, returned to Finland with his new wife and set up home at the Karelian town of Kuusa near Vyborg in the northwest, which was well served by river links to both Helsinki and St. Petersburg. Here Massalin developed a profitable business trading to timber merchants in the two capitals; the trade was so successful that his timber paved the streets of St. Petersburg.[6] Massalin's wife bore him a son and two daughters, and when the girls were of age, they were taken off to find good society matches in the imperial capital.

Mikhail Domontovich was a young guardsman serving in the Pavlovsky regiment; as in Tolstoy's *Anna Karenina*, it was the custom to attend the Italian opera at the Mariinsky Theatre to seek out the beautiful young women of the aristocracy. It was here that Domontovich first caught sight of the young Alexandra Massalina with her sister and mother—who together merited the reputation in society circles of "the three northern beauties"—in their box at the Mariinsky. The young guards officer proved more honorable than Tolstoy's Vronsky; at once falling in love, he resolved to ask for Alexandra's hand, yet met with an abrupt rejection from the old Massalin. Domontovich was too high-society for Alexandra's family—the marriage of a distinguished guards officer of the Pavlovsky regiment to the daughter of a *nouveau riche* merchant was improper.[7]

Indeed the Domontovich family was among the most illustrious in the empire and could trace its lineage back to the thirteenth century.[8] The earliest known family member was Prince Dovmont of Pskov, a Lithuanian pagan who Timothy of Pskov had converted to Christianity and whose father-in-law was Alexander Nevsky. Dovmont was ruler of the ancient kingdom of Pskov and one of the semimythical, saintly warriors to emerge during the Russian princedom's defense of its independence against the Teutonic Knights. Dovmont died from the plague in 1299, and his ceremonial sword is still kept in the Pskov monastery.[9] The descendants continued to serve the Russian cause after moving to Ukraine, where the family name was Ukrainized. Nonetheless, the olden times were not forgotten; when a Domontovich returned to the town of Pskov, the church bells were rung in commemoration of entrance in the hometown of the ancient lineage.[10]

The old Massalin, the self-made man from Finland who had married into the Russian *beau monde* and built his own mansion in the style of the finest country houses of the day, feared a public scandal when Mikhail Domontovich appeared at his door. The liaison ended suddenly when Domontovich was called to military service in the Balkans. For the old Massalin, Domontovich was conveniently out of the way, at least for the time being; therefore, when Konstantin Mrovinsky turned up shortly afterward, Massalin had no trouble accepting him as a son-in-law, *hors de combat* and a high-status career in the civil service to his credit.

It was thus that in 1870, following ten years of wedlock, a chance meeting at a society ball led to Alexandra renewing her relationship with Domontovich. They began an *affaire d'amour*, and Alexandra had already conceived a child by her lover by the time Mrovinsky discerned his wife's infidelity. Alexandra demonstrably left Mrovinsky, taking the daughters with her to the family home of Kuusa. Regardless of the social consequences, Konstantin Mrovinsky initiated proceedings against his wife.

For the age, divorce was unheard of, and the affair assumed scandal proportions, enjoying its supporters and opponents. A special sitting of the Holy Synod was required to judge the matter, yet the annulment after many months, on grounds of adultery, arrived quickly with intercession by court officials, though only after the birth of a girl to the two lovers in March 1872.[11] If the conception had already ripped asunder the Mrovinskys, the new daughter, christened Alexandra, was to have a decisive role in the future of her country. Now with old Massalin dead, Mikhail and Alexandra quickly married, and they lived in *beau idéal* for the next thirty years.[12] Domontovich brought up the Mrovinsky daughters while Alexander stayed with his father.[13] Now, his career having survived the damage done by his wife's desertion—in what became a cause célèbre—Major-General Mrovinsky was to suffer yet another blow. In March 1881, by the Malaya Sadovaya and the bank of the Griboyedova Canal, an area under Mrovinsky's jurisdiction, a bomb was thrown at the Emperor Alexander II's carriage, and he died in great agony. Grinevsky, who threw the explosives, expired immediately, while his accomplices and a host of other suspects were arrested. It was wholly unexpected when Mrovinsky was among those taken into custody.[14]

Mrovinsky was considered negligent in allowing access to the underground passages near the scene of the assassination. The secret police had requested Mrovinsky to carry out an inspection of subterranean tunnels, and it was assumed that he had failed to discover those that the plotters had used.[15] There was scanty evidence for the prosecution, nevertheless Mrovinsky was found guilty—it was clear that the authorities needed a scapegoat—and he was sentenced to twenty years penal servitude.[16] Few doubted Mrovinsky's loyalty and dedicated service to the emperor, and the emperor's widow, Alexandra, attempted to save him by urging Mikhail Domontovich to appeal to the new monarch—Alexander III.[17]

The new tsar was averse to pardoning Konstantin Mrovinsky, but rather than exile him to Siberia, he dispatched Mrovinsky to the town of Archangelsk in the Far North. Some twenty years later, Mrovinsky settled in Moscow, and he outlived by three years the Romanov Dynasty that he and his ancestors had so loyally served.[18] The matter led to Mrovinsky's son Alexander changing his surname by just one letter—from Mrovinsky to Mravinsky—and at once the new family name appeared more aristocratic and noble. One other member of the family, Jenny, was to attain recognition throughout Europe for her magnificent artistic gifts, but by the spring of 1886, the once proud and celebrated family name of Mrovinsky had all but vanished.

Yevgeniya (Jenny) Konstantinovna Mravinskaya was born on 4 February (16 February new style) 1864. Jenny's education began at home, where she was taught by her mother, with her elder sister and her brother. Alexandra's youngest child by Konstantin Mrovinsky, Jenny revealed musical gifts when she was three years old, singing arias and lullabies with her English nanny, and her first music lessons were with the German piano teacher Frau Gattendorf. At twelve, Jenny joined the Yekaterinskaya Gymnasium in the fourth-year class—advanced for her years—where she learned her mother's native tongue of Finnish, along with Italian, English, French, and German. Her stepfather was appointed provisional governor of the Bulgarian city of Tyrnova and later military consul in Sofia, thereby interrupting her studies for a whole year. In Bulgaria, Jenny's hours were spent in parties and picnics in the mountains and countryside around the city; Jenny sang at receptions and parties hosted by her stepfather. The sojourn ended abruptly when Domontovich was suspected of sympathizing with the Bulgarian nationalist community and was assigned to other duties in St. Petersburg in May 1879.

Back in the imperial capital, Jenny prepared for examinations fulfilling two of the subjects she had missed when in Bulgaria. Despite being absent for a full year, she passed her exams as a teacher. The most memorable times for Jenny were those spent at her grandparents' home at Kuusa in Finland. The wooden building, a typical two-story structure of the Russian gentry as depicted in Pushkin's *Yevgeny Onegin*, enjoyed a vista overlooking the Finnish woods and the lake of Eurpyanyarvi, with the Kannilan rapids and pine trees close by. The house had two wings, one of which was entirely given over to housing a vast library where Jenny would immerse herself in scores assimilating operatic roles. Jenny would accompany herself at the piano, in a wonderful voice unforgettable to anyone who heard her: clear, melodic, and evocative of a violoncello's timbres. With her father's implication in the assassination of the tsar, a stigma of association endured for his three children, so much so that Adéle married a man forty years her senior—Senator Konstantin Domontovich, Mikhail's elder brother—in a *mariage de convenance*.[19] The Domontoviches kept their own box at the Mariinsky, and Jenny's first visits there stirred in her the desire to become a singer. Long after the performance, swept away by the wonderful music, the singing, and the fairy-tale passions encountered at the theater, she could not sleep.

The first person to give Jenny assistance in making the decisive step was the wife of the Minister of Finances Julia Abaza, who heard Mrovinskaya at a soiree.[20] Abaza was an amateur singer, and she introduced Jenny to Ippolit Pryanishnikov, one of the finest teachers of the period. Pryanishnikov had prepared a whole group of brilliant singing actors at the Mariinsky Theatre; he created Lionel in Tchaikovsky's *The Maid of Orleans* and the first St. Petersburg Onegin and Mazeppa in Tchaikovsky's eponymous operas. Upon hearing Mrovinskaya's voice, he at once guaranteed that she would sing on the stage and that he would teach her for no fee, the sole condition being that she should rest her voice for six months. Jenny began her studies with him in 1883; to complete her education, she went with her teacher, mother, and younger stepsister Alexandra to Italy in the spring of the following year.

The three Russian women arrived in Milan and took a little flat near the Galleria Vittoria Emanuelle. Visits to the art exhibitions, the resplendent churches, and the historical monuments of the city all made their mark. Jenny had the daring to ascend to the roof of the cathedral, promising her sister some delightful local ice cream if she would be adventurous enough to accompany her to the dizzy heights. Jenny was "beautiful as the Raphael Madonna, modest, serious, . . . singing without any affectation, like the birds."[21] Jenny assimilated Italian culture, studying the history of the town and polishing up her Italian. Indeed Jenny was already looking ahead: "this will help me to re-create the living images of the historical roles that I will sing in opera."[22]

Many years later, she wrote, "I want to recall the 'spring of my life,' when I, my mother, and young sister lived by Lago di Como, in preparation for my Italian debut. . . . I clearly remember when sailing on a boat, my little sister was at the rudder and Pryanishnikov would tell of the local legends about the famous singers Malibran and Pasta, and how they caught a little fish, eating it raw, and then discovered they had wonderful voices."[23] Jenny completed her vocal studies, and a few months later, on 7 August 1885, made her professional debut in the part of Gilda in *Rigoletto* at Teatro Vittoria Veneto. Her debut was well received, as she sang without restraint; her sister wrote, "It seemed that she had only to open up and there would flow forth pure, wonderful sounds."[24] In this age, daughters of the aristocracy did not take up the stage as a career, and notwithstanding a love for music, her mother opposed her daughter singing professionally; it was one thing to perform at soiree for friends and family, but quite another to perform on stage for the general public. Nevertheless, Jenny defied her mother and convention: "I can cope with upholding my honor and dignity."[25] Her mother knew of the tradition of actresses becoming the lovers and mistresses of the royal family, a famous example being Praskovya Zhemchugova,[26] yet this carried no weight with Jenny. The stage had bewitched her, and nothing would distract the young aristocrat from this dream.

Jenny was auditioned at the Imperial Opera Theatre: "the singer Frey with whom one would later sing on stage at the Mariinsky, the singer R, who later sang only minor roles, and I auditioned. Soon I was on stage where the prima donna P was seated who at the time in the directors office had '*la pluie et le beau temps*,' and some undue influence, very talented with a great repertoire. When the singer R sang (quite poorly) the prima donna, in tears, threw herself on her, thanking her for the enjoyment. She said not a word. Therefore R received a contract very quickly and I got my debut."[27] Jenny's first performance at the Mariinsky was again in the role of Gilda, on 6 January 1886. Subsequent to this, she was asked to sing Marguérite in Gounod's *Faust*, and the conductor Kondratyev wrote in the *Journal d'Théâtre*[28] "Her great achievement is in her self-possession. If her voice develops then one can expect that she will be a useful acquisition. . . . [T]he public took to Mravina very sympathetically."[29] Tsar Alexander III and the entire court arrived to hear this new singer; it was of no little interest that the daughter of an aristocratic family was on the stage of the Imperial Court Theatre. Her appearance was the talk of the beaumonde, and Jenny was invited to the tsar's reception suite, where the tsar praised her both for the beauty of her voice and her portrayal of the part.[30] In concluding a contract for three years, she was transformed from Mrovinskaya to Mravina, which was her new stage name.

Pryanishnikov advised his protégée that she spend two months studying with Désire A'rto in Berlin; later she studied with Mathilde Marchési and Professor Bakst in Paris. The experience of absorbing the finest of Parisian theater and life was yet another seminal, refining stimulus. French music became a focal point in many of her finest portrayals, and she developed sensitive collaborations with Charles Gounod and Jules Massenet, who both accompanied her Paris recitals in years to come. The summer of 1886 was spent studying the parts of Lyudmila (Glinka's *Ruslan and Lyudmila*) and Elsa (Wagner's *Lohengrin*). Mravina sang the first of these roles at the opening of the season on 31 August. "My partners were all famous, great artists; Melnikov was the best Ruslan, Farlaf was Stravinsky, an artist and actor giving a mass of outstanding visions and images. . . . I was just happy, without feeling, to sing the first phrases, and only when one has to sing an aria did my hands freeze."[31]

The appearance of the new soloist evoked interest from the local press: "Mravina is a young singer who has been recently accepted onto the Petersburg stage. She has a high, fresh soprano and performs to the highest degree, being very attractive. She sings correctly with fine intonation and clever phrasing but is still unassuming—somehow too reserved, obviously due to her inexperience."[32] On one of her appearances, Mravina was introduced to Camille Saint-Saëns when he was visiting the Russian capital, and she was highly praised by the French composer. Her next *comprimario* role was in German romantic opera, that of Elsa: "this is an ideal role for her; she performs the part very well, like no one else, her voice suits this role excellently."[33] Her singing in this admired work transformed her into a foremost personality. It was now challenging to obtain tickets for her performances at the Mariinsky Theatre; the entire elite of the city wanted not only to hear her but to see her—Mravina had become the adored singer of the "gallery."

In her second season, Jenny assumed more fresh parts: Micaëla, Antonida (*A Life for the Tsar*), Tamara (*Demon*), Ännchen (Weber's *Der Freischütz*). "Outstanding for her coloratura technique, Mravina, however, did not limit herself to such roles, possessing a fine vocal range."[34] A major challenge for Mravina was the role of Tatyana in *Yevgeny Onegin*, and once again, the critics were impressed. "The singer has much intelligence, feeling, natural taste, and attractive charm. In Tatyana—Mravina is everything, complete, poetic, and wonderful."[35] Mravina was asked to sing the role of the *Snow Maiden*, one of Rimsky-Korsakov's finest creations, and it became one of her greatest roles—so much so that in his next work, based on Gogol's *Christmas Eve*, Rimsky-Korsakov wrote the part of Oksana for Mravina's voice. Mravina wrote to the composer: "Dear respected Nikolay Andreyevich! Allow me to ask you a great favor. I am so delighted with the great aria of Oksana that I would like to do something which may appear out of place and untactful. Before the staging of the opera, can you permit me to sing this aria at some kind of suitable concert?"[36] Mravina did receive the composer's permission, allowing her to attain her part and conduce to its *succès fou*.

Tchaikovsky admired Mravina and wrote the role of Lisa for her in *The Queen of Spades*. However, things did not materialize as the composer wished, as he explained to the conductor Eduard Napravnik: "as he [Figner] is studying the opera with his wife, then it certainly will be more comfortable for him to sing with Medea than with Mravina. Incidentally I initially wanted the role of Lisa for Mravina, never thinking that Medea would be able to perform the part."[37]

Despite not getting this role for Mravina's appearances at the Mariinsky— there appeared glowing reports in the *Journal d'Théâtre*: "Mravina is the favorite prima donna"; "Mravina was met with great applause" (Rossini's *William Tell*, 21 December 1889); "From the beginning of the first act, applause began for her. The *Brindisi* was repeated to fearful applause; Mravina's aria was greeted with a roar from the public" (*La traviata,* 22 October 1890).

Mravina's success did not always favor her with fame and glory, and she was met with both intrigue and envy at the theater, causing her to consider leaving, and this led to stormy demonstrations: "Today all around the city there was gossip that Mravina is going to give her farewell to the public. They met Mravina with applause at her first entry on stage; after the end of each act, they called for her and brought, apart from flowers, a silver memorial and a wreath of silver, on the ribbon of which was inscribed all the roles she had performed."[38] Later, Kondratyev described another evening: "when I entered the theatre before the performance [4 October 1895] the foyer of the Mikhailovsky Theatre beheld an unusual sight; full of school students, students, nurses, army cadets and officers. The public filled the upper seats behaving noisily to the most unpleasant degree. They shouted, cheered and clapped all the arias and demanded Mravina sing encores. By request she had to repeat all the duets, . . . the whole concert was an unambiguous manifestation."[39]

The famous critic Vladimir Stasov wrote that Mravina made the Russian public appreciate the beauty of Russian opera of the nineteenth century: Glinka, Dargomizhsky, Rimsky-Korsakov, and Serov. With her superb voice and unusually sensitive characterizations, she revived the role of Antonida from *A Life for the Tsar* and that of Fornarina from *Raphael*, by Arensky. Her portrayal of the part was realized through her vocal artistry, her acting, and her subtle movement—Mravina possessed a natural gift—causing audiences to "believe" her interpretation. Among other roles at the theater were Zerlina (*Fra Diavolo*), Miss Ford (*Falstaff*), Olympia (*The Tales of Hoffmann*), and Musetta (*La Bohème*).

Artists at the Imperial theaters were subject to intense attention from their public, as well as the media. Many opera lovers would descend to the most disconcerting behavior. "Artistic reputations were made and undone by casual remarks of the leaders of the stalls. . . . [T]hey were a tyrannical public. . . . [A]fter the stalls have emptied and the lights gone down in the auditorium, the gallery raved. . . . A last rite was to be performed yet—waiting at the stage door. Manifestations at the stage door varied in proportion to the popularity of each artist. They ranged from silence to delirious outbursts. Sometimes a group of young people would follow their idol, keeping at a distance, a silent escort."[40] Mravina's step-sister Alexandra said later that "when I walked on my own through the foyers of the Mariinsky Theatre, the public would comment in passing— 'look that is Mravina's sister, she's also a spruce young girl.'"[41] It was a major surprise when Mravina decided to enter wedlock, following an *affaire du cœur*, with the guards officer Ludwig Koribut-Dashkevich.[42]

Jenny made three major tours of Europe, in 1891–1892, 1902–1903, and 1906, and enjoyed the same degree of success as at home. In Berlin, it was reported that "Miss Mravina enchanted delightfully with her freshness, her force, and the sensitivity of her voice."[43] At Covent Garden, she sang in Verdi's *La traviata* and Meyerbeer's *Les Huguenots*: "The success of Miss Mravina is even more considerable for in *Les Huguenots* her partners were the De Reszke brothers, Lassall, Maurel, Miss Albani and Ravolli, amongst whose company it is always difficult to distinguish oneself."[44] Mravina's triumph at Covent Garden led to a second successive summer season there in Gounod's *Faust, Roméo et Juliette*, and *Philémon et Baucis*; a third visit to Covent Garden was planned, as was a visit to the United States, yet Mravina declined due to consequences on her health from a difficult winter.

As her father had his enemies in the Civil List, Mravina too had her opponents at the Imperial Theatre in the court favorites—Medea and Nikolay Figner. As Count Alexey Volkonsky wrote, he (Figner) "worked for himself, not for arts sake." And it was apparent that Medea "worked for herself."[45] Seeing Mravina's success, the husband and wife singing partners spread rumor after rumor, so much that Tchaikovsky complained to Napravnik about this scandalous behavior.[46] On 25 April 1895, a petition with three hundred signatures supporting Mravina was sent to the minister responsible for the Imperial Theatres.[47] The composer Alexander Glazunov wrote to Napravnik: "we should be proud of Mravina. Miss Mravina is our sole outstanding coloratura soprano of European standing. She possesses a rare stage art, and such an artist would be looked after at any other theater, but here. . . ."[48]

An article appeared in the *Petersburg Gazette* expressing the hope that the theater would offer new terms to Mravina.[49] Gossip circulated that new terms had been offered for a smaller fee. At last Mravina wrote to the tsarina herself, and a revised arrangement was finally concluded through to May 1900. There were other motives, however, behind the determination to rid the theater of Mravina, besides her popularity among the liberal youth. The Tsarevich Nikolay, heir to the throne, had fallen for her, as Veresayev recalls:

> Alexander III suggested to him a choice of those at the Opera or Ballet whom he liked. The tsarevich preferred Mravina, and when this high honor was transmitted to Mravina, she responded, "Not for anything!" One must remember what an honor and benefit it would have been for an artist to be the lover of the tsar or tsarevich, for such a great honor even the princesses and fraüleins related to the royal family dreamed of yet admired this display of elementary woman's honor by Mravina. On every performance by her on stage, we wildly applauded her and with wonder looked at her dear, pure face and laughed at the mood of the tsarevich, who realized that not all was possible for him in this world.[50]

For weeks, the young tsarevich sent bouquets of flowers and numerous gifts to Mravina's flat, all of which were sent back. The rejection of the tsarevich caused wide social consequences; apart from the determination to dismiss her, a section of the press also derided her popularity with the public, calling her supporters hysterical and offensive. Mravina demanded her rights to a pension from the directorate, which she received only on the condition that she resign her position as an artist of the theater, giving health reasons. Mravina retired from the Imperial Theatre on 1 May 1900 with a half-pension worth a miserly 1,140 roubles. Her public was so shocked at her leaving the Mariinsky that an appeal was sent to the Tsarina Maria Fyodorovna, mother of Nikolay II, along with some nine hundred signatures supporting her.[51]

Mravina found her future in touring extensively throughout Russia. Her greatest artistic success was at the Kharkov Opera Theatre, where she sang *Roméo et Juliette, La traviata, Rigoletto, Snow Maiden*, and *Ruslan and Lyudmilla*. It was during a particularly traumatic tour in February and March 1902 that Jenny contracted smallpox while in far-off Siberia. The treatment she received in Irkutsk was not beneficial, and following the abandonment of her next concerts, she returned to recuperate at the family home at Kuusa in Finland. However, back in St. Petersburg, she received a double blow. The stress of her career had caused intense problems—her marriage had proved a disaster as Koribut-Dashkevich had become a womanizer and had taken half of her property. Mravina attempted to leave her past behind, yet family grievances seemed to follow; her mother had died in 1900, and two years later her stepfather passed away. In Mravina's later years, she suffered from her cup of sorrows, so much so that the poet Igor Severyanin described her as "a tragic nightingale."[52]

Mravina now had little to cling to in the damp, cold of St. Petersburg, and she was advised to rest at one of the European spas; however, she chose to settle in the Crimea, and it was in the delightful resort of Yalta that she found her last refuge, arriving in late September 1903. Mravina had first visited Yalta in her childhood, and she had been enchanted by the wonderful soothing air, the cloudless sky, the hills and mountains looming over the bay, and the sparkling waters of the Black Sea. Here she could recover her spirits with the golden haze of fresh sea air together with the aroma of the trees and plants in this exotic resort. It was also attractive in possessing an artistic community including the composer Spendiarov and hosting many visiting musicians in Arensky, Cherepnin, Glazunov, and Grechaninov. It was Spendiarov whose home proved a welcome venue for musical evenings and soirees.[53] Mravina felt well enough to visit Constantinople and Vienna for recitals and to make her farewell concert in the capital—where she saw her young nephew Zhenya for the first time—at the packed People's Assembly in March 1906.

Following an unsuccessful operation in Yalta, Mravina developed tuberculosis and died of a heart attack there on 25 October 1914 at the age of only fifty.[54] The great poet and family relative Severyanin met her shortly before her death and wrote of her as being "a shadow of a shadow."[55] Her last request was to be dressed as Juliette and for her gravestone to be decorated in marble cross woven by her favorite roses. Mravina's grave at the Massandra Cemetery stands on the heights above Yalta, looking over the beautiful bay she loved so much, beside the composer Vasily Kalinnikov.[56] Her passing during the Great War went almost unnoticed, and the most touching of obituaries appeared in the city she had graced in recent years: "Like the Snow Maiden she portrayed so well, . . . she melted the snow for us like the warm rays of the sun in springtime."[57] No recordings remain, and all that is left to us are the reminiscences of her enchanting, fairy-tale voice, like that of a nightingale singing in the deep Russian forest.

NOTES

1. V. Fomin, *Dirizher Yevgeny Mravinsky* (Leningrad: Muzika, 1983), 11.

2. *Geroicheskaya oborona Petropavlovsk-Kamchatsovo v 1854* (Kamchatka: Dalnevostochnoe knizhnoe izdatelstvo, 1979), 107–109.

3. Fomin, *Dirizher Yevgeny Mravinsky*, 11–12.

4. A. Kollontay, *Vospominanii—Proletarskoi Revolutsie* (Odessa: Vseukgosizdat, 1921), 3: 261–302.

5. Kollontay, *Vospominanii—Proletarskoi Revolutsie*.

6. Beatrice Farnsworth, *Aleksandra Kollontai* (Stanford, California: Stanford University Press, 1980), 4.

7. Kollontay, *Vospominanii—Proletarskoi Revolutsie*, 261–302.

8. "Mikhail Alexeyevich Domontovich," *St Piterburg Voennaia Entsiklopedia 1912*, 9: 178.

9. Kollontay, *Vospominanii—Proletarskoi Revolutsie*, 261–302.

10. Kollontay, *Vospominanii—Proletarskoi Revolutsie*, 261–302.

11. A. M. Kollontay, *Den forsta ётappen* (Stockholm: Bonniers, 1945), 80–84.

12. Kollontay, *Vospominanii—Proletarskoi Revolutsie*, 261–302.

13. Kollontay, *Vospominanii—Proletarskoi Revolutsie*, 261–302.

14. A. P. Grigoryeva, *Mravina* (Moscow: Sovetsky Kompozitor, 1970), 12.

15. A. Kollontay, *Den forsta ётappen*, 80–84.

16. Ariadne Tyrkova-Vilionis, *Na putakh k svobodu* (New York: Chekhova, 1952), 401.

17. Tyrkova-Vilionis, *Na putakh k svobodu*, 401. Ariadne Tyrkova-Vilionis (Williams) suggested that Mravinsky was a police agent and should have caught the plotters.

18. A. M. Vavilina Mravinskaya, author interview, October 2001.

19. Igor Severyanin, *Tragichesky solovei, Tost bezotvetny* (Moscow: Respublika, 1999), 482.

20. Y. F. Abaza was on friendly terms with Charles Gounod and Franz Liszt. In 1883, at her salon, the second staging was given of *Yevgeny Onegin*, in which Abaza sang the role of the Nanny.

21. Kollontay, *Den forsta ётappen*, 80–84.

22. Kollontay, *Den forsta ётappen*, 80–84.

23. Y. Mravina, *Stranichka memuarov*, 99.

24. Y. Mravina, *Stranichka memuarov*, 99.

25. Y. Mravina, *Stranichka memuarov*, 99.

26. N. Popova, *Krepostnaya Aktrisa* (St. Petersburg: Avrora, 2001). Praskovya Kovaleva-Shemchugova (1770–1803) was a serf girl possessing a great voice who worked in the theater and became the lover of Count Sheremetyev, causing a major scandal during the reign of Catherine the Great.

27. Y. Mravina, *Stranichka memuarov*, 99.

28. Official journal published by the Imperial Theatres.

29. *Imperial Russian Opera Season 1885–86*, vol. 2, 164, State Central Theatre Museum.

30. Y. Mravina, *Stranichka iz Artisticheskikh vospomiannii*, in A. P. Grigoryeva, *Mravina* (Moscow: Sovetsky Kompozitor, 1970), 137.

31. Y. Mravina, *Stranichka memuarov*, 100.

32. *Russikiye Vedomosti*, 5 September 1886, no. 243, 3.

33. *Imperial Russian Opera 1886–87*, vol. 3, 2.2.

34. E. Stark, *Peterburg Operniye masteri 1890–1910* (Leningrad: Iskusstsvo, 1940), 26–28.

35. *Russikiye Vedomosti*, 16 October 1888, no. 285, 2.

36. V. V. Yastrebtsova, ed., *Nikolay Rimsky Korsakov, Vospominaniye, Vol. 1, 1886–1897* (Leningrad: Muzgiz, 1959), 238.

37. E. Stark, *P. I. Tchaikovsky on Stage of the Kirov Opera and Ballet* (Leningrad: Kirov Theatre, 1941), 106.

38. *Imperial Russian Opera 1894–95*, vol. 11, no. 117191.

39. *Imperial Russian Opera 1895–96*, vol. 12, no. 177192.

40. T. Karsavina, *Theatre Street* (London: Constable and Company, 1930), 126.

41. Karsavina, *Theatre Street*, 126.

42. E. K. Spendiarova to A. P. Grigoryeva, 9 February 1965, *Y. K. Mravina* (Moscow: Sovetsky Kompositor, 1970), 120.

43. *Birzhevii vedomosti*, SPB, 18 March 1891, no. 77, 3.

44. *Birzhevii vedomosti*, 16 May 1891, no. 134, 3.

45. Sergey Mikhailovich Volkonsky, *Moi vospominaniyi*, Vol. 1 (Berlin, 1923–1924); Igor Severyanin, *Tost Otvetny,* 482.

46. P. I. Tchaikovsky to E. F. Napravnik, 5 August 1890, E. F. Napravnik, *E. F. Napravnik—avtobiograficheskiye, tvotchesckiye materialii, dokumentii, pisma* (Leningrad: Muzika, 1959), 159.

47. G. Sokolov to I. A. Vsevolozshky, 3 April 1895, TsGIA, Ff. no. 497.

48. A. K. Glazunov to E. F. Napravnik, 12 April 1895, Napravnik, *E. F. Napravnik—avtobiograficheskiye*, 362–63.

49. *Teatralnoye echo, Piterburgskaya Gazeta*, 7 February 1897, no. 37, 3.

50. V. V. Veresayev, *Sobraniye sochineniye*, Vol. 5 (Moscow: Pravda,1961), 228.

51. TsGALI, f. no. 497.

52. Igor Severyanin, *Tost Otvetny* (Moscow: Respublika, 1999), 482; L. V. Belyakaeva-Kazanskaya, *Siluetti Musikalnovo Piterburga* (St. Petersburg: Leninizdat, 2001), 3.

53. E. K. Spendiarov to A. P. Grigoryeva, 25 January 1965, in *Y. K. Mravina*, 123.

54. A. M. Kollontay to chairman of Yalta City Council, 12 October 1935, Archive of Yalta Region Museum, *Mravina*, 133.

55. Severyanin, *Tost Otvetny*, 483. Igor Severyanin (Igor Vasilevich Lotarev, 1887–1941) was a cousin of Mravina related through the Domontovich family, and he was among the great poets of the Russian "Silver Age."

56. Vasily Sergeyevich Kalinnikov (1866–1901), composer of two symphonies and a small number of orchestral works.

57. E. Embe, *Pamyati Snegurochki-Mravinoy, Yuzhny krai*, 29 October 1914, no. 12329, 7.

Chapter Two

"Zhenya"

I grew up in a family where there was a love and knowledge of music.

—Y. A. Mravinsky

Alexander Konstantinovich Mravinsky had loyally stayed with his father after the divorce; a career in the armed forces no longer held an attraction, and he opted for a tranquil career in law. Alexander sought a life of appeasement, venerating the principles of the Scotsman Adam Smith and the intensifying, dynamic pace of technology.[1] The young man epitomized the new class of industrialists and democrats who supported alliance with France and England. Despite the ignominy of his father's decree nisi and the affair of 1881, Mravinsky enjoyed a wide circle of friends.[2] Graduating from university and owing to his stepfather's contacts, Alexander Mravinsky was appointed to serve as a jurist in the General Staff of the emperor.

At the opening of the twentieth century, Mravinsky met Yelizaveta Nikolayevna Filkova, the second daughter of a prosperous family of the gentry, at a soiree in St Petersburg. Despite differing generations and temperaments, the couple shared a belief in knowledge and scholarship in the sciences and fine arts. The Mravinskys set up home in a large first-floor flat in a district long associated with the family on 9 Srednaya Podyacheskaya Street, near the Griboyedova canal, and with the Imperial Opera and Ballet Theatre and Nikolsky Cathedral just a few moments walk away.[3] It was a prosperous union; the Mravinskys spent their free hours at the theater and weekends at Pavlovsk partaking in musical concerts al fresco. All their aspirations were focused on a child who would protract the family's devotion to the arts. This was the epoch of the "Russian Seasons" in art, when an innovative wave of poets, painters, and musicians gave birth to dreams of a world in concord. Yelizaveta yearned for a girl who would become a pianist or a painter, believing the opening century would tolerate free-thinking women in the arts.[4]

Their first and only child, Yevgeny Alexandrovich, was born on 22 May (4 June new style) 1903. Beloved by his family—notably Jenny and Alexandra— Zhenya revealed much of his mother's gifts in his sketching of animals and nature. In a photograph taken when he was two years old, Alexander looks dispassionately, far into the distance, while mother and son look resolutely at the lens, as if possessed by a single-mindedness. Yelizaveta cast all her love and aspirations into her son, and Zhenya's first years found himself enrobed in girls' clothes. Zhenya took a heartfelt, zealous constitution from his mother, while from his father he attained benevolence and a love for perfection.[5] Alexander Mravinsky was a disciplined father who inculcated prudence in his son. Zhenya one day found money lying in the doorway; discovering him with the newly found coins, his father insisted he return them. In later years he would count every foreign coin and change them down to the last one before leaving for home.

Yelizaveta and her sister Shura had attended the Smolny Institute, a finishing school for daughters of the gentry founded by Catherine II, where they had become proficient in several foreign languages and were encouraged in the fine arts—writing, drawing, singing, and playing musical instruments. Yelizaveta's love for music and the poets of the "Silver Age" was to greatly influence her son and his path in life; there reigned a high moral ideal, a desire for knowledge, duty, and resolute dedication in the family. The Mravinskys always observed religious festivities.

> Palm Week was a break from the long monotony of Lent; an anticipation of Easter, of all the holy days, the holiest in Russia. Noisy bazaars swarmed in the streets, their chief wares grotesque toys, whistles, golden fish, and big roses made of bright tissue paper. Oriental sweets and wax cherubs—heads and wings only. The approach of Christmas and its celebrations brought home to children that feeling of wonder about to happen, great expectations and something still more wonderful, a mystic benevolence prevailing. Around churches, on boulevards and even in the middle of the streets, Christmas markets appeared in great number and forests of fir trees on their stands.[6]

At the age of six, Zhenya was taken to a performance of Tchaikovsky's *The Sleeping Beauty* conducted by the Englishman Albert Coates at the Mariinsky Theatre.[7] On his first visit, to the satisfaction of his parents, the young boy was bewitched by the spectacle. Zhenya, sitting with his family, beheld a vision of paradise, the colors, lights, the huge crystal chandelier in the cupola; he was in such a state of exhilaration that at moments his heart rose throbbing at this first experience of the Mariinsky.[8] This was the first time he had ever

seen or heard a symphony orchestra. At home a Pathéphone playing 78 rpm
records would reproduce the sound of the piano and human voice, but this all-
embracing, exciting sound enraptured the child. He later recalled, "At our
home there hung portraits of the great composers, including Brahms,
Tchaikovsky, and Wagner, and famous singers, including our close acquaintance the bass Mayboroda."[9] The young boy manifested an enchantment for
ballet—the plasticity of movement and music captivated his artistic fancy. On
his tenth birthday, his mother gave him a season ticket for the theater.[10]

> I managed to catch *Siegfried* under the direction of Albert Coates with Ivan Yer-
> shov singing.[11] Returning home devastated, I searched for the piano and tried,
> as best I could, to recollect the notes. A cold chill trickled up one's spine re-
> membering Erda's motif. . . . Stirred by a new, enigmatic sensation, one began
> to look at the composers' portraits with both reverence and excitement. The
> composer of *Siegfried* appeared equally as a magician and sorcerer capable of
> some mysterious force. It was impossible to perceive him as a real person, only
> as a genius. The musicians in the pictures represented beings from another
> higher world, inhabitants of Valhalla, not of this earth. One could no longer re-
> gard Mayboroda, who often visited our home, and chatted and joked with me,
> as a normal human being. He was also from that higher dimension, the "other
> world."[12]

From this time forth, the young Mravinsky's world became that of the theater,
his dreams full of the fantastic sounds and imagery created in the wonderful
Nibelungen legend, or the magic of Tchaikovsky's *The Sleeping Beauty*. Here
among the fantastic riches of the glorious Imperial Mariinsky Theatre was another vista offering a fascinating future, motivated with the triumphs of his
aunt and all part of the family's tradition: "The years passed and I became familiar with many details from the life of my childhood idols and with those
aspects of their personality which made them quite real, of this earth and
closer to me."[13]

Zhenya began studying the piano with Valentina Avgustovna Strem, whose
exquisite, stimulating manner schooled in the German tradition left a constant
influence.[14] Music, however, was not an exclusive passion for the young boy;
Zhenya was also captivated by zoology and botany, and he pursued a close,
abiding interest in them throughout his life. Rather than competing with his
obsession for music, they assimilated into his character and psyche—a constant being his love for nature. He would explore flora and fauna through long
walks in the countryside and in the abundant wild woods beyond the city,
spending entire days there, delighting in the sunsets, the colors of the sky, the
seasons and their effects on the environment. The young Mravinsky's pastimes of hunting, fishing, rowing, and swimming in the rivers and lakes be-

came enduring aspects of his lifestyle; harmony and communion with the earth were ever linked in his expression. Concord and affinity with the world were a quintessential part of the family's aesthetics, and he began to study languages. Every summer, the Mravinskys would holiday in the fashionable spas of Switzerland and Germany, often visiting Zurich and Baden Baden, delighting in Lake Geneva and the Swiss Alps. Speaking the tongue of the great composers and frequenting their haunts became another point of veneration. Zhenya, at the age of eleven, entered the second year at one of the most distinguished schools in the capital—the Alexander I Gymnasium. The subjects included French, German, drawing, philosophy, natural sciences, geography, history, jurisprudence, physics, mathematics, religion, Latin, and calligraphy. Zhenya's weekly report cards reveal he rarely received less than five (the highest mark given) in all his subjects.[15] Zhenya's main interest was the natural sciences; drawn to study entomology, ornithology, and botany, he collected a large number of insects and preserved them in little glass cases. In parallel were his music lessons at home with his new teacher Olga Achkasova-Brandt. On 6 December, the emperor's name day, Zhenya would attend a special matinee at one of the three Imperial Theatres.

> Huge samovars steamed outside the stage door. The theatres were an unusually pretty sight on these days, full of children and young people, tiers of boxes tightly packed with girls in uniform dresses, blue, red, pink with white fiches. The parterre was reserved for boys, schools, lycée, military and naval cadets, and the gallery for public schools. Every child received a box of sweets with a portrait of the Tsar, Tsarina or Tsarevich on the lid. In the interval, tea and refreshments were served in several foyers, and the waiting staff wore their gala red livery with the Imperial eagles. Cool almond milk, deliciously fragrant, was a special feature of this treat.[16]

Zhenya's fecundity was not limited to music, but also extended to poetry, in which he revealed an abstruse passion and an affinity for nature, art, and the church. In his youth, he recited his poems at literary gatherings, winning the admiration of a close friend, Georgy Balanchivadze, who set several poems to music. "We met each other at the Mariinsky Theatre. . . . He wrote poetry, not understanding verse very well at the time; but I looked at him—he seems to be a fine poet. Would it not be a good idea to write romances to Mravinsky's poems?"[17] The two remained friends until Balanchivadze's departure for the West, where he was to gain fame, under the name of George Balanchine—choreographer of ballets by Glazunov, Stravinsky, and Tchaikovsky, collaborator of Diaghilev, and most significantly, founder of the New York City Ballet. Mravinsky's secondary education was completed in the spring of 1920, by which time events in the city had transformed life in his homeland.

The Bolshevik Revolution broke out with sporadic shooting in the afternoon of 24 October. Only a few streets away from their flat, loyal troops had barricaded the Winter Palace Square, access from side streets and the other side of the river was cut off, and all the bridges were up; the destroyer Aurora faced the Palace from the Neva; the fortress was in the hands of Bolsheviks; a battalion of cadets and women defended the Palace from inside, and a few loyal troops still held the positions outside. The wine cellars all through the town were being looted. At the Mariinsky, it was a ballet night, only a few hundred yards from the Palace Square. A machinegun rattled with renewed zest, the sounds of field guns, machine-guns and rifle-fire were deafening. As winter light stole through the chinks of the curtains, the fighting had died down—only an occasional boom of gunfire. In the morning, a new regime was in place and Lenin was Prime Minister.[18]

Alexander Mravinsky had been afflicted by the notorious Petersburg climate; nevertheless, the tragic fate of the Russian armies in the catastrophic defeats of 1914 inflicted a greater blow to his self-esteem. The fate of the Russian Empire grieved him, and its collapse in the February 1917 Revolution left Mravinsky little more to live for. He had been wounded while serving in the armed forces and had been discharged in 1916. For the dying Mravinsky, it was as if all his dreams and beliefs had been shattered at a single stroke, and these tragic events would have a profound effect on young Zhenya's character. During these painful, scarring months, Yelizaveta Nikolayevna tried to immunize her son from the happenings, but following her husband's death from tuberculosis, this became impossible. Subsequently, the flat was searched for weapons, itself a horrific and traumatic ordeal, as the Red Sailors showed total contempt for the gentry and their property.[19] The Mravinsky apartment was confiscated, transformed into a communal flat by the Petrograd Soviet, and given over to the poor. The cart bearing the remaining belongings of the family, evicted from their home, rumbled slowly over the cobblestones, accompanied by urchins shouting abuse, throwing stones at the Mravinskys, and stealing their bread rations. This episode forever cast a shadow over Zhenya's life; it was one calamity to lose one's father, another to be ostracized in one's own country. In these October days of 1918 there echoed through the streets the steady firing of the Kronstadt naval batteries, for only a short distance from the city the forces of the White General Yudenich were advancing on the Bolshevik citadel. The situation was so grim that the Commissar Anatoly Lunacharsky predicted a future of only a few months for the Soviets.

The Mravinskys moved a short distance away, to a building on 12 Theatre Square, opposite the Mariinsky and adjacent to the Conservatoire. This was a communal flat that his aunt Shura shared with other families—occupying one room.[20] Zhenya and his mother were now bound to work at the same theater they had previously visited as patrons. The fall from grace was not so great a volte-face, and Yelizaveta took well enough to working on the costumes at the Mariinsky and taking private pupils. Still at the gymnasium in 1919, Zhenya now took employment as a mime actor at the theater; little did he know this was to be a second education for him.

During the Great War and in the months of the two Russian Revolutions of 1917, the theaters and concert halls operated normally. The torments of living through the revolutions of 1917 were difficult, but having a job at the former Mariinsky Theatre was an enriching experience. One could be transported to another world—for a few short hours—forgetting the horrendous occurrences on the streets of the giant city.[21] It was here Zhenya entered into a lifelong friendship with Nikolay (Kolya) Cherkasov.[22] Auspiciously, their meeting was in the coronation scene of *Boris Godunov*, and the tall Cherkasov and Mravinsky were placed at the front of the boyars following Boris in the procession:

My partner, dressed and bearded exactly as myself, was a well-built youth, Yevgeny Mravinsky, later one of my closest friends. . . . "Follow Shalyapin a step away straight up the dais," the *régisseur* told me. "Only don't rush Shalyapin," he continued. "Keep a little behind and walk in step with your partner. . . ." The chorus greeted Boris Godunov with "Glory." The coronation procession was beginning. Shalyapin took his place before us and walked on to the dais amidst thunderous applause from the audience. Keeping in step with Mravinsky, I followed him. This was the first time one saw the auditorium from the stage. I took up my place next to Shalyapin. It was a thrilling experience taking part in the ceremonial scene that one knew so well and had so often applauded with all my youthful fervour.[23]

During these months, the theater was confronted by a labyrinthine predicament. The above-mentioned performance of Musorgsky's great opera was prestaged by Lunacharsky, declaring the young Soviet Government's aspiration for high art and to sustain the Mariinsky Theatre for the masses.[24] Cherkasov continues:

The atmosphere at the Mariinsky was one of full-blooded, brisk creative activity. Despite all difficulties it proved worthy of the tasks it had been set popularising Russian classical music and improving the quality of its performances. The Revolution was exerting a vast influence on the theatre, and this could be seen in its productions. Very often, the theatre was the venue of congresses that were usually rounded out by concerts and pageants on revolutionary themes. There were no admission fees for the shows, and the tickets were distributed among workers, students and school children. Most of the shows were for the Red Army and Navy.[25]

By the time Mravinsky joined the Mariinsky staff, over half of its former staff members had left, leading to a constriction of the repertoire. However, by the spring of 1920 the repertoire at the renamed State Academic Opera and Ballet had expanded to twenty-seven operas, centered on the Russian classics of Glinka, Dargomizhsky, Serov, Musorgsky, Borodin, Tchaikovsky, and Rimsky-Korsakov.[26] The two young men, Cherkasov and Mravinsky, embraced the tasks entrusted them with all the fervor of youth. Because of the curfew, tram services terminated at about the same time as the theater closed its doors, and life in the streets soon came to a standstill. Therefore performances usually began at 6:30 or even 6:00 p.m. Mravinsky arrived at the theater promptly at four and ascended quickly, taking giant steps to the dressing room on the third floor. The heating was minimal, and it was so cold that the water in a glass would freeze. Mravinsky and Cherkasov warmed themselves with hot carrot tea and began to prepare carefully for the evening's performance, in which they would switch costumes five or six times. The two young men learned every opera and ballet in the repertoire, amplifying their love for music and the theater's dramaturgy. Performances would end just before ten, and now and then special tram services would be provided for the audience. While for Mravinsky it was only a short distance home, for Cherkasov it was a long, lonely walk every so often met by army patrols. During the spring and summer of 1919, the front line was just a few miles away, on the outskirts of Petrograd.

The two friends managed to make use of their free moments and were drawn to the orchestra's handiwork, eavesdropping on practically all the sessions.

> My friend Mravinsky and I had our favourite seats too—in the lower box immediately above the timpani—from which we had an excellent view of the orchestra and its conductor. With time, I learned to understand his gestures and could guess correctly, why he stopped the orchestra. I might add that I probably suffered even more than the musicians themselves when things went wrong, as they are apt to do during rehearsals. The musicians waged a bitter, but vain struggle against the cold; the theatre was heated very rarely and very little, the temperature on the stage and in the auditorium was seldom above 40 degrees F., and because of that the sounds produced by wooden and brass instruments were sharp to the point of jarring on the ear.[27]

Akin to a moth attracted to light, Mravinsky would observe the artists at close quarters, and one who caught his attention most of all, apart from Shalyapin, was the tenor Ivan Yershov. "Ivan Vasilyevich was a living reincarnation of Art; without any gratuitous words, ornate expression, or deceit."[28] Mravinsky was fortunate to hear Shalyapin in his finest roles; not only did Mravinsky pick up the splendid and unique nuances in Shalyapin's voice, but he was also able to study the singer's genial creations of some of the great roles: Boris, Varlaam, Dosifei, Don Basilio, Méphistofélès, and Don Quixôte.[29] There could be heard in Shalyapin's singing "an endeavor to throw down the gauntlet at the source of evil. The quest of the ordeal of the human spirit forever remained in the soul of Shalyapin."[30] In Serov's *Judith*, in which Shalyapin portrayed Holoférnes, Cherkasov and Mravinsky acted as bodyguards to the great bass-baritone:

> Shalyapin gave such a vivid performance of a man overcome by passion — without once losing his majestic bearing — that I trembled when he fell exhausted at Judith's feet. Controlling a gripping fear, I helped the other bodyguards to carry him to a bed at the rear of the stage, and was surprised to hear Shalyapin whisper softly: "Thank you, comrades, thank you." Shalyapin was then at the peak of his career, and his art knew no equal. I liked him most in tragic roles, which revealed him as a master in conveying its psychological depth, in perfecting each little detail and portraying emotional fervour.[31]

Another instructive story of the artist Shalyapin was of his staging in 1919 of Serov's *Power of Evil*.

> He knew all the roles by heart, oversaw the rehearsals and taught the singers how to sing their roles. He would softly hum the music, inculcating all the necessary intonations and inflections. At one of the rehearsals, Shalyapin told the conductor that he wanted a pause after a certain remark, and the latter asked how long it should last. "Never mind that," Shalyapin retorted angrily. "Follow my acting and you'll see for yourself when it should end." He wanted the players and conductor to feel the music. That was one of the unwritten laws of his art.[32]

The young Mravinsky's compulsive attention to all aspects of the performances caught the eye of the tenor Yershov, who empathized with the aspiring musician and initiated a long-lasting friendship. "Among contemporary Tristans, in his talent and strength of dramatic expression Yershov has no equals."[33] Among the "roles" often given to young Mravinsky were minor ones, such as the "seaweed" in the undersea kingdom in Rimsky-Korsakov's *Sadko*. However, in Stravinsky's ballet *The Firebird*, Cherkasov and Mravinsky portrayed the roles of Knight of the Day and Knight of the Night in which the former (played by Cherkasov) had to "dispatch" his friend Mravinsky in the latter role. Such interpretations were vastly important in developing their plasticity and movement on stage. One of their first ballet performances was in Glazunov's *Raymonda*, in which the composer himself was conductor. This experience was fascinating, for the audience loved to see this musician at the rostrum. However, the venerable musician did not always secure the best results: "Glazunov conducted somewhat sluggishly," wrote Cherkasov. "Now and then, he would look at a musician and nod approvingly. There was nothing extraordinary in the way he conducted *Raymonda*, and yet there was something bewitching in it all."[34]

The performances during the darkest days of the Civil War were unforgettable, as special concerts were given for the Red Army and Navy. The theater was filled with soldiers and sailors on leave from the front line. They would pack the cold, unheated auditorium, often with rifles in their hands, bayonets unsheathed. Sometimes up to thirty servicemen would crowd into the six-seat boxes, and the management was afraid that one day the boxes would collapse. Cherkasov wrote:

> One shall never forget the extremely cold days that year, so freezing that the radiators in our theatre burst and the lobby floor was covered with such a beautiful layer of ice one could skate on it. We young actors volunteered to go to the woods to get fuel. Working in a blustering snowstorm, we felled trees, dragged them several kilometres to the railway line, loaded them on to flat cars and triumphantly returned to the theatre. One shall never forget how the theatre looked nor the square with its shops closed down, with snow piled up so high, we had to break a path to get into the theatre. Desolation seemed rife, yet the theatre was pulsating with creative life.[35]

Nevertheless, following graduation from the Gymnasium, Mravinsky had a perplexing choice before him. In September 1920, taking advice from Yelizaveta Nikolayevna, Mravinsky entered the natural sciences faculty of Petrograd University. However, the long hours he spent at the theater forced him to drop out in the first year. The daily regime of full evenings at the theater as well as morning rehearsals persuaded Mravinsky that music was his future; it was bewitching to watch the greats of the world stage performing just a few feet away from him. At home, before wall mirrors, Mravinsky copied the entrancing movements of the conductor's arms and hands, as if sculpting the performance of the artists on stage.

> We were young and so in love with the theatre that one evening, with the permission of the firemen on duty, we spent the whole night there just to enjoy its atmosphere. Mravinsky made believe he was conducting an orchestra, while I recited monologues and sang arias to the deserted auditorium. On the backdrop illuminated by a few lamps hung a décor—a mountain with the ruins of a castle in the distance, and this detail added to the fantastic character of our impromptu performance which so originally reflected our dreams of the future.[36]

If Cherkasov had yet to find his calling in life, the art of conducting was a magical, bewitching art, and in the end, Yevgeny Mravinsky was enchanted by its spell. The aspiring maestro followed the work of the English conductor

Albert Coates, and he studied the breathtaking dancing of Yelizaveta Gerdt and Yelena Lyuk and the plasticity in the creations of Agrippina Vaganova. The greatest impression made on the young man, however, was by the theater's artistic director—Emil Cooper:

> I remember the man who somewhat similar to Wagner or Napoleon expressed marvelous talent, indefatigable energy and enormous willpower. Emil Cooper combined the roles of chief conductor and artistic director, bearing upon his shoulders the entire repertoire of the theatre. Cooper inspired one to take up the art of conducting for the rest of one's life. At this time, one was engrossed in the legend of music making in the theatre, appreciation and finding an affinity for the symphonic spirit of opera and ballet music.[37]

While Mravinsky continued his theater travails, he sought additional employment as a *répétiteur* in the dance class of Vecheslova-Snetkova at the Vaganova Dance School.[38] This was the preparatory institution for the Ballet Troupe of the former Mariinsky, and both dancers and accompanists were expected in time to progress to the theater. The situation was difficult and demanded not only astute musical gifts but also a finely honed feeling for rhythm. It engaged dancers in monotonous, repetitive exercises and involved constant improvisation by the pianist. Mravinsky was well equipped, as his hands perfectly encompassed the full octave; the third finger was unusually long, allowing him the greater range.[39] It was at the Vaganova that he first made the acquaintance of another life-long friend in Konstantin Sergeyev.[40] His debut in the evening class was also that for Zhenya Mravinsky, as Sergeyev himself later described: "I suddenly saw this tall, young man walk into the rehearsal room and walk casually across to the piano and begin accompanying and improvising—amazing this was his first day working there!"[41]

In the Civil War and later during the New Economic Policy, with limited private enterprise, the inflation rates were horrifying; money in one's pocket would disappear in value within a few hours. Those commodities valued most of all were fresh meat and fish, and many would have died of starvation if it were not for the allotments families kept on the city's perimeters. Mravinsky and Cherkasov would spend summers out far away to the east, in the Tver province, where they lived with Cherkasov's aunt, spending their days fishing and walking through the endless Russian forests.[42] Back in Petrograd, free hours would be spent reading poetry and debating their future careers. Cherkasov had pretensions to be an opera singer, but this was to be an unrealized dream—his vocal chords were unsatisfactory—nevertheless, the two would play piano duets endlessly. Mravinsky insisted that his companion join him in enrolling at the Conservatoire. However, in 1923, Cherkasov finally chose to enter the Petrograd Institute of Stage Art.[43]

The 1920s was an intensive period for laying the groundwork for Mravinsky's future career. Together with studying music and perfecting the art of accompaniment, he had acquired a reputation as being resilient and hardworking, and he developed the working relationships he would enrich for many years with Ulanova,[44] Sergeyev, and Dudinskaya.[45] In later years, Galina Ulanova recalled meeting this "tall, imposing very serious man in the corridors of the Ballet School, often accompanied by his elegant mother. He had a great reserve, was very composed and intense within himself, and was able to express vocally his distinctive strength of will very well."[46] Mravinsky's term at the Ballet School lasted a full ten years, during which he was appointed Head of Music in 1929. Mravinsky followed a tough and arduous schedule, working at the theater in rehearsal, attending classes at the Conservatoire, and spending the evening accompanying at ballet classes, subsequently to which he would regularly play in cinemas to earn his daily bread. It was the most exhausting, engrossing, and torturous labor of love, yet it was to prove the ideal preparation for his future career.

NOTES

1. Adam Smith, author of *The Wealth of Nations*.
2. A. M. Vavilina Mravinskaya, author interview July 2001.
3. A. M. Vavilina Mravinskaya, author interview, July 2001.
4. A. M. Vavilina Mravinskaya, author interview, July 2001.
5. Y. A. Mravinsky family archive.
6. T. Karsavina, *Theatre Street* (London: Constable and Company, 1930), 111–12.
7. Coates (1882–1953), born in St. Petersburg, conductor and composer, studied with Nikisch, spent his early career in Russia, and later worked in Europe and South Africa.
8. Karsavina, *Theatre Street*, 23.
9. Vladimir Yakovlevich Mayboroda (1852–1917) was a distinguished opera and chamber singer who worked with Mravina, Yershov, Sobinov, Shalyapin, and Stravinsky.
10. Y. A. Mravinsky, "Tridzat let s muzikoi Shostakovicha," in *D. Shostakovich,* ed. L. V. Danilevich (Moscow: Sovetsky Kompozitor, 1967), 103.
11. Ivan Vasilyevich Yershov (1867–1943), tenor, was renowned for his interpretations of Wagner.
12. Mravinsky, "Tridzat let s muzikoi Shostakovicha," 103–104.
13. Mravinsky, "Tridzat let s muzikoi Shostakovicha," 104.
14. V. Fomin, *Dirizher Yevgeny Mravinsky* (Leningrad: Muzika, 1983), 12.
15. Y. A. Mravinsky archive.
16. Karsavina, *Theatre Street*, 76.

17. S. Volkhov, *Strasti po Tchaikovskomu: razgovori s Georgem Balanchinem* (New York: Slovo Word, 1999), 88.

18. Karsavina, *Theatre Street*, 264.

19. The detachments of Red Sailors were the shock brigades of the Revolution, and their severity and brutality in dealing with former members of the regime were often called into question, even by the Bolsheviks.

20. Y. A. Mravinsky archive.

21. Karsavina, *Theatre Street*, 262.

22. Nikolay K. Cherkasov (1903–1966) became one of the country's finest actors, notably starring in Sergey Eisenstein's classic films *Alexander Nevsky* and *Ivan the Terrible*.

23. N. Cherkasov, *Notes of a Soviet Actor* (Moscow: Foreign Languages Publishing House), 13–14.

24. State Academic Theatre of Opera and Ballet, or GATOB for short; the Mikhailovsky Theatre was renamed the Maly State Opera and Ballet Theatre, or MALEGOT.

25. Cherkasov, *Notes of a Soviet Actor*, 17–18.

26. E. Bronfin, *Muzikalnaya Kultura Petrograda pervovo poslerevolutsionnovo pyatiletiya 1917–1922* (Leningrad: Sovetsky Kompozitor, 1984), 9.

27. Cherkasov, *Notes of a Soviet Actor*, 19.

28. M. V. Yudina, *V Luche Bozhestvennie Lyubov* (Moscow, Universitetskaya Kniga,1999), 110.

29. A. Gozenpud, *Russkiye Operniye Teatr mezhdu Dvuch Revolutsiye 1905–1917* (Leningrad: Muzika, 1975), 30.

30. Gozenpud, *Russkiye Operniye Teatr*, 30.

31. Cherkasov, *Notes of a Soviet Actor*, 22–23.

32. Cherkasov, *Notes of a Soviet Actor*, 24.

33. V. Kolomytseva, *Novaya Rus*, No. 16, 1910.

34. Cherkasov, *Notes of a Soviet Actor*, 21.

35. Cherkasov, *Notes of a Soviet Actor*, 27.

36. Cherkasov, *Notes of a Soviet Actor*, 28.

37. Y. A. Mravinsky, "Schastliva pora," in *Leningradskaya Konservatoria v vospominaniyax, 1862–1962* (Leningrad: Gozudarstvenniye Muzikalniye Izdatelstvo, 1962), 218.

38. Y. A. Mravinsky family archive.

39. Y. A. Mravinsky family archive.

40. Konstantin Sergeyev became one of the great ballet dancers and choreographers.

41. Konstantin Sergeyev, interview for Sankt Piterburg TV, *Russian Video*, 1992.

42. N. Cherkasova, *Ryadom s Cherkasovym* (Leningrad: Lenizdat, 1978), 193.

43. Cherkasov, *Notes of a Soviet Actor*, 31.

44. Galina Sergeyevna Ulanova became one of the finest ballerinas in the country, portraying Juliet against Sergeyev's Romeo in Prokofiev's great ballet in 1940.

45. Natalya Dudinskaya became a noted ballerina at the Leningrad Ballet, giving the first portrayals of many new productions.

46. A. A. Zolotov, *Myzhlenie o Mravinskovo*, Ekran TV, 1978.

Chapter Three

The Conservatoire

The eye listens.

—Paul Claudel, *L'oeil ecoute*

A victim of the October Revolution, Yevgeny Mravinsky attempted to enroll in the Conservatoire in 1923, yet was not accepted. He very much wanted to study composition there, but his theoretical knowledge was deemed unsatisfactory, and the only opening was through a roundabout means—applying to enter the double-bass class of Professor Yegorov. At the audition, Yegorov asked the young man to play any note on the instrument and to take it a fourth higher, and Mravinsky's performance of this task prompted the professor to cry: "Ah so he can really hear!"[1] Papers discovered many years later reveal that, following the passing of his entry examinations in the summer of 1923, Mravinsky could not be taken as a student because of his kin.[2] The education policies of the new Soviet government were fashioned to encourage the children of the working class and the poor and not those of the disfranchised gentry.

If this affair proved an early blow for the young man, nevertheless he found diversion to console body and soul. Barely into his twentieth year, Yevgeny Mravinsky indulged in a love affair with a woman some fifteen years his senior. Marianna Ignatyevna Schwalck was the wife of a Polish merchant living in Petrograd. Her husband was frequently away on business trips, and Marianna was left in Petrograd with little on her mind. . . . Yevgeny's mother Yelizaveta Nikolaevna taught Marianna Schwalck French and German privately; a friendship developed between the two women, both of whom were without their husbands in a difficult period. Yevgeny would visit Schwalck's house assisting his mother in her work, and the Polish woman was taken with the young aspiring musician.

26

Not the type to go unnoticed in a crowd, Mravinsky was tall, gallant, and strikingly handsome, and he attracted many women both young and old throughout his career. The affair with Schwalck went on for some months, until it was eventually discovered by Marianna's husband, who abruptly left for Poland, leaving his wife destitute. Yelizaveta felt it just and honorable that her son should marry Marianna and restore her to respectability in society. In early 1923, leaving his mother on 12 Theatre Square, Mravinsky moved into Marianna's flat on Kirochnaya Street in the northern Petrograd district.[3] The marriage, however, was not propitious, and they parted some years later. Marianna Ignatyevna Mravinskaya died in her ninety-first year, and her former spouse watched over her regularly until her death in 1979, ensuring that she had medical care (Mravinsky's fourth wife was delegated to take her prescriptions) while living alone in a spacious apartment opposite the Pushkin Theatre.[4]

Following the rebuff at the Conservatoire, Mravinsky did not lose heart; if anything, his resolve to make music his profession became even stronger. The young man, with his friend Alexey Zhivotov studied musical theory and harmony with Ivan Vishnevsky. The Capella housed the first music school in Russia, its buildings forming an entire complex of offices, classes, concert hall, and residential flats. Yelizaveta was insistent that nothing hinder her son's career, and she invoked help from her half sister. The daughter whose conception predestined the breakup of the Mrovinsky marriage forty years previously had become a professional revolutionary. Alexandra Kollontay (née Domontovich) became a Marxist in 1898,[5] an ideologue of feminism who fluctuated between the Bolsheviks and Mensheviks, and who was imprisoned on several occasions. Vladimir Lenin appointed her a commissar for social welfare in November 1917.[6] A passionate lover of the arts and well familiar with her nephew's yearning to become a professional musician, Alexandra acceded to Yelizaveta's request for help.[7] Kollontay conferred with Anatoly Lunacharsky, the commissar for enlightenment, and he advised her to write to the rector of the Conservatoire and pledge Mravinsky's political reliability. Providing Mravinsky passed the entrance examination, Lunacharsky promised that he would be accepted as a student.[8] Kollontay wrote to the rector, Alexander Konstantinovich Glazunov, in the spring of 1924, and without divulging her lineage, impressed on the respected composer the distress of the family circumstances (because of the 1881 affair) and that Mravinsky had a prodigious musical savoir faire and merited assistance. This document along with Mravinsky's success on the necessary tests ensured his entry into the composition class in September 1924 as a non–fee-paying student.[9]

Yevgeny Mravinsky thus enrolled in the musical theory class of Mikhail Chernov. He thrived on the atmosphere there; the professors at the Leningrad

Conservatoire were among the finest in Europe, and Mravinsky's seven years
there were the most euphoric of his life. Just strolling through its inner halls
one could grasp the musical heritage and tradition. Following his first two
years of studies with Chernov, Mravinsky attended the lectures in polyphony
by Khristophor Kushnarev[10] and in musical form by Pyotr Ryazanov, laying
a secure basis for the young man in methodology and musical theory.
Kushnarev was an exceptional teacher; he was "always inner collected,
somewhat reserved, yet always open and simple in speech, a man of exceptional high moral fiber, and it was with his name that major reforms began at
the Conservatoire, to be precise, in the change of teaching methods of
polyphony."[11] Mravinsky reminisced: "This was an extraordinarily interesting period, as the old school of Rimsky-Korsakov continued through
Glazunov, Shteinberg, and Ossovsky, who represented one musical tradition,
and on the other hand was the new music epitomized by Shcherbachyov,
Kushnarev, Tyulin, and Ryazanov."[12]

The most prevalent of Mravinsky's teachers was Vladimir Shcherbachyov,
a skilful and unprejudiced composer who assembled around him the most
gifted young composers; he was a sage of the "new wave" in Russian composition—"a wonderful man, complex, tragic, enlightened with a sharp and witty
character together with a scintillating type of charisma."[13] Shcherbachyov took
his students, playing each piece in four hands, through the symphonies of
Bruckner, Tchaikovsky, and Brahms with diversions to modern composers
such as Hindemith and Stravinsky. "I well remember the Leningrad Philharmonic concert season of 1927–1928 when one of the finest conductors of the
day and an enthusiast of Soviet music—Vladimir Dranishnikov—conducted
the admirable Second Symphony by Shcherbachyov, 'Blok.' This was an occasion in Leningrad's concert life, as the symphony reflected the emotional
color of the first postrevolutionary years."[14]

If talent and knowledge flourished in the wonderful creative ambience at
the Conservatoire, this was set against the desperate situation in Leningrad in
the 1920s—a lack of electricity, inadequate heating, and terrible economic
problems resulted from the Revolution and Civil War. The paramountcy of
the institution was much owed to the Rector Glazunov, whose large, bloated
figure moving through the corridors of the building—leaving a wisp of his
beloved Cuban cigars everywhere—contributed to a beneficial and inspirational aura for students and teachers alike. Another person at the Conservatoire in those years who enjoyed great reverence and esteem—the petite
Leonid Nikolayev—presented a different, and miniature, vision than did
Glazunov. Also to be seen in the classrooms was the patrician-like vocalist
Ivan Yershov and the composer Maximilian Shteinberg. A patriarchal figure
was that of Boris Asaf'yev, as one of his pupils Dmitr'yev wrote: "Thirty

years have passed, yet the memory of his words remain with one, not just the ideas, but the very manner of speech and the clarity of his voice."[15] Not only were his lectures compelling, but also Asaf'yev's love of nature led to his taking students on long walks outside the city.[16] For the young Mravinsky, it was a time of debates, discussions, listening to and playing music: "On all these long corridors there were always dark forbidding doors; however for us they were doors into the 'sunlight,' entry into new, different musical experiences. . . ."[17] The twice-weekly soirees at Anna Fogt's home were a focal point where musicians of the day would play contemporary pieces. It was here that Shcherbachyov, Asaf'yev, Malko, and others would debate the controversial new work by composers such as Stravinsky, Hindemith, Schoenberg, and *Lés Six*. Counterpoising the austerity in everyday life, there was an *embarras de richesses* in the arts. We can glimpse at Otto Klemperer's first visit to Soviet Russia in November 1924 an early sympathizer with the young republic and one among the first to achieve fame and recognition there.[18] During rehearsals with the Leningrad Philharmonic, he seemed to have "a kind of diabolic madness,"[19] and he was baptized "the black devil."[20] The German musician received a hearty response. "The enthusiasm that Klemperer has evoked . . . might be considered naïve in Europe. But an ability to derive intense enjoyment from art is a token of a youthful joie de vivre that has not yet been obscured by European satiety or mere American curiosity."[21] Klemperer himself said that he had never witnessed such scenes following his concerts as he did in Moscow and Leningrad. "It was not just that everyone stood. They surged around the platform (continuing applauding) for about a quarter of an hour."[22] The critics were equally overwhelmed and acclaimed him as one of the great conductors of the age, the local paper *Krasnaya Gazeta* comparing him with Nikisch, Mahler, and others who had appeared on the city's concert bills.[23] The *succès fou* naturally led to more concerts, producing the following tribute from the young conductor: "I have no public better disposed to me than the people in Leningrad."[24] An American music critic wrote "Klemperer's popularity in Russia is quite extraordinary—it is a kind of phenomenon—and has never been surpassed by that of any foreign conductor, including even Nikisch."[25] The influential Asaf'yev described the Hamburg musician's visionary work on the podium: "It is as though he focuses the will of the masses in the movements of his arms."[26] Oscar Fried was the first conductor to arrive in the country following the revolution:

Lenin received me and we discussed new tactics of the workers' government in music. He told me about this new public. One problem took my attention, and I explained my concern to the Soviet leader. We conductors take to the podium in coat and tails. In my opinion, this is customary as it is for a doctor in white gown. However, this might be hostile to Soviet audiences as representing bourgeoisie and could only be used in the theater. The question arose, could I appear before workers' audiences in such a bourgeois array? I thought this a very important problem and asked Lenin, who gave it a lot of thought and then responded that one should appear in a festive form. One should be in fashion no worse than the bourgeoisie.[27]

Mravinsky's composing won recognition at the Conservatoire; his most accomplished pieces were the sonata for wind and piano ensemble and a trio, while his piano sonatas, preludes, fox-trots, and études were deemed immature and confined to a bottom drawer. The chamber pieces from the late 1920s, which were heard at the Conservatoire, were his Suite for Flute, Violin, and Oboe and the Fragments for Voice, Cello, Trombones, Oboe, and Percussion performed on 4 March 1929 and 23 May 1930, respectively.[28] The latter allowed him one of his first conducting engagements. There was an unquestionable polyphonic mastery in these publicly presented works, and a feeling for color and musical form reflecting the late romantic style, with traces of influence from Scriabin, Debussy, and Richard Strauss.[29] There was quickly emerging in Russia a richly talented crop of composers in the young Khachaturyan, Shebalin, Popov, Kabalevsky, and Shostakovich—a group just as exciting as previous generations in Russian music. Also, Sergey Prokofiev returned to Russia in 1927 for an extended concert tour, and the mature Nikolay Myaskovsky was keeping the symphonic tradition very much alive while the older generation of Glazunov and Glière was still full of life. Shostakovich impressed Mravinsky in particular—here was the language and music he himself aspired to write. Relinquishing composition, he took the decision to recreate the works of the fresh generation of Soviet composers. Mravinsky felt drawn to this great mysterious challenge of recreating someone else's composition. "The principle of individualization melts in the fire of such mystico-musical union, and nothing can be more real or experienced more securely than this mysterious act of unification between us, the work, and its creator."[30] Not forsaking creativity, Mravinsky was persuaded that the brave new generation needed interpreters who sympathized with and could portray their music.

The entry into the country's universities and colleges by sons and daughters of the peasantry and working class, together with a fresh literate and hungry audience, witnessed the rise of the phenomenon of proletarian-oriented poets, writers, painters, and musicians. Guilds and societies were formulated to cast aside the arts of the past and sanctify Soviet Communist art. The music of Tchaikovsky and Rachmaninov was regarded as recidivist; proletarian art must create new music, and the works of Beethoven and Wagner were regarded as "revolutionary" and to be followed as the true creed. The Revolutionary Association of Proletarian Musicians (RAPM; less prevalent in Leningrad) attracted many of these "new" composers and influenced others, led by Davidenko, Koval, and Mosolov. The Revolutionary Association diverged from the Association for Contemporary Music, which maintained the traditions of classical music and counted among its adherents Asaf'yev, Shebalin, and Myaskovsky.

The Conservatoire's RAPM members preached the need to give up professional studies, that it spoiled the natural talents, making them routine and mediocre. The most damaging aspect of RAPM was its rejection of the Russian romantics, especially Tchaikovsky. There appeared a "commission" in the Conservatoire under the guidance of a "scientific consultant," Krivosheina, whose purpose was to exclude Tchaikovsky from all aspects of the Conservatoire. This was the last straw for the professors, who decided to use their influence to decisively contest this attempt. At a meeting in debate with Krasnukha, who supported RAPM, Professor Tomars said laconically, "I am not going to argue with Krasnukha[31] because it is an infantile disorder and will soon fade away."[32] Wisdom arrived in a significant document penned by Lunacharsky, who wrote in "Answer to the Komsomols of the Conservatoire": "I cannot call Myaskovsky, Alexandrov, Shebalin, and Krein *our composers* in the sense that they are composer-Communists or ideological fellow travelers. I call them *our* because they are composers living and working in the USSR. The environment in which they live is undoubtedly reflected in their creative work. This group of composers remain faithful to the homeland and work in the spirit of the classics—perhaps not of our entire country, but certainly as part of the intelligentsia."[33]

In November 1929, Yevgeny Mravinsky was obliged to take part in a musical performance on Uritsky Square (formerly Palace Square) celebrating the twelfth anniversary of the Revolution. Among those who took part were distinguished figures in the city's musical life of the 1930s: Brusilowsky, Grigoryev, Teplitsky, and Birger. Mravinsky was set a disconcerting charge in his final year at the Conservatoire to change the bell tones of the Peter and Paul Fortress from the former tsarist anthem of "Bozhe Tsarya khrani" to that of "The Internationale"—the new Soviet anthem. This was a rather unenviable task for someone whose family credo was to serve the Romanov Empire, yet Mravinsky set about the work with his customary zeal.

Mravinsky's composing had a great bearing on his development as a musician, in his thought processes and throughout his musical career. The young musician was drawn to the intoxicating experience of performing a piece of music—in charge of musicians—akin to Dmitry Karamazov in Dostoyevsky's novel, charging forward on his troika: "I! I am going at full tilt!"

As Bruno Walter wrote, "Exactly how the recreative musician feels at his great moment when a notable work is challenging all his powers. . . . No it is *his* ego which rises to its utmost heights."[34] Following three years of study, in September 1927, Yevgeny Mravinsky finally resolved to cross the Rubicon, and he entered the conducting class of Professor Nikolay Malko.

At his Class 28 on the second floor, Malko had his own partialities, and Mravinsky was not among them. Malko "was always surrounded by a multitude of potential conductors. (If they all became conductors, then our profession would not be so sanctified as it has now become.) Working with Malko was fascinating, in spite of the fact that his classes gave me little. Students had hardly any practical experience in working with an orchestra."[35] Prior to conducting Gounod's *Faust*, Mravinsky worked only to a piano accompaniment, having to divine orchestral sound: "I remember having only two rehearsals for *Faust* at the Opera Studio," he wrote.[36] Malko had too many pupils to cope with and was always busy with engagements in the city and elsewhere. A fellow student, Valerian Bogdanov-Berezovsky, commented: "He didn't look for those traces of matter which would bring Malko and the student closer together."[37] If Yevgeny Mravinsky was to find someone who could allow him to lift the mask, then kismet favored him, as Malko was invited to take up the conductorship of the newly formed Danish Radio Symphony Orchestra and left Russia in April 1929.

Mravinsky's prospects were transformed when he entered Alexander Gauk's class in September later that year. There were several very prodigious students under Gauk's wing: Alexander Melik-Pashayev, Yevgeny Mikeladze, Nikolay Rabinovich, Ilya Musin, Eduard Grikurov, Issay Sherman, and Nikolay Shkolnikov. "One instantly felt at ease by Professor Gauk's amiability."[38] To enroll in Gauk's class, one had to conduct two pieces played to a pianist's accompaniment and then play a work by memory on the piano and from the score. The ambience reigning in Gauk's class came like a breath of fresh air. Gauk was free of dictatorial tendencies; should disputes arise, students would be taken to a concert and encouraged to form their own opinion of a particular piece of music.[39]

Alexander Gauk was not only a fine pedagogue but also a very distinguished conductor. A pupil of Nikolay Cherepnin and a follower of Nikisch, he had evolved his own style, based on the closest assimilation of the work, its milieu, and its spirit. Mravinsky wrote, "Gauk was a natural teacher who never detached theory from practice."[40] Gauk believed that the conductor had to know the music as intimately if not more so than its composer, that the conductor must *a priori* arrive at the basis of reasoning for the music. There was a rapport between teacher and student in his class that was impossible with Malko, and Gauk taught his students how to master the craft of reading a score, teaching contemporary music as well as the classics. "In performing a particular piece, he would never demand his students follow his own reading or manner of conducting"; he allowed them their independence of thought and aesthetic credo.[41] Gauk inculcated that his students should bequeath an expressive gesture, imparting exigency in "a conductors word"—to recreate a complete work as an architectural concept.

Alexander Gauk created many contemporary Soviet works, notably Shostakovich's Third Symphony, several of Myaskovsky's symphonies, and those of Shaporin, Prokofiev, Khachaturyan, and Kabalevsky. Gauk discovered neglected pieces by Glinka in the Leningrad Public Library and gave the "second premiere" of Rachmaninov's forgotten First Symphony in D minor in 1944.[42] Constants in his programming were works by Bach, Handel, Beethoven, and Berlioz. One of his disciples, the Armenian Melik-Pashayev, wrote that Gauk "attempted by placing all his knowledge, talent, and art in the rehearsal to generate a standard of concert performance."[43] His interpretations were distinguished by an emotional freedom following Safonov's example by relinquishing the baton—ostensibly controlling the orchestra in his own hands, sculpting the music with his gestures.

If Arthur Nikisch "discovered" the real genius of the late symphonies of Tchaikovsky, Alexander Gauk was the first Russian to follow Nikisch studying the original scores and insisting his students do likewise. Gauk read Tchaikovsky's works as dark, world-weary, and philosophical masterpieces at the very period when the composer's symphonic legacy was undervalued and neglected. If they were not "decadent," Tchaikovsky's orchestral works were wrongly interpreted as being naïve, sentimental, and unsymphonic. Mravinsky perceived three main qualities: "Gauk gave us professionalism, a system and a specific technique, matched with a clear performing style and true conducting method."[44]

Following the auspicious tours by Klemperer, the German conductor Heinz Unger visited Russia during the 1920s:

> The city (now renamed Leningrad) *had* been the imperial capital, and here European traditions survived more persistently than anywhere else in the Soviet Union. In the streets, everything spoke of the revolution. As soon as one left the badly repaired Nevsky Prospekt, one came across the torn-up paving of the side streets and the ruined houses and the blind, glassless windows of the palaces of the rich; and these ruins seemed left here purposely, as monuments to the victory of the Bolsheviks. The fruits of this victory so far were typified by the grey mass, which, once it had thrown off its festival disguise, looked as depressed, elbowing their way along the great boulevards. . . . [T]hese things being so, how could one escape from the present into the past, simply by means of a visit to a concert?[45]

The problems of day-to-day life continued, and filling in gaps between his studies and work at the Ballet School, Mravinsky worked as a pianist in cinemas in the Nevsky Prospekt area (renamed Prospekt 25 October), sharing a job with the young Shostakovich at the "Odeon" cinema. Through the 1920s, his path embraced playing in factories and Palaces of Culture as an accompanist with the "Youth" ballet troupe.[46] This struggle to make his daily bread drained the capacity of Mravinsky in a city torn apart by the Revolution. With so many of the former ruling class leaving, it would have been relatively easy for the Mravinskys to emigrate.

The Mravinskys knew European culture intimately; nevertheless, whatever political regime was in power, Russia was their home. Soviet power could not take that from them. The Mravinskys cherished the city of St. Petersburg/Petrograd/Leningrad. If it was the cradle of the October Revolution, it was more significantly the temple of Russian culture—the result of the assimilation of more than two hundred years of great world art and music. Those who stayed behind were proud of their heritage and sought to uphold its magnificent traditions. Whatever the cause, they could not forsake it. Mravinsky's fate was tied to his city and its Melos.

> No. I lived not under foreign skies,
> Sheltering under foreign wings:
> I then stayed with my people,
> There where my people, unhappily, were.[47]

Religion and a sincere belief in a better life were a lasting source of moral and spiritual strength, giving them succor and solace in their everyday lives and hope for better days ahead. Mravinsky, when a spare moment allowed, would stroll through the many parks and gardens of the city. The seasons interested him; he cared after animals as warmly as he would his closest friends. Throughout his life (although this may have been somewhat dangerous), Mravinsky kept a diary; here were his most intimate thoughts, ranging from his daily working schemes to accounts of his wandering through woods and fields. His love of writing too saw him recording his experiences in frequent letters to friends and colleagues. In the summer of 1928, Mravinsky wrote to the ballerina Tatyana Vecheslova:[48]

> I am fine here, Tanya. There are trees all around; in the distance I can see the rye bowing in the wind and beyond endless, deep forests. In some places it is difficult to make one's way. . . . I am walking a lot; yesterday I returned from a six-day hike covering 50 miles. I found myself beyond Mologa and stayed with a woodsman, and together with his friend we drank tea and honey from an old brass samovar. Walking through the countryside, I followed the riverbank along

the forest edge, and beyond the distant hills one could see like mushrooms—the roofs of cottages and small little village churches .The wind swept through the shimmering fields bringing a fresh and pleasant taste to one's senses. . . . Here quite alone, I live in a little hut with three tiny windows. I write both for myself and to various people, I read a little, and as I write, walk a great deal.[49]

In 1929, opportunities to conduct were so hard to come by that Mravinsky had to forge his own openings. He approached an amateur ensemble led by Yakov Genshaft (himself an aspiring musician and conductor) and affiliated with the trade union for shop and trade workers. Mravinsky sat in on the rehearsals, and when Genshaft opportunely fell ill, Mravinsky took over and conducted the public concert. The program comprised the *Andante* from Tchaikovsky's Fifth Symphony, "Panorama" from *The Sleeping Beauty*, *A Night on a Bare Mountain* by Musorgsky, the *Waltz Fantasy* by Glinka, and *The Toreador and the Andalusian Girl* by Anton Rubinstein. Ivan Sollertinsky, a young music critic, wrote a glowing appraisal.[50]

It was an auspicious beginning for the youthful conductor, and for a relationship with Sollertinsky that in future years would become vastly important. More dates arose with the Conservatoire Orchestra, and in 1929 Mravinsky was directing fragments from Glazunov's *Raymonda*; later, in 1930, in an evening presentation for students in Professor Gauk's class, he conducted Mozart's *"Haffner" Serenade* no. 9 in D major K. 320. One of Mravinsky's fellow students, Eduard Grikurov, explains: "In five years of study, I only conducted the overture to *Prométheus* by Beethoven, *Francesca da Rimini* by Tchaikovsky, and Liszt's First Concerto. That was all!"[51] The real test for developing conducting experience was at the Opera Studio in the third year. There were daily performances, and this was much owing to the efforts of Yershov: "he was always affectionate with his students, at least those who he said had 'a touch of God' in them."[52]

In the spring of 1931, Mravinsky undertook *Carmen* for his graduation work at the Conservatoire. He already had conducted Gounod's *Faust* and Verdi's *Rigoletto* in collaboration with Yershov:

His creations of *Tsars Bride*, *Rusalka*, *Marriage of Figaro*, or the *Merry Wives of Windsor* were major sensations of the period. Yershov was the founder of a school of opera direction, unmatched by anyone before or since. Yershov however did not have the benefit of an easy nature and conductors were afraid of him, refusing to accept their authority in opera production. However, behind the storm and thunder of Yershov there was a transparent and innocent soul. . . . Ivan Vasilyevich loved to speak in public, however never prepared his speeches, always improvising. . . . He could speak eloquently and sometimes very willfully. In 1938, at a Kremlin reception for a group of professors hosted by President Kalinin, Yershov being the most senior present, had to give a speech in reply. He quite lost his way and began talking about the walls of the Kremlin, who had built them, and talking about philosophy, in which subject he was weakest of all.[53]

Bizet's *Carmen* was an old warhorse; nevertheless, Mravinsky revived it, bringing in a chorus and singers from the State Academic Opera Theatre. Mravinsky was credited with attaining a harmony of singers, chorus, and orchestra, and despite aged sets and costumes, he reinvigorated it as if for a new production. In concert performances, Mravinsky often returned to the score with the Philharmonic. In April 1931, Mravinsky graduated from the Conservatoire with a diploma in conducting to follow that in composition.[54]

Yevgeny Mravinsky was isolated because he was a member of the gentry, and on every disposition upon enlisting for work, he had to cite his family circumstances. Because of his diligence and excellence at both the Ballet School and the Conservatoire, Mravinsky just kept his head above water. In 1924, when Mravinsky enrolled at the Conservatoire, three hundred of the almost eight hundred students were members of the Young Communist League (Komsomol); a branch of the Communist Party had been set up in 1922, and its influence carried a majority of students, and among their ranks originated a culture of intimidation, of informants. During the 1920s, the secretary of the Party organization was a student at the vocal faculty, Zakhar Zabludovsky, "a man of intelligence and sharp character [whose] simplicity in approach and preparedness to help students removed many of life's incongruities."[55] There was opposition from Komsomol and party members, and "candidates" would suffer written denunciations, which had to be investigated. Mravinsky was the subject of one of these anonymous letters, and an inquiry was made into his alleged "absenteeism." The ensuing investigation was revealed to be the result of an intrigue—the first of many.[56] An unsettling factor was the disappearance of Mravinsky's cousin from his research job at the Timiryazev Institute in Moscow. As Kollontay confided in her diary, "the son of my sister-in-law Adéle—a doctor and a very promising man—has committed suicide. He was a Bolshevik since 1905 and later as a student went abroad, returned, and worked with us in 1917. It's difficult to inform my sister about this; the very thought sends a chill down my spine."[57]

Employment in the Soviet Union depended on recommendations from voluntary organizations, and if this avenue failed, then only someone in a respected position could grant means of entrée. If Mravinsky owed his entry into the State Conservatoire to the influence of his aunt, then his appointment as a staff conductor in September 1931 at the State Academic Opera and Ballet came only upon the recommendation of his teacher. Alexander Gauk's class of 1931 laid the foundations of the Soviet school of conducting. Alexander Melik-Pashayev proceeded to work regularly at the opera theaters in Tbilisi, Baku, and Yerevan. However, his greatest achievements were during his tenure at the Bolshoi Opera Theatre during the 1950s and 1960s; it was there he gave the stage premiere of Prokofiev's *War and Peace* in 1959. "Melik-Pashayev made a great impression; he was an accomplished professional conductor, and everyone looked up to him as an paradigm."[58] Ilya Musin's own practical crafts were limited—his sole posting was at the Belarus State Symphony between 1938 and 1941, and his last concert with the Philharmonic was in 1954—but he began teaching in 1928 and brought up a whole string of fine conductors.[59] Nikolay Rabinovich carved out a niche as a great Mahlerian, and he would be an assistant at the Philharmonic from the late 1930s to the 1960s, his teaching work at the Conservatoire no less impressive than Musin's.[60]

The path of Yevgeny Mikeladze, however, suffered one of the most ghastly fates of this era. "Mikeladze was noble, honorable, and sincere, Malko said of him that he had a disposition in his hands as if they were a 'living baton. If he had not suffered such an untimely tragic death, I am convinced that Mikeladze would have become one of the greatest Soviet conductors. As a colleague, during the difficult student years, I was indebted to him, for he always gave me firm support in periods of doubt, and restored to me my self-belief."[61] Mikeladze had started as a horn player in his native Georgia before enlisting in Malko's class in 1928.

A short, compact, muscular man with shaved head, Mikeladze had a physique that was somewhat uncomely for a conductor, yet he possessed a natural charm, charisma, and a hypnotic power on the podium. Mikeladze undertook a season of concerts in his hometown during the summer vacation, including new pieces in his repertoire. Mikeladze won the most admiration for his performances of the late romantics, particularly Brahms's Third Symphony—rarely heard in the Caucasian republic—and he insisted on rehearsing his musicians twice a day. Seeing such fine conductors as Walter and Klemperer, Mikeladze claimed that one must instill one's individuality: "you know that there is only one Bruno Walter—an exceptional musician. But there are many fine conductors; one must develop one's own personality."[62]

Regarded as a promising opera conductor, Mikeladze upon graduation returned to Tbilisi and worked as conductor at the State Opera and Ballet Theatre (becoming chief conductor in his third season) and at the newly formed Georgian State Symphony Orchestra. Mikeladze achieved critical acclaim in recruiting many fine singers and encouraging leading artists from Moscow and Leningrad to sample the hospitality of the musical Georgian people.[63]

Yevgeny Mikeladze's wife, Ketevan Orekhelashvili, was the daughter of the chairman of the Georgian Council of Ministers. In what became known as the Lakoba Affair,[64] Lavrenty Beria had the chairman executed by the Georgian secret police in a terror campaign before Beria was appointed head of the NKVD in Moscow.[65] Mikeladze, being part of this clan, was seized together with his wife and children and shot without trial in 1937.[66] Alexander Gauk paid tribute: "Mikeladze was dissimilar to any other young conductor, and I believe that he had a great future before him."[67] This episode was one of the most dehumanizing in Soviet art, although a small part of the greater Soviet tragedy; it emphasizes how close Yevgeny Alexandrovich Mravinsky was himself to suffering a similar fate.

NOTES

1. Y. A. Mravinsky, *Schastlivaya Pora, Leningrad Conservatoire 1862–1962*, edited by G. Tigranov (Leningrad: Gozudarstvenniye Muzikalniye Izdatelstvo, 1962), 215.

2. Y. A. Mravinsky archive.

3. Y. A. Mravinsky archive.

4. A. M. Vavilina Mravinskaya, author interview, July 2001.

5. A. Kollontay, *Iz Moyei Zhisni i Raboti* (Moscow: Sovetskaya Rossia, 1974), 90.

6. *Izvestia*, 27 October 1917.

7. A. M. Vavilina Mravinskaya, author interview, July 2001.

8. A. M. Vavilina Mravinskaya, author interview, July 2001.

9. Y. A. Mravinsky archive.

10. Kushnarev's major work was *Questions of the History and Theory of Armenian Monodic Music*.

11. T. G. Ter-Martirosyan, "Klass kompozitsii K. C. Kushnareva," in *Leningradskaya Konservatoriya v vospominaniyakh 1862–1962* (Leningrad: Gozudarstvenniye Muzikalniye Izdatelstvo,1962), 175.

12. Mravinsky, *Schastlivaya Pora*, 215.

13. Mravinsky, *Schastlivaya Pora*, 215.

14. A. I. Dmitr'yev, "Moy lyubimiye uchitelya," in *Leningradskaya Konservatoriya v vospominaniyakh 1862–1962*, ed. K. C. Kushnareva (Leningrad: Gozudarstvenniye Muzikalniye Izdatelstvo,1962), 163.

15. Dmitr'yev, *Moy lyubimiye uchitelya*, 157.

16. Dmitr'yev, *Moy lyubimiye uchitelya*, 158.

17. Dmitr'yev, *Moy lyubimiye uchitelya*, 217–18.

18. P. Heyworth, *Otto Klemperer: His Life and Times*, Vol. 1 (Cambridge: Cambridge University Press, 1983), 214.

19. G. Y. Yudin, *Za gran yu proshlihk dnei* (Moscow: Muzikalnoe Nasledtsvo-Muzika, 1966), 107–120.

20. Yudin, *Za gran yu proshlihk dnei*, 107–120.

21. B. Asaf'yev, *Kriticheskiye statyi, ocherki, retzenzti* (Moscow: Muzika, 1967), 273.

22. Otto Klemperer, interview with Philo Bregstein 1, manuscript, 1972: 10–11.

23. N. Malkov, *Zhisn iskusstvo*, 28 April 1925.

24. Klemperer to his wife, in Heyworth, *Otto Klemperer,* Vol. 1, 222.

25. Y. Braudo, *Musical Courier*, 11 February 1926.

26. B. Asaf'yev, *Krasnaya Gazeta*, 2 December 1925.

27. O. Fried, *Pariser Nachrichten*, 21 January 1935.

28. The latter score is marked for three celli and three trombones.

29. V. Fomin, *Dirizher Yevgeny Mravinsky* (Leningrad: Muzika, 1983), 18.

30. B. Walter, *Of Music and Music-Making* (London: Faber and Faber, 1961), 28.

31. Krasnukha is a children's illness similar to chicken pox.

32. Boris I. Zagursky, "Moy Konservatorskiye gody," in *Leningradskaya Konservatoriya v vospominaniyakh 1862–1962* (Leningrad: Gozudarstvenniye Muzikalniye Izdatelstvo,1962), 117–18.

33. A. Lunacharsky, *Otvet Komsomolstii Konservatorii, V Mire Muziki* (Moscow, 1926), 308–311.

34. Walter, *Of Music and Music-Making*, 28.

35. Mravinsky, *Schastlivaya Pora*, 216–17.

36. Mravinsky, *Schastlivaya Pora*, 216.

37. V. M. Bogdanov-Berezovsky, *Sovetsky Dirizher* (Leningrad: Muzika, 1956), 42.

38. O. A. Dimitriadi, "Dni Yunosti," in *Leningradskaya Konservatoriya v vospominaniyakh 1862–1962* (Leningrad: Gozudarstvenniye Muzikalniye Izdatelstvo,1962), 226.

39. A. V. Gauk, *Memoiri, izbranniye stati, vospominaniye sovremminikov* (Moscow: Muzika, 1975), 179.

40. Mravinsky, *Schastlivaya Pora*, 215–17.

41. O. A. Dimitriadi, *Dni Yunosti*, 227.

42. V. Y. Shebalin, *Zabytaya simfoniya Glinki*, Shebalin, *Literaturnoye naslediye* (Moscow: Sovetsky Kompozitor, 1975), 177.

43. A. Melik-Pashayev, *Sovetskaya Muzika*, no. 9 (1963): 77–78.

44. Mravinsky, *Schastlivaya Pora*, 215–17.

45. H. Unger, *Hammer, Sickle and Baton* (London: Cresset, 1939), 62–64.

46. Y. A. Mravinsky archive.

47. A. Akhmatova, *Requiem: Anna Akhmatova Works*, Vol. 2 (Munich: Inter-Language Literary Associates, 1965), 353.

48. Tatyana Vecheslova was a promising ballerina who created the Komsomol Girl in Shostakovich's *The Age of Gold*.

49. Y. A. Mravinsky family archive.

50. I. Sollertinsky, *Zhisn i Iskusstvo*, no. 34 (1929).

51. E. Grikurov, "Gody minuvshiye," in *Leningradskaya Konservatoriya v vospominaniyakh 1862–1962* (Leningrad: Gozudarstvenniye Muzikalniye Izdatelstvo,1962), 222.

52. E. Grikurov, *Gody minuvshiye*, 223.

53. Zagursky, *Moy Konservatorskiye gody*, 113–14.

54. Archives of the St. Petersburg Philharmonia Library.

55. Zagursky, *Moy Konservatorskiye gody*, 111–12.

56. Y. A. Mravinsky family archive.

57. A. M. Kollontay, *Diplomaticheskiye dnevniki 1922–1940*, Vol. 2 (Moscow: Akademiya Izdatelstvo, 2002), 21.

58. Mravinsky, *Schastlivaya Pora*, 215–16.

59. Between 1928 and 1996, Ilya Musin taught at the Leningrad Conservatoire; among his pupils were Vladislav Chernoushenko, Yuri Temirkanov, Valery Gergiyev, and Mark Ermler.

60. Rabinovich taught several outstanding young conductors in Yuri Simonov, Neemi Jarvi, and Mariss Jansons.

61. Mravinsky, *Schastlivaya Pora*, 215–16.

62. I. Andronikov, *K Muziki* (Moscow: Sovetsky Kompozitor, 1975), 219.

63. Andronikov, *K Muziki*, 220–21.

64. The Lakoba Affair was an alleged plot gone wrong in 1933 to assassinate Stalin at his dacha in Georgia. It is believed that the affair was based on false accusations and contrived by Beria to achieve his own ends.

65. S. Beria, *Beria, My Father* (London: Duckworth, 2001), 25. The NKVD (Narodny Kommissariat Vnutrenye Delo, or Committee for Home Affairs) was the forerunner of the KGB.

66. M. Oleinik, "Kutaisskiye vechera (pamyati Evgeniya Mikeladze)," *Muzikalnaya Zhizh*, no. 24 (1988).

67. Andronikov, *K Muziki*, 223.

Chapter Four

"A Future Conductor of World Class"

> Our conductor is possibly a composer himself: able to build up a fugue,
> variations, or sonata form, and to take them to pieces.
>
> —Frederick Goldbeck, *The Perfect Conductor*

The resplendent Italian rococo building of the Mariinsky Opera and Ballet Theatre bequeathed a wealth of associations for the Mravinskys; here on its stage Mravina had enchanted with her singing and acting, and here Yevgeny Mravinsky was first bewitched by Tchaikovsky's great ballets. Passing by daily going to the Alexander II Gymnasium, Yevgeny was haunted by this veritable treasure house of musical delights. Yet he could never have expected that his primary experiences would be to work there as a mime artist. Nevertheless, the young Mravinsky held no pretensions, boundlessly happy just to be part of this great institution. Everything that became possible for Mravinsky was attained through grueling toil together with a God-given talent.

In September 1931, once again Mravinsky entered the stage door of the theater and felt himself completely at home. Here reigned an atmosphere of thriving creativity, with constantly renewed repertoire, a wealth of tradition, and a respect for the older generation.[1] Contemporary life had failed to inspire libretti for modern opera; however, the ballet troupe was producing the most entrancing work in the emergence of young exciting dancers such as Chabukiani, Sergeyev, Dudinskaya, and Ulanova. New Soviet ballets by Glière, Shostakovich, Khachaturyan, and Prokofiev were keeping safe the legacy of Glazunov, Rimsky-Korsakov, and Tchaikovsky. While they did not forsake the classics, the current works had a freshness and novelty, and Mravinsky was naturally attracted to the genre. His status was initially as a *répétiteur*, preparing with dancers and producers for ongoing stage productions at both state theaters. Toward the end of his first season, Mravinsky took

41

charge of a production of Glazunov's *The Seasons* on the stage of the Maly Opera and Ballet Theatre on 29 March 1932 in a well-received showcase of graduates from the Ballet School.[2]

The arrival of Sergey Radlov as the new artistic director at the State Opera and Ballet was a major step for the theater. This appointment of the city's leading theatrical producer heralded much, and there arrived in his wake the musicologists Adrian Piotrovsky, Boris Asaf'yev, and Alexey Gvozdev, artists Valentina Khodasevich and Vladimir Dmitr'yev, choreographers Agrippina Vaganova and Vasily Vainonen, and conductor Vladimir Dranishnikov. "Radlov managed to create a *milieu* and advanced level, unknown before or since."[3] A few months after his engagement, Radlov said "we are entering a season very important for us. We want it to be better, more meaningful, and more valuable than all the preceding ones."[4]

Radlov's first productions through the 1932–1934 seasons were *William Tell*, *Das Rheingold*, *Il Trovatore*, *The Love for Three Oranges*, *Swan Lake*, *The Fires of Paris*, and *Bakhchisaray Fountain*. Not all secured success; the Verdi opera was credited in its publicity as produced by Radlov and Khodasevich and duly received Sollertinsky's witticism: "since the poster does not make it clear who 'supervised it' then the staging might be called somewhat impersonal." Radlov aspired to a synthesis of the text, music, singing, pantomime, dance, color, and light on stage. In bidding to portray "musical tragedy" on stage, Radlov cast away tradition in an attempt to create a complete realization of opera and ballet.

Mravinsky's own opportunity duly arrived in the 1932–1933 season, when he was entrusted with *The Sleeping Beauty*, by an astonishing coincidence, the same ballet Mravinsky saw on his first visit to the theater as a child. Following his year of apprenticeship, Mravinsky now appeared at the same daunting rostrum as masters of the not so distant past—Rachmaninov, Cooper, Coates, Napravnik, and in recent times Klemperer, Glazunov, and Walter.

The Sleeping Beauty production used the celebrated choreography of Maurice Petipa, revived by Fyodor Lopukhov, directed by Gauk and by the theater's chief conductor Dranishnikov, and naturally Mravinsky felt no little apprehension in following in their wake. Gauk read the ballet close to the text, with great attention to inner detail, while Dranishnikov took the work more eloquently, underlining its emotional expression. The young man being so intimately acquainted with the music nevertheless considered it important to impart his own conception and deliver a fresh dramatic concept to the ballet.

That Mravinsky was allotted just one rehearsal rendered his task even more formidable. Nevertheless, he displayed such independence of thought and purpose that he won respect both on stage and in the orchestra pit. The premiere on 29 September 1932 became Yevgeny Mravinsky's first artistic success, so much so that following the second act, he was awarded an ovation by his musicians and the applause of the public in the theater.[5] The young conductor's triumph was in transforming the ballet from "a mixture of different ballet numbers through symphonic-like movements into an integral conception."[6] Mravinsky studied the score perceptively, feeling each nuance, bringing an emotional force and depth to the listener. The young dancer Natalia Dudinskaya also made her debut that night in the central role of Aurora, and she remembered the performance as being quite exceptional: "There was a different sound created by the orchestra, a richness and a color I had not heard before. Only Mravinsky did this, yet how he could do this from a single session is uncanny."[7]

Mravinsky's first victory in the musical profession resulted in audiences coming to the theater not just to see Dudinskaya and Sergeyev in *The Sleeping Beauty*, but also to hear Mravinsky's conducting.[8] In attendance at Mravinsky's debut was his aunt, the ambassador to Sweden, and Alexandra Kollontay together with the regional secretary and Politburo member Sergey Kirov. In her diaries, Kollontay recalled: "Kirov invited me to his loge for the ballet. Mravinsky, my half sister's son, was conducting. Kirov complimented him, saying he was a 'promising talent.' Mravinsky has a beautiful conducting manner. One feels he compels one, and the public has been quite won over by him."[9] Sollertinsky wrote that Mravinsky "made major lines in the contour of the main musical form, achieving a ingenious contradiction to the nature of performing contrasting numbers, but allowing a cyclic, flowing unity giving a developing symphonic narrative."[10]

Mravinsky spent much of his free hours at the Philharmonic, regularly meeting fellow musicians, among whom were the musicologists Mikhail Druskin and Ivan Sollertinsky; Mravinsky's teachers Gauk and Shcherbachyov; pianists Nikolayev, Sofronitsky, Serebryakov, and Yudina; and the composers Shaporin and Shostakovich.[11] Here began strong, life-long friendships, including with the young student Isaak Glikman. who shared many interests and, most importantly, a love for the music of Shostakovich.[12] This circle regularly debated new names emerging at the city's theaters and concert halls, and occasionally the "club" would be graced by famous figures such as Yur'yev, Radlov, or Steidry and visiting musicians such as Klemperer or Walter. The *bel esprit* was Sollertinsky, whose wit, charm, and biting satire would endear him to Shostakovich; another wag in Irakli Andronikov would imitate the facial gestures of Steidry, taking him to task for his Russian speech, leaving everyone in tears of laughter and causing no little embarrassment for the Austrian, who could only stand and watch.[13]

Following the young conductor's initial success at the theater, Radlov offered Mravinsky a new production of Adam's *Corsair* in October 1932 and

Giselle in February 1933. The response of the press and audience to *Giselle* was unanimously positive:

> To raise one's artistic performance and make the orchestra believe that it is pos-
> sible to play such cliché-ridden music is difficult, particularly as Mravinsky is
> only in his second year as a professional conductor.[14] Mravinsky directs the or-
> chestra very assuredly, the least hesitation in rhythm drawing instant attention
> from his baton and showing restraint in not allowing his temperament to develop
> moments of dramatic tension.[15]

The new *Swan Lake* united Radlov with Yevgeny Mravinsky for the first time at the theater. Asaf'yev was the musical consultant, and this represented their first collaboration in a series of which would lead to both successes and dis-appointments. Agrippina Vaganova provided the choreography, and the sce-nario was by Dmitr'yev; however, this could not save the production from be-ing savaged by local critics when it opened on 13 April 1933. Nevertheless, the musical performance of *Swan Lake* did receive acknowledgment, the con-ductor particularly praised for his clear, lyrical treatment of Tchaikovsky's score. The astute Ivan Sollertinsky wrote: "The thoughtful nature of the sce-nario, the sharpness and lack of pity makes it quite vulgar."[16] Sollertinsky nevertheless recounted Mravinsky's conception as "intense and loving."[17]

As always, Sollertinsky drew a fine line between positive criticism and en-tertainment in his articles:

> In this fresh production of *Swan Lake*, we are taken to the 1830s, and the Prince
> Siegfried of the middle ages is transformed into a romantic youth—a German
> Prince living in an old family castle. For him, the book of poetry he has in his
> hand is not that of Lord Byron but Klopstock. The company has chosen to give
> us something in the style of a Hoffman novella (evident not only from the issued
> program), however, they have forgotten on this occasion to give this opportunity
> to a proven scenic-dramatist. . . . The new musical edition is highly speculative;
> a half way house between that of Drigo and Tchaikovsky. . . . Praise must be
> given to the attentive and veritable labor of love by Yevgeny Mravinsky—a
> gifted young conductor, of somewhat lyrical persuasion, already revealed very
> well by him in a fine portrayal of the *Sleeping Beauty*; it would be of extraordi-
> nary interest to hear Mravinsky in opera. Taking all this into account, the new
> production of *Swan Lake* is an indubitable achievement by the theater. The bal-
> let is freshened up, revived, and more youthful. To retain all of the old produc-
> tion would be irresponsible and pedantic. However, the lessons of this *Swan
> Lake* are the first task for the ballet troupe and something to be tackled with full
> responsibility.[18]

A few weeks following the controversy at the Ballet Theatre, a diversion for Mravinsky was undertaking a setting of Richard Strauss's *Till Eulenspiegel*, staged by the young, brilliant Leonid Yakobson at the Dance School.[19] Mravinsky wrote the libretto, which corresponded closely to a programmatic illustration to Strauss's music. Sollertinsky somewhat caustically berated "the production's unsuitable match of music to dance form."[20] Following the two great Tchaikovsky ballets, a revival of *The Nutcracker* with choreography by the young, exciting Vasily Vainonen now consumed Mravinsky's attention. The opening night, following extensive rehearsals, took place on 18 February 1934. Tchaikovsky's most popular creation became the ne plus ultra in Mravinsky's period at the theater, exceeding that of *The Sleeping Beauty*. The ballet in his hands was no children's fairy-tale made up of brilliant dance episodes executed in small, miniature sketches. Mravinsky's *Nutcracker* was a sophisticated musical drama, artistically enlightened and drawn in fresh and dramatic orchestral colors with the symphonic concept transforming its nature. Wrote the ever perceptive Sollertinsky:

A fine success for the theatre, nevertheless, fault was to be found; in the heritage of Tchaikovsky, *Nutcracker* is both a major achievement and serious failure. Much is great in the score. The richly refined orchestral music contains brilliant novelties (for the first time, the use of a celesta, oboe pitched at a high note and much else) and a rare rhythmic invention. Symphonic methodology continues through the first two acts. . . . Yet contrary to these musical wonders, there is such a surprising lack of subject which seems quite out of context, pictures of Hoffmannesque imagery or moralistic fairy-tales for children of the youngest age. The contradictions of style and subject in *Nutcracker* always created the most difficult of problems for the choreographer. Staged for the first time in 1892 by Petipa and Ivanov, the ballet achieved little success. The monumental delights of Petipa did not suit the intimate miniatures of Tchaikovsky's bejeweled score. Neither did the 1929 production by Lopukhov capture Tchaikovsky's style. The present producer Vasily Vainonen has not created a new choreographic style. He has managed to latently combine elements of former styles and remain on the base of classical ballet. In short, Vainonen is not always compatible with Tchaikovsky's music . . . however, despite his shortcomings . . . Vainonen is capable of fine work in the corps de ballet scenes, in major scenes. . . . The greatest success was that of Galina Ulanova in the role of Masha. The recent work of Ulanova in *Giselle* and this *Nutcracker* reinforces conclusively that she is among our country's leading artists. A fine partner for Ulanova was the elasticity and finesse of Konstantin Sergeyev. At last—a great success for the theater—was the accurate and well-thought portrayal of Tchaikovsky's score by the conductor Yevgeny Mravinsky. Without unnecessary accents, and loud pompous brass, Mravinsky maintains a correct line of interpretation with *Nutcracker*, giving it an intimate-lyrical ambience. Free of traditional layers dictated by routine and misunderstanding, Tchaikovsky's score sounded unusually fresh and in relief.[21]

Mravinsky's next task was to turn to contemporary Soviet ballet and Boris Asaf'yev's setting of Alexander Pushkin's poem, *The Fountain of Bakhchisaray*. The staging was an experiment to introduce so-called dramatic ballet. The production heralded the future and introduced what was to become the sole "legitimate" form of dance, which followed in the traditions of Noverre, the creations of Maurice Petipa regarded now as harmful and old fashioned — Sollertinsky declared that Petipa's choreography was archaic, having outlived itself.[22] The production brought together some of the theater's finest artists: Rostislav Zakharov was choreographer, Valentina Khodasevich was set designer, and Nikolay Volkhov was librettist.[23] Boris Asaf'yev (Igor Glebov) was the doyen of Soviet musicology, brilliant in his field and the only musicologist to be elected to the Academy of Sciences. "The first major work upon Asaf'yev's return to composition was the ballet *Fires of Paris* of 1932. The latter was written on textual works of the eighteenth and the beginning of the nineteenth centuries (Grétry, Lesuéur, Cherubini, Gossêc, Berton, and Méhul) from chansons, village songs and to present intonation of the epoch."[24] *Fires of Paris* was a triumph for the masses, of celebratory revolutionary scenes, the apotheosis of the crowd (and naturally of the corps de ballet), including a chorus.

It would be not reckless to declare Asaf'yev's gifts were more toward writing about music than they were to original composition.[25] The composer explained his own reservations: "I was afraid, admittedly, to use an openly romantic work with a delicate psychological premise: the spiritual rebirth of a tyrant through his love for a young girl."[26] "Asaf'yev held in reserve innumerable notations on customs, songs and dances, folk tunes, harmonisations, and many other details needed for a 'concrete' realization of a given subject. With his theatrical experience and great intellect, he created almost single-handedly a new 'science' of ballet."[27] Before the premiere on 28 September 1934, Asaf'yev attended all the rehearsals and was deeply impressed by both Mravinsky's attention for detail and his ability to grasp the essence of the author's conception as a whole. "Asaf'yev chose an early nineteenth-century musical idiom. It also provided the opportunity for stunning stage effects that were to become the hallmark of Bolshoi ballet productions."[28] Sollertinsky naturally led the assault:

> Orthodox balletomanes are not over the moon about *Fountain of Bakhchisary*; there is too little ballet! Nor are there dazzling variations with thirty-two pirouettes; neither are there any pearls of dance technique of the "Spanish" school, nor a feast of parading corps de ballet scenes in white toupees. This is not the strength of this new GATOB production of *Fountain of Bakhchisary*. The major positive aspect is that it recreates the tradition of real ballet, based on the celebrated reformer of dance in the 18th century Noverre—to Fokin. Therefore, the

artists do not require brilliant technique but maximum artistic expression in *Fountain of Bakhchisary*. This was a considerable triumph for the young choreographer Rostislav Zakharov [a student of Radlov], making his debut in dance form. Zakharov revealed a model of talented, considered, and mature work. Other criticism would impart that while Zakharov is a fine producer, he is not so good a choreographer. Why is it that a choreographer is not in charge? That is because the purpose is to relate a dramatic narrative through dance. What is so controversial is in Boris Asaf'yev's attitude to Pushkin's poem; there is a clear departure from restoration of the period style and the emotional context of the subject. On the one hand embracing the classical form of overtures by Mozart and Cherubini, with sentimental romances of Gyurilev on the other, with a setting from the 1820s and 1830s in the beginning and concluding with salon music and the ballets of Didlo and others. One might call it: "Pushkin in musical chairs."[29] Certainly, these principal complaints do not deter from the unquestionable merits in Asaf'yev's score, clearly written with taste, in part effectual and clearly theatrical (polonaise) although with an ineffective orchestration that sounds both insubstantial and feeble. The conductor Mravinsky balanced out the weak with the dangerous sections in the score, interpreting Asaf'yev's music with care, concentration, and consummate mastery. Praise must first be given to Galina Ulanova, an artist of outstanding lyricism, for whom technique has long been secondary to her characterization. Every line and arabesque in her choreography is full of dramatic expression. The part of Maria following her *Giselle* represents Ulanova's finest role. For the theater, the troupe, and for Zakharov, *Fountain of Bakchisaray* is a major step forward.[30]

Yet, *Fountain of Bakchisaray* is an elegiac poem and a sad tale of the departure of an isolated soul in the death of a lonely despot. The charm of Ulanova's Maria produced a great effect, yet it was the fear of the crowd that created the atmosphere in the theater. Other critics had stronger regrets for Radlov's experiment; "Classical dance was almost among the victims."[31] The ballet nevertheless became one of the triumphs of this period and part of the Soviet repertoire following its premiere under Mravinsky at the Bolshoi Theatre in 1935. The leading dancer in Asaf'yev's ballet, Pyotr Gusev, wrote that "it was from Asaf'yev that for the first time we heard about Mravinsky as a 'future conductor of world class.'"[32] Asaf'yev prophetically added, "Believe me, his career lies in symphonic music when he leaves this theater."[33]

As in tsarist times, many of the dancers at the Leningrad Ballet enjoyed relationships with members of the regime: secretary of the Leningrad Party Sergey Kirov enjoyed several mistresses among the young, beautiful ballerinas at the theater.[34] One of those who served drinks at Kirov's receptions was the young waitress Milda Braule from the Smolny restaurant. She was suspected as being a lover of the popular politician, and her jealous husband Nikolayev shot dead the Soviet leader in December 1934.[35] Many of the innocent "suspects" of the alleged "plot" at the theater disappeared into the torture chambers of the NKVD. It was here in the "cradle of revolution" that Iosif Stalin's purges began and a great shadow hung over the city, there flowing into the river Neva streams of blood from the broken souls of those betrayed by the Revolution.[36] To immortalize Kirov's memory, the State Academic Theatre was named in his honor, as the theater had graced in former times the name of Tsaritsa Maria Fyodorovna.

In May 1935, the Kirov Ballet toured at Moscow's Bolshoi Theatre, and Mravinsky was a natural choice to unveil the theater's rich array of talents in the dancers, choreographers, and set designers. Leningrad artists always aspired to display their greater artistry and class to the Muscovites, and this was an early opportunity for Mravinsky to work with what was then regarded as among Europe's finest ensembles—Klemperer declared that "in my opinion only one orchestra can rival Moscow's and that is the Vienna Philharmonic."[37]

The performances undertaken by Mravinsky at the Bolshoi Theatre were *Swan Lake* and *Fountain of Bakhchisaray*. The orchestra responded splendidly, winning critical acclaim:[38] "we must in particular, point out the work of the conductor in *Swan Lake*. Mravinsky and the wonderful orchestra of the Bolshoi Theatre have managed to reveal the symphonic and lyrical essence of Tchaikovsky's music, allowing its exhilarating beauty and creativity to be savored by his listeners. Nothing has been lost in its dance values, but embodied in the performance is an atmosphere of real romantic melody."[39]

The continuing successes of Mravinsky at the Kirov Ballet and this glowing recognition in the Moscow press only led to relentless study of new and old repertoire, occupying his ever-consuming schedule. On the eve of 1936, he conducted the world premiere of Asaf'yev's ballet based on Balzac's novel *Lost Illusions*, staged by Zakharov with a scenario by Dmitr'yev entitled "a choreographic romance." On this occasion, neither Mravinsky nor his musicians could save it from being a failure, and the ballet was withdrawn following three performances (many years later, Mravinsky would look back at the score and try to fathom the reason why the music failed to win over the audience and critics).[40] There were other reasons for the production's unpopularity and the contrast in fortunes with Asaf'yev's previous ballets. This was in the nature of the themes in the ballets, that of a dictator transformed into a good man in *Fountain of Bakchisaray* and that of Balzac's *Lost Illusions* touching upon hypersensitive nerves.[41] All during a period of turmoil and repression shared with the brief period of the Kirov's "experiment," which ended so abruptly with the resignation of Sergey Radlov.

Radlov received an appointment to the Moscow Art Theatre, and his departure from the Leningrad Theatre was announced in December 1936.[42] His replacement was the exceptionally talented Ariy Pasovsky, who also now attained the chief conductorship. Pasovsky was a student of Leopold Auer at the St. Petersburg Conservatoire and worked at the Minin private opera and Narodny Dom before the Revolution.[43] His arrival coincided with the departure of Dranishnikov to Kiev.[44] A major continuation of the Radlov influence was the presence of Boris Asaf'yev as a musical consultant. A member of the theater's artistic council, he became involved in a myriad of aspects of the Kirov Theatre, and his patient and courteous manner became a considerable asset to the theater if not on a wider horizon. "Everywhere and always, Asaf'yev's sound ear and keen eye noted real artistic potential, distinguishing it from the mediocre, petty, and sterile; in artistic matters it was quite impossible to deceive him."[45] Asaf'yev's flat on Trud Square became one of the musical centers during the 1930s; musicologists and musicians, writers and artists, dancers and singers would congregate there, including Shostakovich and Mravinsky. As a composer and musicologist, Asaf'yev accrued a vast network of contacts and was involved with all the major theaters in the country.[46]

Mravinsky found succor from this first major failure, happy to accept an invitation from the Dance School conducting *Andalusian Wedding*, based on the music of Albéniz and Granados.[47] Mravinsky's first and last opera production at the Kirov Theatre was of Tchaikovsky's complex and dark work based on Pushkin's *Mazeppa*, which opened on 19 February 1937. Mravinsky's background at the Conservatoire and Opera Studio had allowed him to gain invaluable experience in different operatic styles. Tchaikovsky's *Mazeppa*, however, has a difficult orchestral score with several important roles. The Kirov possessed some of the country's finest singers in Mark Reizen, Georgy Nelepp, Pavel Lisitsian, and Sophia Preobrazhenskaya, each magnificent in their vocal range and, with the outstanding chorus, offering Mravinsky all the opportunities of an excellent operatic debut, yet he was not to explore this genre, at least not at the theater.[48] Nevertheless, Mravinsky revealed his gifts in "demonstrating a magnificent feeling for the specifics of opera and brilliantly understanding the characteristics of conducting in opera."[49]

As Boris Asaf'yev had predicted, underlying all Mravinsky's work at the Kirov was an *idée fixe* to the philosophical school of symphonic music. If self-doubt would pose an inhibiting factor, nevertheless, following seven years at the Kirov, Yevgeny Mravinsky was now fully equipped for the next stage in his career.

NOTES

1. S. I. Levik, *Chetvert Veka v Opery* (Moscow: Izkusstvo, 1970), 307.
2. V. Fomin, *Dirizher Yevgeny Mravinsky* (Leningrad: Muzika, 1983), 22.

3. D. Zolotnitsky, *Sergei Radlov: The Shakespearian Fate of a Soviet Director* (Luxembourg: Harwood Academic, 1995), 109.

4. S. Radlov, *Rabochii i Teatr*, no. 23, 10 September 1931, 8.

5. S. Radlov, *Rabochii i Teatr*, no. 23, 10 September 1931, 24.

6. V. M. Bogdanov-Berezovsky, *Sovetsky Dirizher* (Leningrad: Muzika, 1956), 52–53.

7. N. Dudinskaya, interview in *Russkoe Video*, 1989.

8. K. Sergeyev and N. Dudinskaya, interview, *Russkoe Video*, 1989.

9. A. M. Kollontay, *Beseda s Segeyem Mironovichem Kirovym, Diplomaticheskiye dnevniki 1922–1940*, Vol. 2 (Moscow: Akademiya, 2002), 125.

10. Bogdanov-Berezovsky, *Sovetsky Dirizher*, 52–53.

11. I. D. Glikman, *Pisma K Drugu* (St. Petersburg: DSCH, 1993), 7.

12. Isaak Glikman, author interview, July 2002.

13. A. Glumov, *Nestertiye Stroki* (Moscow: Vserossiskiye Teatralnoye Obshestvo, 1977), 309–310.

14. L. Entelis, "E. A. Mravinsky," *Rabochi i Teatr*, no. 36 (1933).

15. Entelis, "E. A. Mravinsky."

16. I. Sollertinsky, *Rabochi i Teatr*, no. 12 (1933).

17. Sollertinsky, *Rabochi i Teatr*, no. 12 (1933).

18. I. I. Sollertinsky, "Lebedinoye ozero," *Rabochi i Teatr*, no. 12 (1933).

19. Fomin, *Dirizher Yevgeny Mravinsky*, 25.

20. I. I. Sollertinsky, *Rabochi i Teatr*, no.15 (1933).

21. I. I. Sollertinsky, "Tselunchik," *Rabochi i Teatr*, no. 4 (1933).

22. V. M. Gayevsky, *Dom Petipa* (Moscow: Artist-Rezhisser-Teatr, 2000), 220.

23. The ballet remains on the repertoire of many theaters throughout Russia.

24. V. A. Dranishnikov, *B. V. Asaf'yev i evo baletnaya muzika* (Moscow: Izdannie Gozmuz Teatra im Nemirovicha-Danchenko, 1936), 60.

25. Gayevsky, *Dom Petipa*, 218.

26. B. Asaf'yev, *Na baleta* (Moscow: Muzika, 1974), 253.

27. B. Schwartz, *Music and Musical Life in Soviet Russia 1917–1982* (Bloomington: Indiana University Press, 1983), 151.

28. B. Schwartz, *Music and Musical Life*, 151.

29. Here Sollertinsky is alluding to an expression about "Pushkin in theatrical chairs" in Leonid Petrovich Grossman's 1926 book on the Russian stage in 1817–1820.

30. I. I. Sollertinsky, "Vpered k Noverru," *Rabochi i Teatr*, no. 29 (1934).

31. V. Gayevsky, *Dom Petipa,* 218.

32. P. Gusev, *Drug Baleta* (Leningrad: Lenizdat, 1974), 168.

33. P. Gusev, *Drug Baleta*, 168.

34. P. A. Sudoplatov, *Spetzoperatsia—1930–1950* (Moscow: OLMA, 1997), 83.

35. Sudoplatov, *Spetzoperatsia*, 84.

36. Sudoplatov, *Spetzoperatsia*, 84.

37. O. Klemperer, *Izvestia*, 1 January 1925.

38. N. Volkhov, "Obnovleniya Spektakli," *Sovetskoye Izkusstvo*, 29 June 1935.

39. Volkhov, "Obnovleniya Spektakli."

40. Y. A. Mravinsky archive.
41. V. M. Gayevsky, *Dom Petipa*, 219.
42. *Vechernaya Krasnaya Gazeta*, no. 296, 27 December 1936, 2.
43. E. Orlova and A. Kryukov, *Akademik Boris Vladimirovich Asaf'yev—monografiya* (Leningrad: Sovetsky Kompositor, 1984), 203.
44. Vladimir Dranishnikov's career at the Kiev State Opera and Ballet was short lived, as he died in the following season of a heart attack.
45. A. N. Dmitr'yev, *Vospominaniye o B. V. Asaf'yeve* (Leningrad: Muzika), 121–22.
46. E. Orlova and A. Kryukov, *Akademik Boris Vladimirovich Asaf'yev*, 206.
47. Fomin, *Dirizher Yevgeny Mravinsky*, 28.
48. S. Yu. Levik, *Chetvert Veka v Opery*, 325.
49. V. Fomin, *Orkestrom dirizhiruet Mravinsky* (Leningrad: Muzika, 1976), 46.

Chapter Five

The Leningrad Philharmonic

Distinguishing those that have feathers, and bite, from those that have whiskers and scratch.

—Lewis Carroll, *Alice and Wonderland*

The Summer Gardens on the Neva River is a sacred pantheon in Russian culture; Alexander Pushkin was inspired there to write his classic poem *Yevgeny Onegin*; the tree-shaded grounds found their locus, too, in the novels of Dostoyevsky and Gogol, as they did in the scene of Lisa's suicide in Tchaikovsky's *Queen of Spades*. Today the large park with paths flanked by lime trees has a wild and unkempt look brought to life by statues from Russian history and culture, and the white swans inhabiting a large circular lake evoke Tchaikovsky's great ballet. It was in this picturesque setting in July 1931 that Yevgeny Mravinsky made his conducting debut in a matinee concert with the Leningrad Philharmonic Orchestra. The bill included Beethoven's overtures *Egmont* and *Leonora III*, and Musorgsky's prelude to *Sorochinsky Fair*. The engagement was an award for graduating from Gauk's conducting class; regardless of the short program and minimal rehearsal time, Mravinsky made a distinct impression with the players and arts council of the Philharmonic.[1]

The Philharmonic Orchestra, following the 1917 Revolution, had attained state support in a resolution by the Soviet government of 21 May 1921 and was granted as its home the former Hall of Nobility—the finest large concert venue, possessing admirable acoustic qualities. The building offered excellent facilities for rehearsals and a superb music library. The first performance on 12 June was undertaken by Emil Cooper and devoted to Tchaikovsky: the *Pathétique*, the Violin Concerto (Cecilia Hansen as soloist), and the sym-

52

phonic fantasia *Francesca da Rimini*. Despite the privations of the Civil War and the loss of most of the Philharmonic's former audience, some fifty-four performances were presented during that summer. "The Philharmonic is the sole institution where there is maintained the culture of symphonic music and the sole orchestra that has continued regular concerts during the entire period of revolution."[2] For a long period, however, there was no chief conductor, simply a director responsible for artistic planning.[3] Numerous guest conductors made an impression—Golovanov, Suk, Saradzhayev, and Glazunov (the latter gave the first factory concert in 1926). However, considerable problems emerged with regular change in artistic directors; following Cooper's resignation in 1924, the Committee for Arts asked the head of the Capella Mikhail Klimov to assume the mantle of music directorship.[4] Klimov nevertheless demanded a triumvirate to resolve arts planning: Boris Asaf'yev, composer, teacher, and music critic; the leader of the cello section, Ilya Brik, erudite, polymath, and fine musician; and the head of the hall administration, Boris Khais. This troika became accountable for repertoire and inviting artists.[5]

Following Mravinsky's debut, his next invitation would not be for another eighteen months, yet by then much more experience would be at his disposal. In November 1932, Mravinsky gave his first concert at the Philharmonic Hall in Rimsky-Korsakov's *Scheherezade*. Mravinsky acquired a circle of admirers for his warm, impassioned readings of works both familiar and not so well known to audiences, all apart from his tall, handsome elegant figure.[6] "There was a more varied repertoire, with a more perceptible inclination to Western music than in Moscow."[7] There was a long tradition of musical performance, further oriented to European standards, bel canto, and clarity and precision in orchestral playing. "In Leningrad there prevails a special culture of sound in the orchestra. In Moscow there was the Golovanov school—more substantial and heavy bass sound."[8]

If Tchaikovsky gave Mravinsky his entrée into the theater, then it was the same composer's music that was featured in his initial phase with the Leningrad Philharmonic—in the first months of 1934, when there arrived frequent invitations.

A visit to a Philharmonic concert created a strong impression; its huge hall was always overfilling with people, the two rows of white marble columns on each side of the auditorium with the splendid chandeliers gave off an almost festival-like atmosphere to everyone there. On the right-hand side were the places occupied by distinguished visitors; in the directors loge sat the bespectacled, scowling chief conductor Fritz Steidry; beside him was the elderly artistic director Alexander Ossovsky wearing a goatee, *à la Henry III*. Ensconced there too was the patrician-like Ivan Yershov, the dramatic tenor of great Wagnerian operas. There looked out the youthful modest Shostakovich, his face framed by spectacles,

nervously twitching his fingers and arms, hardly keeping still a single second.
Next to the young composer was conductor Alexander Gauk, his round, ruddy
cheeks and bearing a self-assured pose. There would appear in the loge the tall
figure of Ivan Sollertinsky, somewhat awkwardly dressed in an ill-fitting suit as
if he had left a tailor's in a hurry. There would emerge from the artists' rooms
several elderly men; these were the professors and academics of the Academy
of Sciences led by its President Alexander Karpinsky, a constant patron of these
concerts. In the body of the hall, sitting in row five, was the large mass of the
former Count Alexey Tolstoy, his graying hair swept back to hide his encroach-
ing baldness. Another notable personality present in the parterre was the angu-
lar, thin actor from the Pushkin Theatre, Nikolay Cherkasov. On his right was
the director of the Hermitage Academician, Isaak Orbeli. The audience was full
of distinguished actors and writers; here were the crème de la crème of the old
Petersburg mixed with the youth of Leningrad arts and sciences. This was the
regular Philharmonic audience at subscription concerts of the 1930s.[9]

This audience was gathered to attend a concert of Tchaikovsky's music; first
on the program was *Francesca da Rimini* from Dante, a favorite piece, one of
the first to be performed by the Philharmonic, by Emil Cooper in 1921, and
performed again in 1924 by Vyacheslav Suk and in 1927, in one of his scintillating concerts, by Bruno Walter. On this evening, it was the opportunity for
Yevgeny Mravinsky to offer his portrayal of the work; recognized as a fine
conductor at the Leningrad State Ballet, he had already won a reputation for
his fine, intelligent work with the most difficult orchestral pieces. Before the
conductor went on stage, the musicians listened from their places on the platform to the opening words of the tall and elegant actor from the Pushkin Theatre, Elga Unger, announcing the program. Yet her function was only to introduce Ivan Sollertinsky, who in his forceful speech, intently listened to by
his audience, told of the "tragic-comedy," the tale of the maiden Beatrice, and
Dante's love for her.

Finally, there would appear the tall, thin figure of the conductor Mravinsky,
emerging from under the scarlet curtain to the left of the organ, striding quickly
to the podium. Met with applause from the audience, Mravinsky bowed somewhat imperiously, quickly turned around, and confronted his players. There he
awaited the complete silence of the hall. He waited and waited with arms
motionless—there had to be total, absolute quiet before he could begin. For several moments the noise and expectation would gradually come to a hush of expectation, during which Mravinsky's figure looked as if a sculpture, severe and
foreboding as any of those in the city's parks; this as it were granite figure represented a monument to the music about to be heard. Suddenly, as soon as there
was stillness, an unrelenting shock wave of sound was unleashed upon the listeners. The burst of orchestral music, of passion and torment, swept over everyone; as never before, this torrent of Tchaikovsky's tense emotion caught the

mood of the audience like a whirlwind. To this venerable hall of music lovers, it seemed as if the love passions of Francesca and Paolo were being drawn out before them; such was the powerful effect of Mravinsky's direction of the Philharmonic's musicians. Despite his youth, Mravinsky had captured the minds of his audience, making them understand his portrayal of this great symphonic poem. At last, one caught one's breath before a storm of applause for the conductor and the orchestra.[10]

Following this Tchaikovsky evening,[11] in April, Mravinsky tackled more late romantic repertoire at another Philharmonic evening by Cesar Franck: *Le Chasseur Maudit* and the *Variations Symphonique* (Pavel Seryabryakov). The other pieces were by Wagner, Brahms, and Bizet, making a highly colorful offering for Leningrad's musical elite.[12] In between engagements at the theater, Mravinsky would study works, most frequently under preparation by other conductors at the Philharmonic, including Fritz Steidry.

Once I went to the Philharmonic for a morning rehearsal of Beethoven's Fifth Symphony; there were a few musicians sitting in the hall listening. On his own, Mravinsky was ensconced in the score. While on stage, the chief conductor Fritz Steidry approached the podium, smart and lively, wearing thick glass spectacles, looking daggers. He removed his jacket and began at once with the opening bars of the "theme of fate" as written by Beethoven. Steidry endlessly repeated this passage, returning to the building of tempi and trying to attain rhythmical unity of all instruments. The orchestra became tired and angry; "it will be alright on the night," the musicians said with their typical indolence. Yet, these promises were as nothing to Steidry; this top ensemble, the best in the country, an "academic" orchestra, must play without fault or mistakes, and for another forty minutes he occupied himself with the introductory phrases of the symphony. Suddenly, Steidry in a storm of anger broke his baton into small pieces and stuffed them into his pocket, buried his face in his hands, standing in complete silence on the podium. The musicians were struck dumb. There reigned complete silence in the hall; it seemed for at least five minutes that the conductor stood there motionless, almost an eternity for the players sitting before him. At last, Steidry pulled himself together, lay the broken pieces of his baton on his desk, and with an abrupt movement of his arms began to conduct again—and as if a miracle happened, the opening *motto* came together. It sounded perfectly, and Steidry continued to conduct through to the end of the Fifth. Finally, he asked for some small changes from the trombones to create a heavenly ringing sound. With trepidation, I listened to the remaining movements of the symphony and what was created on stage! A wonderful resonance came from the strings, and at the end everyone rose in applause for Steidry, "Bravo, bravo!" The exclamations came from his musicians. Steidry gathered his broken baton, put his jacket on, and the grimace at last gone from his face, quickly announced an interval and disappeared into his room.[13]

Despite his love for the stage, the sweep of musical expression, and the fusion with the magic and plasticity of dance, Mravinsky was increasingly drawn to the Philharmonic—symphonic music was his true passion.[14] Mravinsky would explore his ideas and develop experience with amateur, part-time, and professional ones at Palaces of Culture in the city. Several of his future stable works were "studied" with the symphony orchestra of the Conservatoire's Music School, including a difficult program of Beethoven's Fourth Symphony in B major. He directed the same group of players in an event marking the seventieth anniversary of the Conservatoire on 13 March 1933, performing pieces by it's founder, Anton Rubinstein.[15] At the studios of Leningrad Radio, he recorded soundtracks for early Soviet feature films for Lenfilm.[16]

In the 1933–1934 season, Mikeladze returned to give concerts with the Philharmonic, bringing his new wife, Ketevan Orakhelashvili, with him. She was an extraordinarily beautiful woman and enchanted many in the northern capital; multitudes of fine beauties were frequently to be seen on the streets of Leningrad, but few had ever witnessed such a woman bearing the full bloom of her youth, her face and figure of rare Oriental exoticism and elegance. However, Ketevan was not the only chef d'oeuvre brought by Mikeladze, for he unveiled music of contemporary Georgian composers and the Soviet premiere of Schubert's Fifth Symphony in B minor. That evening, Mravinsky could admire those fine musical qualities of his Georgian colleague: nobility and grace in gesture. He would render the most indiscernible glances to the orchestral players for changes that he desired, for which he received in return playing of great virtuosity and clarity. Mikeladze was a model of the ideal conductor, dissimilar to anyone, possessing immediate presence on the podium. Following the Schubert, there were performed in the second half the overture to *Daisy* by Zakhary Paliashvili, the *Tale of Shota Rustevali* by Arakishvili, the wonderful suite by Kiladze, and to end the evening's program, the celebratory march from Ionia Tuskiya's *Carmencita*, written for a theater production at the Rustaveli Drama Theatre.[17] This was the last occasion that the two friends would meet; in the following season, Mikeladze would tour to the Bolshoi Theatre for a Festival of Georgian Art in a performance there of Paliashvili's tragic-heroic opera *Daisy*.[18]

Mikeladze's short spell in charge of the Tbilisi State Opera and Ballet Theatre was a period of ascendancy for Georgian music; new works for the stage were being written by the doyen of music, Zakhary Paliashvili, with his operas *Absalam et Eteri* and *Daisy*, and by an innovative group of composers in Balanchivadze, Taktakishvili, Kiladze, and Tuskiya. Yevgeny Mikeladze's conducting was distinguished by clear emotional empathy, a dynamic tension bearing a strict discipline and rhythm with a thorough preparation. A major event in this season was the arrival in Georgia of Sergey Prokofiev, who played his Third Piano Concerto in G minor, opus 37, accompanied by Mikeladze, "enjoying huge success."[19] Suitably impressed by the young conductor—reluctant to praise his fellow musicians—Prokofiev noted in his diary that Mikeladze was "a very talented conductor."[20]

The culmination of the season on 17 May 1935 was a complete performance of Grieg's *Peer Gynt*, working with the choir of Leningrad Radio and soloists from the Kirov Opera. Mravinsky "sketched a feeling of nature with such color, illumination, exceptional force, and enlightenment that one sensed both the rays of the morning sun and the force of a storm."[21] Grieg's *Peer Gynt* was also collaboration between the Philharmonic and the Pushkin Drama Theatre and a major occasion, for the orchestral suites had been erstwhile favorites, yet the complete production had never been performed in Russia. The thespian Alexander Glumov recounted:

> Pushkin's prophecy for great simplicity was at the center of our conception. Mravinsky was drawn to this music with both warmth and affection. In my opinion, it was with *Peer Gynt* that his great popularity began as a symphonic conductor. I remember one moment, during a matinee when the light of the sun's rays crept through the semicircular windows of the Philharmonic's ceiling and a narrow ray of sunlight fell upon myself and the conductor during the second half in "Early morning" and my narration about beauty and the strength of life and nature seemed so befitting.[22]

Following the brief tour to Moscow, Mravinsky returned to Leningrad on 1 June and accompanied the young David Oistrakh in Tchaikovsky's Concerto in D minor and in the same program directed the contemporary Alexey Zhivotov's *Dance Suite*.[23] The Leningrad Philharmonic Orchestra was the oldest orchestra in the country and held a reputation.

> The Merited Collective of the Republic terrorized conductors, having no respect for anyone. People were simply afraid of conducting them. The orchestra was led by the council of principals—at its head was Ilya Iosifovich Brik, a middle-aged man and quite bald. He was renowned for his knowledge of languages and proved very useful during the 1920s, when many guest conductors came on tour. Brik was the most lively conductor hater and loved to proffer his own guidance to conductors. When a foreign maestro was conducting, he would often translate not what he wanted, but Brik's own directions to the orchestra. There was an occasion when the conductor asked in German the double basses to play *spicatto*. Brik instead translated it as "Trombones—quieter!" Everyone knew that if Brik began to wipe his forehead, then one should ignore the conductor and Brik would direct the tempi tapping his desk with his bow. One had many regretful encounters; however, he is also remembered for his funny side. Mravinsky was

invited to give a concert, and Brik as usual began to wipe his forehead, yet Mravinsky would not allow the orchestra to depart from his tempi. Brik attempted to tap the music stand with his bow; however, Mravinsky instantly gripped his bow with his free hand, and would not let go. This was a genuine augury for Brik![24]

The Philharmonic concerts followed a tradition of preconcert talks from pre-1917 Count Sheremetyev's orchestra, which were now given by Ivan Sollertinsky and Mikhail Druskin.[25] The composer Vissarion Shebalin described Sollertinsky's influence:

He invited many foreign artists who didn't appear in Moscow at all; he presented Fritz Steidry work at the Philharmonic; even though not among the first rank, all the same, he conducted many interesting concerts and left behind a fine musician in Kurt Sanderling. The Mahler cult was wholly due to the concerts arranged by Sollertinsky.[26] Mahler was not well known and Sollertinsky acquainted Moscow with his music (he was accused later of being pro-Western). . . . In Moscow, new music rarely appeared; for instance, I never heard *Pulcinella* by Stravinsky, but they performed it in Leningrad and even in Novosibirsk, thanks to the efforts of Ivan Ivanovich, Yevgeny Mravinsky, and Sanderling.[27]

Following the concerts featuring Grieg's *Peer Gynt*, the Philharmonic intriguingly dedicated an evening to *Ballet in Russia and the USSR* on 28 May. Mravinsky was the protagonist, and he arranged the program under his baton: Glinka's dances from *Ruslan and Lyudmila*, Glazunov's *The Seasons*, Tchaikovsky's *Nutcracker*, "Bercéuse" from Stravinsky's *Firebird*, a suite from Asaf'yev's *Fountain of Bakhchisaray*, and the "March" from Rimsky-Korsakov's *Mlada*.[28] Mravinsky programmed traditional composers with those whose work had fallen under a cloud—Stravinsky and Glazunov had been neglected in recent years—nevertheless, the experiment became a triumph of Mravinsky's unrestrained judgment. Following these weeks of intense work, the summer vacation now allowed him long weeks of rest in the countryside to the east of the city.

If the repertoire of the 1930s was unique and enlightening, what was the orchestra like during these "pre-Mravinsky" seasons? The leader of the orchestra, an exceptionally gifted virtuoso—Viktor Zavetnovsky, following studies at the Paris Conservatoire, had served for twenty years and performed in the premiere of Shostakovich's First Symphony under Malko in 1926—took part in string quartets, and was a gifted organizer of his section, highly disciplined and industrious. Among his assistants was Ilya Shpilberg, who would ultimately replace his superior and work through until the 1960s. Ilya Brik's deputy was Boris Shafran, who eventually took over before the war and served for three decades.

However, the strongest section of the orchestra prewar was the woodwind section, all of whose members were distinguished both for their individual virtuosity and their musicality. The principal flute, Boris Trisno, had been recruited in 1932, and it was his insight and clarity in intonation that integrated the woodwind group. Georgy Amosov was solo oboe and worked in the orchestra for fifty years; his playing was spirited and incisive, combined with faultless technique. Vladimir Gensler as first clarinet won a major musical competition in 1935 and played for a quarter of a century in the orchestra—until the 1960s—delivering the most breathtaking sound and melodic line. The chief bassoonist was Alexander Vasil'yev, who had started his service in 1907, was technically brilliant—producing resonance from his instrument no one else could equal—and was a founder of the Russian school of bassoon playing. On one occasion, Joseph Szigéti was rehearsing the Beethoven Concerto and stopped suddenly; when asked by Gauk what the matter was, the soloist replied that he had never heard such captivating bassoon playing before. All the players in the orchestra taught at the Conservatoire, and it was ultimately their pupils who were the next generation, replacing them in future years. Several musicians of the orchestra would work through into the 1980s, including the trombonist Akim Kozlov. "There was too the Leningrad orchestral heritage: Buyanovsky, the bass player. His son is still without doubt the best horn player in the country, and students come from abroad—this was the Leningrad school."[29] This was an ensemble of incredibly high standard—awe-inspiring in concert and with a fantastic quality of sound (each musician could easily stand and play a solo no worse than many famous names). "The peculiarity of the orchestral playing was in that there was never such routine mistakes 'produced' as articulated in Soviet terminology as in creatively innovative playing. . . . The intensity of professionalism was quite superb."[30]

In the 1935–1936 season, Mravinsky directed for the first time Tchaikovsky's Fifth Symphony in E minor, a work that would be the most compelling of his career. Fritz Steidry worked with Mravinsky during his preparation, playing the grand piano in the Blue Room and demonstrating so admirable an affinity with the symphony that the Austrian congratulated his young assistant: *"Das ist noch echt!"*[31] Mravinsky painstakingly developed his repertoire in the 1936–1937 Philharmonic season, some parts being controversial, as the works of Glazunov had fallen into neglect since the composer's departure from the USSR. Mravinsky gave Glazunov's Fifth Symphony in B flat major and symphonies by Tchaikovsky, the First in G minor, *Winter Daydreams*, and the Sixth in B flat minor, *Pathétique*. A novelty for the period was the Second Symphony in C minor by Alexander Scriabin, another "unfashionable" composer. With the Philharmonic, Mravinsky performed works by Rimsky-Korsakov, Borodin, and Rachmaninov,

Beethoven's overture *Leonora III*, Liszt's *Les Préludes*, and pieces by Wagner, Saint-Saëns, and Lyadov.[32]

With the demise of the conductorless Persimfans, the Soviet government had created a super orchestra that would draw the finest musicians in the country—some sixty orchestras now working all over the USSR. Now based in Moscow, Alexander Gauk masterminded this "elite" ensemble.[33] A sign of Mravinsky's growing authority was the invitation to direct the new state orchestra in Moscow. Mravinsky was Gauk's much-loved pupil, and the latter realized that his "new child"—the USSR State Symphony Orchestra—would be in safe hands with Mravinsky. His debut in August 1937 was the first stage of an eight-concert tour beginning in the capital and encompassing Baku, Kharkhov, and Kiev. Mravinsky directed Tchaikovsky's *Pathétique* and *Francesca da Rimini*, Rachmaninov's Third Concerto (Rosa Tamarkina), Beethoven's Fourth Symphony, and the overture *Leonora III*. This successful series led to his being invited back in November 1937 to conduct Tchaikovsky's Fifth Symphony in E minor, Georgy Sviridov's Piano Concerto (Pavel Serebryakov as soloist),[34] and Alexey Zhivotov's *Dance Suite*.

In March 1938, Mravinsky was invited to participate in a ten-day festival of Russian music in Moscow performing Tchaikovsky's Second Symphony in C minor, *Little Russian*; arias from his operas; the *Rococo Variations* (Daniil Shafran as soloist); and *Francesca da Rimini*. Shafran was the recent winner of the Young Musicians Competition in Moscow. There was an explosion of brilliant young string players; among the most prominent was Boris Goldstein. Mravinsky conducted a highly novel program with Goldstein of violin concertos: by J. S. Bach in E flat and Beethoven in D major, together with the Bach *Suite in B minor* and Beethoven's overture to *Prométheus*. The sixteen-year-old "Busya" Goldstein was already a prize winner at the Wieniawsky and Brussels Violin Competitions of 1935 and 1937, and he had been invited to the Kremlin, where Iosif Stalin had taken a keen interest. The Soviet leader reminded Goldstein of the prize money from his competition victories. "Well, Busya, now that you have become a capitalist, you will become so well off, you won't want to invite me to see you!" Stalin joked, to which Goldstein audaciously responded "I would invite you with great pleasure, but we live in a small flat and there would not be anywhere for you to sit!"[35] Stalin liked this riposte so much that he provided Goldstein with a spacious flat and arranged him to be given a Guaneri violin from the State Collection. Following their concert in February 1938, Mravinsky did not renew his collaboration with the Odessa virtuoso.

Yevgeny Mravinsky continued to study visiting conductors in Abendroth, Ansermet, Blech, Kleiber, Klemperer, Knappertsbusch, Scherchen, and Weingartner. It was Leo Blech and Knappertsbusch who particularly impressed him, as he admired in their readings of Wagner and Beethoven a color and dynamic rhythmic control. He observed their relationships with orchestral musicians, analyzing their preparational routines, absorbing what he saw and heard, and evolving his own view on achieving the best results.[36] Mravinsky adored the tinting and phrasing attained by Ansermet in the French masters of Debussy, Ravel, and Bizet. He studied the different styles of Gauk, Golovanov, Dranishnikov, Fried, and Talich. Mravinsky began a long correspondence with Abendroth and Talich that led to invitations to conduct in Leipzig and Prague.[37] Mravinsky's copious notebooks would be filled too with discussions with orchestral musicians, from whom he gathered views of various styles of work and on different repertoire.[38]

In the city, there were several highly gifted young Soviet conductors—Karl Eliasberg, Ilya Musin, Kirill Kondrashin, Eduard Grikurov, Nikolay Rabinovich, and Boris Khaikin—all of whom contributed to an incredibly rich musical life. The Moscow-based conductors Alexander Orlov, Nikolay Golovanov, Konstantin Saradzhayev, Nikolay Anosov, Lev Steinberg, and Konstantin Simeonov would make brief journeys to the northern capital. Leningrad's concert schedule before the war was of the highest international standards, embellished by guest soloists in Heifetz, Enesco, Mainardi, Anderson, Marechal, Neveu, Casadeseus, Schnabel, and Fournier.

However, fate would play its part, for in April 1937 Fritz Steidry, having already signed a three-year extension to his contract, left for Switzerland on vacation.[39] In the Austrian's absence, the incumbent artistic director, Mikhail Chulaki, arranged concerts between Eliasberg, Mravinsky, and Rabinovich, with Mikhail Shteiman (from Kharkov) enlisted for the subscription series.[40] Mravinsky was a popular choice to be offered the curtain raiser for the 1937–1938 term. On 30 October, Yevgeny Mravinsky opened the new season with Glinka's effervescent overture *Ruslan and Lyudmilla*, the Leningrad premiere of Aram Khachaturyan's Piano Concerto (Lev Oborin), and Gavriil Yudin's *Fragments from the Heroic Oratorio*. If the latter enjoyed a short life on the concert platform, then a quite different fortune awaited Khachaturyan's piece: "A great success was enjoyed with the Leningrad debut of this concerto, for which the success lies rightly with its composer, pianist, and conductor. Their duet was beyond reproach, with clear accord in ensemble, and dramatic temperament."[41] Mravinsky took this work to Moscow and conducted it several times outside the Soviet Union, beginning a fruitful collaboration.

Such a fine opening to the concert season would have been sufficient for any aspiring young conductor, yet shortly afterward there took place an event that beckoned a new stage in the career of Yevgeny Mravinsky. On Saturday, 21 November 1937, there took place the world premiere of Dmitry Shostakovich's Fifth Symphony in D minor.

NOTES

1. V. Fomin, *Dirizher Yevgeny Mravinsky* (Leningrad: Muzika, 1983), 22.

2. B. Asaf'yev, *Krasnaya Gazeta*, 9 October 1924.

3. Several conductors worked as chief conductor prior to 1921, such as Serge Koussevitsky (1917) and Grigory Fitelberg (1918–1920). Emil Cooper was elected by the musicians, yet the government appointed Alexander Hessin, not aware of the orchestra's election; thus Cooper was appointed as director before his departure in 1924.

4. The Academic Capella was the former Court Choir and Orchestra, which possessed a school, a concert hall, and a full professional choir. The Philharmonic had been under its auspices before the revolution as the Court Orchestra.

5. M. Reznikov, *Vospominanii starovo muzikanta* (West Germany: Overseas Publications Interchange, 1984), 43.

6. Fomin, *Dirizher Yevgeny Mravinsky*, 28.

7. V. Raznikov, *Kirill Kondrashin rasskazyvaet* (Moscow: Sovetsky Kompozitor, 1989), 67.

8. Raznikov, *Kirill Kondrashin rasskazyvaet*, 67.

9. A. Glumov, *Nestertiye Stroki* (Moscow: Vserossiskiye Teatralnoye Obshestvo, 1977), 266–67.

10. Glumov, *Nestertiye Stroki*, 269–70.

11. Archives of the St. Petersburg Philharmonia Library.

12. Raznikov, *Kirill Kondrashin rasskazyvaet*, 67.

13. Raznikov, *Kirill Kondrashin rasskazyvaet*, 271–72.

14. P. Gusev, "Drug Baleta." In *Vospominanii o B. V. Asafyeva* (Leningrad: Lenizdat, 1974), 168.

15. Fomin, *Dirizher Yevgeny Mravinsky*, 28.

16. V. Fomin, *Orkestrom Dirizhiruet Mravinsky* (Leningrad: Muzika, 1976), 46.

17. I. Andronikov, *K Muzike* (Moscow: Sovetsky Kompozitor, 1975), 222–23.

18. A number of purges afflicted a group of artists, including some of the finest writers, M. Dzhavakhishvili, T. Tabidze, P. Yashvili, and the brilliant theater director S. Akhmeteli, resulting in their deaths.

19. G. Toradze, *Gruzinskaya Muzika 1917–1941*, edited by G. Toradze (Tbilisi: Istoriya Gruzinskoi Muzika, Tbilisi Gosudarstvennaya Konservatoriya imeni Saradzhishvili, 1998), 112.

20. S. S. Prokofiev, *Dnevniki*, 17 May 1933 (London: sprkiv, 2003), 17 May 1933, 832.

21. V. Bogdanov-Berezovsky, *Sovetsky Diriizher* (Leningrad: Muzika, 1956), 74–75.

22. Bogdanov-Berezovsky, *Sovetsky Diriizher*, 291–92.

23. Fomin, *Dirizher Yevgeny Mravinsky*, 16.

24. V. Razhnikov, *Kirill Kondrashin Rasskazivaet*, 213–14.

25. O. Sarkisov and V. Fomin, *Zasluzhenniye kollektiv RSFSR akademicheskiye simfonicheskiye orkestr filarmonii* (Leningrad: Leningradskaya Philharmonia, Lenizdat, 1972), 123.

26. This is misleading, as Sollertinsky followed Professor Scherbachyov's authority in Mahler.

27. V. Shebalin, *Literaraturnoye Naslediye: vospominanii, perepiska, statii, vystpleniye* (Moscow: Sovetsky Kompozitor, 1975), 68.

28. Archives of the St. Petersburg Philharmonia Library.

29. Raznikov, *Kirill Kondrashin rasskazyvaet*, 67.

30. D. Shafran, *Daniil Shafran-Violoncellist solo* (Moscow: ACT, 2001), 23.

31. Y. A. Mravinsky, interview with A. A. Zolotov, Ekran TV, 1982.

32. Archives of the St. Petersburg Philharmonia Library.

33. V. Shebalin, *Literaturnoye nasledi* (Moscow: Sovetsky Kompositor, 1975), 71. Glinka's Symphony on Two Russian Themes was completed by Shebalin and first performed in Moscow by Gauk on 14 March 1938.

34. M. Goldstein, *Zapiski Muzikanta* (Frankfurt: Posser-Verlag, 1970), 78.

35. Y. A. Mravinsky family archive.

36. Fomin, *Dirizher Yevgeny Mravinsky*, 31.

37. Regrettably, the score is now lost.

38. Y. A. Mravinsky, interview with A. A. Zolotov.

39. Fomin, *Dirizher Yevgeny Mravinsky*, 31.

40. S. Khentova, *Molodiye gody Shostakovicha*, Vol. 2 (Leningrad: Sovetsky Kompositor, 1980), 182–83.

41. Bogdanov-Berezovsky, *Sovetsky Dirizher*, 81.

Chapter Six

The Year 1937

To hear with eyes.

—William Shakespeare, Sonnet XXIII

Yelizaveta Nikolayevna Mravinskaya hosted the 1937 New Year celebrations in the age-old Russian fashion, *en famille* exchanging presents under the decorated fir tree. Such pre-Revolutionary customs were now disapproved, but religious holidays were nevertheless reverentially celebrated at the Mravinskys. Enduring friends in the actor Nikolay Cherkasov and fellow conductor Nikolay Rabinovich and their wives would come round. Yevgeny Alexandrovich would modestly drink beer and some vodka while smoking his eternal *papirosi*, and the intimate company would reminisce on the past year's changes, look at the positive things in their lives, and with trepidation long for better days.[1] Soviet life offered no break during this period; Yevgeny Alexandrovich had rehearsals at the Kirov Theatre the following day, and students would be a source of concern as he now shared classes with Rabinovich at the Conservatoire. Nevertheless, although his family had lost so much in the past decades, for the young conductor the next year would prove his *annus mirabilis*.

Nikolay Cherkasov had embarked on a major career at the Pushkin Drama Theatre and attained wider fame in *Children of Captain Grant*, a popular adventure film. Cherkasov was on the verge of an international career and was sought by Sergey Eisenstein for the historical *Alexander Nevsky*.

We saw each other often. Mravinsky was a very fine and mannered guest. He was a home-loving and civilized person to be in company with, bringing to our home the expression "to console and be in comfort." Often and for long spells, Mravinsky and Cherkasov would play four-handed pieces on the piano by

Glinka, Tchaikovsky, Musorgsky, Borodin, Rimsky-Korsakov. They loved to recite opera, from *Boris Godunov*, for example, and Cherkasov in his low, soft voice time and again sang Boris's aria. They were quite unconventional, these two friends. Nikolay Konstantinovich was unusually open, trustful to the point of naïveté. He worked without a care; mixing with others somewhat helped him get by, nurturing him with the necessary juices of life. Mravinsky was his opposite; for him, duty and creativity were both very difficult and oppressive processes. At work, he would soldier through until he dropped and following a concert feel terribly drained and numb. In relations with people, he was also unusually complex and spasmodic. Seeing Mravinsky tender, sociable, even sentimental was difficult to imagine—just yesterday, he was normal; now he was tensed up and looked at one with suspicion. "What happened to you yesterday?" "That is what it is like before a concert." Alternatively, quite simply "I was distressed." Whatever cropped up, he was unusually sincere. This saved their relationship.[2]

The year 1937, for the peoples of Europe, was a year of harsh and cruel fortunes; fascism was on the march in Italy, Germany, and Spain, and the Second World War was already being played out on the fields of Abyssinia and Catalonia. The great conflagration had already begun in the Far East with the conquest of Manchuria by Imperial Japan. In the Soviet Union, 1 January initiated the Third Five-Year Plan; new industrial achievements, improvements, and enlightenment were on the advance, with attainments of literacy among the peoples of Central Asia. Technology was making its mark; radio and the cinema were living miracles for the population, and the possibility of regular music concerts was becoming the norm. The German guest conductor Heinz Unger described these changes:

> New orchestras were founded everywhere, even in the most remote places. For example, Leningrad now possessed four; for in addition to the orchestras of its two opera houses and the Philharmonic, a new Radio Orchestra had been formed. In Moscow, besides the famous Orchestra of the Great Opera (Bolshoi) [*sic*] and the existing Philharmonic Orchestra, a new Radio Orchestra was gradually increasing its numbers until it was a hundred and twenty strong, and could thus easily be divided into two complete orchestras, as the BBC Orchestra in London is divided. The activities of this Moscow Radio Orchestra were by no means confined to the microphone, and in a comparatively short time it developed into the best orchestra of the Soviet Union, and only one comparable in merit to good European orchestras. . . .[3]

Yet not all was so rosy, as Unger met with problems:

> Political conditions, and conditions of housing, made it difficult to transfer players from one place to another. Also, the founding of all these new orchestras, and

the larger number of vacancies to be filled, resulted in students leaving conservatoires and musical academies too early, to take up work for which they were not yet fitted. The Soviets wanted these foreigners to teach their nation, and give it of their very best. Nothing was impossible at that time if the foreign expert declared it necessary; if one needed eight rehearsals for a special programme, I got my eight rehearsals. If one needed ten horns or eight trumpets for a performance, there was never any doubt but that the required extra players would be in their places. . . . It was a joy to work with the number of cultural institutions, steadily growing and a corresponding increase in concerts, before audiences that were as a rule appreciative and eager to listen.[4]

Despite remarkable progress made by Mravinsky at the Kirov Ballet, no operatic productions had come his way. Vladimir Dranishnikov—probably the most industrious *chef d'orchestre* the theater ever possessed: "He could conduct *Die Walküre* one evening and the next conduct *Ruslan and Lyudmilla* or *Prince Igor* at a matinee. It's not strange that he died at work in his forty-sixth year."[5] Upon his return for Mravinsky's first important opening concert for the Philharmonic in October, there came a meeting of the Leningrad Board of the Composers Union to resolve the programming of the Ten Day Festival of Soviet Music commemorating the twentieth anniversary of the Bolshevik Revolution. On 8 October, at the Composers Union on Rossi Street (adjacent to the Vaganov School of Dance) in a session chaired by Isaak Dunayevsky, Mravinsky sat with a group of young composers—Marianna Gramenitskaya, Boris Bitov, Andrey Diderichs, and Ilya Glyasser—listening attentively as Dmitry Shostakovich played his new symphony through with Nikita Bogoslovsky.[6] The autobiographical nature of the freshly written piece was clear—there was an individual perspective, an extraordinary tone and clarity of vision.

Mravinsky's keen enthusiasm for contemporary music allied with his consideration for fine detail and thorough, assiduous preparation were familiar to leading members of the board. Boris Asaf'yev and Vladimir Shcherbachyov had perceived Mravinsky's affinity with current music, and his portrayal of stage and orchestral works along with a reputation as epitomizing the Leningrad tradition left little doubt that Mravinsky would be able to bring this work off successfully. In scheduling the new Fifth Symphony in D minor by Shostakovich, the Board of the Composers Union had no hesitation in asking Yevgeny Mravinsky to give the first performance.

Yevgeny Mravinsky himself had no little anxiety about the task confronting him: "One must confess that in being the first performer of this work, I neither realized the greatness nor indeed the full significance that fell upon my shoulders. If one knew this at the time, and if one could foresee the whole perspective for Shostakovich, then perhaps one would not have accepted the task. . . . Certainly being young helps in such matters. Youth always gives one self-confidence."[7] The success of the opening Philharmonic concert on 20 October accentuated the judgment shown in granting the debut performance of Shostakovich's Fifth to Mravinsky.[8] Mravinsky's natural gifts witnessed on a regular basis both at the State Ballet and the Philharmonic had won widespread admiration and respect, yet what could Mravinsky do for a composer still under a shadow—an unsuccessful rendition would only spell official disapproval and a fall from grace for both men.

In the previous year, Shostakovich had withdrawn his Fourth Symphony: "Steidry clearly did not understand the music, and the orchestra played poorly; a difficult situation arose. It was a terrible time for Shostakovich: he was being destroyed on all sides and so he withdrew the symphony prior to its premiere."[9] Shostakovich had begun writing his new symphony on 18 April 1937. It progressed very well—the slow movement being set down in just three days—and the composer's thrill at its completion was equaled only by that when he finished the First Symphony.[10] Shostakovich and Mravinsky were already *au courant*; this was the first time their professional paths had crossed—they shared common friends yet enjoyed quite divergent tastes away from music. Dmitry Shostakovich came from the Petersburg intelligentsia. He loved football and already had a young family, while Yevgeny Mravinsky was aloof and favored solitude to the crowd. Music was the catalyst for them, and uncovering parallel outlooks in each other. Nevertheless, the rehearsals started with some difficulty; Mravinsky would constantly ply Shostakovich with questions on tempi and phrasing, but the composer was reticent in confiding his intimate ideas to someone with whom he was still unfamiliar: "I discovered Mravinsky more closely when we began to work on my Fifth Symphony. At the beginning, one must admit that I was put off by Mravinsky's methods. It seemed that he was too absorbed in detail; too much attention was in specific parts, and this ruined both the general shape and whole conception. Mravinsky questioned me on each measure and facet, pressing me for answers to all his doubts."[11]

Well aware of the symphony's importance, Mravinsky had hoped that the composer would open up his motives and allow him to grasp its conceptual plan.

My first meetings with Shostakovich were a blow to my hopes. Initially, one could not achieve anything, not even tempi indications for the Fifth Symphony. It was then that I decided to play a trick on him. During our work at the piano, I deliberately played a section at clearly the wrong speed. Dmitry Dmitrevich was angry, stopping me and pointing out at what tempo it should have been played. Soon he caught on and began to offer his own ideas.[12]

Typically for Mravinsky's painstaking character, his absorption in such fine
detail convinced Shostakovich that the former was correct in attempting to
achieve a complete understanding of the symphony: "By the fifth day of our
work together, I understood that such a method was undoubtedly correct. Observing how assiduously Mravinsky worked, I began to respond more candidly to his craft. I understood that the conductor cannot 'sing like a nightingale.' At first, talent can only express itself through long and scrupulous
skill."[13] Mravinsky attained detail on tempi, balance, and general conception
of the symphony, and most significantly, there developed a bond of mutual
trust between the two musicians. Mravinsky wrote many years later:
"Shostakovich and I perhaps shared some words about music, apart from the
Fifth Symphony. This was the first time we had collaborated. It was the latest in a mature stage of Shostakovich's music. No symphonies were ever discussed so much as this one."[14]

The Festival of Soviet Music opened on 16 November with Shostakovich's
Concerto for Piano, Strings, and Trumpet with the composer performing to
Rabinovich's accompaniment. On the same bill were Valery Zhelobinsky's
fragments from his opera *Mother*, a chorus from Mikhail Gnessin's *Symphonic Monument*, Nikolay Myaskovsky's Eighteenth Symphony, and the patriotic song "On Parade," by Soloviev-Sedoy. Mravinsky was asked to give
two of the ten concerts, the first of which included the suite *Episodes from the
Civil War*, by Viktor Tomilin, the Piano Concerto by Georgy Sviridov, and
Moldavian Songs, by Yuri Weisberg.

Scheduled for the third evening of the Ten-Day Festival, the latest
Shostakovich symphony was the only world premiere undertaken by Mravinsky, and the most keenly awaited performance of the festival. This was certainly the most important presentation in the city since that of Tchaikovsky's
Sixth Symphony of 1893. Fate had played its part in that Tchaikovsky's last
symphony did not enjoy a successful premiere; the composer failed to deliver
a convincing reading, and only later did Nikisch present it as a chef d'oeuvre.
Nevertheless, academician Vladimir Shishmarev, who attended the premieres
of both the *Pathétique* and Shostakovich's Fifth, said that "there was a stunning atmosphere at both concerts enjoying a far-reaching social resonance."[15]
On 21 November, Shostakovich's symphony came first in the program, followed after the interval by a short entracte from the Asaf'yev's ballet *Fires of
Paris*, and once again, Khachaturyan's fresh and colorful Piano Concerto
(Lev Oborin as soloist).

There had been much anticipation in the city's musical community, which
generated an electric atmosphere on the night of the performance. It was
thought that a major event was about to happen; everyone knew the fate of
the composer was at stake, and the whispers had circulated that this new sym-

phony was a magnum opus. "The composer was in the hall encircled by a group of friends."[16] Mravinsky knew very well that he could not afford to fail in producing a worthy performance, and the auditorium was alive with a thrilling tension:

> Following the ringing of the first bell, everyone was firmly in their seats, with many standing huddled around the beautiful marble pillars adorning the hall. At the third and final ring, the curtain was pulled back and Yevgeny Mravinsky calmly emerged from under the crimson curtain—the lights in the hall, having been dimmed before, suddenly come to a full and stunning brightness. Almost theatrically, and with resolute stride, Yevgeny Mravinsky, bearing a frozen, severe mask, walked toward the rostrum at the center of the stage; everyone could feel his complete confidence and assurance in what he was about to do.[17]

It was the calm assurance and self-belief emanating from Mravinsky that reinforced for the audience that this was to be a special night:

> Everyone understood that something great was being born, philosophically profound, a suffering of colossal dynamic forces in which the mastery of the music transforms not in single parts but in an affluence of factura, at once winning the listeners to the subject matter of its ideas, and its concept. The Leningrad public enjoyed an intense love and loyalty in their favored son—Dmitry Shostakovich; his modest, almost timid features had become the property of all who valued honesty and sincerity in art.[18]

The listeners in the hall grasped what this new symphony was about and recognized their Shostakovich—their musical son—and knew too how he had been reduced to almost nothing by the tirade of abuse from the Party's press. Now the mature Shostakovich had written a work not only about himself as hero—here they, too, were the participants: the heroes and heroines, in this vast symphonic canvass, of love and joy, of irony and hate, of great evil, and within its closing bars, a glimpse of a victory in this struggle. Here was a young man writing about their lives and their passions and offering a hero in his original, brilliant Fifth Symphony. "Shostakovich's orchestral music swept over the audience at the Philharmonic Hall, holding them silent, aghast, enrapturing them until the finale brought them to their feet cheering like no audience had done for many years."[19]

During the finale, many listeners one by one began to rise spontaneously from their seats. Such behavior happened only at Yermolova's performances. (Maria Yermolova was an actress at the Moscow Arts Theatre). The music's electrical energy brought everyone in the hall to their feet. The thunderous ovation shook the white columns of the Philharmonic Hall.[20]

The premiere was a magnificent triumph; no less than seven times Shostakovich had to return to the stage to take a bow, yet the applause developed to a gathering crescendo. Not only was everyone standing, applauding, stamping their feet, they now crowded around the stage cheering the musicians, Shostakovich, and Mravinsky. "Following the performance of the symphony, there was a burst of applause, a stormy expression of love by the Leningrad people to their idol. It was impossible to get to the artists' rooms to congratulate the composer."[21]

This demonstration of Leningrad's musical public led to Vissarion and Alissa Shebalin (who had traveled from Moscow for the premiere) spiriting the composer away, making their exit through the artists' stage door, and returning home, where they celebrated this fresh and brilliant success into the small hours.[22] In a letter to a friend, Shostakovich wrote: "My Fifth Symphony was performed and was a very big success. Mravinsky performed it wonderfully. Everything was thought through very attentively, and apart from the technical aspect, on a very high level, and the artistic side was above praise (standard)."[23] The actor Glumov recounted traveling especially for the concert:

> This was the first new piece to be performed following the opera *Katerina Iz-mailova*, apart from his music to the theatrical production of *Salute, Spain*, for almost two years. Both Elga and I took our places on the Red Arrow and traveled to Leningrad on the morning of the concert. There sounded the first bars, and a theme of great energy. The aesthetic, severe voice of the tribune "The idea of my symphony," said the composer, "is the formation of a personality."[24] Man with all his experiences was really at the core of this work's conception. However, the symphony was not only a deep personal confession in the awakening of a conscience; its significance [was] much wider. . . . [H]ere, wrote Alexey Tolstoy, "is a sweeping breath of the wings of a bird before it ascends to the heights. Here is a personality bound in the mean of our epoch untying itself and speaking in concord with its time."[25] I consider that this concert was a Rubicon of my Leningrad times.[26]

The repeat performance met with no less success—the venerable seventy-year-old Ivan Yershov (on one occasion having been shocked by the composer's ballet *The Age of Gold*) descended to the artists' room and bowed low to the composer, who was so taken aback that he could not make any response. At a banquet of Leningrad's arts and intelligentsia in the Yevropeiskaya Hotel, the writer Alexey Tolstoy proposed a toast: "To that member of our company who we all may justly call a genius!" The performance of the Fifth created such an impression that the Party convened a special meeting in Leningrad to discuss the symphony, to which the composer was duly summoned, and it was here the epithet of the Fifth as "an optimistic tragedy" was born.

The upturn in Shostakovich's fortunes was the result of some skillful organization by Mravinsky, Sollertinsky, and Glikman.[27] They all inspired leading figures in Leningrad life—beyond strictly musical circles—to write letters and articles into the local press. These were precisely the same tactics used by Shostakovich's enemies when his works had been attacked in the mass media the previous year. The campaign extended through their friends and colleagues in Moscow and nationwide. Before the conservatives could act, a train of support for Shostakovich had been instigated that could not be halted. There duly followed a wave of articles devoted to the Fifth all over the country. What was noticeable was that the authors were not musicologists but ordinary members of the public, and this was a determining element in its wider popularity. Shostakovich had discovered in his original creation an ability to express in complex musical language the atmosphere and epoch in which people were living and working.

If the initial impact of the Fifth Symphony was euphoric, it was not until a month afterward that analysis began to appear, and therein came the first criticism. Those first reviews by composers such as Anatoly Alexandrov and Vladimir Nechayev lacked any thorough analysis, although conceding: "At this point, it is difficult and premature to appraise or to give a detailed analysis: there is so much to reflect and take account of. However, it is clear that in his Fifth Symphony Shostakovich has accomplished a major transformation in creating his most outstanding work."[28] As Bogdanov-Berezovsky illustrated, the conundrum was because "musicians of 'traditional nature' couldn't grasp different characteristics and elements of its language, the rhythmic intonation, polyphony, harmony, and orchestral language."[29] Following the Moscow premiere (directed by Alexander Gauk) several members of the Composers Union, Muradeli, Chemberdzhy, and Ostretsov criticized the symphony: "in several elements, the pathos of suffering is reduced to naturalistic shouts and cries. The music in part causes one almost physical pain."[30] If the greatest criticism was for the *Largo*, the musicologist Israel Nestyev found cause for concern in the finale: "one loses that feeling of humanity and living emotion, so clearly expressed in the first three movements. . . . [T]here is a danger of exaggerating narrow subjective human experiences and the risk of unnecessary extremes in their portrayal."[31] The Soviet writer Alexander Fadeyev wrote in his diary: "The finale doesn't sound like a culmination (quite unlike a celebration or victory), and more as if a punishment or admonishment is being given someone."[32]

"The terrible emotional force is overwhelmingly tragic and leaves in one unpleasant feelings," wrote Alexander Fadeyev.[33] Myaskovsky expressed more sober comments in a letter to the conductor Malko: "The Scherzo is wholly Mahlerian (brilliant, yet orchestrally screeching) and an impassioned, gushing finale (D major screaming through three pages of the score)."[34] The composer Dunayevsky was so concerned at the public sentiment that he wrote to the Leningrad Branch of the Composers Union: "there is an unhealthy ambience around this composition which attains the degree of some kind of psychosis which can only serve as a disservice both to the work itself and its author."[35] The resident composer for Leningrad's Music Hall added "that [Shostakovich] is far from the model to be followed in Soviet symphonic music."[36] On 29 December, Mravinsky explained his own analysis at a meeting of the Leningrad board of the Composers Union and played examples at the piano together with Shostakovich. "Shostakovich's Fifth Symphony is the most important work written in the past twenty years," Mravinsky wrote.[37] The conductor emphasized the singular, unequivocal concept of the Fifth: "It has staggering strength and depth of philosophical conception embodied in strict classical form."[38]

The man who premiered the Fifth Symphony became its most enthusiastic protagonist, as Mravinsky revealed directing a Moscow concert. "As soon as he lowered his baton the audience in the Large Hall of the Conservatoire erupted; everyone stood up and poured toward the stage, [and] as if in one voice excited shouts could be heard. I remember well the imposing and elegant gray-headed figure of Vladimir Ivanovich Nemirovich-Danchenko, who rose and with out-flung arms approached the stage applauding for a long time."[39] The influential pianist and teacher Heinrich Neuhaus became a passionate champion: "after Mravinsky's performance it became clear to everyone that, as in any true artistic masterpiece, the intrinsic parts of this symphony form an integral artistic concept."[40]

Neuhaus expanded: "Shostakovich, who devoted so much to the grotesque and satire in his youth, producing distaste and pain among his listeners, has now created the most profound tragic music, humane and simple: he who once expressed his resistance has now conformed, and how!"[41] One musicologist wrote: "there are a number of novel qualities in Shostakovich's symphony: melody, affinity to Russian folk music, simplicity of language, and monolithic orchestral individuality."[42] There was no doubt of the nature of the Fifth; the musicologist Yevgeny Braudo reflected that "the new symphony bears a clearly expressed biographical character."[43] Georgy Khubov, another music critic, concurred in finding similarities: "the symphony is conceived as a great lyrical tragedy, with clear (undisguised by the composer) autobiographical features."[44] The great significance of the Fifth is that it was lined with the time and period in which it was written, reflecting the composer's fears and doubts, preserving a belief in his own ideas and of regeneration through struggle.

Mravinsky knew of its nature and content more than anyone, and the conductor expounded in a newspaper article: "I consider that this symphony is an event of world significance. It shatters one with its force and depth of philosophic thought, enriched in severe, real classical form in all its simplicity and greatness."[45] As always, Asaf'yev wrote colorfully and thoughtfully: "the nervous challenge to the gigantic conflict of modern times is heard in this music . . . as a justified narrative of the concerns of present-day civilization—actually not individual personalities or groups of people, but of mankind."[46]

However, Mravinsky considered that Shostakovich "places great effort in the finale being a declaration of objective positive content, . . . and this conclusion is attained by superficial means."[47] Bogdanov-Berezovsky articulated that "the optimism so prevalent in the tone of performance produces the impression of some spontaneity and not as an organically decisive conclusion."[48] Nevertheless, Shostakovich argued that "linked with the principal theme of the finale, it appears as an answer to all the questions posed in the opening movements."[49]

The composer himself gave high praise to the conductor's achievement in portraying the Fifth: "the fate of a musical work is usually very often dependent on its successful premiere. I think that the favorable reception for my Fifth Symphony is a very great achievement of its first interpreter—Yevgeny Mravinsky."[50] Shortly afterward, in March 1938, Mravinsky set down his first gramophone recording of the Fifth. No longer their bête noire, Shostakovich almost overnight became *primus inter pares* among his fellows, and quickly the Fifth became the most sought after and popular piece of Soviet music. Mravinsky himself performed the Fifth no less than ten times in this first season. Neuhaus reiterated: "for me personally, the performance by Mravinsky of Shostakovich's symphony convinced me that this is the work of a genius."[51]

In a year of conducting the Fifth, Mravinsky established a magnitude in performance and a grandeur—as he described its characteristics: a will of resolute ideas, reserved lyricism, "masked emotion, clarity, laconism, timbre color, impulsiveness, firmness, and tense, inflexible rhythms."[52] The triumph of the Fifth was for Mravinsky his "Royal Début," and in the emerging school of Soviet musicians the conductor would take his place alongside Emil Gilels, David Oistrakh, Boris Goldstein, Yakov Zak, Lev Oborin, Daniil Shafran, and others who were winning reputations throughout Europe.

Meanwhile, the Fifth Symphony toured the world; Desormière gave the Western premiere in Paris on 14 April 1938, and Stokowski and the Philadelphia Orchestra recorded it in April 1939. "Shostakovich sounds so Slavonic to a greater degree than we have heard before. He can rank with Musorgsky, Tchaikovsky and Borodin. In the slow movement as in the first, the composer it seems particularly well feels the national ties linking him with his musical forebears."[53] The complete mastery of the writing was so obvious to Mravinsky that for him it did not require any additional comment: "As the first musician to perform this symphony, I can only compare my feelings with what I experienced when coming into contact with the finest examples of world musical literature."

During the 1930s, the genre of the modern symphony had slowly reestablished itself in concert programs; Shostakovich's glorious Fifth Symphony in D major presented a chef d'oeuvre. Shostakovich's symphony became a classic of the times: "the most human symphony of the twentieth century."[54] The great importance to the composer of the Fifth Symphony was that he had won a faithful interpreter in Yevgeny Mravinsky—a musician who implicitly shared the composer's world and musical outlook. The Fifth Symphony brought forth a master symphonist and *tout de suite* a virtuoso conductor. The world of music was changed after the premiere on 21 November 1937, for it revealed that symphonic music was not dead, classicism was alive, and heroes were still being born in the harsh and cruel world of the 1930s.

NOTES

1. A. M. Vavilina Mravinskaya, author interview, February 2002.

2. Nina Cherkasova, *Ryadom s Cherkasovym* (Leningrad: Leninizdat, 1978), 193–94.

3. H. Unger, *Hammer, Sickle and Baton* (London: Cresset, 1939), 91.

4. Ungar, *Hammer, Sickle and Baton*, 91.

5. S. Y. Levik, *Chetvert veka v Opere* (Moscow, Izkusstvo, 1970), 315.

6. Leningrad branch of Union of Composers of the USSR minutes, LGALI F. 9709 OP. 1 C. 37, 26.

7. Y. A. Mravinsky, "Tridzat let s muzikoi Shostakovicha," in *D. Shostakovich*, ed. L. V. Danilevich (Moscow: Sovetsky Kompozitor, 1967), 112.

8. S. Khentova, *Molodiye gody Shostakovicha*, Vol. 2 (Leningrad: Sovetsky Kompositor, 1980), 199.

9. A. V. Gauk, *Memoiri, izbranniye stati, vospominanii sovremminikov* (Moscow: Muzika, 1975), 223.

10. Khentova, *Molodiye gody Shostakovicha*, 184.

11. D. D. Shostakovich, "Yarkii talent," *Smena*, 18 October 1938.

12. Mravinsky, "Tridzat let s muzikoi Shostakovicha," 113.

13. Shostakovich, "Yarkii talent."

14. Y. A. Mravinsky, interview with Zolotov, *Shostakovich Pyataya*, Ekran TV, 1973.

15. From a conversation with the author, July 2002.

16. K. Kondrashin, *Moy vstrechi s Shostakovichem*, *Dmitry Shostakovich—stati i materiali*, ed. Grigory M. Shneerson (Moscow: Sovetsky Kompozitor, 1976), 87.

17. V. M. Bogdanov-Berezovsky, *Dorogi Izkusstsva*, Vol. 1 (Leningrad: Muzika, 1971), 188.

18. Bogdanov-Berezovsky, *Dorogi Izkusstsva*, 188.

19. Bogdanov-Berezovsky, *Dorogi Izkusstsva*, 188.

20. A. N. Glumov, *Nestertie Stroki* (Moscow: VTO, 1977), 316.

21. Kondrashin, *Moy vstrechi s Shostakovichem*, 87.

22. A. M. Shebalina, "S Alisoy Maksimovnoy Shebalinoy," in *V Mire Shostakovicha*, ed. S. M. Khentova (Moscow: Kompositor, 1996), 128.

23. Shostakovich to G. Yudin, 21 November 1937.

24. D. Shostakovich, "Moy tvorchesky otvet," *Vechernaya Moskva*, 23 January 1938.

25. A. Tolstoy, "Pyataya simfoniya Shostakovicha," *Izvestia*, 28 December 1937.

26. Glumov, *Nestertiye Stroki*, 315–16.

27. L. Mikheyeva, *Zhisn Dmitriya Shostakovicha* (Moscow: Terra-Terra, 1997), 204.

28. A. N. Alexandrov and V. V. Nechayev, *Pyataya simfoniya D. Shostakovicha: vpechatleniye slushateliye* (Moscow: Muzika, 26 November 1937).

29. Bogdanov-Berezovsky, *Dorogi Izkusstsva*, Vol. 1, 190.

30. A. A. Ostretsov, *Pyataya simfoniya Shostakovicha, Sovetskoye Iskusstvo*, 2 February 1938.

31. I. V. Nestyev, "Pyataya simfoniya Shostakovicha," *Komsomolskaya Pravda*, 3 February 1938.

32. A. A. Fadeyev, *Subjectivniye noti, Tridzat letiya* (Moscow: Sovetskiye pisatel, 1957), 891.

33. Fadeyev, *Subjectivniye noti, Tridzat letiya*, 891.

34. Myaskovsky to N. Malko, 10 February 1938, *N. A. Malko, Vospominaniya. Statii. Pisma* (Leningrad: Muzika, 1972), 281.

35. TsGALI, f. 2048 op. 1 ed. Ch. 160, 1–3.

36. I. O. Dunayevsky letter, 29 January 1938, TSGALI, f. 2048, op. 1, ed. Khr. 160, 1–3.

37. Y. A. Mravinsky, "Proizvedenie potryasayuschie sili," *Smena*, 28 December 1937.

38. Mravinsky, "Proizvedenie potryasayuschie sili."

39. V. A. Josefivich, *Razgovori s Igorem Oistrakhem, David Oistrakh* (Moscow: Muzika, 1978), 312.

40. Heinrich Neuhaus, "Yevgeny Mravinsky," *Sovetskoye Iskusstvo*, 18 October 1938.

41. Heinrich Neuhaus, "Pyataya simfonia," *Vechernaya Moskva*, 31 January 1938.

42. M. Chulaki, "Vydayuschashisya proizvedeniye," *Smena*, 23 December 1937.

43. Y. Braudo, "Pyataya simfoniya Shostakovicha," *Rabochaya Moskva*, 1 February 1938.

44. G. I. Khubov, "Pyataya simfonia Shostakovicha," *Sovetskaya Muzika*, no. 3 (1938): 17.

45. Y. A. Mravinsky, "Proisvedeniye potraschashyuschaya sily," *Smena*, 28 December 1937.

46. B. V. Asaf'yev, "Cherez proshloye k Buduyuschemu," *Sovetskaya Muzika* (1943): 27–28.

47. Mravinsky, "Proisvedeniye potraschashyuschaya sily."

48. Bogdanov-Berezovsky, *Dorogi iskusstva*, 189.

49. Shostakovich, "Moi Tvorchesky otvet."

50. Shostakovich, "Yarkii talent."

51. Neuhaus, "Yevgeny Mravinsky."

52. Mravinsky, "Proizvedenie potryasayuschie sili."

53. *Christian Science Monitor*, 4 December 1940.

54. S. Koussevitsky, quoted in Leichtentrit, *Serge Koussevitsky, the Boston Symphony Orchestra, and the New American Music* (Cambridge: Cambridge University Press, 1946), 180.

Chapter Seven

The Chief Conductor

Here am I, here are you—what does it mean, what are we going to do?

—W. H. Auden

With the onslaught of war in Europe, the presence of foreign citizens on Soviet territory became wholly untenable.[1] The refusal by Georges Sebastian to
cancel a performance of *Aida* on the day of Kirov's assassination was un-
helpful, as was his sending a telegram to Mussolini congratulating him on
Italy's conquest of Abyssinia. Vyacheslav Molotov—chairman of the Council of Ministers—said enough was enough and that foreign conductors would
have to take up Soviet citizenship or go;[2] the sole foreigners to stay behind
were Sanderling and the Mahlerian disciple Oscar Fried.[3]

The First All-Union Conducting Competition accordingly took place at a
providential period, in the wake of the unearthing of such talents as Oistrakh,
Gilels, Shafran, and Oborin. The laureates would naturally be expected to fill
the vacancies opened up at orchestras throughout the land with the departures
of the foreign conductors. The distinguished veteran Samuil Samosud led the
jury and serving with him were fellow conductors Lev Steinberg, Alexander
Gauk, and Ariy Pasovsky; composers Nikolay Myaskovsky, Dmitry Kabalevsky, Useir Abdul Gadzhibekov, and Isaac Dunayevsky; and the pianists
Heinrich Neuhaus and Alexander Goldenweiser. In the first round, the forty-
five competitors had to take the USSR State Symphony Orchestra through a
one-hour rehearsal. Mravinsky picked the first draw and quickly gained the
jury's attention.[4] He rehearsed the *Second Suite* BWV 1067 by J. S. Bach and
a movement from Scriabin's Second Symphony in C minor. "One felt that
here on stage there was a real conductor in charge—a musician with exceptional talent equipped with indefatigable technique and bolstered by passion

and a capacious culture," wrote Moisei Grinberg. "It became quite clear that Mravinsky was guaranteed to go through not only the next stage but straight into the final."[5] One of the jury members, the influential pianist Heinrich Neuhaus, confirmed Mravinsky's opening success:

> it is revelatory that Mravinsky began with a rehearsal of Bach. He explained to the players the specific characteristics of Bach's style, in both technical and artistic terms. During the session, this became a disposition revealing the conductor's wide knowledge. The musical performance of Bach is considered most difficult and complex, yet Mravinsky managed to express his own views and artistic understanding with surprising clarity and simplicity.[6]

The competition drew a wide degree of interest from the press, as dozens of features appeared daily throughout the fortnight. One of the competitors who dropped out after the second round, Kirill Kondrashin, remembered many years later: "My father collected everything that was written about the First Conducting Competition of 1938.[7] The general press coverage from the first round of the competition was extensive; correspondents interviewed members of the jury, who each made their prophecy."[8] In the second round, the remaining sixteen competitors had to take the ensemble through a full rehearsal in three different works; Mravinsky chose Mozart's overture *Impresario*; Tchaikovsky's First Symphony in G minor, *Winter Daydreams*; and the *Andante* and Scherzo from Shebalin's Third Symphony, having received the score a day before.[9] "There remains an impression of admirable technique over mediocre creativity,"[10] commented David Rabinovich of Mravinsky. For the third and final round, five candidates remained in contention, including Mravinsky's former fellow student, the opera specialist, Alexander Melik-Pashayev. The quintet of finalists included the composer Konstantin Ivanov from Moscow, the self-taught Nathan Rakhlin from Kiev, and Mark Paverman from Rostov on Don. In the final, each received the opportunity of a full concert in the Large Hall of the Conservatoire, preceded by three days of rehearsal. The whole process was exceptionally grueling, yet Mravinsky had his wife and mother there to offer proper backing, and the conductor's ebullient style attracted an enthusiastic cluster of devotees from among the public. Destiny once more beamed upon the Leningrad man, as Mravinsky again was drawn first in the ballot.

Mravinsky conducted the first movement of Khachaturyan's Piano Concerto, Tchaikovsky's *Francesca da Rimini*, and Shostakovich's Fifth Symphony in D minor. It was the Shostakovich and Tchaikovsky works that earned the greatest acclaim from critics, jury, and audience, and following the last concert there was no doubt Mravinsky would be given the first prize. Melik-Pashayev and Rakhlin shared second prize, with the third going to Ivanov and the fourth to Mark Paverman; Karl Eliasberg, Zhukov, and Kirill Kondrashin received diplomas.[11] Mravinsky by right should have taken part in the Brussels Conducting Competition the following year; however, it was canceled due to the outbreak of war.

Mravinsky's achievement was assured, and in a rare interview he expressed gratitude to those who had assisted him in recent years: "This successful outcome is first of all due to the creative ambience and sympathy received during my first years at the Kirov Theatre and Leningrad Philharmonic Orchestra."[12] The Moscow triumph had an immediate impact, not only winning for the laureate a nation-wide reputation but also drawing interest from ensembles and theaters. All the same, Mravinsky was candid in gauging his victory, thinking of tomorrow's problems, and seeking new avenues: "I shall continue to work for the development of Soviet art and my own maturity. The profound significance of the competition is that throughout the Soviet Union, the questions of style, interpretation, and in passionately searching for the Soviet interpretative method, we must consciously help Soviet composers in their work."[13] Shortly afterward, Rakhlin was appointed to the USSR State Symphony, Melik-Pashayev to the Bolshoi, Ivanov at Moscow Radio, and Eliasberg and Kondrashin to the two Leningrad Radio orchestras.[14]

Mravinsky was expected back at the Kirov for the new season; however, he received a posting from the Committee for Art under the Council of Peoples Commissars of the USSR as chief conductor of the Leningrad Philharmonic Orchestra.[15] At first, the young man was overwhelmed and, incredibly, turned down the offer. He was still happy with and committed to the theater, enjoying the camaraderie there; another more personal factor was his obsessive self-doubt and apprehension.[16] Mravinsky was skeptical at the notion of being the isolated chief of such a formidable orchestra. The position was different from that at the theater, where several staff conductors shared the workload. Nevertheless, Mravinsky was bound to accept a challenge he might never be offered again in the rapidly changing world of the Soviet Union.

The thirty-five year old now led one of the finest and most fastidious orchestras of the day. Mravinsky had never guided the métier of a symphony orchestra, and the responsibility over such an ensemble and its immensely complex structure was awesome. Yet he was not bereft of help, for the artistic triumvirate of Chulaki, Sollertinsky, and Brik would aid him in his task. Mravinsky's first engagement began almost immediately, on 18 October 1938, when he repeated the programs of the Moscow competition final, omitting the Tchaikovsky piece and substituting for it with Mozart's *Impresario* overture, Musorgsky's prelude *Dawn on the Moscow River*, Shostakovich's Fifth Symphony, and Khachaturyan's Piano Concerto (Lev Oborin as soloist).

His enthusiastic listeners greeted Mravinsky's first appearance since his Moscow triumph euphorically. For the cultured musical audiences in Leningrad, his victory was fresh evidence of the prevalence of the old performing traditions; here in Leningrad was the font of Russian classical praxis, the birthplace of the Russian composing school, and the cognoscenti who valued great art. Mravinsky's public was familiar with Tchaikovsky and Rimsky-Korsakov, Scriabin and Rachmaninov, and remembered their concerts in the city. Following all the traumatic transformations of the past twenty years, Mravinsky's Moscow triumph—for the beau monde—showed the great Petersburg school was still very much alive in the Leningrad of 1938. Mikhail Druskin portrayed the setting of the evening:[17]

> This gifted conductor's talent has grown in measure, with this program's performance culminating in complete triumph. Mravinsky revealed his potential as a distinct and sophisticated musician last season able to cultivate his conducting ability in opening up a composer's ideas. Recently, Mravinsky's talent has developed to its full potential, revealing him as a thoughtful, deeply artistic and accomplished master, possessing a flowing and expressive stylistic impulse. Mravinsky has all the hallmarks of a great musician: the ability to express in a single gesture, both strength of will and real imagination, with reserved intelligence and a burning heart.[18]

The initial period of work for Mravinsky at the Philharmonic was beset with problems, leading to frequent disputes and distress. The players had enjoyed years of experience with the world's finest, and their traditions were among the most respected in the country. The Achilles heel of the Philharmonic was that there had never been a continuity in artistic leadership, Koussevitsky, Fitelberg, Cooper, Berdyayev, Malko, Gauk, Steidry all having enjoyed brief sojourns as chief conductor. There was no stability in leadership, too much independence, hesitation and a lack of consistency, particularly in artistic matters and repertoire policy, and insubordination; harmful, too, was a spirit of self-belief and a lack of accuracy in ensemble.[19] The orchestra at its finest possessed a sound quality and a quite unsurpassed color in tone.[20] There was great professionalism, yet there also existed complex internal politics and a religious adherence to modus operandi.

Yevgeny Mravinsky was met by the section leaders of the orchestra with some resistance, many of them contemptuous of his youth, his lack of a previous chief conductorship and tenure at the Kirov Ballet influencing the general skepticism.[21] Mravinsky's initial attempt to introduce a strict disciplinary regime was met with an active resistance. The issue was not a new one, as Meyerbeer wrote: "At the same time he (the conductor) ought to have the power of attracting to himself the love of all his artists, who should at the same time love and fear him."[22]

The young Kirill Kondrashin's experiences were similarly traumatic when he made his own debut: "It was a matinee. I can't remember the whole program, but the last item was Liszt's *Les Préludes*, and afterward, the principal bassoon Vasil'yev came to me upset, 'How can you conduct the finale so quickly. It should be a magnificent march, not a gallop.' At the time, I took his words as a veteran trying to 'sort out' a young man."[23]

Mravinsky was lambasted for a lack of knowledge of the repertoire and for being appointed above their heads by the government. The latter was an echo of an episode when the orchestra had "elected" Cooper against the dictates of the Committee for Arts in Moscow, which veteran players remembered with bitterness. The essence of the conundrum was that musicians regarded themselves as above reproach and veritable "apostles of virtue." Mravinsky had conducted the Philharmonic in a varied and different repertoire in forty concerts through seven seasons. To reestablish itself as the leading orchestra, the Philharmonic needed a music director who would work with them consistently on both playing performance and ensemble praxis. Bruno Walter wrote of the chief conductor's role: "he is in the middle of things, all is set in motion by him, he is everything, ego, work and creator, and there is no room for 'another person' or an external object in this enhanced, transmuted ego and in what issues forth from it."[24]

In the year since the premiere of Shostakovich's Fifth, a series of fine conductors had worked with the Philharmonic: Leo Blech, Fritz Busch, Clemens Krauss, Eugene Széngar, and Arthur Rodzinsky. In reviewing the 1937–1938 season, the Moscow press wrote that the Philharmonic "required a real chief conductor, not only able to take on full control but to feel personal responsibility for the ensemble's artistic standards."[25] Because of Mravinsky's championing of Soviet composers, notably Shostakovich, musical opinion in the city was that they now possessed a *chef d'orchestre* of great artistic potential. The twin achievements of Mravinsky's championing of Shostakovich in the previous season and his Moscow victory had already given him an overwhelming reputation that made it difficult for any enemies to attack him.

Mravinsky refused to make concessions and stood firm in his principles. The young conductor painstakingly pursued his goal, through work rate, enthusiasm, and knowledge, and the critics were won over by his persuasive abilities and the example he set. The single most important factor in his success was that Mravinsky introduced a strict discipline, imposing sectional rehearsals for each orchestral program. The new chief found that he had trustworthy disciples; the concertmaster Zavetnovsky had arranged chamber groups within the string sections, and they had their own rehearsal structure already in place.[26] In the interregnum following Steidry's departure, these groups had maintained elementary ensemble standards. Before a concert, each musician would have to learn his part thoroughly before joining section

rehearsals that would be held before the orchestral run-through. A strict daily
time schedule was established whereby musicians would arrive to work
through their parts at 9:00 a.m. in their own room, and the general rehearsal
would begin at 11:00 a.m. and last three hours. These group sessions—each
led by its principal—had to prepare the particular work thoroughly before the
collective session. Mravinsky himself would take an active part in most of the
sectional workouts. The regime soon brought its results in greater homo-
geneity and a refined ensemble playing in the orchestra.[27]

In his first three prewar seasons, Mravinsky based the main part of the
repertoire on the Western classics, concentrating on the Beethoven symphonies. In 1939, he performed the Second, Fourth, Fifth, and Ninth symphonies and the *Choral Fantasy*, with the great Maria Yudina as soloist.[28] In
the 1940–1941 seasons, Mravinsky added the First in C major, the programmatic *Pastoral*, *Music for Egmont* (with the great thespian Yuri Yur'yev[29]
from the Pushkin Drama Theatre as narrator), the vast *Missa Solemnis*, the Violin Concerto (with the legendary Miron Polyakin as soloist), the Fourth Piano Concerto (Vladimir Nilsen as soloist), and the overtures to *Coriolanus*,
Prométheus, and *Consecration of the House*.

Mravinsky pursued a methodical approach to the problem of interpreting
Beethoven, studying the style of performance and building his repertoire
through the performing praxis of the time. Mravinsky's art was in searching
for and reading the classics and romantics, from Beethoven, Handel, Bach,
and Mozart to Bruckner and Wagner. Mravinsky's love for the musical dramaturgy, and specifically for Tchaikovsky and Wagner, led him to combine both
stage and symphonic works in his schedules. Beginning in January 1939 and
following the Petersburg Wagner School, opera fragments by Wagner became
an inseparable aspect of Mravinsky's repository. Overtures and preludes from
the Ring cycle—the "Flight of the Valkyries," "Forest Murmurs,"
"Siegfried's Funeral March," the overture from *Tannhäuser*, the "Prelude" to
Acts I and III of *Die Meistersinger von Nürnberg*, the overture to *Die
fliegende Höllander*, and the "Prelude" to Act III of *Lohengrin* and "Die
Liebestod" from *Tristan und Isolde*.[30]

The Wagnerian repertoire was controversial, because the operas were now
rarely performed in the Soviet Union, which scorned the great pre-1917 Wagnerian tradition in St. Petersburg.[31] The symphonic thread in the operas was
the *beau idéal* for Mravinsky, and the fairy-tale fantasy contrasted with the
ideology of the Ring cycle. Mravinsky invited distinguished singers from the
Kirov for these concert performances; if the theater would not stage this
repository, then he would mount his own revival in the city.[32]

If there was one Viennese composer to whom he gravitated, it was Bruckner. This was a repertoire no other Russian conductor embraced, and he re-

membered the impression made by Hermann Abendroth conducting the great symphonies at the Philharmonic.[33] With their broad canvasses of spiritual, philosophical music embedded in the Austrian tradition, Bruckner's symphonies' restoring values, forgotten in contemporary Russia, attracted Mravinsky. The composer was so fundamental to Mravinsky that within weeks of his appointment, on 24 December 1938, he conducted the *Romantic* Fourth Symphony in E flat; he added the Seventh and Ninth Symphonies in successive seasons.

It took some years, however, for Mravinsky to bring to light the genius of Mozart; his readings of the Mozart symphonies, no. 40 in G minor K.550 and the *Jupiter,* no. 41 in C major K.551, were well received; nonetheless, they did not remain in his programs. Other Mozart works under his direction were found to be lacking in warmth and color by critics. Nevertheless, these setbacks did not halt Mravinsky reviving his readings for a celebration of Mozart in a 1941 festival. It was much later that Yevgeny Mravinsky found the secret to Mozart, when he found a warm response to his interpretations in 1956 at the Mozart Bicentennial in Vienna.

One of Mravinsky's triumphs was a magnificent performance of the great monumental oratorio *Judas Maccabaeus*, by George Frederick Handel. In the spring of 1939, he performed the work on five occasions, twice in Moscow with the State Orchestra. During the same period, Mravinsky conducted the *Concerto Grosso* no. 6 in E flat, no. 12. Mravinsky frequently gave readings of works from the eighteenth century by J. S. Bach, Corelli, and Haydn, the virtuoso soloists of the woodwind section allowing a unique musicality to the concerts.

One of the most peculiar aspects at the Philharmonic was the cult for Mahler; there was a long-standing Leningrad Mahler heritage dating to the composer's own concerts and those given in the city by his disciples in Walter, Fried, and Steidry. The cult was encouraged, too, by the influential consultant at the Philharmonic since 1928, Ivan Sollertinsky. Mravinsky introduced Gustav Mahler's Fifth Symphony and one of the gems of his early period. Along with the song cycle *Das Lied von der Erde*, the symphony was performed as part of annual Mahler Festival with other symphonies and under various conductors, with Walter, Steidry, Unger, Klemperer, Krauss, Zemlinsky, Steinberg, Talich, Sebastyan, and Széngar all taking part through the late 1930s.

Amid Leningrad's championing of unfashionable Western music, Mravinsky turned to two Russian composers whose symphonic works were ignored and misrepresented during the 1930s. At the onset of Soviet power, the creativity of Alexander Scriabin was enthusiastically supported by no less than the Bolshevik commissar of enlightenment: "The music of Scriabin is the supreme expression of the musical romanticism of the Revolution."[34] However, fashion seemed to distract interest from the late romantic and toward more extreme modernists. "In Russia, the dominating influence—until recently exerted by Scriabin—now seems to shift toward Prokofiev."[35] Nevertheless, the crusade led to many finding disapproval, and Scriabin was now attacked from unfamiliar sources: "Scriabin's music tends towards unhealthy eroticism, also to mysticism, passivity, and a flight from the reality of life."[36]

Although the music was labeled as "decadent," the Leningrad pianists Sofronitsky and Yudina were impassioned interpreters of Scriabin in the recital hall, and Mravinsky became the composer's most loyal protagonist in symphonic music.[37] "Can anyone forget Mravinsky's performance of Scriabin's *Le poèm de l'extase!*" remarked Sergey Shlifstein.[38] One of the memorable triumphs, the solo trumpet part was admirably played by Iosif Volovnik. Mravinsky initially programmed the Scriabin in December 1938 with a fine, sensitive interpretation of the suite from the neglected opera by Rimsky-Korsakov, *The Tale of the Legend of Kitezh and His Daughter Fevronia.*

One composer famously championed by Mravinsky was the doyen of Russian romantic music—Pyotr Ilyich Tchaikovsky. The late symphonies had been misread with a penchant toward sentimentalization, distorting the profundity and tragic trait in his music. However, this was not an exclusive fault of Russian musicians. "Tchaikovsky has been the victim of the conductor. Year after year, interpretations have become increasingly exaggerated, increasingly hysterical and filled with false emotion, and inevitably, his music has become a symptom of bad taste. . . . The bad taste is not in his music. It is in the people who have interpreted the music."[39] Critics in the Soviet Union of this period regarded Tchaikovsky as pedantic, unfashionable.[40] Full recognition came to fruition in 1940, when the country extensively marked Tchaikovsky's birth centenary. Asaf'yev wrote that great writers of Tchaikovsky's day "had an affinity in Tchaikovsky's love for everything Russian: people, children, village life, nature, life, and language—Russian language is something endlessly rich, powerful, and great."[41] Mravinsky conducted the late symphonies as philosophical and deeply tragic sound canvasses wholly divorced from the romanticism of the past. "Tolstoy was attracted to Tchaikovsky's music, and Tchaikovsky, in turn, recognized that he understood the 'oppression of doubt and tragic misunderstanding that Tolstoy endured.'"[42] That Tchaikovsky was no longer "decadent" and back in vogue was much to the credit of Boris Asaf'yev.[43] "Critics, in 1940, awoke national sympathy to his work, which grew particularly during the Great Patriotic War."[44] "Our time, a time of great titanic patriotic force, hears in Tchaikovsky's music the song of glorious motherland and pride in their own country."[45]

Mravinsky's reputation was of an active propagandist of Soviet music—one month after winning the conducting competition, he made a return to Moscow to take part in a ten-day festival of Soviet music. Mravinsky directed the world premiere of the Moscow composer Yevgeny Golubyev's Second Symphony and repeated those works with which he had achieved so much recent success: the Fifth Symphony by Shostakovich and Khachaturyan's Piano Concerto. In the New Year of 1939, the exploration of new music continued, as Mravinsky directed the Leningrad Philharmonic in several world premieres: Boris Arapov's *Tadjik Suite*, Zinovy Kompanietz's *Rhapsody on Jewish Themes*, Yuri Kochurov's *Preludes in Memory of Pushkin*, and Mark Teplitzky's *Suite on Karelian Themes*. Pieces of a more popular character were unveiled in Abraam Paisin's *Two Songs about Lenin* and Viktor Tomilin's suite from the film *Fedka*. This all in the same bill as fragments from Isaak Dunayevsky's music from the films *Children of Captain Grant*, *Volga-Volga*, and *Seekers of Happiness*, somewhat a turn to popularism, and a beau geste to the chairman of the Composers Union board.

Two years following the premiere of the Fifth, Mravinsky was now asked to introduce Shostakovich's next major orchestral work—the Sixth Symphony in B minor. There had been some talk that this was to be based on a poem by Mayakovsky on Lenin; however, when the composer played the first two movements on the piano, there was disenchantment at the Composers Union. At this audition in August 1939, expectations had been understandably high following its predecessor's triumph, yet the controversy over the Sixth Symphony would not abate following its public performance. The world situation had changed greatly in recent months; with the signing of the German-Soviet pact, Nazi troops now faced Soviet troops in Poland, and only a short distance from Leningrad, the Red Army was already engaged in a territorial conflict with the Soviet Union's northern neighbor—Finland. The threat of war loomed ever closer, and a tragic and pessimistic color permeated the new work by Shostakovich.

However, the composer's elucidation of the piece emphasized emotions contrary to this: "Music of a contemplative and lyrical order predominates in my latest symphony. I wanted to convey the moods of spring, joy, and youth in it."[46] In a letter to his confidant, Isaak Glikman, Shostakovich wrote: "this is the first time I have written such a successful finale. It seems to me that not even the most hostile of critics will be able to fault it."[47] In October, Shostakovich had given the completed score to Mravinsky, who quickly assimilated it with his orchestra. The world premiere was scheduled for 21 November. The composer wrote to his friend Levon Atovmyan: "Tomorrow my Sixth Symphony will be performed. Mravinsky is doing all that he may, and everything is fine. If the premiere is a failure and is repeated, it will be admirable. Just now, there is some uncertainty about the last movement."[48]

Once again, an opening for Shostakovich's symphony took place as part of a Festival of Soviet Music in Leningrad. There were two other premieres that evening: the suite *Peter the First* by Mravinsky's former composition teacher, Vladimir Shcherbachyov, and the Romantic Poem for Violin and Orchestra by Valery Zhelobinsky, performed by Ilya Spilberg (assistant concertmaster). Following the premiere, Shostakovich wrote: "the symphony went very well."[49] Indeed there was no reason for the composer to have had doubt in his finale, as the Leningrad public was so enthusiastic that it had to be encored. The Sixth was given under Mravinsky with the USSR State Symphony Orchestra in Moscow two weeks later. Shostakovich, however, could not travel to the capital for the concert: "on 3 December, I heard the symphony on the radio. Despite the bad reception, it was very well performed. I am indebted in many ways to Mravinsky for his magnificent performances of my Fifth and Sixth Symphonies."[50]

Reviews of the two concerts found common footing in just one characteristic, that in Mravinsky "we have a first class conductor of European stature."[51] More doubts emerged from the composer's opponents about the Sixth. Because of the absence of a *symphonic allegro* in the first movement, critics christened Shostakovich's Sixth "The Headless Symphony"; the opening *Largo* was called too static and the dramaturgy unsatisfactory with a lack of contrast and no cohesion, each movement having a separate motif.

The critics sensed a return to the irony and parody of old, particularly in the Scherzo, which surprised many for its abrupt changes of rhythm and tempo and for the transition from the almost ideal proportions of the "classical" Fifth Symphony to the vast tragic opening *Largo*, rendering an overwhelmingly dark backcloth to the whole work. Expecting a continuation in the style and mood of its predecessor, officialdom found Shostakovich's latest symphony a major disappointment: "It is natural to expect profound and interesting artistic ideas from such a gifted master, however, there was none of this in the Sixth Symphony. The brilliance and refinement of the orchestration cannot mask the lack of an integral symphonic concept."[52] This statement appearing in the central journal of Soviet music seemed to sum up the perceived faults.

The Composers Union, following the new symphony's Moscow premiere, summoned a discussion on the work. Shostakovich wrote: "It appears that composers are upset by my symphony; what can one do if one has proved unsatisfactory to them? One has to compromise oneself to meet with their good will."[53] Regardless of Shebalin—his friend inviting him to the meeting—Shostakovich responded, "your last telegram upset me terribly. It seems that this audition is being arranged because they think it's rubbish."[54]

However, not all the critics were so negative, and the composer did not have so much to fear. "With every new symphonic work, Shostakovich reveals himself as a maturing artist, continuing to develop his own creative fantasy and musical conscience. In the Sixth Symphony, he has achieved new heights, particularly in the first movement . . . it becomes clear, after one has heard it three or four times, its unusual depth of expression."[55] Boris Asaf'yev judged the Sixth Symphony as sharing a common identity with the Fifth, as "a living reflection of the storms and tempests of the present, and he himself is akin to Shakespeare's Prospero transformed into an observer in images of sound, and of the imperceptible electric current: as if it is not music, but the flow of nervous mighty tension."[56] By the summer of 1940, the Sixth began to be accepted by the musical authorities: "the symphony has won recognition as one of the most interesting and outstanding works of Soviet symphonic music."[57]

This was much to the relentless advocacy of Yevgeny Mravinsky; similar in his championing of the Fifth, he conducted the Sixth Symphony relentlessly throughout his career, believing it a deeply tragic composition epitomizing the finest of Shostakovich's work. Later, during the war years, the composer described receiving the first recording of the Sixth Symphony by Stokowski: "I must say honestly that I do not like his reading very much. It's well thought through and precise, but the character of his reading does not quite suit. He plays it very slowly and sadly, particularly in the last movement. There is not the abundant lightness and gaiety, which characterizes Mravinsky's interpretation."[58]

The Piano Concerto by the Leningrad composer Orest Yevlakov (a pupil of Shostakovich) was heard for the first and last time in May 1941, scheduled with Khachaturyan's *Poem to Stalin* and Shostakovich's Sixth Symphony at a concert arranged by the Union of Composers in Leningrad. As is often the fate for modern pieces, only Shostakovich's Sixth Symphony emerged in the constant repertoire of the orchestra in seasons to come, and solely Vladimir Shcherbachyov's orchestral suite was performed again during the war years.

In the summer of 1939, the Leningrad Philharmonic Orchestra gave a series of concerts at the mountain holiday resort of Kislovodsk in the Caucasus, renewing a pre-Revolutionary tradition of summer music there. The retreat and nearby watering places at Mineralny Vody and Essentuki possessed a comprehensive network of theaters, concert halls, and hotels drawing many tourists from the big cities of the South and the Caucasus. There prevails a wonderfully exotic atmosphere with stunning vistas of the Caucasus, the surrounding woods and forests, and invigorating fresh mountain air. Shalyapin had owned a villa there, and there at the birthplace of the first great Russian conductor, Vasily Safonov, a memorial remains at the Kurhaus Theatre.[59] The concerts given by the Philharmonic there were always enthusiastic, allowing Mravinsky the opportunity of spending time in this Caucasian resort reminiscent of the Switzerland he knew before the Revolution. It was an extraordinary few days, spent *en famille* in this almost idyllic location away from the hardships of the northern capital.

It is remarkable that the *succès d'estime* achieved by Mravinsky and the Philharmonic was during a period when an enormous shadow hung over the peoples of the Soviet Union. Many thousands had been arrested as part of the purges unleashed by Yezhov and Stalin. In this process, distinguished artists, poets, and musicians suffered; notable stage directors such as Meyerhold were murdered, as was his actress wife; the poetess Tsvetaeva took her own life, the writer Babel was shot, and many others were arrested. The composer Mosolov was briefly imprisoned, and the influential musician Zhilyaev was sent to die in the Gulag, yet musicians were curiously treated in comparison with other artists.[60] There were several personages in this period who, for some reason known only to Stalin, were sacrosanct, including the playwright Bulgakov, the poetesses Akhmatova and Berggollts, the actor Yur'yev, and theater directors Stanislavsky and Nemirovich-Danchenko. Soviet power leaned heavily on sources of information in every establishment, whether it be a school, a factory, a hospital, or indeed a symphony orchestra. Party and Komsomol members would collect information about each other and their work colleagues about whom they had suspicions. This could range from details of their sex lives to their hobbies and pastimes, all apart from their political views. Whatever was unfashionable, extreme in taste, was deemed suspect and punishable, and the culprits would be questioned and jailed for the slightest breaches of the law. Yet these were times without laws.[61]

Whatever his background, and there were other former aristocrats who found their niche within Soviet power, there was nothing unusual in Mravinsky's lifestyle, which could be deemed unimpeachable. His close circle of friends—Cherkasov, Rabinovich, and Yershov—all shared his views, and they went back many years together; a great loyalty bound their friendship. Mravinsky's work rate was admirable; the creation of a disciplined work regime within the wider state apparatus was widely respected, even by the Party clique. The finely tuned, homogenous, and rich sound produced by Mravinsky's musicians was almost the perfect instrument. For the Party, a full program of concerts with enthusiastic audiences represented success—a symbol of the preeminence of Soviet cultural policies. Mravinsky and his orchestra in years to come would become cultural ambassadors for the USSR. The essence of Mravinsky's terrifically drawn and passionate performances of Brahms, Beethoven, and Shostakovich was for the system immaterial.

In December 1939, Mravinsky was nominated as a candidate to represent electors in the first All-Union Soviet of Peoples Deputies, having been selected for this by the musicians and staff of the Leningrad Philharmonic Orchestra who made up electoral district No. 389; his name had been proposed by Vladimir Gensler, principal clarinet. His published biography noted that "Yevgeny Alexandrovich Mravinsky is a talented representative of Soviet art, having won great popularity among Soviet listeners."[62] The conductor was awarded the Order of Merit for his work with the orchestra, the first of many awards and honors he was to receive from the Soviet state. The titles and medals allowed protection and fashioned his public persona in Soviet life.

In March and April 1940, Mravinsky traveled to the capital for a series of concerts with the Moscow Philharmonic Orchestra:

> With his performance of the Sixth Symphony of Tchaikovsky, Mravinsky showed that he is a deeply profound artist. He allowed us to hear the tragic side of this symphony with unusual force—the first *Allegro* and finale. What deep tragic pathos and with such reserve, detachment, and superficial expression! This is the first time in many years that the Sixth Symphony of Tchaikovsky has been revealed in such a light. One would prefer more lyrical beauty, poetic breathing in the second movement. . . . In reviewing Beethoven's Ninth Symphony, Shlifstein discovered some lack of experience in the conductor: "One needs long years of knowledge in this work, before an artist (if capable of it) can come to a profound understanding. . . . Naturally, Mravinsky, who conducted this Ninth Symphony on only the fourth occasion, is just beginning such an undertaking. Yet there was so much that was positive in his interpretation, correctly taken tempi, proper relations between dynamics in sound. . . . Yet there lacked the most important factor—the daring enchantment of Beethovian fantasy, poetry, and grandiose conception.[63]
>
> Mravinsky not only possesses the necessary physical technique and resources (he has a beautiful expressive gesture, enough variation, well-developed technique), but great inner will power and energy. This is in a gesture—imperious and powerful—which so distinguishes the master conductors. This is what organizes an orchestra and binds them to his artistic will. Moreover, this characterizes Mravinsky as a complete and expressive conductor. There are those ordained to be pianists or violinists, but Mravinsky is a born conductor. In hearing him, you notice the wonderful enlightened orchestral sound; under his baton, the orchestra acquires that inner artistic discipline with which there can be a living creative relationship of each musician to the performed work. Really, this defines a general style of orchestral performance. (I have in mind the technical aspect.) However, the real major achievement of Mravinsky in recent times is his interpretation of Shostakovich's Fifth Symphony. It is difficult to exaggerate Mravinsky's triumph.[64]

The culmination of Mravinsky's early period quickly followed these performances, with the tour to the Soviet capital in May 1940. This was the first time that the Leningrad Philharmonic Orchestra had performed in Moscow, unquestionably lending the visit a special character; there had always been a keen rivalry between the two major centers. Of the seven concerts given at the Large Hall of the Moscow Conservatoire, one each was taken by Mravinsky's assistants, Rabinovich and Eliasberg.

The programs embraced the range of Mravinsky's Leningrad repertoire, all designed to show off the universality and indeed preeminence and virtuosity of the Philharmonic.[65] On 20 May the program included the suite *Peter the First* by Shcherbachyov, Tchaikovsky's *Francesca da Rimini*, and Shostakovich's Fifth Symphony in D minor; on 23 May it included the *Romantic Poem* by Zhivotov, fragments from *Till Eulenspiegel* by Maximilian Shteinberg, and Tchaikovsky's *Pathétique*. Mravinsky's last program came on 25 May with the "Prélude and Liebestod" from *Tristan und Isolde* by Wagner, Paganini's First Violin Concerto (soloist Ilya Spilberg), and Bruckner's Seventh Symphony in E major.[66] As if arriving from another planet, the Philharmonic caused an almost unprecedented wave of warmth and excitement among the Moscow public. "For a long time, such accomplished orchestral playing has not been heard in the Soviet Union,"[67] wrote *Izvestia*. Dozens of reviews recorded the exceptional musicianship of the Leningrad Philharmonic Orchestra: "The playing of the Leningrad musicians is noted most of all for its ideal ensemble, its unity and integrity in performance, attained through many years of interactivity, the distinguished culture of the musicians, and their exquisite artistic leadership." Solovtsov wrote: "the outstanding consistency, warm and clear string sound, fine brass instruments, but perhaps the woodwind deserve most attention. In each solo phrase, one realizes that here is a real artist and master giving expression to the music performed, clearly understanding his part within the whole conception."[68] The performances with the Kirov Theatre of some five years before had not been forgotten—a feature in the government broadsheet *Izvestia* commended Mravinsky's "magnificent and deserved success."[69] Particular enthusiasm was given to the symphonic performances of works by Tchaikovsky, Shostakovich, and Bruckner, the latter a novelty for Muscovites: "These scores not only revealed the depth of the conductor's repertoire and quite justifiably can be considered no less outstanding in his triumph."[70] In recognition of the orchestra's achievements, the government presented awards to Mravinsky and several musicians; the title of Merited Artist of the Russian Federation was given to the double bass player Mikhail Kravchenko, the flautist Yuri Bayer, and the cellist Boris Shafran. The bassoonist Vasil'yev was given the even more eminent title of Honored Art Worker of the Russian Federation, making him the first to receive such an honor at the Philharmonic. The Philharmonic was presented later in the year with the Order of the Red Banner for its concert prowess. During a break in the Moscow schedule,

Mravinsky and his orchestra made an early television recording with dancers from the Kirov Ballet in fragments from Tchaikovsky's *Nutcracker*. This was shown on Pathé-type newsreels all over the country together with Galina Ulanova's enticing dancing, enchanting millions of filmgoers. Mravinsky was seen conducting without a score before musicians who it seemed could play anything; Mravinsky's eyes were caught in their hypnotic glance, making it seem as though the sound was heard through his eyes as much as through the tip of his baton.

In February 1941, Mravinsky was back in the Soviet capital, albeit without the Philharmonic, as we can read: "once more we became convinced of the magniloquent work of this profoundly interesting musician." On this fresh visit, Mravinsky offered Bruckner's Ninth, Schumann's Fourth, Shostakovich's Fifth and Sixth Symphonies, Tchaikovsky's *Pathétique*, Scriabin's *Le poème de l'extase*, and Wagner overtures. "Mravinsky is an example for our young conductors in his intense and untiring search for new goals." Rabinovich wrote that few were familiar with the Bruckner, "however, Mravinsky works systematically on both Bruckner and Mahler, for which we should be seriously and wholly grateful!" The critic commented that a few days prior to Mravinsky's performance, the German conductor Leo Blech gave a concert of Wagner overtures, and Mravinsky could be found at Blech's rehearsal, studying the German's work. However, Mravinsky's reading of the same Wagner pieces was quite different and deeply individual. "Mravinsky—an independent and creative artist and still avaricious for knowledge—could not but hear how Blech played the very same pieces of music."[71]

The spectrum of work at the Philharmonic involved regular guest conductors augmenting that of Mravinsky's work; Ivan Sollertinsky now organized programming as well as the selection of soloists replacing Chulaki. The month of April 1941 was almost typical—as many as seven different maestri presenting wholly contrasting programs at the Philharmonic. On 10 April, Mravinsky conducted Russian works, including Glazunov's Fifth Symphony in B-flat major, the suites from *Raymonda* and Rimsky-Korsakov's *The Tale of Kitezh*, and Serge Koussevitsky's Concerto for Double-Bass (Getrovich as soloist). Karl Eliasberg conducted Tchaikovsky's Third Symphony in D major, *Polish*, and his *Francesca da Rimini* and *Rococo Variations* (Knushevitsky as soloist); on 16 April Mravinsky conducted Berlioz's *Requiem* with the Glinka State Choir, and two days later Kurt Sanderling gave his debut with Vivaldi's *Concerto Grosso*, Richard Strauss's tone poem *Also Sprach Zarathustra*, and Schumann's Cello Concerto. Mravinsky's assistant, Nikolay Rabinovich, directed a concert performance of Beethoven's *Fidelio* using singers from the Maly Theatre, whose chief conductor, Boris Khaikhin, arrived to undertake a Tchaikovsky night of the Second Symphony in C minor,

Little Russian, and the one-act opera *Iolanta*. A Beethoven evening was given by the local composer Iosif Miklashevsky. On the bill were the Seventh Symphony in A major, the *King Stephen* overture, and the *Emperor Concerto* (Lev Oborin as soloist). On 29 April, Mravinsky directed Beethoven's great *Missa Solemnis*, again using forces of the Glinka Choir. In addition, Alexander Melik-Pashayev came to conduct the orchestra,[72] revealing the depth of artistic planning of the Leningrad Philharmonic Orchestra before the war.

Although Mravinsky gave only three concerts that month, his work could not go unmentioned at the Leningrad Philharmonic Society conference held a month later. Artistic director Ivan Sollertinsky reported:

> In his position as chief conductor, Mravinsky has taken upon himself the entire monumental world repertoire. . . . One can declare without any exaggeration that any other conductor of lesser status would break under such pressure; nonetheless, there was never any doubt that he would not falter taking on such work previously shared between excellent Western conductors. It is to Mravinsky's credit—and I am speaking now as a fellow musician—that he has come through this test of fire brilliantly.[73]

The conference was to discuss the fate of the symphony in the Soviet Union; Shostakovich's symphonies had inspired a revival, for almost all composers in the country were now writing in the genre.

Mravinsky's first marriage lasted until the late 1930s, when he encountered Olga Alexeyevna Karpova. Meeting Mravinsky at a soiree, Olga fell for the young, stunningly handsome conductor, and following his divorce, the two married in 1938 and set up home at 13 Borodinsky Street on the northern Petrograd side. This marriage was long-lasting and ostensibly successful; Olga shared the most difficult years of his life, during a period of *Sturm und Drang*, giving him everything he needed in support, understanding, tenderness, and love. Olga, however, played a finely drawn public role. In his diaries, Mravinsky complained of her ignoring domestic responsibilities and going off to the cinema or theater with her friends. Cherkasov's wife remembers: "both our families lived with difficulty. Often the phone would ring and it would be Olga Mravinskaya on the line, [asking] 'Zhenya has a concert coming up, can he have a loan of Kolya's tails?' and I would return, 'Of course, but in a couple of days Kolya will need it for a concert himself.'" Cherkasova wrote in her memoirs of the period that Olga and Mravinsky were of dissimilar characters and background, and his mother unfailingly noticed this; for Yelizaveta Nikolayevna, this was a mésalliance. Throughout her son's remarkable career, Yelizaveta was his most devoted and enthusiastic critic, attending all his concerts, giving herself wholeheartedly to his career. Always there would lie before the rostrum a bouquet of freshly picked flowers with a handwritten dedication from Yelizaveta to her beloved son.[74]

In 1941, Yevgeny Mravinsky gave two performances, both of music by Wagner and Tchaikovsky, during the famous "White Nights" at the Central Park of Culture and Rest on Vasilostrovsky Island. On 3 June—the eve of his thirty-eighth birthday—neither Mravinsky nor any of those attending the last of these open-air productions could know it would be a long three years before the orchestra played again in the city. For many Leningrad citizens, a worse fate would beckon.

If the European war had missed the peoples of the Soviet Union since 1937, it had become an almost foregone conclusion that the country would become involved in war with Nazi Germany; yet no one could have predicted that it would begin as it did on 22 June 1941. Finding the defenses weakened by summer leave in Western Ukraine and Byelorussia, the Germans destroyed the Soviet air force on the ground and made rapid advances toward their two main objectives of Moscow and Leningrad. By late August 1941, the city in the north was already under siege.

NOTES

1. There were also many foreign specialists working in different parts of Soviet life.

2. V. Razhnikov, *Kondrashin rasskasivayet* (Moscow: Sovetsky Kompositor, 1989), 53.

3. Oscar Fried was invited by Lenin in 1921 to give concerts in the Soviet Union, returned many times, and died in 1943 in Moscow.

4. V. Fomin, *Dirizher Yevgeny Mravinsky* (Leningrad: Muzika, 1983), 35.

5. M. Grinberg, "E. A. Mravinsky," *Sovetskoye Izkusstvo*, 4 October 1938.

6. Heinrich Neuhaus, "Yevgeny Mravinsky," *Sovetskoye Izkusstvo*, 18 September 1938.

7. Four hundred newspaper articles around the country were dedicated to the competition.

8. K. Kondrashin, *Mir Dirizhera* (Moscow: Muzika, 1976), 174.

9. The full symphony had to wait another six years for its first complete performance.

10. D. Rabinovich, *Sovetskoye Izkusstvo*, 4 October 1938.

11. *Pravda*, 1 October 1938.

12. Y. A. Mravinsky, "Blizhaishi zadachi," *Izvestia*, 17 October 1938.

13. Y. A. Mravinsky, "Za novi pobedy sovetskovo iskusstzva!" *Leningradskaya Pravda*, 18 October 1938.

14. The Leningrad Radio possessed two ensembles: one a large symphonic orchestra and the other a chamber orchestra. Eliasberg was appointed to the former.

15. The Committee for the Arts under the Council of Ministers, established in 1934, was the predecessor of the Ministry of Culture. The latter took over in March 1953.

16. A. M. Vavilina Mravinskaya, author interview, September 2002.

17. Mikhail Druskin was a young music writer and a consultant at the Philharmonic.

18. M. Druskin, "Prekrasni konzert," *Smena*, 20 October 1938.

19. V. Fomin, *Stareischey Russki simfonicheski Orkester* (Leningrad: Muzika, 1982), 30–31.

20. G. Yudin, *Za gran yu proshlihk dnei* (Moscow, Muzikalnoe Nasledtsvo-Muzika, 1966), 107–120.

21. Mravinsky at the age of thirty-five was the youngest chief conductor in the orchestra's history.

22. G. Meyerbeer, "Musical World," in *Notes on Conductors and Conducting*, by T. R. Croger (London: Willam Reeves,1907), 50.

23. V. Razhnikov, *Kirill Kondrashin rasskasivaet* (Moscow: Sovetsky Kompozitor, 1989), 55.

24. B. Walter, *Of Music and Music Making* (London: Faber and Faber, 1957), 27.

25. "Itogi leningradskovo simfonicheskovo sezona," *Sovetskoye Iskusstvo*, 4 July 1938.

26. Fomin, *Stareischii simfoniscesky russkiye orkester*, 29.

27. V. Fomin, *Dirizher Yevgeny Mravinsky* (Leningrad: Muzika, 1983), 39.

28. Maria Yudina was an eclectic pianist with a vast repertoire who was a wonderful interpreter of Bach and Beethoven and of new music, but she was frequently admonished for her behavior by the Soviet authorities.

29. Yur'yev was a legendary actor at the theater, celebrated before the Revolution and decorated by Nikolay II. His roles were universal: works of Shakespeare, Schiller, Chekhov, Tolstoy, and Gorky were among his favored plays.

30. Y. Yelagin, *Ukroshchenie iskusstv* (New York: Chekhov, 1952), 220.

31. L. E. Gakkel, "Yevgeny Mravinsky—Patritzii za pultom," *Delo*, 2 October 2000, 14–15.

32. D. B. Shafran, *Daniil Shafran—Violoncellist solo* (Moscow: ACT, 2001), 24.

33. Y. A. Mravinsky, interview with A. A. Zolotov, 1983.

34. A. Lunacharsky, *V mire muziki* (Moscow, 1926), 145.

35. N. Zhilyaev, *K novym beregam* (Moscow, January 1923).

36. D. Shostakovich, *New York Times*, 20 December 1931.

37. M. Yudina, *Luchi Bozhestvenniye Lyubvi* (St. Petersburg: Universitetskaya Kniga, 1999), 725–26.

38. S. Shlifstein, "Konzerti E. Mravinskovo," *Sovetskoye Iskusstvo*, 24 April 1940.

39. O. Klemperer, *New York Times*, 5 May 1935.

40. V. V. Protopopov, *B. V. Asaf'yev—Vol. 1, Isbranniye trudi* (Moscow: Akademiya Nauk SSSR, 1953), 6.

41. Protopopov, *B. V. Asaf'yev—Vol. 1*, 6.

42. B. V. Asaf'yev, *Velikiye Russkiye Kompozitor, Isbranniye trudi*, Vol. 2 (Moscow: Akademiya Nauk SSSR, 1952), 22.

43. Asaf'yev, *Velikiye Russkiye Kompozitor, Isbranniye trudi*, Vol. 2, 22.

44. Asaf'yev, *Velikiye Russkiye Kompozitor, Isbranniye trudi*, Vol. 2, 22.

45. Asaf'yev, *Velikiye Russkiye Kompositor, Isbranniye trudi*, Vol. 2, 22.

46. D. D. Shostakovich, "Novy Raboty D. Shostakovicha," *Leningradskaya Pravda*, 28 August 1939, 4.

47. Y. Makarov, *Muzikalniaya Akademiya*, no. 1 (1993): 153.

48. Shostakovich to Atomyan, 20 November 1939, GTsMMK, f. 32, ed. Khr, 1762.

49. Shostakovich to Atomyan 22 November 1939, GTsMMK, f. 32, Khr, 1927.

50. Shostakovich to Atomyan 5 December 1939, GTsMMK, f. 32, ed. Khr, 1763.

51. L. V. Danilevich, "Posle decady," *Sovetskaya Muzika*, no. 12 (1939): 47.

52. Danilevich, "Posle decady," 45.

53. D. D. Shostakovich to Shebalin, in S. Khentova, *Molodiye gody Shostakovicha*, Vol. 2 (Leningrad: Sovetsky Kompositor, 1980), 233.

54. D. D. Shostakovich to Shebalin, in Khentova, *Molodiye gody Shostakovicha*, Vol. 2, 233–34.

55. G. M. Shneerson, *Sovetskaya Musika*, no. 5 (1941): 105.

56. Asaf'yev, *Akademik B.V. Asaf'yev Isbranniye Trudi*, Vol. 5 (Moscow: Akademiya Nauk SSSR, 1952), 128.

57. Y. Vainkop, "Leningrad compoiztori za raboty," *Sovetskaya Muzika*, no. 8 (1940): 36.

58. L. Mikheyeva, *II Sollertinsky* (Leningrad: Sovetsky Kompositor, 1988), 151.

59. Shalyapin was so famous that upon rising in the morning, he would often give impromptu recitals, singing from his balcony!

60. "In the years of the Great Terror there were three 'privileged' categories of population who remained practically untouched: musicians, aviators, and chess-players; the friendship with Tukahachevsky cost Zhilyaev his life. A charismatic personality, musicologist, critic, and professor at the Moscow Conservatoire, Zhilyaev had exerted an influence on Shostakovich's creative development. In Tbilisi, Dmitry Gachev (1902–1945), a political émigré from Bulgaria who had become one of the most active RAPM writers, perished in the GULAG. The pianist Maria Izrailovna Grinberg (1908–1978) suffered serious troubles as a member of the family of an enemy of the people. Music critic Viktor Yulievich Delson (1907–1970), musicologist Pavel Alexandrovich Vulfius (1908–1977) were among those who passed through prisons and camps." Yevgeny Yelagin, *Ukroshchenie iskusstv* (New York: Chekhov, 1952), 302.

61. P. Sudoplatov, *Spetzoperatsia 1930–1950* (Moscow: OLMA, 1997), 84.

62. Archives of the St. Petersburg Philharmonia Library.

63. S. Shlifstein, *Sovetskoe Iskusstvo*, 24 April 1940.

64. S. Shlifstein, "Konzerti E. Mravinskovo," *Sovetskoye Iskusstvo*, 24 April 1940.

65. The first and last programs were repeated during the series.

66. O. Sarkisov and V. Fomin, *Zasluzhenniye kollektiv RSFSR akademicheskiye simfonicheskiye orkestr filarmonii* (Leningrad: Leningradskaya filarmoniya, Stati, Vospomianiya, Materiali, Lenizdat, 1972), 123.

67. L. Ginzburg, "Dva Konzerta," *Izvestia*, 23 May 1940.

68. V. Solovtsov, "Koncert v bolshom zale conservatory," *Vechernaya Moskva*, 21 May 1940.

69. Radtsev, "Velikiye izkussvto," *Izvestia*, 28 May 1940.
70. D. Rabinovich, "Dirizher i orkester," *Leningradskaya Pravda*, 24 May 1940.
71. D. Rabinovich, *Sovetskoe Izkusstsvo*, 2 March 1941.
72. Mikheyeva, *II Sollertinsky*, 128.
73. Fomin, *Dirizher Yevgeny Mravinsky*, 47.
74. A. M. Vavilina Mravinskaya, author interview, September 2002.

Chapter Eight

Evacuation

Beat, heart! Hammer away—no matter how tired. Listen! The city has
sworn that the enemy will not enter.

—Olga Bergoltts, *Dnevnye Zvezdy*

In modern times, no other experience brought the Soviet people together as
did the Nazi invasion of 1941; as in the Napoleonic Wars, the country mobi-
lized its forces for what was to become a Great Patriotic War. Though 22 June
1941 became a deeply tragic day for the people of Leningrad, the conflict was
indeed a turning point in the life and work of the Philharmonic and its chief
conductor. In the end, the involvement of the Soviet Union in the Second
World War turned out to be a key to the final victory over the Nazis.

The announcement of war with Germany found the country basking in a
warm Sunday holiday; examinations were being held at the Conservatoire
and the Philharmonic's players were there preparing their pupils. Since 1936,
Mravinsky had taken a class of students, and their fortunes were matters for
his concern.[1] Mravinsky was at the Kirov Theatre undertaking a tribute performance for the ballerina Yelizaveta Gerdt, and he was to take part both on
stage and at the podium directing *Giselle*.[2] Cherkasov was also there acting,
in *Don Quixôte*. With the outbreak of war, many thought the gala would be
canceled; however, it ended as a magnificent triumph, and for those jubilant
crowds emerging through that summer night, few could suspect what would
unfold in coming months.[3]

The first natural reaction to the war was enlistment of many into the Red
Army, Air Force, and Navy; however, employees of state collectives were exempted, and that loophole saved musicians from losing their lives in the unfolding conflagration. Nevertheless, musicians enlisted in the People's Volunteers and built defense structures and bomb shelters, all presided over by

Mravinsky, who was now appointed a lieutenant-major.[4] For some weeks, many believed that the Soviet army would throw back the Germans and fight on foreign soil, and that the war would not involve Leningrad. This opinion was shared by Mravinsky and many of his colleagues; because of their respect for the "cultured Germans," who refused to bomb Paris in 1940, few actually expected an attack upon the beautiful city of Leningrad or indeed that they would threaten the city's arts treasures.[5]

In the first weeks, uncertainty reigned in the city, but life followed its usual course as, with the borders far away, no immediate concern was prevalent. In July, the war became much closer when the Baltic Fleet suffered catastrophic losses and evacuated from Tallinn to Leningrad. Rationing was introduced and private shops opened, offering a wide variety of foodstuffs albeit at extortionate prices.[6] With the relentless advance by the Germans upon the city, hundreds of thousands of Leningrad men and women enlisted in the Volunteers. At the end of July, incredibly, it was the efforts of these units by sheer weight of numbers and brave determination that stopped the Nazi advance at the very gates to Leningrad.[7]

In August, as the magnitude of the Nazi progress became apparent, the government ordered the withdrawal of all Leningrad's main arts institutions to the deep rear of the country. Mravinsky did not want to leave, yet to forgo disaster removal of the Philharmonic was the only viable option; there had been a long-standing plan for evacuation for the arts treasures, theaters, and ensembles.[8] The options for the Philharmonic would be Tashkent and Novosibirsk; the former might be acceptable with a Conservatoire and professional orchestra because of its a warm climate and fresh fruit and vegetables. However, "life" could become congested with another performing ensemble. The Philharmonic opted for the more enigmatic city of Novosibirsk. This was the center of a vast region of large industrial towns with little musical heritage; however, their sojourn could serve to stimulate cultural life—and the chance to bring music to a fresh audience was duly relished by both Mravinsky and Sollertinsky.[9]

On the evening of 22 August, as Leningrad was being slowly encircled by enemy forces, the Philharmonic Orchestra together with the staff of the Pushkin Drama Theatre[10] quietly collected at the Finland Station, on the northern side of the city.[11] The musicians and their families, clutching their instruments and a few precious items of clothing, gathered on the station concourse awaiting their evacuation. Their departure on a specially prepared train was wholly dependent on the security of the railway line leading to the east of the city. The approaching threat could be heard in the thundering, mighty guns of the Baltic fleet firing on the advancing German army, while air-raid balloons, antiaircraft defense, and unseasonable weather kept the enemy from making direct raids on the city center.[12] On the platform, the tall figure of the Philharmonic's chief wore a beret, nonchalantly smoking his eternal Belomor *papirosi*, giving the scene a degree of normality; beside him were his elegant mother and the *bon ton* Olga, both clutching several domestic cats.[13]

Many believed that with the suddenness of the war, together with a sustaining belief in the courage of the Russian soldier and the country's ability to defeat the Germans, that they would soon be able to return home. Few thought that their invaders would be so inhumane as they had heard. Both ensembles left behind members who would follow later; "see you soon!" they cried out, thinking that they would return shortly.[14] Everyone in the orchestra was able to take their immediate family members—others were left to embark on a later train—and the exodus was to go on for another few weeks until no way out remained. The direct route to Moscow was already cut, and the train had to take a slow, circuitous route through the northern towns of Mga and Volkhov and onto Vologda and Cherepovetz and the east. During the first night on the train, they had to make an emergency stop before the train could cross the bridge over the Volkhov River. German bombers had bombed the track in advance and were attempting to destroy the bridge itself. In the early dawn hours, the musicians could see from the carriage windows the light of antiaircraft fire and German Junkers dropping their deadly loads. All of the bombs fortunately missed their target, while everyone watched, relieved to see them fall harmlessly into the water. It was the first time that the war had come so close. The Philharmonic had to wait a few more hours, following repairs, before they could move on to the relative safety of the East. Three days passed, and in capturing the town of Mga, the Germans took the railway line, and the circle finally closed, cutting Leningrad off from the outside world.[15]

There now followed travel across endless, eternal Russian steppe for Mravinsky and his orchestra. On this stretched-out journey across Russia's central plain, they made unscheduled stops in the middle of the countryside, or at quiet railway sidings in the depths of the virgin forest, and for a few hours they could disembark from their cramped rail compartments and walk around, easing the tension for the musicians and their anxiety for the present. In wartime, the barriers between the musicians and the illustrious actors from the Drama Theatre were shed. The sole privilege allowed was the availability of a conventional railway carriage for the elderly veterans of the theater, while everyone else had to make do with modified goods wagons with rudimentary, makeshift seating. The children played around, unaware of the terrors they were leaving behind them, while their parents made bonfires for barbecue, and for a brief hour their problems seemed to disappear.[16] Somehow, the two tall figures of Cherkasov and Mravinsky—eternal friends—personified steadiness and order and gave these wartime scenes a sense of *bonhomie*. The acting of Cherkasov was famous to all from his magnificent interpretation of Alexander Nevsky in Eisenstein's eponymous classic film. Here he was beside them, sharing their joys and sorrows.

Along the way, there were many incidents of bombing of the orchestra's train, many scenes of cruelty, despair, and destruction caused by the hideous war raging around them. Columns of goods wagons would overtake them taking loads of factory parts out to the Urals and Siberia. Passing them, too, were the hospital trains taking wounded to safe treatment in the East; and they could see passing their compartments more and more troop trains speeding Westwards full of fresh reinforcements. For the artists on board, it would be an unchanging picture, night and day, until they reached their goal.

Among the dramatic events on one fateful evening of bombing was the complete loss of Leningrad's food supplies. Left behind in the besieged city were Mravinsky's fellow student in Shcherbachyov's composition class, Valerian Bogdanov-Berezovsky, his assistants Karl Eliasberg and Nikolay Rabinovich, Boris Asaf'yev, and Dmitry Shostakovich. On 9 September, as the ring closed around Leningrad, the storm on the city began in earnest, yet every attack was turned back and the Nazis were eventually forced to change to siege tactics—starving the population to death—and turned their attention to the capture of Moscow. Every radio bulletin was devoured with grim attention as there unfolded far away on the Neva the fate of the northern capital.[17]

There was a feeling of helplessness in being sent into the distant rear of the country, and there was concern about what they would do there. Would there be an audience for them in Siberia without their beloved and devoted Leningrad public? However, the evacuation to Novosibirsk was a decision Mravinsky approved; it would be another challenge bringing music to a completely fresh public at the heart of a developing industrial region. The landscape of the undulating Russian countryside could be monotonous, yet following their crossing of the vast Volga, near the ancient fortress of Kazan in Tatarstan, days and nights were spent traveling through the most beautiful and wondrous forests, visible from the compartments. The panorama of the awe-inspiring wild and stunning nature of the Ural Mountains embraced in the golden autumnal shades of color offered a picturesque vision for Mravinsky and his fellow travelers. Their train now steadily began to make speed across the vast, expansive plains of Western Siberia.

On Wednesday morning, 4 September, the train of tired and hungry musicians, actors, and their families made its way across the Garin-Mikhailovsky Bridge spanning the expanses of the River Ob and finally steamed into the blue-and-white art-nouveau railway station. Following two weeks of travel, with constant halts and diversions across the vast tracts of Russia and after surviving enemy aircraft bombing raids and shelling, the staff of the

Leningrad Philharmonic Orchestra and the Pushkin Drama Theatre were greeted at Novosibirsk by an enormous welcoming party. Flowers and the traditional Russian greeting of bread and salt were proffered to Cherkasov and Mravinsky by young Siberian girls trying their best to hide their blushing cheeks from the world-famous actor. Cherkasov had little time for pleasantries, however, for his infant child had become gravely ill with diphtheria, and Olga Mravinskaya and Nina Cherkasova had to take young Andrey to the hospital. Within a few days, his situation improved, and he made a full return to health. Meanwhile the Mravinskys and Cherkasovs were first allocated the Sibir hotel before moving to a sixth-floor flat.[18]

The first impression arriving at this great city is of the abounding flatness of the lush and green—wild—almost virginal countryside, of the silence of the encircling wild nature. Founded as a railway junction of Novonikolaeyevsk in 1893, Novosibirsk had become the biggest industrial city of this vast region—a center of the armaments industry with a population of over one million. The metropolis was spread over a territory where space was bountiful, together with undulating, unspoiled forests and swarming hosts of mosquitoes, offering an unequivocal proposition. The orchestra was domiciled in the spaces offered in the city's railway station, but within twenty-four hours, the musicians were moved to more appropriate accommodation. Housing their "guests" was a major problem for the city authorities; housing was a perennial dilemma in Novosibirsk, and to find quality homes for up to a thousand dislocated artists and their families for an indefinite period was a predicament that few concerned themselves with. The Siberians' "visitors" included the Leningrad Drama Institute, the Tretyakov Art Gallery, the Central Puppet Theatre from Moscow, the Leningrad Jazz Orchestra, and the Byelorussian Jewish Theatre from Minsk.[19]

An everlasting broad avenue called Krasny Prospekt dominated the city center. Along this thoroughfare, all the principle buildings of importance could be found—the Central Hotel, the main cinema, the zoo, all the main shops, cafés, and restaurants—yet no custom-built concert hall; there were only a Drama Theatre and a Youth Theatre, as well as several untried venues. Shortly before the onset of the war, the two theaters had been provided with a large building housing the staff and the families in a purpose-built House of Actors. To make these accommodations on 35 Romanov Street available for the Leningrad musicians, both theaters were dispatched to nearby Kuzbass.[20] Here the Mravinskys were to occupy a spacious two-room apartment with modern furnishings. Despite the lack of available water during the day, and the interminable power cuts, the conditions were better than elsewhere. A concert hall was made accessible in the I. V. Stalin Palace of Culture, which possessed a capacity of some five hundred seats lined by marble columns beyond which another two hundred people could be accommodated with makeshift seating. Thus on 5 September, the orchestra began their rehearsals and preparations for their first season "in exile."[21]

Enormous problems were presented in evacuating the orchestra to a city without a tradition of classical music and a constrained musical life. In Novosibirsk, a philharmonic society had been established in the 1930s, but it had been restricted to chamber recitals, while orchestral music was confined to a radio band playing light music. The local authorities believed that the Leningrad Philharmonic would perform exclusively patriotic music to inspire the war effort and would tour to neighboring towns. Lengthy discussions were held with local council dignitaries on the question of repertoire, political leaders believing that the Philharmonic in this great megapolis would fail to attract public interest.[22] But Mravinsky and Sollertinsky were adamant, insisting that they construct their evenings with an educational, and indeed "evangelistic," emphasis, performing the finest of classical and Soviet music for all. A season of concerts was quickly arranged along these lines, and a major feature by Ivan Sollertinsky published in the main daily newspaper promoted the opening concert on 4 October.[23] By the end of 1941, time had vindicated their confidence in Novosibirsk's public; concerts of Tchaikovsky, Beethoven, Glinka, Rimsky-Korsakov, Mozart, and Brahms were drawing large, enthusiastic audiences. The optimism generated led to more performances with chamber orchestra and with brass and wind quintets, given at the House of the Red Army, the Chkalov Factory Club, and smaller venues across the city. A lecture theater became available in December and a recital hall for chamber concerts opened its doors in the new year.[24]

Having the orchestra live together in one building allowed Mravinsky the opportunity of organizing sectional rehearsals and welding the cohesion and ensemble of the orchestra even more tightly. During the Siberian period, the entire orchestra as a creative and organized body was under Mravinsky's direction—he evolved plans of work and concert schedules and, with artistic director Ivan Sollertinsky, masterminded the concert repertoire.[25] Sollertinsky wrote in a letter to Shebalin: "Shostakovich's Fifth Symphony was performed here for the first time to huge success. The concerts are for all tastes, from evenings of waltzes and *Dmitry Donskoy* by Rubinstein to Mahler's Fifth and Stravinsky's *Chamber Suite*. Soon we're arranging a Mozart Festival to celebrate his 150th anniversary."[26]

On their first local tour to the neighboring city of Tomsk during the Siberian winter, Mravinsky's Philharmonic experienced temperatures of –53°C; despite the cold, Yelizaveta Nikolayevna insisted on accompanying her son. In Tomsk, Mravinsky could find books to pore over from the famous Stroganoff collection, a celebrated pre-Revolutionary library—one of the finest in the entire country.[27] He would have little time to peruse these volumes, as in this first winter Mravinsky was the sole conductor; his assistant Nikolay Rabinovich was still in besieged Leningrad and only arrived much later. The local conductor of the radio band—Nikolay Shkolnikov—lacked first-class experience, and help was urgently needed to share the workload. Sollertinsky heard that Kurt Sanderling was in Alma Ata with no work and in some distress; just a year before, the Prussian exile had given his debut, having found himself like a "fish in water" with the Philharmonic. Following the outbreak of war and escape from Nazi-occupied Ukraine, Sanderling found himself—without an orchestra—in Kazakhstan, where his son Thomas was born. Sollertinsky made contact and immediately summoned him to make the train journey to Siberia. "I recall when I arrived in Novosibirsk Mravinsky was rehearsing the second movement of the *Jupiter* Symphony. From Moscow, I had travelled in a cattle wagon. Just to go into that hall and hear that kind of music-making, well it was like being transported into another, happier world. Mravinsky was of course the acknowledged musical director—a marvellous trainer and rehearser—and I was simply entitled 'conductor.' We each took about half the concerts at first but later, when he was often ill, I had to conduct more and more programmes. I conducted all kinds of works and for me it was a very hard-working but happy, satisfying period. I learnt an enormous amount from the orchestra."[28]

It was to be a long and fruitful relationship for everyone, Sanderling ushering singular experience in the central European tradition.[29] The Mozart Festival was taken to neighboring towns and cities in the region, and local radio was utilized to facilitate broadcast concerts to the vast areas of Central Siberia—the success of which led to regular radio concerts. The sheer amount of work for the Philharmonic far exceeded that of the prewar period, yet everyone set to their task with enthusiasm despite difficult conditions, with the bitter cold and frequent power cuts. Due to the wartime restrictions, the musicians experienced irregular or no pay, an erratic food supply, and an even more problematical climate than the damp icy cold of Leningrad. In recalling their Siberian period, Mravinsky reminisced "wherever the orchestra performed, we felt ourselves as ambassadors for Leningrad, and this . . . added to everyone's responsibilities, and we couldn't allow our standards to fall below that of our concerts in Leningrad."[30]

During the war years, the Leningrad Philharmonic Orchestra played 538 concerts for audiences of troops, workers, schoolchildren, and students and extending to a wider audience through 240 radio concerts.[31] The Leningrad Philharmonic Orchestra together with the Pushkin Drama Theatre furnished such a diet of culture as to inspire the whole city and region to metamorphose into a major arts and musical center that later possessed several music schools and its own conservatoire and formed its own symphony orchestra and an opera and ballet company.

The war had not silenced the voice of Soviet composers, and the patriotic theme was quickly adopted in all genres; Prokofiev arranged the cantata *Alexander Nevsky* from his eponymous film music and the orchestral suite *The Year 1941* and *Ode to the End of War*. Myaskovsky had written a new symphony—the Twenty-First in F-sharp minor—Khachaturyan composed an orchestral suite to the *Battle of Stalingrad*, and Kabalevsky produced his dramatic Fourth Symphony. The most significant offering, however, was that of Dmitry Shostakovich's freshly written *Leningrad* Symphony. In March 1942, a broadcast of its Moscow performance was heard in distant Novosibirsk.[32]

Yevgeny Mravinsky listened intently to the faint strains of the transmission coming through the crude loudspeakers. In coming months, another chapter would be opened in the collaboration between Yevgeny Mravinsky and his closest musical ally—Dmitry Shostakovich. However Mravinsky's reading would portray not only the trauma of a people at war, but also a greater and more far-reaching characterization of evil and malignance.

NOTES

1. A. M. Vavilina Mravinskaya, author interview, July 2001.

2. Yelizaveta Gerdt, 1891–1975, was a leading ballerina performing at the Mariinsky Theatre whose career spanned the pre-1917 period and the Soviet era.

3. N. Cherkasova, *Ryadom s Cherkasovym* (Leningrad: Lenizdat, 1978), 64.

4. V. Fomin, *Dirizher Yevgeny Mravinsky* (Leningrad: Muzika, 1983), 47.

5. Cherkasova, *Ryadom s Cherkasovym*, 64.

6. *Voyenniyie Istoricheskiye Zhurnal*, no. 8 (1966).

7. A. M. Vavilina Mravinskaya, author interview, September 2002.

8. *Voyenniyie Istoricheskiye Zhurnal*, no. 8 (1966).

9. Fomin, *Dirizher Yevgeny Mravinsky*, 48.

10. The Pushkin Drama Theatre was formally called the Alexandrinsky Theatre.

11. From this railway station on the northern, Vyborg, side of the city, over a few days the city's great ensembles were dispersed all over the country, the Conservatoire to Tashkent and the Maly and Kirov Opera and Ballet Theatres to the Urals, to Orenburg and Perm, respectively.

12. *Voyenniyie Istoricheskiye Zhurnal*, no. 8 (1966).

13. A. M. Vavilina Mravinskaya, author interview, September 2002.

14. Cherkasova, *Ryadom s Cherkasovym*, 66.

15. L. Mikheyeva, *II Sollertinsky: zhisn i naslediye* (Leningrad: Sovetsky Kompositor, 1988), 131.

16. Mikheyeva, *II Sollertinsky: zhisn i naslediye*, 131.

17. Fomin, *Dirizher Yevgeny Mravinsky*, 48.

18. Cherkasova, *Ryadom s Cherkasovym*, 66–67.

19. Fomin, *Dirizher Yevgeny Mravinsky*, 48.

20. Archives of Novosibirsk Oblast, GANO, f. 1376, op. 1, d. 42.

21. Mikheyeva, *II Sollertinsky: zhisn i naslediye*, 133.

22. "Leningradskaya Philharmonia vosvratilas v rodnoy gorod," *Leningradskaya Pravda*, 8 September 1944.

23. I. I. Sollertinsky, *Sovetsky Sibir*, 28 September 1941.

24. Mikheyeva, *II Sollertinsky: zhisn i naslediye*, 137.

25. Mikheyeva, *II Sollertinsky: zhisn i naslediye*, 134.

26. Mikheyeva, *II Sollertinsky: zhisn i naslediye*, 137.

27. Mikheyeva, *II Sollertinsky: zhisn i naslediye*, 135.

28. Kurt Sanderling, interview with Alan Blyth, *Gramophone* (April 1974): 1844.

29. Mikheyeva, *II Sollertinsky: zhisn i naslediye*, 160.

30. Y. A. Mravinsky, "Tri Goda v Sibiri," *Sovetsky Sibir*, 16 June 1944.

31. V. Fomin, *Orkestrom dirizhiruet Mravinsky* (Leningrad: Muzika, 1983), 49.

32. Mikheyeva, *II Sollertinsky: zhisn i naslediye*, 144.

Chapter Nine

The Great War

Let this tale live forever in our hearts, forever heard! Let its memory be our conscience.

—Olga Bergoltts, *Dnevnye Zvezdy*

Of the patriotic works that flowed from Soviet composers' pens, it was the *Leningrad* Symphony that became an unvarnished symbol in music of the Soviet people's defense of their country against the Nazis. The spectrum of popularity realized worldwide for Shostakovich's symphony went far outside the listeners normally attracted to classical concerts. Shostakovich's music won unprecedented attention and served to epitomize the Soviets' struggle, championing their minds and souls in a common unity against fascism. Paradoxically, the symphony's origin dated from the prewar period; Shostakovich announced the symphony at the Composers Union board in May 1941, saying that a movement had already been written and promising to complete it by the end of the summer. The Seventh was set for an October premiere as curtain opener for the new 1941–1942 season.

The invasion changed all these peacetime plans and, indeed, the character of the whole composition, the remaining three movements of which were ostensibly influenced by the first weeks of the siege of Leningrad. The symphony was completed only following the composer's flight to Kuibyshev on the Volga. Shostakovich, however, was dissatisfied by its first performances and frustrated that the orchestra was inadequate, and he lacked faith in Samosud as a symphonic interpreter.[1] Every one of his previous orchestral works had after all been introduced by the Leningrad Philharmonic; "Shostakovich desperately wanted his designated Leningrad Philharmonic to perform the Seventh, and Yevgeny Mravinsky to conduct it as he had the Fifth and Sixth."[2]

Mravinsky received the score on 7 May 1942 and spent a month in study before initiating sessions with the Philharmonic.[3] Regardless of the constraints, no little energy was sacrificed in attempting to find affinity with the symphony; an extra source of anticipation and responsibility for the Leningrad musicians was that Shostakovich was planning to arrive for the first performance. However, travel from Moscow by any means was arduous. "There is no direct flight, and going by train is frightening. . . . All apart from the fact I can't leave my large family, . . . so I am not going anywhere."[4] Shostakovich, however, was drawn by the desire to hear Mravinsky's interpretation: "in every way, it is sad that I cannot hear the Seventh in his performance. How splendidly he would have done it. Samosud does it very well but one wants to hear it in Mravinsky's performance."[5]

Shostakovich was compelled to travel and make his way out to Siberia, and he eased the load of his journey by breaking it up to meet up with friends and colleagues en route. At Sverdlovsk, he listened to his ally Shebalin's *Slavonic* string quartet. Further on through the Urals, Shostakovich made his next sojourn at Chelyabinsk, where the Moscow Maly Theatre was in residence.[6] As a curtain raiser, in Novosibirsk, Sollertinsky wrote a feature in the local broadsheet embellished with Shostakovich's portrait.[7] On 3 July, the composer, after being met at the railway station, went directly to the rehearsal session with Sollertinsky and Sviridov. Mravinsky and Shostakovich discussed questions regarding tempi and dynamics in the score, reviving the affinity and rapport from previous symphonies. Shostakovich wrote that evening: "Not one of the orchestras that have performed my work has attained such a perfect fulfillment of my ideas. I never had any doubts that this orchestra would characterize my conception with maximum precision."[8]

Mravinsky's portrayal of the Seventh on 9 July drew stormy, impassioned playing from the Leningrad musicians. Scorning an interval between the first and second movements, Mravinsky played the Seventh straight through and drew a tumultuous response from his audience. The conventionally reticent Leonid Utesov recorded his impressions: "this was so grandiose and compelling that one finds it difficult to find words. One thing is sure; this is immortal as is all grand art. There was everything in this concert that makes great music—a masterly composer, a brilliant conductor, and a virtuoso orchestra."[9] The distinguished thespian Yuri Yur'yev described the surprising synthesis of emotions reflected in the symphony: "It is so moving and impels one to feel that we are sharing a single heartbeat."[10] The composer himself gave his own grateful response: "Yevgeny Mravinsky's is the most faithful performance of my symphony."[11] Mravinsky repeated the *Leningrad* during the next seven days in another three concerts, all drawing packed audiences in Novosibirsk, and Sollertinsky wrote at length: "Shostakovich's Seventh

Symphony is the first really monumental work of Soviet art" dedicated to the war against the Nazis, and Shostakovich has "with complete responsibility and dedication approached this mammoth task avoiding the slightest prejudice. He has not been tempted in using noisy battle musical paraphernalia, or picturesque illustrations, . . . allowing the music a stunning abstract canvass of all the emotions, tragic experiences, and passionate hopes. . . ." Sollertinsky emphasized the classical form and restraint in, "creating this individual, intonational style and language chosen by the composer, . . . to follow the heritage of world symphonism from Beethoven and Tchaikovsky to the recent masters of Mahler, Ravel, and Stravinsky. Moreover, the symphony is unambiguous for everyone. . . ."[12] All this in the middle of a Shostakovich month, when the composer played his Piano Quintet with the Glazunov Quartet[13] and accompanied Arkanov in his four Pushkin romances, and the Tretyakov Gallery mounted an exhibition of sculptures and paintings, including a bronze statue of Peter I in the uniform of the Preobrazhensky regiment.[14] Shostakovich reminisced later: "I was terribly relieved to meet my friends in Novosibirsk. . . . Ivan Sollertinsky as always was in good form."[15]

The Seventh was performed no less than eight times that summer, and Mravinsky discovered new and fresh colors in its score, on each playing finding a different clarity both in the integrity of its form and tempi, characteristics that opened up inflections with the diversity of its movements, grasping a polyphonic unity and equanimity in sound. Each performance was prefaced by additional rehearsals and more demands from Mravinsky. Shostakovich sat in on all the sessions and the concerts on 11, 13, and 15 July, untiring of the persistent search by the Philharmonic to achieve precision and effusing: "Yevgeny Mravinsky is a brilliant conductor, and the Leningrad Philharmonic Orchestra is quite magnificent."[16] The composer further expanded: "Far off in the middle of Siberia, one suddenly felt so much the Leningrad milieu one has been familiar with and which one misses so much. During the rehearsals and concerts, I again experienced that creative process—that noble musical culture that is so characteristic of the city of Lenin."[17] Shostakovich chose unusually to honor musicians in the Philharmonic: Vasil'yev, Shpilberg, Levitin, Shafran, Gensler, Zamiralov, and Nazarov.

In Novosibirsk, Ivan Sollertinsky as always would open the concert dashingly attired in tails, starched shirt, and bow tie. His prologue—an art form in itself—was laconic and witty, indeed as eloquent and virtuosic as the playing of the orchestra. "Today we privileged guests of this bizarre city share with Novosibirsk citizens an occasion extraordinary in the history of art—and not only of art!"[18] He always carefully chose his language depending on his audience—be they schoolchildren or soldiers about to go to the front. Sollertinsky closed his opening talk with a *coup de théâtre*; "center stage he met with

Mravinsky, and drawing a roar of applause, the conductor with an energetic gesture brought the entire orchestra to its feet."[19]

Far off in distant Sweden, Mravinsky's aunt—Alexandra Kollontay—was sitting in her office at the Soviet Embassy when suddenly the broadcast of the *Leningrad* Symphony came on the radio, and without further ado she made plans to have the work performed in neutral Sweden. In the previous year, the distinguished Russian musician Issay Dobrowen had given the premiere in Göteborg of Musorgsky's *Khovantschina*. It was to Dobrowen that she entrusted the microfilm of Shostakovich's new symphony and in October 1942, the *Leningrad* was unveiled in Göteborg.[20] When Shostakovich was listening to Toscanini's famous recording of the *Leningrad* with the musicologist Sergey Shlifstein, the latter exclaimed "Isn't it wonderful?" Shostakovich, however, was reserved in his agreement. Later, he said "you know, the symphony sounds very well, but I don't quite value or accept Toscanini's reading. Really a great artist is correct to play a work in his own way, but without being detrimental to the author's conception."[21]

The appearance of the *Leningrad* Symphony in the West was not in every respect accepted; Virgil Thompson and Olin Downes in the *New York Times* attacked it for its lack of aesthetics and its links with what was perceived as Communist ideology. Nevertheless, the Shostakovich work was defended by Serge Koussevitsky: "Those musicians and critics who attack the Seventh Symphony so brusquely today will strongly regret what they have said in the near future. . . . [M]y deep conviction is that there has not been such a composer able to speak with such force to the masses since Beethoven."[22] Another distinguished musician to offer his views was the German conductor Wilhelm Furtwängler, following the first performance of the *Leningrad* by the Berlin Philharmonic Orchestra on 21 December 1946 under Sergiu Celibidache. "On Sunday, I heard the Seventh Symphony by Shostakovich. This is a wholly well-conceived work, having a historical significance in that it appears to be an attempt to recreate the style of a large-scale symphony, something that has in our times been quite forgotten. . . . As a young artist, he is drawn first of all to expression, and in this he is quite original."[23]

The fate of Shostakovich's Seventh Symphony in C major was to be an ambiguous one. During the war years, the world's finest conductors performed it before huge audiences; nevertheless, it would almost disappear from the repertoire, its sole champion remaining Mravinsky's Philharmonic. The perception of the *Leningrad* Symphony as an epic opus confronting fascism warranted a renascence many years later. However, one knew of what lay behind the *Leningrad* Symphony and its wider significance. Long before the Seventh fell into neglect amid accusations of "formalism," Shostakovich wrote that "the symphony has been performed in many cities in our country, . . . and I am deeply grateful to both Soviet and foreign conductors who have shown love and attention for my symphony. However, the performances closest to me as its composer are those of the Leningrad Philharmonic Orchestra under the direction of Yevgeny Mravinsky."[24]

As in Leningrad, Mravinsky spent almost all his time working on his scores and preparing for concerts, little time given for rest, and rare expeditions out beyond the city precincts limited yet always pleasurable. Nevertheless, he found time for a portrait to be made of him by the Leningrad artist Yelizaveta Yakunina. Here she recounts this experience:

> Arriving at his flat, I met his wife Olga Alexeyevna. She was a cheerful, sociable person. One felt so much at ease with her! People just melted in her company. I explained the purpose of my visit, but she said: "Oh, he is so intractable! He won't agree to pose for anything!" Yet on this Mravinsky entered the room and complained. "Why are you so mistaken Olechka? Yelizaveta Petrovna: only for a short time." We agreed on the following day. At the appointed hour, Olga Alexeyevna on meeting me put her finger to her mouth: "Oh, Zhenya is disturbed by something. Not all went right at the rehearsals—some manager who didn't know anything about music came and Zhenya chased him away. When he came home, he tore the sheets from the bed, threw them on the floor, and simply lay down on a plain mattress. He hasn't got up since." At this point, I heard a noise from the other room. A pale Mravinsky came out, exchanged good-natured remarks, and asked me, "Where do you want to draw me?" I chose a suitable corner of their flat and a certain angle, but Yevgeny Alexandrovich, sitting on the chair, declared, "I will sit on the chair like this. How much time will you need? Is two hours sufficient? I remained silent and began to arrange my instruments. We sat opposite each other in utter peace; other subjects would sometimes change their pose and chat with me, but here it was quite serene. Unerringly, two hours passed. "That's all. I have no more time today. I beg your pardon. When do you want to come again?" "Tomorrow?" I answered. Making his leave, Mravinsky disappeared: "Well, tomorrow at the same time." Then Olga Alexeyevna appeared, asking me to sit a little longer. I completed some of the sketching without Mravinsky. Olga let slip that he hadn't eaten today and cautioned that no one else should come. On the following day, Yevgeny Alexandrovich himself awaited my arrival. He was in a better state of mind. I asked after his well being and we joked a little. "We can't jest like fools." He sat in the identical setting, assuming his former pose, and there reigned total silence for two hours. Following this séance, I finished the portrait and then brought it for him to view. He scrutinized it assiduously and acknowledged: "It gives the impression of being a bit like me." I was taken aback; it seemed to me that it was a fine creation and deserved a higher appraisal. I declared: "I would like to give it to you." Mravinsky showed his appreciation and kissed me on the hand. Olga Alexeyevna brightened up and voiced her compliments.[25]

Following the defeat of the German army at Stalingrad in February 1943, it was clear that the turning point of the war had occurred and victory over the Nazis was now predetermined. The major theaters and ensembles began to return to the capital, undeterred by the conflict going on many miles to the West. A return to normality for the vast wartime population of Moscow was paramount, and all efforts were now toward rebuilding the country. In August, following a summer of touring throughout central Siberia, Mravinsky received a telegram from the Committee for Arts summoning him to Moscow. His call to the capital was on two factors: Shostakovich had written a new symphony and an important position was open. Mravinsky had worked with the USSR State Symphony Orchestra regularly since its founding, and it was hoped that the Moscow-based ensemble would assume the mantle as the preeminent orchestra in the country.[26]

The invitation to Moscow partly originated from the desire of Dmitry Shostakovich. For a number of years, Shostakovich had been tempted to move to Moscow. On 29 April 1943, he wrote Sollertinsky,

> Yesterday I listened to the USSR State Symphony under Rakhlin. I have heard their concerts a few times and am convinced Rakhlin is not a very good conductor. I spoke with Sergey Shlifstein after the concert, and he wants to raise the question of making you artistic director of the State Orchestra and Mravinsky chief conductor.[27] I want you to write me whether this appointment would suit you. If this is agreeable, then I shall speak about it to Khrapchenko.[28] I would very much like you to be in Moscow, although on the other hand, it's a pity, for the Leningrad Philharmonic, for all its faults, is by far the finest orchestra in the USSR. Think about it and write or just telegraph me with one word that you are agreed. Then I will act upon it. By the way, don't tell anyone about this letter, as well as Mravinsky.[29]

Despite all his friend's encroachments, Sollertinsky wrote Shostakovich that he had no intention to move to Moscow. Shostakovich wrote back: "your last letter did not thrill me. I beg you to come to Moscow. Khanin will give you a directorship on theatrical affairs. I spoke with Shebalin yesterday; he wants to make use of you at the scientific-research institute. I advise you not to make any conclusions, just come to Moscow, have a look around, and then make up your mind."[30] However, it was to be another six months before Sollertinsky would visit the capital. Sollertinsky finally conceded to take up the offer of a position at the Conservatoire and, most importantly, a large spacious flat in central Moscow, but he would still continue his obligations in Leningrad.

The fact that Mravinsky favored a slow rail journey to taking a fast military plane was as if a hint to the Moscow authorities of his mind. Despite traveling far from the frontline, it was a traumatic, difficult task to traverse the

country, let alone enter the capital. It required a number of permits without
which it would be pointless to set off; it normally took a fortnight just to obtain these authorization papers.[31] In any case, the prolonged rail journey was
much preferable to the often hazardous wartime flights, and for the erstwhile
botanist, it could be rewarding, for his route straddled the magnificent Ural
mountain range; the fantastic vistas seen from the railway carriage offered
rare visions of nature. Like every Russian child, Mravinsky had read
Bazhov's wonderful evocative fairy-tales set in the Urals. The rich and colorful variety of plants and wildlife were fascinating to Mravinsky; upon unscheduled stops, he could be seen descending from his carriage to collect rare
species of flora and fauna. The solitude and relative quiet pooled with the opportunity of reading his favorite authors; Prishvin, Chekhov, Dostoyevsky,
and Leskov allowed him transitory sanctuary from the oppressive work
regime in Novosibirsk.

When he reached the capital, foregoing the Committee for Arts, Mravinsky
first visited Shostakovich's new flat on Kirov Street, where the composer
showed him the still incomplete symphony marked in the key of C minor.
Thrilled and excited, Mravinsky found the work grandiose and profound—
almost Beethovian—in its tragic canvas of darkly stirring imagery.[32] "One remembers hearing it for the first time played by Shostakovich on the piano, ex-
periencing feelings as if it was all within me and that one was being reborn
and flowing in a mysterious stillness—a harmonious detachment—a savior
from the whole caboodle, or from something terrible."[33] He resolved to prepare the score as soon as possible and took it with him to Novosibirsk. On 7
September, Shostakovich expanded in writing to Sollertinsky in Novosibirsk:
"I have only just finished my Eighth Symphony. There is so much emptiness
in one's heart accompanying completion of a major work. The symphony is
in five movements: (1) Adagio, (2) March, (3) March, (4) Funeral march, (5)
Pastorale. I am quickly copying the score. Mravinsky is taking it back to
Novosibirsk. . . ."[34]

Mravinsky was met at the Committee for Arts by its secretary,
Khrapchenko; however; the Leningrad man insisted that they respond first to
other important matters before any discussion about the Moscow appointment. The conductor's disquiet was on the orchestra's funding and measures
to return to its home city. Now that the war had turned in favor of the Allies,
Mravinsky wanted the Leningrad Philharmonic Orchestra to return home. His
unwavering stance on their facilitating a speedy restoration revealed that
Mravinsky was unwilling to accept their offer of the state orchestra's conductorship. Material enticements were of no value to Mravinsky; he loved his
own roots and leaving would be tantamount to going into "exile," and neither
could he forsake the orchestra with which he had done so much of his work

in recent years. Regardless of Moscow's compliance in beginning planning of the Philharmonic's homecoming, Mravinsky's refusal to take the Moscow position was to be another factor for the authority's skepticism of the audacious, unswerving conductor.

The broadsheet *Izvestia* informed its readers of Shostakovich's Eighth Symphony on 19 September. Following the audition at the Committee for Arts two days later, copying began to be made for performance that autumn. Sollertinsky had now arrived in Moscow and wrote to his wife, "Yesterday evening I heard this symphony, which is so much better than the Seventh."[35] Now that a date had been set for the premiere, Mravinsky set off for Novosibirsk on 25 September and returned within three weeks for the rehearsals. Dmitry Shostakovich wrote to Glikman on 8 October 1943: "you know I have finished the Eighth Symphony, comprising five movements. It is going to be performed on 3 November under Mravinsky's direction."[36]

Upon Mravinsky's return to Moscow for the rehearsals, his working relationship with the state orchestra followed that of before: "In common with Toscanini's traditions—yet without bursts of anger or impatience."[37] Tranquilly and systematically, Mravinsky engaged in his own program of preparation. He began by making corrections to the tempi markings associated with the pauses in passages of the great opening movement. Mravinsky endeavored to clarify the polyphony and dynamics, the flexibility of the rises and falls, and the balance for the inflexible, primary restraining elements in the score. Exhaustive attention was focused on breathing and rhythm, and on accents; the decisive issue was resolving the problems of phrasing and microdynamics in the articulation of solo instruments and in *tutti* with the orchestra. Mravinsky took care to engage his musicians so the solo passages could be articulated both in detail and integrally. Little or no cause could be allowed for improvisation; freedom of expression was imparted through fidelity and precision. Despite all this, most thought and time in the sessions was given to the chamber-like Passacaglia.

During the rehearsals, Mravinsky made a number of additions to the score; the conductor placed *sul tasto* and a ligature in the exposition, at bar 1; *ff* replaced *f* at bar 3, measure 2, the direction *espressivo* and short fingering. In the third bar, from measure 7, was added *mezzoforte*; at the fourth, *mezzoforte* was also added, in the celli and basses, instead of the composer's *p*, assisting the gradual descent in dynamics. At bar 29, a reworking of unsatisfactory tempi by a fourth = 147, the conductor indicated at half = 96; at bar 41 he placed ligatures and strings in the concluding theme on the celli and basses; in the Passacaglia he considered it necessary for *diminuendo* at the 5th bar in the violins and *pp* instead of the composer's *p* at the 12th measure of bar 112; in the Toccata, he introduced an extra trombone so as to make an unnoticeable change in breathing in the continuous phrasing. Shostakovich agreed with the modifications by Mravinsky, and almost all were corrected in the score.[38] Mravinsky himself was more modest about his own share:

> In all the long years of our collaboration, only once did I suggest a small change to the score: in the Eighth Symphony; where this new music responds to such a courageous and in many ways unusual orchestration, one needed to double the woodwind and trumpets at one place in the second movement and in another in the third movement with horns. These changes were accepted, although not immediately, by the composer and appeared in the printed score.[39]

It was during the rehearsals that Shostakovich decided to dedicate the Eighth Symphony to his conductor, a singular act of thanksgiving and loyalty similar to those made to the Beethoven Quartet. Mravinsky recounted an incident that epitomized the perfectionist in the composer:

> Shostakovich has absolute perfect pitch. He hears both each instrument and the whole orchestra at the same time—as he conceived it and in reality. I remember one incident when we were rehearsing the Eighth Symphony. In the first movement, not long before the general culmination, there is an episode in which the cor anglais has to play quite high, in the second octave. The cor anglais is doubled here with the oboes and celli and is almost indiscernible against the sound of the orchestra. Considering this, the musician played an octave lower at the rehearsal to preserve his lips before the great crucial solo passage; this comes immediately after the culmination. To hear the cor anglais in the general play of the orchestra and to discern a little trick of the musician was almost impossible. I must confess that I did not notice it. However, suddenly behind my back in the stalls there came the voice of Shostakovich: "Why is the cor anglais playing an octave lower?" We were all shattered, the orchestra stopped, and after a few seconds passed we began applauding the composer.[40]

Despite the privations of wartime Moscow, the rehearsal work went very well. Mravinsky recalled that all their meals at the conservatoire canteen were servings of a greenish-colored soup and afterward vodka, regarded as necessary sustenance for the musicians. Social life was improving; the city's restaurants and theaters had begun operating normally; and the Bolshoi Theatre had largely returned to its base and was performing night and day to entertain the vast overflowing population with revivals of great operas of the nineteenth century—*A Life for the Tsar*, *Boris Godunov*, *The Queen of Spades*, *The Tsar's Bride*. The company was at the peak of its powers and employed great singers such as Mikhailov, Lemeshev, Kozlovsky, and Maksakova and the conductors Fayer, Golovanov, Pasovsky, and Samosud, with young men in Kondrashin and Melik-Pashayev.[41]

Following a precedent, the Eighth Symphony in C minor was unveiled before a packed auditorium at the Large Hall of the Moscow Conservatoire on 3 November 1943. "There was an atmosphere of profound concentration reigning in the hall from the very first moments of the symphony's music, the significance of which was in the unique, inspirational artistic majesty of the performance by the State Symphony Orchestra of the USSR under Yevgeny Mravinsky."[42] Shostakovich wrote to Glikman: "I am sorry that you did not hear my Eighth Symphony. I am very pleased with it. Mravinsky has played it here four times and on 10 December will play it a fifth time."[43] The conductor had fashioned in his assimilation and identity with the Eighth his own pièce de résistance, more than with any other Shostakovich opus, even the Fifth. "Of all Shostakovich's symphonies, it was the Eighth that became intimate to Mravinsky for its tragic subject matter."[44] The conductor became immersed in its psychology and was able to recreate its conceptual character unlike any other interpreter. "The significance of the inner content was closer to Mravinsky's psyche, which allowed him to analyze and assimilate the score, regardless of the complexities of the orchestration."[45]

On 5 November, the Moscow papers *Vechernaya Moskva* and *Trud* commented on the premiere, while almost all other broadsheets ignored the new work, despite the wide coverage previously granted the Seventh. It was four days before the first reviews appeared: "It's challenging to say something about this symphony; one simply wishes to listen to it again."[46] Most commentaries were restrained, as the sympathetic Asaf'yev verified: "its demanding to listen to this music, as it was in their time to the moving scales of Bach and Beethoven."[47] The musicologist wrote what amounted to the most substantial appraisal of the symphony, succinctly calling it "a great tragic ballad of our terrible times, an epic and anguished song expressing the boundless ordeals of a human heart." Other musicologists sought to account for its failure, explaining "the concentrated traits of its content" and a "transgression of normal accepted musical laws."[48] Nonetheless, Asaf'yev offered a view that was not only eloquent but also wholly alluding to its moment in time: "Following the triumph of victory, and with the ringing cries of joy, it would be a great injustice not to recognize Shostakovich as a genius, as one of the giants of Soviet music."[49] Asaf'yev induced the epoch of the symphony and its relevance to great Russian patriotic works. "One hundred years following the performance of the genius Glinka, and the final words of the peasant-hero Susanin, Shostakovich again reminds people of the suffering of a great human heart as the wellspring of courage."[50] Asaf'yev's words were not published until much later, however: "suddenly, in the hush there is one lonely heart alive and beating that sings fluently and tenderly, as a bottomless spring streaming through the rocks of a craggy mountain cliff: 'I am alive'"[51]

Furthermore, Asaf'yev drew the analogy from Shakespeare: "Shostakovich is akin to Prospero from *The Tempest*, possessing complete power of expression in using all his musical resources in narrating what appears to be a dispassionate challenge to the spirit of life."[52]

If the reticence of the Soviet press to endorse the new symphony appeared somewhat ominous, this proved an interregnum and the quiet before the storm, as the arranged symposium of the Composers Union to discuss "Creativity for 1943" would unleash another round of attacks from Shostakovich's enemies. Paradoxically, Shostakovich himself presented the main report. He analyzed the works of other composers, taking time to inveigh against the Nineteenth and Twenty-Third Symphonies of Myaskovsky and against *The Suite 1941* and the *Oratorio Ballad of a Boy Who Remained Unknown* by Prokofiev, and to point out shortcomings in the technique of Shaporin and Popov and accuse them of vulnerability in psychological command and lack of conscientiousness.[53] Timofeyev spoke on "Problems of Shostakovich's symphonism and his Eighth Symphony," complaining "the achievement of the Seventh was not continued by the Eighth and the mass of great experiences, suffering through evil wasn't resolved, instead replaced by a Passacaglia and a Pastorale."[54] In the ensuing debate, Prokofiev with his customary sense of humor claimed: "the wayward aspect in Shostakovich is the unsatisfactory clarity of the melodic line. The Eighth Symphony, one cannot say it disappointed; more to the point, it did not suitably charm me. The melodic profile is uninteresting, and concerning its form, it's too prolonged. In its musical development, great indulgence is demanded of the listener; by the beginning of the fourth movement, one is exhausted, therefore the slow movement is unacceptable."[55] Dissident opinions issued forth from Bely, Koval, and Ikonnikov, while endorsements for the Eighth came from Popov, Masel, and Rabinovich. Taking up Prokofiev's argument, Popov said that, "all five movements are united in a single conceptual plan."[56] Rabinovich noted the new maturity in the composer and his "emphasizing the perpetual beauty of life as versus all evil forces and death itself."[57] Masel verified that there was a justified development in the composer's melodic language "connected with the principles of folk song."[58] Masel concluded prophetically that, "only time will tell as to whether this wonderful work will have a future, a creation in which contemporary men and women do not always feel able to evaluate the form of depth of its ideas contradicting accepted common laws of symphonic development."[59]

Shostakovich's Eighth Symphony was particularly close to Mravinsky, "regardless of the degree of compound ideas, positive principles, and detail in factura. The abundant inner material had an affinity to Mravinsky's creative psyche that allowed him to grasp the score more precisely."[60] Shostakovich's

Eighth is a shocking document not only of a time of war but of peacetime tragedy. Listening to Shostakovich's Eighth, wrote one critic, "I feel all the time, that the powerful hand of the composer is taking me as if to a window to peace."[61] For another contemporary writer, "the image of Time was already present in the composer's conception and only later developed and perfected."[62] One other writer found associations created at the symphony's premiere: "This music shakes you, stuns you suddenly; in one word, expressed in a whisper, it takes you into a dream world. . . . [O]ne is captivated by its intimate poetry."[63]

Opinions on the Eighth would continue to diverge greatly, and fresh censure emerged, as Shostakovich was accused of "formalism"; the latest symphony diverged from the *Leningrad* in that the great Passacaglia was a slight to the conventional Soviet musical establishment. Lev Danilevich said that the composer had found exciting and convincing "words" with which to tell of the "sorrow that knows no bounds"[64] and of the "monstrous torments that had befallen the lot of millions of people. Shostakovich's music is alluring in its humanity. . . . In the grand crescendos at the peak of the first *Adagio*, a wrathful protest is to be heard."[65] Danilevich, however, expressed doubt, contending that the specifically gloomy, malignant colors predominated. Dmitry Rabinovich was more upbeat: "the theme of the Eighth Symphony is war, treated by the composer as a tragedy for all humanity. . . . The finale is concrete social history."[66]

There was a moment for humor from Sollertinsky, who laconically commented to Mravinsky following the premiere: "Once again, he still cannot write a proper symphonic allegro!"[67] Nevertheless, the "feeling of dissatisfaction" with the Eighth culminated three years later in the Composers Union journal, which emphasized that "the concluding part of the symphony, with its chamber sonorities and individual ambience, does not answer the questions posed in the symphony. The tragedy remains devoid of a resolution. . . ."[68] The musicologist Dmitry Zhitomirsky nagged: "how can a creative artist of his standard make us slither through barbed wire so one may glimpse the lower depths and feel the chill!"[69] Here was not only a failure to understand the essence of the Eighth, but also these words belie a contemptuous and plebeian view — limitations in evaluating the complete significance of Shostakovich's music and its portrayal of the world and country in which he was living and working. It was clear the essence of the Eighth Symphony and its music — that there was no assurance of sovereignty following the conquest — was acknowledged by the select few of the Composers Union. For the Composers Union's leaders, the Eighth Symphony did not hold to the ideals of "socialist realism" and was a nonconformist creation required to be proscribed.

The composer, in his own commentaries on the Eighth Symphony, said that the finale was "an attempt to look into the future, into the postwar epoch. Everything evil and ugly will disappear, and the beautiful will triumph."[70] For the dedicatee of this great symphony, there developed a closer bond with Shostakovich, who attended almost all of Mravinsky's performances, regardless of location (his sole absence was due to a broken leg in the 1960s).

Ritually, the composer would initial Mravinsky's score, transformed into a worn and dog-eared manuscript decades later. If Shostakovich still suffered problems in his homeland, the reverse was now true in the West: "as soon as Shostakovich writes another work, it is celebrated as if it was another victory over Germany."[71] Carnegie Hall hosted the U.S. premiere of the Eighth on 2 April 1944, by Artur Rodzinsky and the New York Philharmonic.[72]

In the Soviet Union, the score was published only three years later, and a second edition did not appear until 1963.[73] No other Soviet conductor performed the Eighth Symphony for more than a decade.[74] With an interval following the 1948 sessions, in future seasons Mravinsky took the Eighth Symphony with the Philharmonic all over the world, recording it several times. Mravinsky's work on this great tragic symphony lies at the peak of his artistic creativity; it was a work of triumphs and agonies, of hope and despair, and of a philosophical depth rarely met in musical form for its revelations of "the tortures of the human soul."[75]

In the immediate aftermath of the premiere of Shostakovich's Eighth, there were more duties calling for the Leningrad conductor; the other cause for the Moscow visit was the invitation by the Union of Composers to take part in the Tchaikovsky jubilee. On 16 November, a cycle of concerts in the Large Hall of the Conservatoire was opened by Mravinsky conducting the USSR State Symphony Orchestra in the *Pathétique*, the First Piano Concerto in B-flat minor (Lev Oborin as soloist), and *Capriccio Italien*. Additional engagements followed of Brahms's First Symphony, Berlioz's fragments from *La Damnation de Faust* and *Roman Carnaval Overture*, and finally, two movements from Debussy *Nocturnes*: "Nuages" and "Fêtes."[76] Mravinsky was asked to study with Nikolay Myaskovsky on his new Twenty-Fourth Symphony for presentation later that season.

During the years in Novosibirsk, the war symphonies of Shostakovich aside, Yevgeny Mravinsky prepared premieres of works by Soviet composers: Shcherbachyov's symphonic suite *The Storm* (based on Ostrovsky), Vano Muradeli's Symphony *In Memory of Kirov*, Shebalin's *Variations on a Russian Folk Song*, and Alexander Lokshin's vocal symphonic poem *Wait for Me*, based on Simonov's war verses. The great patriotic cantata by Prokofiev, *Alexander Nevsky*, based on the film music of 1938, was performed in February 1943. If Mravinsky only conducted the latter once, he was more enthusiastic for Prokofiev's Second Suite from *Romeo and Juliet*, first performed in April 1942. As he did with symphonic suites from Tchaikovsky's ballets, Mravinsky made changes, withdrawing the "Duke's Command" between "Friar Lawrence" and the "Dance of the Maidens," escalating the work's dramaturgy, emotional feeling, and fatalistic conception.

Mravinsky first conducted Tchaikovsky's Fourth Symphony in F major and Glinka's brilliant and colorful *Jôta Aragonésa* in Siberia. Orchestral suites and overtures, some neglected, by Borodin, Musorgsky, Rimsky-Korsakov, Rachmaninov, Glazunov, Lyadov, Scriabin, Taneyev, Arensky, and Cherepnin were added to their programming. The Viennese classics were fundamental to the concert repertoire of the Philharmonic. Mravinsky directed Beethoven's *Eroica*, Fifth, Seventh, and Eighth symphonies. During the war, Mravinsky conducted Brahms's First and Fourth Symphonies, Schubert's *Unfinished* in B minor, and Weber's overtures *Oberon* and *The Invitation to the Dance* (using Weingartner's orchestration) for the first time. A colorful French season was arranged by Mravinsky: Berlioz's *Symphonie fantastique*, excerpts from *La Damnation de Faust*, Bizet's incidental music to *L'Arlesienne*, Debussy's "Nuages" and "Fêtes" from *Nocturnes*, Chabrier's *España –Rhapsody*, and Arthur Honneger's *Pacific 231*. The inclusion of Claude Debussy was controversial, as the composer was still under the cloud of accusations of "decadence" from Glavrepertkom; nevertheless, Mravinsky programmed his compositions through future years.[77] Collaborations with the Pushkin Drama Theatre, including Beethoven's *Music to Egmont* from Goethe and the complete Grieg's *Peer Gynt* based on Ibsen, became highlights for the intelligentsia of Novosibirsk, who heard great thespians such as Cherkasov, Vivian, Karyakina, and Yuri Yur'yev together with Mravinsky's Philharmonic. Almost all the actors at the theater were legends, and none more so than Yur'yev, whose prodigious acting career at the Imperial Alexandrinsky Theatre was distinguished in his being honored with a gold cigarette case by Nikolay II.[78] The scope of musical styles during the Novosibirsk period embraced Bruckner, Haydn, Liszt, Mozart, Rossini, Smetana, and Wagner. They represented not only enlightenment but also a different world of values during the rigorous war and all its associated privations. Separate concerts for schoolchildren offered ballet music and popular miniatures by Johannes Strauss, Delibes, Saint-Saëns, Drigo, Massenet, and Lacombe.

The orchestra embarked on successful tours to other cities in Central Siberia, Sanderling and Rabinovich traveling up to the Altai Mountains and into Central Asia and extending the concerts given to fifty-six engagements. Among the conurbations visited were the old university towns of Omsk and Tomsk and the mining settlements of Barnaul, Leninsk-Kuznetsk, Novokuznetsk, Prokopyevsk, and Kemerovo. In Barnaul, the concerts took place at the Textile Complex Club and comprised overtures and waltzes by Glinka, *Dawn over the Moscow River* by Musorgsky, and *Polovtsian Dances* from

Borodin's *Prince Igor*. A second performance comprised French and German music: Weber's *Oberon* overture and *Invitation to the Dance*, Saint-Saëns "Le Cygne" from *Le Carnival de Animeaux* (Boris Shafran principal cellist as soloist), the Second Suite from *L'Arlésienne*, and excerpts from Bizet's *Carmen*, with soloists Yevgeniya Verbitskaya and Alexandra Khalileyeva from the Kirov Theatre's war-time refuge of Perm in the Urals. At the university town of Omsk, concert bills were more traditional, including Tchaikovsky's *Pathétique*, *Capriccio Italien*, and the *Swan Lake* Suite. One took the form of a matinee at the Summer Gardens and included fragments from Glazunov's *Raymonda* and Tchaikovsky's *Nutcracker* Suite. In the third of four concerts in Omsk, the program included Shostakovich's Fifth Symphony in D minor.

The sojourn during the Novosibirsk evacuation brought the Leningrad Philharmonic Orchestra to a new, higher level of performance during which it "continued its resourceful expansion, becoming more disciplined in ensemble, richer and cogent in its work."[79] Yevgeny Mravinsky's management of the orchestra created an optimal disciplined system respondent to his own zealous attitude toward work. His exceptional demands and influence on everyone made the Philharmonic Orchestra a regime within a regime. During the war, the "other" conductors included Nikolay Rabinovich, Mark Paverman, Kurt Sanderling, and Abram Stasevich. Organizing and promoting the Leningrad Philharmonic's concerts through this period was the artistic director, Ivan Ivanovich Sollertinsky. A passionate advocate of Mahler and Bruckner, bel esprit, polyglot, and confidant of Dmitry Shostakovich, Sollertinsky was a phenomenally talented teacher and organizer. Following the local premiere of Shostakovich's Eighth Symphony on 10 February 1944, there took place the first performance of a cantata by a local man, Andrey Novikov. The composition was wholly Sollertinsky's idea in encouraging the young composer to write a patriotic work for the Philharmonic with local choral forces. Ivan Sollertinsky egged on Novikov: "Imagine yourself on stage in evening dress and military uniforms."[80] The very idea of writing such a piece for this virtuoso orchestra proved obviously appealing, and the score was ready a few weeks later, when Novikov gave it to Sollertinsky at the Officers Club on Krasny Prospekt. Sollertinsky said: "You know Andrusha, we're going to print it—there are some good things in it."[81] At the opening performance, there occurred a quite extraordinary incident: "Suddenly a bird flew through one of the windows of the concert hall, flying around, chirping, and old people in the audience crossed themselves, quoting an old Siberian proverb—'a bird inside the house means there will be a death in the family.'"[82] Afterward the composer invited Sollertinsky back to his home for a celebration. Sollertinsky was in great form, cracking jokes, telling stories, and the center of attention. It was late when the party broke up. Shostakovich describes what happened next: "Following supper, he felt very tired and retired to sleep, asking to be woken at 9 in the morning. When his friend entered the room where Ivan was sleeping saying, 'Ivan its time to get up,' he did not answer. Approaching him, he found that he was dead. A great many people were at his funeral, and the orchestra played his beloved music. Now he lies in distant Novosibirsk, far from his beloved Leningrad."[83]

The death of the forty-one-year-old artistic director of the Philharmonic was a devastating loss. Sollertinsky had brought an incalculable value to the city of Novosibirsk, organizing musical education, lectures, and concerts there. It was a most important blow for Mravinsky; they had worked closely together, and Ivan Ivanovich was always a critical pillar of support. Ivan Ivanovich had reviewed his debut concert in 1929 and together with Mravinsky "organized" the triumph of Shostakovich's Fifth Symphony. Sollertinsky's death coincided with the date of the lifting by the Red Army of the siege of Leningrad.

For the Leningrad musicians, there were mixed emotions on leaving their Siberian hosts. In his farewell speech to the orchestra, Siberian writer Leonid Lubachevsky said "I can only offer my thanks for all the delights brought to us by your orchestra."[84] Yevgeny Mravinsky promised his new public that he would return and perform in a future, peaceful country. At almost any time during the Great Patriotic War, Novosibirsk railway station was used to vast multitudes making their way through its great concourse, yet on one particular day, in late August 1944, the throngs on the platforms and at the station building were there for a singular purpose. Thousands of folk, young and old, civilians and soldiers, children and pensioners, had all gathered to see off the Leningrad musicians who had become so treasured and dear. The winning of new listeners to classical music was the most lasting achievement of the Leningrad Philharmonic Orchestra's seasons.[85] The Siberians knew themselves that the visit of this magnificent orchestra had been a rare experience, and upon departure for Leningrad, their hosts gave Mravinsky's orchestra a heart-warming farewell as only Siberians may. One commented, "We all know what huge popularity the Philharmonic's orchestra enjoys. Each of us felt how inspiring music can help us in working to win the war."[86] Mravinsky's orchestra gave children a fresh opportunity, opening doors through the special children's concerts and leaving behind a new music school. One teacher commented, "As a teacher of literature, I loved seeing the positive influence of music on young people and am deeply grateful to the Philharmonic in that their concerts helped us to bring artistic values to our younger generation during the war." Julia Manusovich proclaimed: "the orchestra has awoken the finest and highest feelings for music among our youth."[87]

Almost three years to the day from their arrival, Mravinsky, Sanderling, and their musicians stood at the doors and windows of the train compartment engulfed in flowers tossed at them from adoring fans running alongside as the train slowly departed the platform of the Novosibirsk railway station, again heading westward across the vast bridge spanning the River Ob. It was a sad yet joyous leave-taking; as Mravinsky had hoped, they had brought great art to the lives of many. The battle for a new listener and public had been won, the Russian people were now victorious against the Nazis, and the Leningrad Philharmonic could make a safe return to its native city on the Neva.

NOTES

1. Shostakovich to Atovmyan 5 February 1942—GTsMMK, f. 32, yed. Khr., 1772.

2. L. Mikheyeva, *Zhisn Dmitriya Shostakovich* (Moscow: Terra-Terra, 1997), 231.

3. S. Khentova, *D. D. Shostakovich v gody Velikoi Otechestvenniye voini* (Leningrad: Muzika, 1979), 113.

4. Shostakovish to Shebalin, GTsMMK, f. 129, No. 249.

5. Shostakovich to Sollertinsky, 31 March 1942, in Mikheyeva, *II Sollertinsky: zhisn i nasledstvo* (Leningrad: Sovetsky Kompositor, 1988), 151.

6. Khentova, *D. D. Shostakovich v gody Velikoi Otechestvenniye voini*, 113–15.

7. I. I. Sollertinsky, *Sovetsky Sibir*, 24 June 1942.

8. D. D. Shostakovich, *Sovetsky Sibir*, 4 July 1942.

9. L. Utesov, "Do samovo serdtsa," *Sovetskaya Sibir*, 16 July 1942.

10. Y. Yur'yev, "Eto ispytivaeyet kazhdy sovetsky grazhdanin," *Sovetsky Sibir*, 16 July 1942.

11. D. D. Shostakovich, *Uchitelskaya gazeta*, 10 September 1942.

12. I. I. Sollertinsky, "Sedmaya simfoniya Shostakovicha," *Sovetskaya Sibir*, 16 July 1942.

13. Khentova, *D. D. Shostakovich v gody Velikoi Otechestvenniye voini*, 117–18.

14. L. Shinkarev, "Osoby eshelon," *Izvestiya*, 25 May 1971.

15. Shostakovich to Shebalin, GTsMMK, f. 129, No. 250.

16. GTsMMK, f. 129, No. 251.

17. D. D. Shostakovich, "Zamechatelniye orkester," *Literatura i Isskustvo*, 1 August 1942.

18. Ryasentsev, "Perviye vecher i tridzat let," *Sibirskiye ogni*, no. 9 (1976): 138–39.

19. Ryasentsev, "Perviye vecher i tridzat let."

20. Khentova, *D. D. Shostakovich v gody Velikoi Otechestvenniye voini*, 146–47.

21. Boris Khaikhin to Sophia Khentova, in Khentova, *D. D. Shostakovich v gody Velikoi Otechestvenniye voini*, 170–71.

22. S. Koussevitsky, "O Sedmoy simfonii Shostakovicha," *Pravda*, 3 August 1942.

23. W. Furtwängler, *Tagliche Rundschau*, 25 December 1946.

24. "U Shostakovicha," *Uchitelskaya gazeta*, 10 September 1942.

25. P. Merkuryev, "Istoriya odnovo portreta," *Sovetskaya Muzika*, no.10 (1990): 126–28.

26. The Bolshoi Symphony Orchestra had been directed since 1919 (albeit with interruptions) by Nikolay Golovanov, who had consistently worked on a rich color in orchestral sound.

27. Shlifstein was a musicologist and worked at the Committee of Arts and at VOKS, which dealt in cultural relations with other countries.

28. Khrapchenko was the chairman of the Committee of Arts under the Commissariat of Education and a leading writer on literary history. He wrote several authoritative works on Gogol and Pushkin. He left the position after the 1948 debates and took up his full career.

29. Shostakovich to Sollertinsky, 29 April 1943, in Mikheyeva, *II Sollertinsky: zhisn i naslediye*, 250–51.

30. Shostakovich to Sollertinsky, 29 April 1943, in Mikheyeva, *II Sollertinsky: zhisn i naslediye*, 251–52.

31. Mikheyeva, *II Sollertinsky: zhisn i naslediye*, 162.

32. Y. A. Mravinsky, interview with A. A. Zolotov, March 1982.

33. Y. A. Mravinsky, interview with A. A. Zolotov, *Shostakovich Pyataya*, Ekran TV, 1973.

34. Mikheyeva, *II Sollertinsky zhisn i naslediye*, 156.

35. Mikheyeva, *II Sollertinsky zhisn i naslediye*, 163.

36. I. Glikman, *Pisma k Drugu* (St. Petersburg: DSCH, 1993), 60.

37. Khentova, *D. D. Shostakovich v gody Velikoi Otechestvenniye voini*, 190.

38. Khentova, *D. D. Shostakovich v gody Velikoi Otechestvenniye voini*, 190–91.

39. Y. A. Mravinsky, "Tridzat let s muzikoi Shostakovicha," in *D. Shostakovich*, ed. L. V. Danilevich (Moscow: Sovetsky Kompozitor, 1967), 111.

40. Mravinsky, "Tridzat let s muzikoi Shostakovicha," 111.

41. V. Razhnikov, *Kirill Kondrashin rasskazyvaet* (Moscow: Sovetsky Kompozitor, 1989), 86–87.

42. D. Zhitomirsky, "Noviye proisvedeniye sovetskihkh kompositorov," *Informtsionniye sbornik SSK SSSR*, Moscow, no. 5–6 (1944): 10.

43. Glikman, *Pisma k Drugu*, 61.

44. V. M. Bogdanov-Berezovsky, *Sovetsky dirizher* (Leningrad: Muzika, 1956), 268.

45. Bogdanov-Berezovsky, *Sovetsky dirizher*, 195.

46. V. Gusev, "Edinym dykhaniem," 273.

47. B. Asaf'yev, "Vosmaya simfonia Shostakovicha" (Moscow: Moskovskaya filarmonia, 1945), 8.

48. D. Zhitomirsky, "Noviye proisvedeniye sovetskihkh kompositorov," 12.

49. Asaf'yev, "Vosmaya simfoniya Shostakovicha," 6.

50. Asaf'yev, "Vosmaya simfoniya Shostakovicha," 7.

51. Asaf'yev, "Vosmaya simfoniya Shostakovicha," 7.

52. Asaf'yev, "Vosmaya simfoniya Shostakovicha," 9.

53. D. D. Shostakovich, "Sovetskaya muzika v dni voiny," *Sovetskaya Muzika*, no. 11 (1975): 64–77.

54. Shostakovich, "Sovetskaya muzika v dni voiny," 64–77.

55. *Informatsionii sbornik SSK SSSR*, Moscow, no. 7–8 (1945): 52.
56. *Informatsionii sbornik SSK SSSR*, Moscow, no. 7–8 (1945): 57.
57. *Informatsionii sbornik SSK SSSR*, Moscow, no. 7–8 (1945): 70.
58. *Informatsionii sbornik SSK SSSR*, Moscow, no. 7–8 (1945): 70.
59. *Informatsionii sbornik SSK SSSR*, Moscow, no. 7–8 (1945): 71.
60. Bogdanov-Berezovsky, *Sovetsky Dirizher*, 195.
61. L. Leonov, "Pervie vpechatlenie," *Literatura i Iskusstvo*, 7 November 1943.
62. V. Bibergan, *Udarniye instrumenty v proizvedeniye D. D. Shostakovicha 60–70 godov*, *D. D. Shostakovich v gody Velikoi Otechestvenniye voini*, edited by S. Kehntova (Leningrad: Muzika, 1979), 182.
63. Jean-Richard Bloch, "V strane musyki," *Literatura i Iskusstvo*, 7 November 1943.
64. L. Danilevich, *Sovetskaya Muzika*, nos. 8–9 (1946).
65. L. Danilevich, *Sovetskaya Muzika*, nos. 8–9 (1946).
66. D. Rabinovich, *Dmitry Shostakovich* (London: Lawrence and Wishart, 1959), 88–89.
67. Y. A. Mravinsky, interview with A. A. Zolotov, *Myzhleniye o Mravinskovo*, Ekran TV, 1978.
68. L. Danilevich, *Sovetskaya Muzika*, nos. 8–9 (1946).
69. D. V . Zhitomirsky, "Noviye proisvediie sov. Kompozitori," *Informburo Union of USSR Composers, Moscow* nos. 5–6 (144): 12–13.
70. D. D. Shostakovich, *Literatura i Iskusstvo*, 25 September 1943.
71. *Morning Record* (Glasgow), 5 April 1944.
72. Khentova, *D. D. Shostakovich v gody Velikoi Otechestvenniye voini*, 214.
73. Khentova, *D. D. Shostakovich v gody Velikoi Otechestvenniye voini*, 194.
74. The sole exception was when Gauk directed a performance for a Composers Union board meeting.
75. L. Danilevich, *Sovetskaya Muzika*, nos. 8–9 (1946).
76. Mikheyeva, *II Sollertinsky Zhisn i naslediya*, 165.
77. Glavrepertkom was the committee for repertoire sanctioned by the Communist Party for works performed or broadcast.
78. S. Volkhov, *Istoriya Kulturii Sankt-Piterburga* (Moscow: Nezavisimaya, 2001), 201.
79. V. Bogdanov-Berezovsky, *Sovetsky Dirizher*, 148–49.
80. A. P. Novikov, *Zametki-Razmyshleniya*, from a manuscript in the archive of A. A. Asinovskaya, Novosibirsk.
81. Novikov, *Zametki-Razmyshleniya*.
84. Novikov, *Zametki-Razmyshleniya*.
83. Shostakovich to Fritz Steidry, 18 February 1946, GTsMMK, f. 32, ed. Khr. 152/1.
84. L. Lubachevsky, *Sovetsky Sibir*, 2 August 1944.
85. V. Fomin, *Orkestrom dirizhiruet Mravinsky* (Leningrad: Muzika, 1976), 63–64.
86. L. Lubachevsky, *Sovetsky Sibir*, 2 August 1944.
87. J. Manusovich, *Sovetsky Sibir*, 2 August 44.

Mravinsky portrait by Gusev, 1954. Courtesy Mrs. Mravinsky.

Mravinsky portrait, 1956. Courtesy Japan Mravinsky Society.

Jenny Mravina. Courtesy Tully Potter Collection.

Mravinsky family: mother, father, and son "Zhenya," 1905. Courtesy
Japan Mravinsky Society.

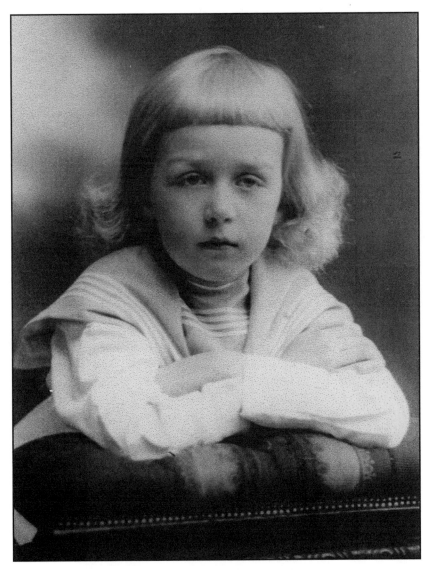

"Zhenya," 1906. Courtesy Japan Mravinsky Society.

"Zhenya" with a helmet, 1906. Courtesy Japan Mravinsky Society.

Alexandra Kollontay photo, card sent from Berlin to Liza Mravinsky with inscription, 1912. Courtesy Mrs. Mravinsky.

Alexander Mravinsky, "Zhenya," and Konstantin Mrovinsky, 1913. Courtesy Mrs. Mravinsky.

Yelizaveta and Yevgeny Mravinsky, 1931. Courtesy Mrs. Mravinsky.

Mravinsky, 1931. Courtesy Japan Mravinsky Society.

Mravinsky at the Moscow conducting competition, 1938. Courtesy
Mrs. Mravinsky.

Mravinsky and Shostakovich during stay in Siberia, July 1943.
Courtesy Japan Mravinsky Society.

Mravinsky conducting at world premiere of Shostakovich's Eighth Symphony, November 1943. Courtesy Japan Mravinsky Society.

Prague Spring Festival: Mravinsky, Shostakovich, Oistrakh, Nina Shostakovich, Olga Mravinskaya, and unidentified person, 1946. Courtesy Japan Mravinsky Society.

Sketch of Mravinsky at the Philharmonic by Vereisky, 1947. Courtesy
Mrs. Mravinsky.

Mravinsky studying a score, 1953. Courtesy Japan Mravinsky Society.

Mravinsky in communion with nature, 1954. Courtesy Japan
Mravinsky Society.

Mravinsky conducting, 1961 (series of five photos). Courtesy Japan
Mravinsky Society.

Mravinsky and Inna Serikova, 1963. Courtesy Mrs. Mravinsky.

Mravinsky's gravestone at Bogoslovsky cemetery, 2003. Courtesy
Japan Mravinsky Society.

Chapter Ten

The Great Victory

Let no one forget, let nothing be forgotten.

—Olga Berggolts, *Dni Mechti, Izbranniye*

In September 1944, the train bearing the Leningrad Philharmonic Orchestra staff and musicians approached their hometown after a journey of five thousand kilometers. Hostile aircraft in the skies and the noise of warfare had long since disappeared, but the reckoning for the peace was to be seen all around. Burned-out houses, scorched fields, shells of factories, wrecked planes, abandoned military materiel, upturned trees, and gigantic shell craters—all bearing witness to three years of conflagration. Nonetheless, this destruction would not prepare Mravinsky's musicians for the terrible shock awaiting them in their native city.

Traveling into the outskirts of Leningrad, they could see devastation that they had not thought possible; almost all buildings in the city had been shelled or hit. Many had been destroyed, including the Hérmitage Theatre, and only shells remained of the tsar's palaces at Petrodvoretz, Oranienbaum, Pushkin, and Pavlovsk.[1] Barely half a million souls remained of the three and a half million inhabitants before the war; when hundreds of thousands of brave Red Army soldiers, sailors, and airmen and women were dying at the gates of Leningrad, millions of civilians were falling victim to bombing, shelling, and most of all, starvation.[2]

Yet the Nazis never stopped the living heart of Leningrad life; during the worst months, the Leningrad Radio Orchestra under Karl Eliasberg performed Shostakovich's *Leningrad* Symphony in the Philharmonic Hall, broadcast to the front line and the outside world, as if daring the Germans to destroy two indestructible entities—their Leningrad and its culture. In those dark days, the music of Beethoven, Mozart, Schubert, Shostakovich, and Prokofiev was food for the impoverished yet courageous citizens who carried on working and living in the besieged city.

Upon arrival, the Philharmonic began work almost immediately, and Mravinsky found there was a fresh gusto in his rehearsals at the Philharmonic Hall.[3] This was a different ensemble from that of the prewar seasons; Zavetnovsky, Brik, and other veterans had taken retirement, and there arrived a new generation, including students and disciples of the old Philharmonic, representing a true continuity of the Petersburg–Leningrad tradition.[4]

There was a clear feeling of a fresh start for the Philharmonic, restored back in its sacred city and anticipating the country's imminent victory in the war. In a beau geste, the city council returned streets and squares to their pre-Revolutionary names: the 25 October Prospekt once again became Nevsky Prospekt, beloved from Gogol's stories, and Uritsky Square was renamed Palace Square. Within a month, the first concerts in the Philharmonic Hall opened the 1944–1945 season. Those who remained of the devoted and long-suffering music lovers, these holdovers from another time, turned up in their festive attire, in furs, elegant dress, and bow ties and bedecked in jewels, to greet their proud Philharmonic with a mighty storm of applause. When Mravinsky and his musicians came on stage, looked into the faces of their public, and met the gleam in their shining eyes, it was worth all that they had endured. Humanity and justice had at last won—for the day and the hour—this was their great victory.

The first work performed on 21 October was Beethoven's glorious overture to *Egmont.* Tchaikovsky almost inevitably followed, with the *Adagio* from the *Pathétique*, the *Adagio* from Schubert's *Unfinished* Symphony, and the finale from Shostakovich's Fifth Symphony. Kurt Sanderling recounted, "there was no ban on German music. As long as it was good music, we played it. In 1944, the orchestra went back to Leningrad. That was a fantastic occasion, unforgettable. We gave ten or so festival concerts. I recall my first concert in Leningrad then: it comprised Dvořák's *New World*, *Eine Kleine Nachtmusik*, and Ravel's *La Valse*."[5]

Each subsequent performance became an event in the city's musical life. Music had never stopped during the siege; nevertheless the Philharmonic's restoration to its rightful home in the Hall of Nobility was a triumph. The "new" Philharmonic earned tributes for upholding the preceding standards: "concerts demonstrate that this estimable orchestra, considered one of the best in the country, continues the exacting traditions of the Leningrad performing school and brings to its playing an even greater clarity in expression."[6]

Upon their return, the Philharmonic had indeed embarked upon a new era. The sound and cogent ensemble had improved and the dynamics and power of the sound picture had been enhanced. Mravinsky's improved orchestra now allowed him to unveil his unfamiliar repertoire to his loyal and constant public. The first was on 11 November, when Mravinsky performed Shostakovich's Seventh Symphony in C major, *Leningrad*; a month later he unveiled the Eighth Symphony in C minor. Mravinsky followed these monumental performances with the premiere of Nikolay Myaskovsky's recently written Twenty-Fourth Symphony, a deeply anguished and philosophical work written in memory of the composer's friend Derzhanovsky.[7] During the same period, Mravinsky introduced three pieces of great significance to his repertoire—Beethoven's *Eroica*, Brahms's First, and Schubert's *Unfinished* Symphonies—all heroic, tragic symphonic tracts. The concerts were fully subscribed, as the contemporary music student Alexey Ludewig recalled: "It was quite impossible to get hold of tickets; however I, together with my friends found a way into the hall, 'capturing' a place at the back of the hall, and listened to the concerts for 'free.'"[8]

Despite the dangers of this period, Yevgeny Mravinsky recorded events in the diary he kept all his life.

Mravinsky's Diary

1 December 1944: I lingered at home and was engaged the whole evening; I played almost all of Bruckner's Ninth (it is a pity one forgets, in part, the intricacy of the nuances in tempi from the third movement). Afterward, I contemplated resurrecting the form and dramatic line of Shostakovich's Eighth (every time, it shakes one, and more acutely, particularly the opening of the first movement. The line of the Great Terror . . .).

2 December: At home, studying Shostakovich's Eighth.

3 December: Shostakovich arrived and spent the evening with us.

5 December: In the evening, I abided with the frustration of one's flawed performance at the opening bar and my "lack of knowledge" to missed opportunities in a number of places. Jumping up from bed in my nightshirt, I checked everything again.[9]

6 December: From 11 until 1:15, through the whole symphony—finished (at the beginning). General rehearsal of the third, fourth, and fifth movements (very clear)—joys of those present (went through the score again for a long time)—calm in one's inner self. Extraordinarily peaceful dreams. Awakening—one of those rare occasions in a long time—from the chain of full happiness. The explanation being in my dreams: an evening in golden clouds and with covetous lucidity of that scene observed near Avdotya's dacha at Medvechova; almaz-like snowflakes distinguished in one's eye against the lamplight and particular kind of upbeat, lively march, coming at one time from somewhere, perhaps from another flat.

13 December: Brahms's Third Symphony reminds one of the relationship with a bright-lit, clear winter's day in simple ionic form ornamented in carnisa. So openly felt and how fitting is this sound of music "at the gates" to the Cathedral of Apollo. The great transparency of this music is—like the cupola of light and temperance. One remembers how sincerely my dearly missed friend, I. I. Sollertinsky, made associations with my feelings on this. . . .

29 December: In the evening—I recalled memories in playing *Illusions* by Asaf'yev.[10] The entire performance is enlightening and reminds one of melancholia. . . . What has vanished in the past is so precious and is unique. . . . What is after all music—it is all functionally and dramatically magnificent, appearing as fine models of form (understanding its synthetics). There is not enough power in one to conceive such ideas. . . .

31 December: With all my faith and soul, I desire so much that those who did not return . . . be at hand when He comes, and suffer His spirit—with a full cup, free of intense despair and desolation. To See and Hear, in belief, praying, and notwithstanding to make just the "notes," one may revisit the Great Departed, in accord just the once, to come to terms with and come into contact with Him (but that can be only while there is still a pulse beating, and not dead blows). And to pass on the word about Shostakovich's course—a brother in Time.[11]

In February 1945, Mravinsky recharged his French programs from Siberia with *Symphonie fantastique* and the "impressionist" Maurice Ravel: the Piano Concerto in G (performed by Leningrad pianist Alexander Kamensky) and *Boléro*. There also surfaced "new" pieces; Mravinsky conducted Schumann's *Incidental Music to Manfred* for the first and last time. Following the world premiere given by the composer, Mravinsky directed Prokofiev's Fifth Symphony in B minor during the last days of the season. There was a startling incident at a concert, attended by the pianist Svyatoslav Richter, that Mravinsky magnanimously illustrated:

Richter is a musician worth his weight in gold. At one point, I adopted the opening of Prokofiev's Fifth Symphony quite "at sea," not knowing the right tempo, not quite "striking" the true ambience. Richter was there and cautiously, in a very tactful manner, he asked me, playing the opening bars on the piano: "What about playing it so?" Suddenly my eyes were opened and playing it in that manner—the whole detail fell into place.[12]

The legendary "White Nights" included magnificent concerts of Bruckner's Ninth Symphony in D minor and David Oistrakh playing Beethoven's Concerto in D, coinciding with Victory Day. To apply the finishing touch, Yevgeny Mravinsky directed the Leningrad Philharmonic in Glinka's *Ruslan and Lyudmilla*, Musorgsky's *Dawn over the Moscow River*, and Tchaikovsky's *Francesca da Rimini*. For the conductor, the summer months would be spent in the austere yet homely Leningrad countryside at Medved-chova, a haven from overwhelming burdens. Here was a special clinic where the conductor would restore body and spirit during coming years.

The summer months of 1945 were made use of by Shostakovich to write a new symphony—the Ninth. In an outspoken discussion, the composer described it as "a short, joyous work."[13] The arts journal *Sovetskoye Iskusstvo* confided in its readers that, "the symphony is full of festive, blissful tones."[14] In early September, the composer and Svyatoslav Richter played the symphony at the Committee for Arts (Shostakovich playing the bass line). This gathering was attended by a keenly enthusiastic audience: Khachaturyan, Shaporin, Neuhaus, Samosud, Gauk, and Goldenweiser.

Khachaturyan acknowledged: "Shostakovich continues to advance in wisdom. One can say with confidence that the Ninth Symphony will be guaranteed great success."[15] Right up to the premiere, the press continued to commentate, "the gamma of its tone in the upbeat delightful light smiling in the closing pages of the finale. The music of the symphony is elegant, captivating, and the score is trouble free and transparent."[16] The writer attempted to take his readers back to the revelry of the springtime and Victory Day with the white charger bearing Marshal Zhukov before his victorious troops, summoning up thoughts that "in this music there is disquiet for the human tragedy and a distressing expression on yesterday's woes."[17] Contrasting the symphony with its immediate predecessors, R. O. Davydov concluded ungraciously that this Ninth was "far from a classic Victory symphony, which the composer contemplated and indisputably has yet to write."[18]

Dmitry Zhitomirsky, however, wrote that the composer had remained true to himself in his refusal to depart from the main tenets of his work. "The world of light comedy descending to parody and the grotesque was always close to Shostakovich. I recall the scherzo-gallop in the First Symphony. . . . Nevertheless, the composer's work shows that his 'Mephistophelian' facet is inseparable from his 'Faustian' side."[19] This was confirmed by the ecstatic reception given to the Ninth's world premiere at the Leningrad Philharmonic on 3 November under Yevgeny Mravinsky. Nevertheless "The Ninth Symphony somewhat disappointed and surprised everyone. Lasting less than twenty-five minutes, it seemed a miniature piece—virtuosic—reminiscent of Prokofiev's *Classical* Symphony and having something in common with Mahler's Fourth. Outwardly unpretentious and classical, it clearly follows the principles of the Viennese symphonies of Haydn and Mozart."[20] Another contemporary reviewer, however, found much to approve of:

Mravinsky feels the temperament of Shostakovich's humor superbly well. One needs to remember that the premiere of the Ninth Symphony has yet again led to fresh discussions about the grotesque and the contradiction of profound and jocular music in Shostakovich. One thinks that the quintessence of this disparity is easier to understand than before. The composer's developing maturity and individual expression illustrates that the wit in his irony comes from the same source as does his romanticism and the divine transparency of its positive form and lyricism. The interpretation of the Ninth Symphony by Mravinsky at any time demonstrates the secret harmony of Shostakovich's style, its organic and creative ideas."[21]

The discord over Shostakovich's Ninth continued: "we were offered a symphony-scherzo, a joke, almost, one might say, a symphonietta!"[22] Israel Nestyev recorded that Shostakovich's new score "enchanted the listener with such ideal form that it looked as if every tintinnabulation had been precisely matched and each tinge of color and secondary timbre acquiesced to sapient determination."[23] Mravinsky candidly summed up his own view of the symphony:

> I interpret the Ninth Symphony as a work directed against philistinism, a primary "symphonic assault" that ridicules complacency and bombast, and the desire to rest on one's laurels—all attributes to a state of mind that was particularly dangerous during a period when the war had just ended and there lay ahead the task of healing its wounds. Of course, not all the symphony is ironic—it contains both tender lyricism and deep sadness. The buoyant or frivolous "light-heartedness" of the first movement (just think of the secondary subject!). Moreover, the element of forced and labored gaiety in the finale express, not the composer's own feelings, but those of his antithesis—the smug, impudent philistine who is essentially indifferent to everything.[24]

If Yevgeny Mravinsky did not view the Ninth Symphony as negatively as some of his compatriots, he did not embrace it, either; Shostakovich's other symphonies intrigued him and drew his interest more compellingly—let others champion the Ninth. Within a fortnight, Mravinsky was in Moscow unveiling the brand new work with the State Symphony. Zhitomirsky wrote: "In orchestral sound this lyrical 'symphonic-scherzo' (as one critic so germanely described it) is more momentous than the work it first appeared to be. With ostentatious simplicity and appeal, the Ninth Symphony possesses that degree of artistic beauty and inspiration that allows one to compare it with the finest works of art. Mravinsky feels so wonderfully the humorous vein in Shostakovich's music. . . . The interpretation of the Ninth Symphony by Mravinsky shows the resolve, inner conviction, and the unity of style of Shostakovich with surprising artistic diversity."[25] Shortly afterward, Mravinsky recorded the symphony at the House of Science in Moscow with the USSR State Symphony Orchestra, attaining a time of just twenty-three minutes![26]

Alexander Gauk performed the Ninth with the Moscow Radio Symphony Orchestra the following January, and Gavriil Yudin directed it in April 1946. While Mravinsky understood the Ninth and its atmosphere, other conductors attempted to minimize the satirical and ironic aspects contained in the Scherzo and Finale and gave emphasis to the symphony's lyricism in the *Moderato* and *Largo* movements. Although the composer's metronome markings for the second movement were 208, conductors took sections at 140–160. As Yudin recalled, "the music seemed distorted; it was pressurized and foreign to Shostakovich's work and appeared to be sentimentalized. Shostakovich himself was concerned about this and asked me not to protract the tempi in the second movement."[27]

There were many mistakes in the score, however, and it was only after the Ninth's premiere that the composer felt confident: "it is impossible to send it abroad before its first performance. My hearing is better than my eyesight, and all the mistakes will be corrected after the first rehearsals."[28] The corrections to the score made during the rehearsals in Leningrad were at bar 27, measures 5–6, to *p. Legato*; at bar 29 there appeared markings to both strengthen and weaken the tone, before bar 31 *diminuendo*. With bar 31 and afterward, *diminuendo* and *pp*—cross-fingering—at 3 bars before 34, Shostakovich changed *poco a poco diminuendo* at bar 42 *pp* and *crescendo*. From bar 81 it is evident Mravinsky's contribution, bar 5, is introduced *crescendo*, at 85, and measures 2–4, *ritardando* and *crescendo*, *poco a poco*.[29] "'You see the Eighth Symphony was pseudotragic for me, and now the Ninth is pseudocomic. I beseech you not to extend the second movement as Alexander Vasilyevich Gauk did.' The tempi taken was 208 compared to 180; it's not so big a crime, but recalling the inspired interpretation by Mravinsky, one sensed a lack of passion in this slow tempo."[30]

In 1946, Mravinsky continued his advocacy of another great Russian in Igor Stravinsky, still neglected in the country of his birth. On 26 January, the Leningrad conductor directed *Petrushka*, the latest in a sequence (Mravinsky had first directed the composer's work more than a decade before in fragments from *The Firebird*).[31] The Stravinsky was billed with other disapproved and "decadent" music in Debussy's "Nuages" and "Les Fêtes" and Ravel's *Boléro*. In the 1945–1946 season, Mravinsky offered two premieres of contemporary Leningrad composers: *The Heroic Poem*, by Alexey Zhivatov, in memory of those who had fallen in the war, and *The Requiem*, by Yuri Levitin, one of Shostakovich's pupils.

In February 1946, as part of a cultural agreement between the Finnish and Soviet governments, Mravinsky together with Kurt Sanderling took the orchestra on its opening international tour—westward to Finland. The concerts took place at two venues in the capital of Helsinki: in the beautiful National

Drama Theatre and the Mëssukhali Hall, a modern multipurpose auditorium that could accommodate some eight thousand people and cope with the massive public demand. Yevgeny Mravinsky directed five of the nine engagements. Mravinsky offered a dazzling display of works by thirteen different composers: Tchaikovsky's *Francesca da Rimini*, the *Nutcracker*, and *Pathétique*; Shostakovich's Fifth, Beethoven's Fifth, and Brahms's Fourth Symphonies; Ravel's *Boléro*; and orchestral fragments from works by Bizet, Borodin, Glinka, Musorgsky, Rimsky-Korsakov, Rossini, Sibelius, and Weber. There were concertos by Rachmaninov and Tchaikovsky, and soloists included three of the finest: violinist Galina Barinova, pianist Yakov Zak, and baritone Pavel Lisitsian—all making their professional debuts in the West. For Yakov Zak, the tour was momentous for his collaborations with Mravinsky:

> Here is a conductor in which there is a harmonic equanimity of "morning" and "evening" performance—Mravinsky is a teacher and artist. An inspired and untiring musician who on every occasion and at each rehearsal discovers in his repertoire something fresh and different. Opening up these new lines in music, he compels his musicians into performing in a more enlightened manner. How refreshed and inspired the orchestra plays for this conductor in the evening concert![32]

This first venture by the Leningrad Philharmonic Orchestra drew many guests from neighboring countries, including press, agents, and impresarios, yet music making was not the only focal point for the local press.

Following the second performance, the media emphasized the diplomatic purpose of the orchestra's visit: "Finland considers it an honor to be the first foreign host for such a distinguished ensemble, . . . this brilliant, world-class orchestra."[33] However, in another review, one can glean something of the impression made by their musicianship: "in our country, we can wait many years to hear such concerts and remember them as great events in our life. . . . It is rare for a conductor and his musicians to form one cogent entity as Mravinsky achieves in conducting this wonderful orchestra."[34] During a break in the schedule, a pilgrimage for Mravinsky was the journey to Äinola—home of the great composer Jean Sibelius. The elderly musician had listened to their performances on the radio, and he conveyed his contentment with their performance of the Lëmminkainen fragment "The Swan of Tuonela." The encounter became the spiritual corollary of the tour for Mravinsky, Sanderling, and Barinova.

The accomplishment of this debut tour was marked with Mravinsky being named the honorary Merited Artist of the Russian Federation and, at the end of the year, being awarded the Stalin Prize First Class for achievements in concert performances in recent seasons. The Stalin Prize was the country's most important honor and recognition that Mravinsky was the preeminent orchestral conductor and representative of the Soviet cultural elite; apart from a solid gold medal, a 100,000-rouble honorarium was presented, an astronomical sum for those years.[35] Mravinsky's second international visit followed quickly afterward—without orchestra—when he joined Dmitry Shostakovich, David Oistrakh, and Lev Oborin at the Prague Spring Festival. Mravinsky traveled there by train from Leningrad with his wife Olga (the others all flew there; Mravinsky had a long-standing dislike of air travel), as spouses were now permitted to accompany their husbands.

The second postwar Prague Spring Festival, in May 1946, was a golden jubilee, and among the liberated cities there prevailed a conspicuously buoyant mood in the country. Soviet music and musicians were very popular in these first difficult years after the war. In two concerts, Mravinsky directed the Czech Philharmonic Orchestra at the Rudolphinium Hall in Shostakovich's Fifth Symphony in D minor (a novelty for these years) and Prokofiev's Second Suite from *Romeo and Juliet*. The two works were repeated, along with Tchaikovsky's Violin Concerto (with David Oistrakh) alternating with Khachaturyan's Piano Concerto (with Lev Oborin), on consecutive evenings. "The Soviet conductor enjoyed a huge success. . . . [F]ew have demonstrated their intricacy of detail and such a relationship of sound together with the inner dynamics of the work plus an ability to link this in one cohesive whole and open up the inner essence of the music."[36]

Appearing in Prague were Ernest Ansermet, Leonard Bernstein, Adrian Boult, Serge Koussevitsky, Charles Munch, Václav Talich, Yehudi Menuhin, and Riccardo Odnoposov. Mravinsky recalled meeting Munch at a function where the Frenchman was drinking from a bottle of red wine. Mravinsky consoled the French maestro when the former asked him why he looked so forlorn, to which Munch replied: "Music is really so sad, is it not?"[37] There began a friendship between the two men, and Charles Munch became a frequent guest conductor with Mravinsky's orchestra in years to come.

Mravinsky opened the 1946 season with a performance of the Fifth Symphony of Shostakovich.

Our Philharmonic opened the concert year with unusual brilliance and triumph on 5 October. Mravinsky, finding new and fresh colors, created wonders with the Fifth Symphony in this work of genius. It was an overpowering triumph, and the orchestra was met with an ovation. It was an unforgettable evening, yet at its heart was the Fifth Symphony. What a pity that its composer was not there to behold it. I particularly regretted his absence, as he doesn't often hear such performances; in a word everyone was taken aback by it.[38]

It appeared the winds of change were in the air, with the opening up of cultural exchange and with foreign musicians once again seen in Leningrad. In January 1947, Josef Krips arrived from Vienna to conduct the Leningrad Philharmonic Orchestra. In interviews with the Soviet press, he expressed his admiration: "I was excited by the first-class mastery of the Leningrad Philharmonic; it can only be through that fine musical tradition led by the wonderful master Yevgeny Mravinsky that one can explain that in just one rehearsal one can find complete rapport with the musicians."[39] Zoltán Kodály visited Leningrad during the summer to conduct his own compositions with the Philharmonic and observed that "The orchestra possesses musicians distinguished for their great finesse and who can quickly settle in to the conductor's wishes. One can in truth argue that they are among the best orchestras in the world."[40]

So successful was Mravinsky's debut in Czechoslovakia that an invitation was renewed for the 1947 Prague Spring Festival. His choice of repertoire was Shostakovich's Eighth Symphony in C minor. The symphony had been a total failure when it was performed in Prague by the FOK symphony orchestra, which was subjected to censure in the local press. The Leningrad conductor made a special request through the Czech conductor that if he were to conduct at all, then it would have to be the Eighth Symphony; Mravinsky genuinely sought to give a truthful interpretation before this *au courant*, music-loving public.

Mravinsky's direction of the Eighth Symphony on 20 and 21 May became the cynosure of the Prague Spring.

> The symphony's performance, carried through by this superb virtuoso orchestra, met with tremendous success: afterward the composer and conductor could not leave the stage, with the ovation lasting more than half an hour. The audience did not merely applaud—they shouted, banged their seats, and stamped their feet. Prague had not seen such a rapturous reception within living memory, and the two concerts at which the Eighth Symphony were performed dominated everything else at the Prague Spring Festival.[41]

In attendance at Mravinsky's concert were the President of the Republic Jan Mazařyk, government ministers, prominent figures in Czech music, foreign guests, and representatives of the European press. Among those present was the distinguished Finnish pianist and musicologist Erik Tavastverna, who wrote:

> I observed how the originator of this monumental creation concentrates as if meditating on this single thematic line, all taken from the piano. Shostakovich is a wonderful example of transforming the miniature into gigantic forms. As

Bach in his preludes, Shostakovich changes the parameters of his spirit into the micro cosmos of the final motif and expands it in a series of variations.[42]

The Czech press wrote that the Soviet conductor "took upon himself the vindication of the Eighth Symphony and confirmed consummately its great merit."[43] The triumph of Mravinsky's conducting of Shostakovich's Eighth led to a heap of animated commentary in the Prague media; more exhaustive judgment was nevertheless hard to find of the musician "who rehabilitated the symphony."[44] The praise was as much for Shostakovich 's music in the aftermath of the war: "Shostakovich again confirmed with this work the secure bond of Soviet art with reality, with Soviet life."[45] Regardless, few could dismiss the connotations for the epoch: "The symphony is an imposing musical testament to the recent world catastrophe, the dominant memory for future generations."[46] Other critics were not oblivious to the Soviet maestro: "Mravinsky opened up for us this almost enigmatic work."[47] While another writer found that the "great strength of Shostakovich's work is that there is no constraint to the melody flowing from such a rich source, verifying in his opinion, Shostakovich's genius."[48]

Mravinsky renewed his acquaintance with Talich, studying his reading of Smetana's great *Má Vlast* at the Rudolphinium and a performance at the National Divadlo Theatre of Janáček's *Kátya Kabanová*. He also heard Honegger's *Liturgique* under Charles Munch and Ernest Ansermet conducting Stravinsky's Symphony in C. Dmitry Shostakovich was impressed enough to write that "the orchestra here . . . is almost on the same level as the Leningrad Philharmonic Orchestra."[49] In portraying his music to a foreign and critical audience, the Prague concerts underlined how constant an interpreter Shostakovich held in Mravinsky. It was to be some time, however, before Mravinsky would be permitted to again travel outside his homeland.

As Shostakovich's Ninth had launched the Philharmonic concert series two years before, a major symphonic work now inaugurated the 1947–1948 season, on this occasion Sergey Prokofiev's newly written Sixth Symphony ushering in a season of sharp contrasts. In the November celebrations, Mravinsky made public his restoration of the *Leningrad* Symphony, in parallel with a conference on Soviet music at the Philharmonic. This fresh reading of the *Leningrad* engrossed many listeners and drew a great deal of interest. Bogdanov-Berezovsky wrote that, "it was surprising the effect of the march in Shostakovich's Seventh where the conductor took a scaled-down dominant measure at each passage—at the beginning and end of each episode—to increase the tempo, in the genuine power of austere measured advance there stirring an imperceptible (as a means) consequence for the listener and creating the feeling of a gigantic and barely audible intensification in dynamics."[50]

In the reprise, Mravinsky made new partitions in the symphonic method, allowing greater expression in the tone of the central section, making it lyrical and triumphant. In the chamber sonorities of the second movement, *Moderato*, Mravinsky, as in 1942, gave color to the intense disposition of the "nostalgic" music, checking it's accent, as Sollertinsky called the "romantic poetry of the Leningrad White Nights." The *Adagio* was clearly at the core of this conception when there appeared a contrasting march section—neither serene nor surprising—as in the first movement, but rather inspiring sort of spiritual anxiety and intransigent resolution. The picturesque nature acquiesced to the heightened mode of emotion and passionate excitement. The exhaustive quintessence assumed a greater magnitude and power.

Mravinsky's suspicions had been verified when he first studied the score of the Seventh Symphony in 1942, when he characterized the development of the first movement, *Allegretto*, as some kind of "banal, illogical, and primordial quintessence. 'A motif with the concept' of unremitting militarism, trivia, and wide-ranging philistinism."[51] Mravinsky's accomplishment in this original reading of the Seventh was more than an "authoritative" portrayal; it was "an organic fusion of the ideas of the composer and the performer, who was able to probe into the aesthetic and ethical core of the work."[52]

Mravinsky, now appointed as artistic director, succeeding Sollertinsky, was unsurprisingly the most energetic protagonist of this showcase of contemporary symphonic music. Yulian Vainkop recounted the festival: "Yevgeny Mravinsky's conducting in seven of the ten concerts resulted in extraordinarily luminous and passionate performances."[53] The programs included Shostakovich's Fifth, Seventh, and Eighth Symphonies, Prokofiev's Fifth and Sixth Symphonies, Revol Bunin's new First Symphony, Khachaturyan's Third Symphony (*Symphonic Poem*) and Piano Concerto, the orchestral suite *Poem to Stalin*, yet another choral work by Yuri Levitin (the oratorio *Motherland*), and *Celebratory Overture* by Alexey Zhivotov.[54]

Every concert became a platform for Soviet symphonic music—a case in point being the world premiere of Aram Khachaturyan's Third Symphony: "I was proud that my symphony, magnificently executed by Y.A. Mravinsky, was incorporated in the same bill with Prokofiev's Fifth."[55] Khachaturyan's new symphony, regardless of Mravinsky's advocacy and that of Stokowski in America, enjoyed a partial success; the work was dear to the composer, according to the musicologist Shneerson: "Aram Ilyich loved and cherished his Third Symphony (*Symphony Poem*). I remember once he invited me to listen to a recording of its performance with Mravinsky conducting. I remember his woe that this piece had suffered such a miserable destiny."[56] Time, outside of Mravinsky's powers, would be the arbiter of this.

The new masterpiece unveiled by Mravinsky was Prokofiev's new Sixth Symphony in B-flat. Sergey Prokofiev had collaborated with the conductor for some weeks at his home at Nikolina Gora during the late summer. The two men had rarely crossed each others' paths, yet they found that they enjoyed each other's company and that they shared a passion for perfection and meticulous performance.[57] The world premiere took place on 11 October, and the performance was repeated on the following evening and broadcast live on Soviet radio. The success of the Prokofiev symphony was beyond anyone's anticipation. In Mravinsky's deep, penetrating, and harshly dark reading, the Sixth assumed an almost Shakespearean feeling of tragedy; the composer, rarely content with interpretations of his own work, valued Mravinsky's both in analysis and rehearsal. The symphony bore the shadow of the grim war years, most of the themes having been composed in 1944–1945 and the work having been completed only on 18 February 1947. There was no specific program, although in Prokofiev's own words: "Now we are celebrating the victory, but each of us bears unhealed wounds: some lost their dear ones, others their health . . . we should not forget this."[58] The jubilant Prokofiev presented to Mravinsky his signed portrait, with rays of the sun sketched by the composer representing his appreciation.[59]

The Moscow premiere took place on 25 December, and among those present was Alexander Werth:

> For the British there it was still Christmas; but the new Prokofiev symphony, conducted by the great Leningrad conductor, Mravinsky, was something not to be missed, even if it meant arriving late at Sir Maurice Peterson's Christmas Party. For a fortnight ahead all tickets had been sold out, and I had to resort to a ticket-profiteer and pay three times the marked price. On the stair leading up to the hall, I met one of the V.O.K.S. critics, a man called Shneerson, who wrote many articles boosting Soviet music for publication in the United States. "I heard it in Leningrad" he said. "It is wonderful; better than the usual Prokofiev, it is philosophic, has the depth of Shostakovich. You'll see![60]

However, the new Prokofiev symphony fell under a cloud, for no other conductor would take up the work. The composer's biographer, Israel Nestyev, wrote that the press welcomed the new work "but missed certain contradictions in the symphony," adding somewhat sinisterly: "life soon brought significant corrections to that evaluation."[61] The Sixth was brusquely disapproved of and dropped by Glavrepertkom. Nevertheless, Mravinsky remained its most dedicated champion, preferring it to the more fashionable Fifth Symphony in B major.

If shadows were falling over cultural relations, other doors were already closing within the country. In the late summer of 1946, the first cycle of an offensive on the arts community had been opened in a resolution by the Central Committee of the Communist Party of 14 August, On the Magazines *Zvezda* and *Leningrad*, in which the writers Mikhail Zoschenko and Anna

Akhmatova were bitterly attacked for "bourgeois and harmful morality." The newspapers unleashed an appalling onslaught on the authors, yet this proved only the beginning of a crusade; on 26 August, another judgment was issued, on The Repertoire of Drama Theaters and Measures to Improve It, in which theaters were censured for producing predominately Western plays and ignoring modern Soviet life. The leading writer Alexander Fadeyev said in Warsaw that "if hyenas could use fountain pens, and jackals could use typewriters, they would write like T. S. Eliot."[62] A disturbing opinion wholly symptomatic of the belligerent atmosphere prevalent in the Soviet arts establishment. The film industry was similarly lambasted with a Party indictment, one of the film *The Great Life*, that issued a disparaging critique of the film's director and scriptwriter. Among those "unsuccessful" film directors put down were the internationally respected Sergey Eisenstein, Mikhail Pudovkin, Grigory Kosintsev, and Mikhail Trauberg—all accused of "light-mindedness and irresponsibility" in their work.[63] Eisenstein, the creator of some of the twentieth century's greatest films—*The Battleship Potemkin*, *Ivan the Terrible*, and *Alexander Nevsky*—was accused of "inconsistency in historical facts, misrepresenting the progressive force of the oprichniki as cast in the form of degenerates such as the American Ku Klux Klan, and Ivan the Terrible, a man of strong will, portrayed as being weak in character."[64]

In January 1948, the Composers Union discussed a Resolution of the Central Committee of the Communist Party that severely censured Vano Muradeli's opera *The Great Friendship*. In the Moscow meetings, the leading group of composers was sharply criticized for writing music that was neither populist nor easy to listen to. The charges were humiliating for many, and indeed the distinguished composer Vissarion Shebalin was so distraught by the attacks that he stood up and declared that he believed Shostakovich to be "a genius,"[65] for which Shebalin was ostracized and removed from his position as rector of the Moscow Conservatoire. Shostakovich, Khachaturyan, and Myaskovsky were all sacked from their teaching appointments, and a long list of their works was barred from public performance.[66]

Mravinsky took part in the Union's meetings, and at sessions of the Leningrad Board called to discuss the Party resolution on 2–3 March 1948, he defended Shostakovich's music, declaring that "rather than attacking formalism one should combat dilettantism in music."[67] The arts historian Isaak Glikman recalls that "Mravinsky handled himself nobly and courageously, publicly speaking in defense of [Shostakovich] with a very fine statement."[68] Normally, the texts of the Composers Union Board would be published in full; however, on this occasion pages 57 to 65 of the minutes were removed by the censor.[69] In his surviving notes, Yevgeny Mravinsky praises the Shostakovich symphonies, which themselves had been discussed fully at their own previous conferences and enjoyed great success with audiences all over the country, and he maintained that he would continue performing Shostakovich's work with his orchestra.

A genuine manifestation of esteem for Shostakovich took place at the Philharmonic later that year. Glikman wrote: "At one of the concerts at which the Fifth Symphony was performed, without Shostakovich being present, Yevgeny Alexandrovich raised the score above his head to a massive roar of applause. Those present at the Philharmonic mentioned this event, and 'the unforgivable behavior of the conductor, was censured in the Moscow press.'"[70]

The performance referred to by Glikman took place on 7 December 1948, when the Fifth was performed following an interpretation of Tchaikovsky's *Francesca da Rimini* at a subscription concert.[71] A leading member of the Composers Union and former Philharmonic director, Mikhail Chulaki, in *Kultura i Zhizh* launched a particularly vehement attack on the Philharmonic and its chief conductor for engaging in a repertoire that was "formalist and decadent."[72] Echoing the period of the censure of Shostakovich's work in the 1930s, history was repeating itself. The country was in the throes of repression and political blackmail; however, at this juncture the composer had his allies. The experiences of the past had been assimilated and there now stood powerful figures in "Maria Yudina a genius and courageous pianist who side by side with Yevgeny Mravinsky, David Oistrakh, Nina Dorliak, Svyatoslav Richter, Zara Dolukhanova and Mstislav Rostropovich . . . managed to save the honour of Russian music during those obscure times."[73]

The attacks on the arts were a symptom of the terrible inner-party struggle involving Andrey Zhdanov and the Leningrad Party leadership that became known as the "Leningrad Affair," in which some two thousand leading figures were murdered and all mention of the heroic siege was obliterated. A great shadow now covered the metropolis, and the ambitious plans to rebuild the devastated buildings and historical sites were put on ice for fifteen years, almost as if the modern municipality were damned by the two-hundred-year-old curse set by Tsaritsa Yevdokiya—Peter's estranged wife who condemned his new capital on the Neva marshes.[74]

Mravinsky's stature during the postwar period was considerable in that he was regularly invited to work with orchestras in the capital:

> This talented musician never fails . . . in his artistic development, and his control of the orchestra has become increasingly compelling. This was particularly evident in Berlioz's *Requiem*, which we heard under Yevgeny Mravinsky in the spring of 1941. These recent concerts of Berlioz's wonderful music sounded better than six years ago. Mravinsky reads the *Requiem* with reserve, restraining correctly the disparate mystical introduction of the bitter struggle with death, and the conductor takes this consistent line, beginning with conflict rising in the

first part of the requiem through the *Dies Irae* and the *Lachrymosa*, to the celebratory and triumphant two fugues in the penultimate fragment. Such a portrayal
of the *Requiem* is intelligent and draws out the humanity reflected in this Berlioz
score, complementary with the Catholic ideas of confession before death and
God. The programs also included a novelty in the oratorio by Yuri Levitin—*In
Memory of the Fallen Heroes* (based on Lebedeva-Kumach). For the performance of this multifaceted oratorio, Yevgeny Mravinsky approaches not only with
a sense of duty but also indisputable care. The State Symphony Orchestra played
admirably for Mravinsky.[75]

On a subsequent visit, the reviewer found cause for grievance:

The performance by Yevgeny Mravinsky of the Sixth (*Pathétique*) Symphony
was a considerable artistic triumph for the conductor. The reserve and control
well thought through to the fine details together with genuine and clear emotion.
Mravinsky opened up the depth of ideas and imagery exciting in Tchaikovsky's
greatest work. . . . It is impossible, however to ignore the controversial decision
by the conductor to play the third and fourth movements without a break, as if
to underline the tragic concept of the symphony. This innovation, however, is
scarcely defensible. The fragments from the *Nutcracker* were magnificently
played. In a masterly performance, Oborin took the First Piano Concerto in a
broad epic form. The Tchaikovsky concert is a momentous musical experience
of this season. However, those of the Brahms and Wagner fashioned a dissimilar reaction. The foremost criticism one needs to make to the conductor is in his
ineffective selection of program. The Second Symphony by Brahms does not
belong among the composer's finest works. . . . I[I]t is devoid of both ideas and
emotional content and cannot be rated as popular among listeners. Insignificant
and pretentious, the overture *Faust* by Wagner does not warrant recognition. Superlative were the "Bacchanalia" from *Tannhäuser* and the "Flight of the
Valkyries" by Wagner. The USSR State Symphony Orchestra performed both
programs consummately.[76]

Another Moscow writer found similar appeal in his work, yet also found criticism for his repertoire:

Following a long interval, Yevgeny Mravinsky has returned to give concerts
with the USSR State Symphony Orchestra. As at all times, this conductor
catches the attention of a wide number of the public who love his talent and
mastery. Mravinsky reveals himself best in works of scale and "great moment."
He is one of the most accomplished interpreters of leading Soviet symphonic
composers. However, Mravinsky gave only three concerts, repeating works by
Glinka, Tchaikovsky, and Kalinnikov. On those of 5 and 6 April were given the
overture and "Oriental Dances" from *Ruslan and Lyudmila* and the *Waltz Fantasy* and *Jôta Aragonésa* by Glinka and the Kalinnikov Second Symphony. The
most impressive by Glinka was *Jôta Aragonésa*—among the most sparkling

symphonic creations by this great composer. This performance fixed a challenging responsibility: the spontaneous brilliance of the folk-dance imagery with the azure orchestral canvass of short phrases, as if flying from one instrument to another, and transparent *piano* with energetic flights of *tutti*—all demand a flexibility and total respite in idiom, and a virtuoso control of all the colors in a precise and accurate ensemble. Both conductor and orchestra showed these qualities to full measure. The *Waltz Fantasy* was played with the most poetic effect. Less successful, however, was the overture to *Ruslan and Lyudmila*. There was an insufficient breadth of dynamics and sparkling energy, which make such a successful piece. In the second half, Kalinnikov's Second Symphony in A major lacks the artistic appeal of its sister First Symphony. No less so, the Second Symphony has its distinguishing qualities, clearly defined national character, expressive, song-like melody, and beauty of orchestration. With great attention and care, and no little mastery, Mravinsky drew out the finest from the score and presented it in a winning light. . . . It's impossible not to express regret that the conductor limited himself to only three programs and that there were no major classical works or contemporary Soviet composers featured. The USSR State Symphony Orchestra under Yevgeny Mravinsky played magnificently with real artistic enthusiasm, and this was appreciated by the audiences greeting both orchestra and conductor.[77]

Mravinsky relented little as an enthusiastic protagonist of contemporary repertoire. In December 1948, two major symphonies by Leningrad composers, Yuri Levitin's First Symphony *Youth*, and his former teacher Vladimir Shcherbachyov's Fifth Symphony *Russian* were given their world premieres. The young composer Sergey Slonimsky was present at the rehearsals of the latter piece: "I would christen this a symphonic 'passion.' The slow movement is heart-stirring, lyrical, deriving from Russian mourning laments, and in the finale there appears the toll of doom on the basses. Mravinsky knew so well how to epitomize death and tragedy."[78] There prevailed a custom of entitling symphonies to differentiate them from the dominating influence of Shostakovich and Prokofiev. The outstanding cellist Daniil Shafran gave performances with alternately Mravinsky and Sanderling, playing for the first time concertos by Boccherini, Haydn, Schumann, and Dvořák. Shafran found time to describe his admiration for Mravinsky: "The spiritual, inner strength and care for restraint and to concentrate on the most important feature in cold and measured bursts, emotion and passions, . . . always 'focused' on the next page, and the measure of the score reflecting artistic professionalism of the highest order."[79]

A concert on 15 November 1949, under the auspices of a Festival of Soviet Music, included premieres of Alexander Arutunyan's *Festive* overture, Arno Babadjanyan's Violin Concerto (played by Leonid Kogan), and Shostakovich's oratorio *Song of the Forests*, based on texts by Yevgeny Dolmatovsky. The idea of a song cycle based on the forest amelioration campaign of those years was much to Mravinsky's liking. Mravinsky was also appointed in charge of the Moscow premiere with the USSR State Symphony Orchestra and the Sveshnikov Boys Choir, among whom was a future student of the conductor, Eduard Serov, who recalled Mravinsky's arrival at the choir's rehearsals, "listening with great attention to our singing fragments from the choral work."[80] The conductor championed the new composition, and not only for its program:

> I have been fortunate to conduct many of Shostakovich's most complex works. However, perhaps one feels his mastery more visibly in such an effortless work as the first appearance of *Song of the Forests*—how the composer brings into play such imperfect and flexible means here! He divulges so much invention and fantasy in an original seven-part fugue! Moreover, this is presented so wonderfully: the listener does not lose his concentration for a second hearing more and more delights! Yet his means, I repeat, are wholly constrained.[81]

Notable premieres during this period were of the Twenty-Seventh Symphony by the late Nikolay Myaskovsky and of Prokofiev's oratorio *On Guard of Peace*. The symphony was one of Myaskovsky's finest in a long symphonic line, and unfortunately the composer did not live to hear it. Myaskovsky died from cancer, never having recovered from the censure of 1948. Nikolay Myaskovsky was of the pre-Revolutionary intelligentsia, which epitomized the finest in Russian art and European culture, and his music, reflecting the nostalgia for the sad yet heroic tsarist past, never found a spiritual home in Soviet society. Myaskovsky's canon caught a tragic theme so typical of the loss of many values and that the composer could never relinquish. If he chose titles for his symphonies dedicated ostensibly to the air force and collective farms, the subject matter was far away, an austere, nostalgic melancholia predominant, reminiscent of Tchaikovsky's late work. Asaf'yev portrayed his compositions as "wholly gray, as if painted under a muddy and funereal cloudy sky transfigured to the dark of a moonless black night."[82] Myaskovsky was a crucially fundamental figure in Russian music who had sustained the symphonic medium, forming a bridge between Tchaikovsky and Shostakovich's symphonies.

New large-scale works given by Mravinsky included Kuddus Kuzham'-yarov's *Rizvangul* and Arno Machavariani's Violin Concerto (soloist Mark Vaiman). More secure in the repertoire was Kabalevsky's Violin Concerto, pioneered with David Sheiderman, concert-master, and having colorful passages brilliantly written for the virtuoso. Among those Leningrad composers whose creations were championed by Mravinsky were Vadim Salmanov's *The Forest*, Vadim Kotlyarevsky's cantata *The Kremlin*, Vladimir Deshevov's *The Russian Overture*, Galina Ustvolskaya's symphonic poem *The Man from the High Mountains* and, for bass voice and orchestra, *The Dream of Stepan Razin*, and Boris Klyuzner's *Overture*.

Mravinsky's attraction to Western music showed no signs of diminishing; among major revivals were the Fourth, Seventh, and Ninth symphonies of Beethoven, Berlioz's *Symphonie fantastique* and *Requiem*,[83] Bruckner's Seventh and Brahms's Second Symphony, and programs of fragments from Wagner's *Ring* tetrology. In May 1949, the symphony in E major by the eighteenth-century Moravian composer Frantisêc Mici was unveiled. The score was discovered by Mravinsky on his Prague visit two years previously and recorded for posterity. "New" for contemporary audiences was the Twenty-First Symphony by one Nikolay Andreyevich Ovsyaniko-Kulikovsky given on successive evenings at the Philharmonic Hall in early February 1952. This composition had been performed by conductors in Kiev and Moscow in recent months, and it was believed to be the handiwork of an aristocrat of the late eighteenth century, yet here were horns and trumpets being used in such an early period piece![84]

Mravinsky was not the only one to suspect that not everything was as it should be in this newly "unearthed" symphony; nor did anyone know of any of the composer's other symphonic works. There was indeed a nobleman who possessed his own serf orchestra and helped found the Odessa opera theater, yet despite searches for other "symphonies" nothing by this "composer" was to be found anywhere. Moreover, additional research revealed that the Ovsyaniko-Kulikovsky work originated from the pen of one Mikhail Goldstein, a violinist from Odessa (elder brother of the child prodigy) who did some composing in his spare time.[85] Needless to say, the work was set aside as a joke, but not before the Moscow militia held conference with "Ovsyaniko-Kulikovsky" at their famous Petrovka headquarters![86]

Soviet film cameras documented the outing to the huge Electrosila plant on 6 December 1948 by Mravinsky's Philharmonic in performances of short orchestral pieces by Glinka, continuing a tradition of the 1920s. This was a renewal of the pre-Revolutionary custom of touring the country with philanthropic summer seasons at Sochi on the Black Sea and in the northern Caucasus, when the area was a popular tourist spot for the royal family. A new affiliation developed with music lovers in the nearby Baltic States "liberated" by Soviet forces. Between the 1947 and 1951 seasons, the orchestra paid regular visits to the Riga coastal resorts and to Tallinn and Vilnius, where there lingered a European cultural tradition historically linked to Germany and Sweden.

The appointment of the Latvian Arvids Jansons as staff conductor followed his success at the Second All-Union Conducting Competition, in 1946. Jansons proved himself an admirable orchestral trainer, a musician of steadfastness, integrity, and inimitable artistry building a most important role over many years. In 1947, the orchestra gave five concerts in Tallinn, as a result of which Mravinsky was awarded an Honorary Diploma by the Estonian government; one of the local newspapers remarked favorably that "this is the first time Tallinn audiences have heard such high artistic standards."[87] In February 1950, the Philharmonic reawakened its acquaintance with Tallinn and was met with ecstatic acclaim, particularly in response to its performances of Shostakovich's Fifth and Brahms's First Symphonies. The Estonian conductor Roman Matsov commended Mravinsky's musical analysis, transparent technique, and idiosyncratic affection for elegance: "all these qualities find all-round articulation in the playing of the orchestra."[88]

In May 1950, Dmitry Shostakovich marked the twenty-fifth anniversary of his First Symphony, inviting close colleagues and friends to an evening at the *Aragvy* Georgian restaurant in central Moscow. Those present were Khachaturyan, Mravinsky, Shebalin, Oborin, and members of the Beethoven Quartet with their wives. It was an extraordinary episode that united friends who had all remained by the composer through many years.[89]

The 1948 denunciation of the leading composers had led to a falling off in the excellence of contemporary music and to not many contemporary works settling into the repertoire. But Mravinsky glimpsed the treasure chest of Russian symphonic music and bowed to revivals of the "Mighty Handful" and beyond. Mravinsky unveiled the First and Second Symphonies by Alexander Borodin, and for the first time he performed Serenade for Strings by Tchaikovsky and Glazunov's *Suite from the Middle Ages*.[90] In 1950, the nationwide celebrations of Glinka led to Yevgeny Mravinsky taking the Philharmonic into the studios of *Lenfilm* to record the soundtrack for Georgy Alexandrov's biopic *Mikhail Glinka*, which also featured the young Svyatoslav Richter acting and playing piano in the part of Franz Liszt.[91] On 28 December 1950, Mravinsky's orchestra gave the deferred world premiere of Sergey Lyapunov's Second Symphony, written in 1917 (Mravinsky having been given the score by the composer's daughter),[92] and on 18 January 1952, after thirty years absence, Vasily Kalinnikov's Second Symphony was returned to the concert platform. A few weeks later, Mravinsky resurrected Balakirev's First Symphony in C minor on 27 February 1952. These rediscoveries became striking delights leading to other conductors adding these late-romantic pieces to their repertoire.

On 5 March, Mravinsky's former composition teacher, Professor Vladimir Shcherbachyov, passed away. Mravinsky had championed many of Shcherbachyov's orchestral works, including his most recent, the Fifth Symphony. Shcherbachyov was a foremost influence and guiding figure in Leningrad life in the 1920s, having marked down a "new" course in contemporary music, having faltered through the difficult 1930s, and in his late work having turned to neoromanticism. Yevgeny Alexandrovich played at a memorial meeting at the Composers Union House with other former pupils, including Yudina and Sofronitsky.[93] Within a few days, on 9 March 1952, the death of Alexandra Kollontay was announced in the Soviet press. A great survivor, Kollontay had retired with honors after many years service in the diplomatic corps. How different might Mravinsky's fate have been without her help and advice.[94] It was a poignant loss for Mravinsky and his mother, who both attended the state funeral in Moscow.

Mravinsky's work with the principal orchestras in the capital extended to broadcasting, and on one occasion, the playing on Moscow Radio of the Shostakovich *Leningrad* Symphony was so impressive that its composer wrote:

> Yesterday [18 April], the orchestra of the Radio Committee performed my Seventh Symphony. Of course, there can never be a quite perfect performance of my work. The orchestra played magnificently, and in a word, shook me with their playing. It is difficult to say which section is best; listening to the strings there is a surprising beauty of sound, possessing the most delicate nuances. The woodwind and the brass have all the possible dynamics of sound, from *fff* to *ppp*. The percussion and harps are magnificent. I am not a music critic nor am I a musicologist, and I do not know how to write about music, but as a listener to my own works, one cannot describe what joy I experienced yesterday. The orchestra of the Radio Committee has been turned into a first-class ensemble with great performing technique and high musicianship.[95]

Golovanov had built the orchestra into a fine virtuoso orchestra; however, this is a case in point of the results that Mravinsky was realizing outside his own Philharmonic. The conductor Mravinsky matched Shostakovich's enthusiasm for his work by privately delighting in Shostakovich's film scores, as we can read from Mravinsky's diary:

> 1952 Summer: At Medvedkovo in Tverskaya oblast. One caught the end of the film *Pirogov*, from Skorobogatov's play, [and] one feels particularly in Shostakovich's music (as something forgotten today) Great Art. How magnificent is Shostakovich's talent in all this! So wonderful, surprisingly communicative, and appealing all created by him spontaneously and as if by accident! Popularity such as this grows from an image of a piece of action, a motif that becomes just a reason for great expression . . . and there is such sensitivity in proportion, structure packed into one part of the music, where it is at one with the elements of synthetics in art (here—in the cinema).[96]

The postwar years were a dark period for the Soviet people; the recovery from the horrors of war, rebuilding of their homes, and moral uplift from the victory could be heard in the music making of Yevgeny Mravinsky's orchestra, as could the tragedy of lost illusions. Evoking memories of the war years in Siberia, the people crammed into the Philharmonic Hall, around the sides of the hall and underneath the massive white marble columns, young and old alike quite lost to the harsh and often forbidding Leningrad outside. Here for a few short hours, a forgotten world of fantasy and adventure—a realm of lost values, of nobility and virtue, of love and poetry—could be discovered. Here was sanctuary from all the evils and wickedness outside the walls of the Philharmonic Hall. Yevgeny Mravinsky and his orchestra gave listeners spiritual comfort in their darkest times to a degree rarely matched—music touching the deepest parts of the human soul, where few others could penetrate.

NOTES

1. The total damage was cited at 45 billion roubles: 716,000 homes, 526 schools and kindergartens, 15 scientific institutions, 101 museums, 187 of 300 historic monuments, 840 factories, 71 bridges, and most of Leningrad University were destroyed. Thirty-two shells fell on the Hermitage, causing 300,000 sq. ft. of damage.

2. Avakumov, senior ed. *Leningrad v Velikiye Otchestvenniye Voine-Dokumenti i Materiali*, Vol. 2 (Leningrad, 1947), 687.

3. Only one shell, causing little damage, hit the building during the three years.

4. V. Bogdanov-Berezovsky, *Sovetsky Dirizher: ocherk deyatelnosti E. A. Mravinskovo* (Leningrad: Muzika, 1956), 148–49.

5. Kurt Sanderling, in conversation with Alan Blyth, *Gramophone* (April 1974): 1844.

6. N. Bolshakov, "Na otchetnykh konzertakh Leningradskoy filarmoniya," *Leningradskaya Pravda*, 13 January 1945.

7. Vladimir Derzhanovsky (1881–1944) was a distinguished music critic and writer. In the 1900s, he organized concerts in Moscow, and he continued to have a central role in music publishing in the Soviet era.

8. Alexey Ludewig, author interview, July 2002.

9. This entry refers to a rehearsal for Shostakovich's Eighth Symphony, the first in Leningrad.

10. This refers to the score of the ballet *Lost Illusions*, which was dropped by the Kirov in the 1935–1936 season after three performances.

11. Y. A. Mravinsky, "Iz Dnevniki," *Muzikalnaya Akademiya*, no. 4 (1997): 98–99.

12. *Iskusstvo*, no. 4 (November 2000): 13.

13. "Novaya simfoniya Shostakovicha," *Pravda*, 5 September 1945.

14. *Sovetskoye Iskusstvo*, 7 September 1945.

15. "Devyataya simfoniya Shostakovicha," *Vechernaya Moskva*, 11 September 1945.

16. R. O. Davydov, "Devyatoy simfoniya Shostakovicha: perviye vpechatleniya," *Trud*, 16 September 1945.

17. Davydov, "Devyatoy simfoniya Shostakovicha."

18. Davydov, "Devyatoy simfoniya Shostakovicha."

19. D. Zhitomirsky, *Devyata simfoniya Dmuitriya Shostakovicha* (Music Department of the Cultural Relations Organization, 1945) no. 9.

20. L. Mikheyeva, *II Sollertinsky-zhisn i naslediye* (Leningrad: Sovetsky Kompositor, 1988), 121.

21. D. Zhitomirsky, "Pervoe ispolneniye devyatovo simfoniya D. Shostakovicha," *Sovetskoye Iskusstvo*, 30 November 1945.

22. D. Rabinovich, *Dmitry Shostakovich* (London: Lawrence and Wishart, 1959), 99.

23. I. Nestyev, "Shestaya simfoniya Prokofieva," *Sovetskoye Iskusstvo*, 18 October 1947.

24. Y. A. Mravinsky, "Tridzat let s muzikoi shostakovicha," in *D. Shostakovich*, ed. L. Danilevich (Moscow, Sovetsky Kompozitor, 1967), 106–107.

25. D. Zhitomirsky, "Pervoe ispolneniye devyatoi simfoniya D. Shostakovicha."

26. The recording has been lost, despite attempts to find the original masters.

27. G. Y. Yudin, "Razroznenniye stranitsii iz vospominaniye o DD Shostakoviche," in *D. Shostakovich, Tridzatiletiye, 1945–1975*, ed L. V. Danilevich (Leningrad: Sovetskie Kompositor, 1982), 15.

28. GTsMMK, f. 32, No. 136.

29. GTsMMK, f. 32, No. 99.

30. Memoir by Gavril Yudin, GTsMMK, f. 441, ed. Khr. 693.

31. Archives of the St. Petersburg Philharmonia Library.

32. Y. I. Zak, "Posle Konkurs Dirizherov," *Sovetskaya Muzika*, no. 4 (1972): 74.

33. *Sansan Sanomat*, March 1946.

34. *Uusi Suomi*, March 1946.

35. Mravinsky used this award to buy a coat and tails, having never possessed his own concert garments and always having had to borrow from friends.

36. D. Sollertinsky and L. Sollertinsky, *Pages from the Life of D. Shostakovich* (London: Hale, 1981), 124.

37. Y. A. Mravinsky, interview with A. A. Zolotov, Ekran TV, 1982.

38. Sophia Shostakovich to L. T. Atovmyan, 8 October 1946, GtSMMk, f. 32, ed. Khr, 1982.

39. "Nashi zarubezhni gosti," *Leningradskaya Pravda*, 25 January 1947.

40. "Nashi zarubezhni gosti," *Leningradskaya Pravda*, 18 June 1947.

41. G. Shneerson, "Zhisn musiki Shostakovicha za rubezhom," *Sovetskaya Muzika*, no. 2 (1948): 246–47.

42. Erik Tavastverna, "Vstrechi s Shostakovichem," in *D. Shostakovich—stati i materiali*, ed. G. M. Shneerson (Moscow: Sovetsky Kompozitor, 1976), 285–86.

43. *Rude Pravo*, 20 May 1947.

44. *Svet Kultury*, 29 May 1947.

45. *Rude Pravo*, 20 May 1947.

46. *Svet Kultury*, 29 May 1947.

47. *Svobodni Noviny*, 22 May 1947.

48. *Prace*, 22 May 1947.

49. D. D. Shostakovich to L. O. Arnstam, 15 May 1947, TSGALI archives No. 73.
50. Bogdanov-Berezovsky, *Sovetsky dirizher*, 159.
51. Mravinsky, "Tridzat let s musikoi Shostakovicha," 107.
52. V. Bogdanov-Berezovsky, *Sovetsky dirizher*, 137.
53. Y. Vainkop, "Festival sovetskoi muziki," *Vechernaya Leningrad*, 25 December 1947.
54. Archives of St. Petersburg Philharmonia Library.
55. A. Khachaturyan, *Stranitsi zhisni i tvorchestvo* (Moscow: Sovetsky Kompositor, 1982), 147.
56. Khachaturyan, *Stranitsi zhisni i tvorchestvo*, 22.
57. A. M. Vavilina Mravinskaya, author interview, September 2002.
58. I. Nestyev, *S. S. Prokofyev* (Moscow: Gosudarstvenniye Muzikalniye Izdatelstvo, 1957), 419.
59. A. M. Vavilina Mravinskaya, author interview, February 2002.
60. A. Werth, *Musical Uproar in Moscow* (London: Turnstile, 1949), 24.
61. Nestyev, *S. S. Prokofyev*, 418.
62. Werth, *Musical Uproar in Moscow*, 9.
63. R. H. McNeal, ed. *Na filmax Velikovov Zhiznya: Resolutions and Decisions of the CPSU* (Toronto, 1974), 240–43.
64. *Na filmax Velikovov Zhiznya*.
65. A. Shebalina, "S Alisoy Maksimovnoy Shebalinoy," in *V mire Shostakovicha*, ed. S. M. Khentova (Moscow: Kompositor, 1996), 130.
66. Works included Prokofiev's Sixth Symphony, Shostakovich's Seventh and Eighth Symphonies, Khachaturyan's Third Symphony, Myaskovsky's Twenty-Third Symphony, and works by Popov, Polovinkin, Shebalin, and others.
67. Y.A. Mravinsky personal archive.
68. I. Glikman, *Pisma k Drugu* (St. Petersburg: DSCH, 1993), 286.
69. Minutes of Composers Union, 2–3 March 1948.
70. Glikman, *Pisma k Drugu*, 286.
71. Archives of the St. Petersburg Philharmonia Library.
72. M. Chulaki, *Izkusstvo i Zhizh*, 2–3 March 1948.
73. L. Hakobian, *Music of the Soviet Age* (Stockholm: Melos Music Literature, 1998), 211.
74. S. Volkov, *Istoriya Kulturii Sankt Piterburga* (St. Petersburg: Nezasimaya, 2001), 209.
75. D. Rabinovich, "Konzerti Y. Mravinskovo," *Sovetskoye Iskusstvo*, 28 March 1947.
76. S. Konstantinov, "Konzerti Yevgeniya Mravinskovo," *Vechernaya Moskva*, 27 November 1948.
77. G. Yudin, "E. Mravinsky v Moskve," *Sovetskaya Muzika*, no.6 (1952).
78. S. Slonimsky, interview with G. Enfaldt, May 2002.
79. D. B. Shafran, *Daniil Shafran: Violoncell solo* (Moscow: ACT, 2001), 93.
80. E. Serov, *Dirizher Eduard Serov* (Volgograd: Nizhnevolzhskoye, 1993), 131.
81. Mravinsky, "Tridzat let s muzikoi Shostakovicha," 110.
82. B. Asaf'yev, *Kriticheskiye statyi ocherki i retzenzti* (Moscow: Muzika, 1967), 223.

83. D. D. Shostakovich, "Vydadyuchy konzert," *Leningradskaya Pravda*, 13 February 1947.

84. M. Goldstein, *Zapiski Muzikanta* (Frankfurt: Posser-Verlag, 1970), 72–73, 74–75.

85. Goldstein, *Zapiski Muzikanta*, 103.

86. Petrovka is the headquarters of criminal investigations for the Moscow City Police.

87. *Eesti*, 2 March 1950.

88. R. Matsov, "Konzert simfonicheskovo orkester Leningradskovo filarmoniya," *Rakhva Khyael*, 1 March 1950.

89. Shostakovich to E. P. Makarov, 9 May 1951, GTsMMK, f. 461, ed. Khr, 60.

90. Archives of the St. Petersburg State Philharmonia Library.

91. Iz istorii "Lenfilm," *Iskusstvo* (Leningrad, 1968–1975), vypusk 1–4.

92. V. Fomin, *Orkestrom dirizhiruet Mravinsky* (Leningrad: Muzika, 1976), 88.

93. M. Yudina, *Luchi Bozhestvennoi Lyubvi* (St. Petersburg: Universitetskaya kniga, 1999), 116.

94. A. M. Kollontay, *Diplomatischekiye dnevniki*, Vol. 1 (Moscow: Academia, 2001), 30.

95. GTsMMK. F. NS Golovanova, No. 1372.

96. Y. A. Mravinsky, "Iz Dnevniki," *Muzikalnaya Akademiya*, no.4 (1997): 99.

Chapter Eleven

The Year 1953

In Shostakovich's music one can hear the voice of civil conscience. . . .

—Y. A. Mravinsky, "Tridzat let s muzikoi Shostakovicha"

The year 1953 was an auspicious one for the people of the Soviet Union, and no less so for the artistic director of the Leningrad Philharmonic Orchestra. The postwar years had suffered a period of storm and stress, and no cessation of the tyranny and lawlessness ruling the land was in sight. The onslaughts by conservatives on the country's people and intelligentsia had intensified the oppressive hold on the arts, and an anxious expectation for a crack in the system and some lightening in the unceasing burden prevailed.

At the beginning of January, the orchestra made a studio recording of Shostakovich's Seventh Symphony, set down over several days by the Leningrad Accord studio engineer, David Gaklin. It proved an exhausting experience, and as always, Mravinsky, seeing the metal cases containing the apparently endless reels of magnetic tape, had second thoughts about "putting music into a tin can."[1] By the end of the month, Yevgeny Mravinsky retired to recover his vigor at a clinic at Mednichny stream near Leningrad.

Mravinsky's Diary

The Seventh of Shostakovich. One has quite lost both sentiment and the necessity for this recording—there is no enlightenment in this. On each and every time one has to raise the stakes once more![2]

Mravinsky rarely returned to the *Leningrad*, passing over performances to Sanderling or Jansons and looking at other works for revival later that year:

"Thoughts about the tempi and form of the Mastersingers. I leafed through the pages of Shostakovich's Sixth Symphony (great work!)."[3]

The recording was among the first to be released on the new format of long-playing records, and it would be several weeks before one could listen to the finished product. If Mravinsky was half-hearted toward the medium, the composer had been dissatisfied by Toscanini's wartime recording and impatiently awaited having his *Leningrad* Symphony set down by Mravinsky's orchestra.

> I have listened to the release of my Seventh Symphony played by the Leningrad Philharmonic under Y. Mravinsky. It is a magnificent performance. In respect to the recording, one would like to say the following: I have never heard such an excellent gramophone record. Alongside a profusion of dynamic tension from *pp* to *fff* there should ensue the breathtaking sound of the whole orchestra—*tutti*. It is admirable that one can perceive sound in the orchestra, both in full sections and on solo instruments. The sound engineer David Gaklin has again verified his great mastery and venerable musical refinement.[4]

In March 1953, the death of Iosif Stalin heralded a wave of change sweeping the length and breadth of Eastern Europe. Few figures imparted so much influence in the twentieth century as the Georgian in the Kremlin; his shadow was indeed a long one—Stalin and his associates overlooked every aspect of life in the Soviet Union and Eastern Europe. While musicians had performed for kings and queens in medieval times Stalin's regime had transformed the country's arts into playing the role of court jester. Absolute power reigned in the figure of the Soviet leader; the paradox was that the people believed him and now with his passing all would be refashioned—something that they feared.

The Leningrad maestro was preparing a series of concerts in Moscow when the death was announced, and Mravinsky along with the conductors Melik-Pashayev, Gauk, Kondrashin, and Konstantin Ivanov were detailed to the funeral ceremonies as Stalin's body lay in state in the Hall of Columns. The most respected musicians in the country—Oistrakh, Gilels, Richter, the Beethoven Quartet—performed tragic funereal music, and Mravinsky directed the State Orchestra in Tchaikovsky's Fifth and Brahms's Fourth Symphonies. The serenity of the closing pages of the music contrasted sharply with the chaos on the streets outside, where thousands of tightly packed people were being crushed among the masses pouring into the city center. Mravinsky spent the evening with the Shostakovich family.

Yevgeny Mravinsky never met the Soviet leader, but he had been moved to take the advice of the president of the Academy of Sciences, Sergey Vavilov, and had written to Stalin requesting his consideration in enhancing the status of the country's leading ensembles. Mravinsky commented that a new leaf had been turned and the cultural well being of the people had been enhanced, and the motherland should safeguard the rank of its leading elite ensembles by elevating their rating, bestowing titles of merited collective or academic, and boosting their salaries accordingly. By introducing an agreed contract system on a specific number of hours per week, the orchestra would fulfill an all-around system as determined between management and musicians. In other words, a pyramid structure would allow a grading for all musicians throughout the country. Those considered worthy of a higher salary structure by Mravinsky, apart from the Leningrad Philharmonic Orchestra, were the Bolshoi and Kirov Theatres, the USSR State Symphony, and the Large Orchestra of Soviet State Radio and Television.[5] This was implemented as sine qua non until the demise of the Soviet Union in 1991. The salaries of these "super" orchestras would be as much as three times higher than those of other ensembles, orchestral musicians would have facilities to use as rest homes throughout the country, be able to set payments for recordings and radio broadcasts, and have priority in housing. Mravinsky himself would receive as much as one thousand roubles a month, ten times higher than the national average.[6]

With the death of Stalin, a critical moment arose in all aspects of Soviet life. Not only was an amnesty declared for many unjustly detained prisoners, but also new legislation quickly appeared; initially these developments, while hardly visible, nevertheless attained immense consequence for everyone in the arts. This would be most prevalent in exchanges with other countries and in information. Slowly, new freedoms emerged in that most tenuous and sensitive of mediums—the theater. Music had presented a key threat to the old order—Mravinsky's presentation of contemporary orchestral works were influential social events disseminating far beyond the solemnity of music itself.

In closing the 1952–1953 season, Mravinsky and Richter offered two magnificent concerts. The performances of Liszt's Piano Concerto in E minor and the *Mephisto Waltz*, with Tchaikovsky's Fifth Symphony in E minor in between, were an intriguing blend; the partnership between Mravinsky and Richter was a magnificent gem of this period in Soviet music. During this same period, Mravinsky's fiftieth birthday was commemorated, but among only a small coterie of friends and relatives at his flat on Borodinsky Street— rather than mark such occasions, the conductor preferred a quiet room and a score to study there. Mravinsky would still visit Moscow and would usually stop over with his former teacher, Alexander Gauk. The pair would use up time at Gauk's dacha outside the city, where there was a splendid, old-fashioned bath decorated in art nouveau style in which Mravinsky loved to immerse himself. It was constructed of brass and rare fittings of pre-Revolutionary origin probably belonging to a rich merchant's family. Here Mravinsky would study scores, smoking his *papirosi*, often drinking a tipple of vodka. The bath became the focus of any visit by the Leningrad maestro. Following Gauk's passing, Mravinsky no longer visited, and the ancient vessel was thrown out. The Kondrashin family happened to move in next door, and spotting the derelict artifice, Kirill Kondrashin asked Gauk's son about it. Hence, the "Mravinsky bathtub" came into the possession of the Kondrashins, who immortalized the Leningrad maestro's former usage of this ornate and historical bath with a plaque.[7]

On 22 October 1953, the legendary relationship of Mravinsky and Richter was renewed for the memorial concert for Sergey Prokofiev. The program included *Romeo and Juliet* (using Mravinsky's edition), the Fifth Symphony, and the First Piano Concerto with the USSR State Symphony Orchestra. Mravinsky and Richter produced an electrically charged event that staggered their listeners and was talked about for years afterward. Aside from the long-standing affinity with Shostakovich, Mravinsky's collaborations with Prokofiev were deeply rewarding—Mravinsky directed premieres of several works, bringing to light a darkly tragic Shakespearean tint in the composer's late lyrical period.

Except for the miniature Ninth, it had been a full decade since Shostakovich had written a symphony. In the last days of April, the Shostakoviches visited the resort of Kislovodsk. Normally, this mountain town with its clear air and waters would provide the almost perfect conditions for rest and recuperation; however, something oppressed the composer. He wrote to Shebalin, "it's often raining and windy. . . . In general everything is all right. The food is fine. It's pleasing to take the Narzan baths here. There is a nice view from the window, but I cannot stand the regime in the sanatorium and dream of getting out of here as soon as I can."[8] Almost immediately upon his return to Moscow, on 15 May, he visited Shebalin in the hospital and shared with him his first thoughts of the Tenth Symphony.[9]

During the summer months, staying at his family's dacha in Komarovo, near Leningrad, Shostakovich began setting down his symphony. Nevertheless, he found the time to write to his pupil, Kara Karayev:

> Although no one interferes, the work is going poorly. When creative potential is at a high, then nothing can stop one writing. Yet, when it is mediocre or down in the depths, even at the House of Rest, no degree of comfort can help. Just now its difficult in the first movement; I really don't know how it's going to go.[10]

On 1 October, before the opening of the new season, Mravinsky traveled to Moscow and heard the still unfinished piece at Shostakovich's flat on Kutuzov Prospekt.[11] Mravinsky spent more than a month in intense study of the symphony, returned to Moscow on 7 November, and two days later brought back portions of the copy, along with the completed score. On the following day, Shostakovich himself arrived in Leningrad to continue their tête-à-tête; according to Mravinsky's diary, the conversation was mostly around tempi. In ensuing weeks, Mravinsky worked daily four to five hours on the score, during which Shostakovich came to meet with the conductor at either Mravinsky's or his mothers' flat. At last, following the completion of the finale, Shostakovich and Wainberg twice played the Tenth in a four-hand version. On the following day, they returned to several episodes where problems remained, by now the time spent on this symphony far outweighing that of any previous occasion. Mravinsky suggested changes relating to speeds and dynamics that he thought the composer needed to make. Their assistant, the composer Mozhei Wainberg, played the changes on the piano.[12]

In the third movement, there is a dedication to Mravinsky; there is a wonderful shimmer of hope following the terrible brutality of the Scherzo. There pours forth warm elegiac tones from the horn repeated several times as if heralding a better, brighter future. The motif begins in the notation E-A (Evgeny Alexandrovich), as if the composer is conversing with Mravinsky.[13] The orchestra began its work on 4 December, two weeks before the premiere; Mravinsky began to go through the symphony with the ensemble. (In his diary entry for 4 December, for the hours of noon to 3:00 p.m., Mravinsky remarks: "Rehearsal. Run through of the first movement of Shostakovich's Tenth Symphony: play through the problematic sections and the second movement: progress through the third and fourth movements, repeat the fourth and first movements—the orchestra read it very well.")

The alterations to the Tenth proposed by Mravinsky clarified the music's structure, allowing the ideas to be more accurately revealed through the precision of tempi and dynamics: In the first movement, in the main theme at bar 5, in the secondary at bar 17, the place of the reprise at bar 44, at the coda, from bar 65, in the second movement, he wrote for the second motif, from bar 79, the third as from bar 114, the beginning of the entry in the fourth movement from the last markings at the start of the second, third, and so on. The orchestral organization linked with tempo and dynamic markings clarified its emotional mood, form, musical idea, and concept, allowing the music to breathe more freely.

There were some forty modifications in total. However, not all of Mravinsky's proposals appeared in the score, some proving unnecessary after subsequent run-throughs on piano and orchestra. The pianoforte score markings are limited to *agitato* at bar 22 and in seven measures before bar 26, *animando* at bar 42, and in place of *p legato* at bar 5 in the score, there appeared *p semplice*. And apart from these alterations, there came slight shifts in the tempo instructions. Shostakovich wanted to determine the very precise tempo markings not by listening, but by the metronome. For instance, in the second movement, the indication of 200 was altered to 116. The degree of the corrected tempi of diverse elements of the Tenth is revelatory: in the first movement, instead of 76 there is a change to 96, while at bar 65, the tempo is modified to 96.[14]

Original Manuscript	**Original Score**
1st Movement	
76	96
Bar 5 104	108
Bar 14, 5 *rit*	*poco rit.*
Three bars before 21 *poco stringendo*	No instructions
Bar 29 *meno ma tranquillo* = 120	108
Bar 31 *rit. Poco a poco*	No instructions
Bar 35 *a tempo*	No instructions
Bar 41 *poco sostenuto*	No instructions
Bar 57 32	*a tempo* 32
Bar 65 70	116
2nd Movement	
Bar 87 *piu mosso*	No instructions
3rd Movement	
Bar 114 *poco sostenuto*	No instructions
Bar 117 *Largo* 76	96, measure 4—*rit.*
Bar 118 *a tempo, Adagio*	108
Bar 130 *poco accel.*	No instructions
Bar 132 176	80
4th Movement	
116	126
Bar 148 116	No instructions
Bar 153 184	*Allegro* 176[15]

From 10 December there began daily rehearsals with the Philharmonic. Mravinsky wrote in his diary:

> Rehearsal 12:30–1:30: with percussion of the Tenth. Before the sessions, with Shostakovich at his hotel—clarification of questions on the score.
>
> 11 December: 11–3: Rehearsal of the Tenth: strings—first, fourth, and third movements; *4.30-8* rehearsal of the Tenth, brass—first, fourth, and third movements.
>
> 12 December: 11–3: 11–12 strings in second movement; then together in second; full orchestra run-through of complete symphony; complete and third and fourth movements once more.

13 December: 11–3: Rehearsal two repeats of yesterdays noted places; in third repeat run-through of second movement. Middle of second and all of fourth movement.

15 December: 11–3:15: Complete *pp* in finale; *pp* in second movement; beginning of first; general rehearsal of whole symphony. Completion. Tired to exhaustion.

16 December: General rehearsal.

17 December: 11–1: Rehearsal. A little part of the symphony. Concert in the evening. Shostakovich's Tenth—the world premiere. Very successful.

18 December: Evening concert. Repeat of yesterday's concert, not only successful but really good.

The diaries reveal how meticulously the Leningrad maestro organized a new opus for performance. To allow his musicians to grasp a piece of music, it was characteristic for Mravinsky to go through it initially as on 4 December, yet this was just a preamble to the rehearsals. At the very same time, Mravinsky was also priming the world premiere of Salmanov's First Symphony, scheduled for early December. Mravinsky frequently unloaded his inner feelings to friends:

This is a difficult time for me; I am preparing Dmitry Shostakovich's recently completed Tenth Symphony for performance. This work is Great both in its depth of ideas and expressive power. Nonetheless, the symphony demands of its performers maximum resources and complete sympathy with both the world of sorrow and the terrible struggle for one's dignity. The fate of this work, whether it will be a success or failure, almost entirely depends on me; . . . hours of peace, clarity, happiness in my life are linked only with *nature*. However, to leave it now and give oneself up in homage is impossible; beyond the window, there is a fragment of sky and the frozen, icy, autumnal streets of Leningrad.[16]

Mravinsky was acutely sensitive to the dilemma posed by the Tenth. Customarily, Shostakovich symphonies would be programmed as part of the November Festivities, however the première was listed much later. Nevertheless, the musical event of the year for the Leningrad public was the world premiere of Dmitry Shostakovich's Tenth Symphony in E minor. On 17 December 1953, Mravinsky, "with imposing veracity and expression, exposed the emotive and deeply tragic content of the score, with color, agility of thought, and feeling."[17] The Tenth Symphony clearly followed in the tradition of the Fifth, Seventh, and Eighth as great epic symphonic canvases set against a starkly tragic and autobiographical background. Yevgeny Mravinsky "allowed one to see through this work as 'panoramic' associated with different styles of Shostakovich gathered here as in focus; the timbre-intonational affinity from the Fifth, Seventh, and Eighth through to the Piano Concerto and *Lady Macbeth* all prevailed in the Tenth."[18] Leonid Gakkel has written of the Tenth:

The Tenth unforgettable Symphony. From the day of its first performance under Yevgeny Mravinsky, it has shone like an indefatigable beacon of inspiration, both intense and courageous in its language. The Tenth Symphony is synonymous in my listener's consciousness . . . with premieres remembered as events in one's whole life.[19]

There awaited a most different fate in the capital after the Leningrad premiere had proved such an undisputed triumph. The first Moscow performance was scheduled shortly afterward, on 29 December, with Mravinsky in charge of the USSR State Symphony Orchestra. There was still a cloud over Shostakovich following the 1948 Party resolution, and problems almost inevitably emerged for this concert. The rumor that circulated throughout the Composers Union was that the Tenth was "a pessimistic work foreign to realism,"[20] however, few were as perceptive of this conundrum as was Yevgeny Mravinsky. During the final rehearsals, Mravinsky advised Shostakovich that the matter would have to be resolved one way or another. In order to save the Moscow concert, Mravinsky went to speak to Panteleimon Ponomarenko, the newly appointed minister of culture. Ponomarenko was a Leningrad man, his reputation wholly owing to his courageous leadership of the partisan movement, and his credentials in the arts were limited; however, he was not from the Party hierarchy, and he was as yet to reveal his potential for the "thaw" threatening to stimulate the country's artistic life. On the eve of 1954, traditionally a time of celebration, opting for the easy route, the minister consistently refused to see Mravinsky, claiming he was too busy.; however the conductor was persistent and at last managed to gain a meeting.

At the art nouveau Ministry of Culture, Yevgeny Mravinsky listed sixteen different questions on the work's merits and emphasized the need to support its performance. He argued that this was a composition of deep philosophical content, continuing the great symphonic traditions of Russian and world symphonism. The conductor's assiduity and resolve to bolster his long-standing friend impressed the former army commander. It was clear to Ponomarenko that this man was a versatile and eloquent advocate, and one not used to being denied. It was because of Mravinsky's persistence that the minister ultimately conceded to his arguments and asked how he could help. Mravinsky simply requested him to attend the premiere and hear the Tenth for himself— a suggestion that Ponomarenko readily acceded to, thinking that he had gotten off lightly.

On the day of the premiere, Mravinsky was asked permission to issue three hundred complimentary tickets to the Union of Composers. Mravinsky refused this apparently innocent request, keenly aware that this was for a claque who solely wanted to hinder the performance. Mravinsky instructed the box office to sell the tickets to the public. Following the triumphant concert, several leaders of the Composers Union, including Tikhon Khrennikov, Vasily Kucharsky, and Marian Koval, went to Ponomarenko complaining that Shostakovich's Tenth Symphony was a formalist, negative work and needed to be banned, but the minister responded that he personally liked the new symphony and would support its future performances. Rarely had officials from the Composers Union received such a rebuke; they were now forced to beat a retreat. The conservatives were powerful enough to cause damage, albeit of a limited nature; Mravinsky's participation in a Festival of Soviet Music was revoked, and invitations to work with Moscow-based ensembles were restricted.[21]

The Moscow premiere nevertheless evoked a multitude of conflicting judgments and opinion. Almost inevitably, there saw a repeat of the controversy in the Soviet press, leading in turn to intensive discussions in the musical papers. This involved polemics about the future of contemporary music as much as it did the Tenth. In the journal *Sovetskaya Muzika*, there appeared a series of articles on the symphony in 1954, and three days were given to a full debate at the Moscow Composers Union.[22] At this symposium, leading supporters of the Tenth proved to be Kabalevsky, Shaporin, Khachaturyan, and the musicologists Sokolsky and Khubov. Yuri Shaporin found that Shostakovich's piece possessed a deep philosophical nature and that the latest turn to symphonic tragedy as portrayed in the Tenth "is impossible not to recognize as historically justified."[23] Khachaturyan declared that "this was a real symphony," emphasizing its dramaturgy and ability to build and develop in major forms.[24] Sokolsky found an analogy with the philosophical concept of the Tenth and those of J. S. Bach and Musorgsky. "It is impossible to forget the suffering of recent times; one cannot ignore that the forces of darkness again wish to indulge in bloodbaths, with dark clouds again threatening on the horizon."[25]

By force of habit, many still thought in terms of the recent past, reproaching the composer for the complexity of his musical language—giving too little prominence to the underlying heroic and optimistic features of the work—and for its predominantly somber tone. Once again, the new piece attained an epithet: "The 'discordant' Tenth Symphony."[26] The most severe censure was from Yuri Kremlyov: "there are no real themes, genuine song, rhythm, or harmonic relief, based on realistic music; the themes of the symphony are diffuse, weakly formed, and build neither consciousness nor emotion."[27] Shostakovich's usual critics took aim at his new opus, Yarustovsky complaining that "there is too great a depiction of evil and insufficient forces for good. . . . [W]here are the positive ideas in the Tenth Symphony?"[28] More positive points of view prevailed, however. "I am deeply convinced that the conflict it portrays arises from the tension now existing throughout the world,"[29] wrote Kabalevsky. In a major feature, David Oistrakh offered a sober appraisal: "The Tenth Symphony is imbued with noble moral principles, innate humanity, and indisputable affection of a great artist and patriot. Its strength lies in its enormous dramatic consequence, tormented struggle, and the discordant beauty and refinement of its idiom."[30]

Most of the concern was surrounding the third movement, with its autobiographical nature, enclosed within a subtext. The comments of musicologists divulge the incongruous sentiments: "It gives the effect of a gigantic whirlwind engulfing a community."[31] However, the most pertinent review came from a Soviet writer: "Can we find sources for such tragic narration in the reality surrounding us? This is the first question that arises as one listens to the symphony. Moreover, there is the answer: yes, we can. There are profoundly tragic events in social life in our present-day world and great sorrow to be met in the lives of individuals—our contemporaries. Here we can grasp at last the essence of the Tenth. . . . In Shostakovich's symphony we feel the tragedy of a profoundly isolated individual. It seems that the hero of the symphony has to meet the forces of evil single-handedly. Out of his purely personal and hence narrow world. . . . Such a conception of the world is far from that experienced by the majority of Soviet people."[32]

Rabinovich was prepared to allow the music to speak for the composer: "The symphony is primarily a picture of a man who reacts keenly and in different ways to the events of life, who listens carefully and attentively to the voices of life and of his own inner world. This figure strides through all four movements of the symphony. However, who is this man, what are his thoughts and emotions? For the answer, we must listen to the music of the symphony."[33] Dmitry Kabalevsky maintained his support, writing: "as before, I remain convinced of the symphony's profound fidelity to life, in his portrayal of a power hostile to mankind. . . . This may not yet be the dazzling ray of the sun, but it is still the sunrise. The day is dawning."[34]

Mravinsky quickly set down the Tenth Symphony in the studios with the Leningrad Philharmonic Orchestra, and his long-playing records became a benchmark. The cold war had set its own particular tone, yet within a calendar year, Dmitry Mitropolous and the New York Philharmonic performed the Tenth, on 14 and 15 November 1954.[35] The composer Aram Khachaturyan gave succinct appraisal of this symphony: "following the passing of Nikolay Myaskovsky and Sergey Prokofiev, whose fine work developed the classical traditions of the great symphonists of the past, the significance of [Shostakovich's] work in this genre is particularly important now."[36]

As always, little was expressed by the composer himself, apart from this covetous remark: "this is my most free-thinking symphony."[37] This outlook can find analogies in Chekhov describing his plays ubiquitously as "comedies." The American musicologist Boris Schwartz wrote perceptively that the Tenth Symphony "was a work of inner liberation, a human document that astounded listeners. . . . [I]ts role in Soviet music is comparable to Ehrenburg's *The Thaw* in literature."[38] During this era of change, Mravinsky in his assimilation, defense, and ultimately, portrayal of the Tenth proved the greatest champion in heralding the liberalization of the human spirit. One writer commented: "The performance of Yevgeny Mravinsky was glorious; it traumatized with its tragic force, as if in devastating energy. . . . However, no performance anywhere has ever made such a powerful effect as with Mravinsky."[39]

At the opening of the rebuilt Vienna State Opera in 1955, Herbert von Karajan asked Shostakovich which account of the Tenth Symphony was preferable to him; the composer replied without hesitation that Mravinsky's was the finest. Many years later, when the Austrian maestro conducted the Tenth with his Berlin Philharmonic on tour in Leningrad, afterward Karajan rather immodestly asked Mravinsky's opinion of his interpretation. Mravinsky soberly replied that he was indeed impressed, however, he thought that the maestro must have listened to his own recording.[40]

NOTES

1. A. M. Vavilina Mravinskaya, author interview, October 2001.

2. Y. A. Mravinsky, "Iz Dnevniki," *Muzikalnaya Akademia*, no. 4 (1997): 99.

3. Mravinsky, "Iz Dnevniki."

4. D. D. Shostakovich, 27 February 1953, *Muzikalnaya Akademiya*, no. 4 (1997): 94.

5. V. Razhnikov, *Kirill Kondrashin rasskazyvaet* (Moscow: Sovetsky Kompozitor, 1989), 180.

6. A. A. Zolotov, author interview, October 2001.

7. Conversation with P. K. Kondrashin, May 2002.

8. TsGALI, f. 2048, op. 1. ed. khr, 14.

9. S. Khentova, *Shostakovich—Tridzatiletiye 1945–1975* (Leningrad: Sovetsky Kompozitor, 1982), 80.

10. K. Karayev, *Statii, Pismo, Vospominanii* (Moscow: Sovetsky Kompozitor, 1978), 52.

11. Khentova, *Shostakovich—Tridzatiletiye 1945–1975*, 80.

12. Mozhei Wainberg was unfortunate to be related through his wife to the murdered Jewish actor Mikhoels and so spent several months in prison. He was, however, released after Stalin's death and a general amnesty.

13. Kurt Sanderling, quoted in Hans Bitterlich, *Portrait of a Dictatorship*, CD-ROM (Berlin Classics, 0090182BC, 1995), 10.

14. Khentova, *Shostakovich—Tridzatiletiye 1945–1975*, 84–85.

15. Khentova, *Shostakovich—Tridzatiletiye 1945–1975*, 85.

16. Mravinsky, "Iz Dnevniki," 90.

17. V. M. Bogdanov-Berezovsky, *Sovetsky Dirizher* (Leningrad: Muzika, 1956), 169–70.

18. Bogdanov-Berezovsky, *Sovetsky Dirizher*, 170.

19. L. Y. Gakkel, "Iz nablyudeniye nad konzertnoy zhiznyu Leningrada 50–60 godov," in *Muzika i Muzikantov Leningrada* (Leningrad: Sovetsky Kompositor, 1972), 134.

20. Y. Kremlyov, *Sovetskaya Muzika*, no. 5 (1954): 48.

21. Y. A. Mravinsky, "S Yevgeniyem Aleksandrovichem Mravinskovovo," in *V Mire Shostakovicha*, ed. S. M. Khentova (Moscow: Kompositor, 1996), 193–94.

22. Khentova, *Shostakovich—Tridzatiletiye 1945–1975*, 86.

23. Y. Shaporin, "Diskussionaya zametki o simfonisme," *Sovetskaya Muzika* , no. 5 (1955): 42–43.

24. A. M. Khachaturyan, "Desyataya simfoniya Shostakovicha," *Sovetskaya Muzika*, no. 3 (1954): 23.

25. M. M. Sokolsky, "Zrelost i masterstvo," *Sovetskaya Kultura*, 23 February 1954.

26. Y. Kremlyov, *Sovetskaya Muzika*, no. 5 (1955): 48.

27. Y. Kremlyov, *Sovetskaya Muzika*, no. 5 (1955): 48.

28. B. Yarustovsky, *Na Shostakovicha desyataya simfoniya, Sovetskaya Simfonicheskaya Muzika* (Moscow: Muzika), 501.

29. D. B Kabalevsky, *Sovetskaya Muzika*, no. 5 (1954): 3.

30. Y. Soroker, *David Oistrakh* (Jerusalem, Tarbut, 1981), 149.

31. F. Youen, *Shostakovich Symphony No. 10* (London: Saga Records, 1964).

32. D. Rabinovich, *Dmitry Shostakovich* (London: Lawrence and Wishart, 1959), 132.

33. Rabinovich, *Dmitry Shostakovich*, 132–33.

34. D. B. Kabalevsky, *Sovetskaya Muzika*, no. 5 (1954): 3.

35. Khentova, *Shostakovich—Tridzatiletiye 1945–1975*, 88.

36. A. I. Khachaturyan, "Desyataya simfoniya Shostakovicha," *Sovetskaya Muzika*, no. 3 (1954): 25.

37. D. D. Shostakovich, "O Desyatoy simfoniya," *Sovetskaya Muzika*, no. 6 (1954).

38. B. Schwarz, *Music and Musical Life in Soviet Russia 1917–1982* (Bloomington: Indiana University Press, 1983), 273.

39. A. Vieru, "Neskolko mysley o Shostakoviche," in *Dmitry Shostakovich*, ed. Grigory M. Shneerson (Moscow: Sovetsky Kompozitor, 1976), 271.

40. A. M. Vavilina Mravinskaya, author interview, July 2001.

Chapter Twelve

Inna

I had great affliction.

—J. S. Bach, *Cantata for All Time*

The bestowing of the title "Peoples Artist of the USSR" on Yevgeny Mravinsky was a foremost tribute corresponding to the honor awarded to his great compatriot Fyodor Shalyapin and gratitude for the conductor's constancy in his devotion to both his city and its prowess in the arts. It also manifested a buffer of impregnability between him and his enemies. All the same, the title was of little consequence; more important to him was that he could still find spiritual comfort in the church. Consolation for Mravinsky's soul was that his roots lay here. He could always find release in the wild Russian countryside. The streets, squares, and gardens of Leningrad were those upon which the great Russian composers and writers had walked; Mravinsky had lived here for half a century, and Leningrad's quarters were as close to his spirit as his orchestra and music. Here was spoken that so treasured and exquisite Petersburg tongue. However, for the honored Yevgeny Mravinsky, there was still much that eluded him in his private life.

In 1953, the Leningrad Regional Party planned to disperse the orchestra of Leningrad Radio—a proposal that Mravinsky vigorously opposed. Since 1928, this refined ensemble had served the public admirably through its radio concerts and had broadcast famously to Western Europe; Karl Eliasberg conducted the *Leningrad* Symphony at the height of the siege in August 1942. Mravinsky urged that the musicians be taken under the auspices of the Philharmonic and that it act as a reserve, filling in when Mravinsky's Philharmonic was on tour. Mravinsky argued that he would find funding from the ministry by taking the Radio Orchestra under his wing at the Philharmonic.

This complementary Philharmonic would perform at the large towns in the Leningrad region: Vyborg, Gatchina, and Volkhov. The concern of the Regional Party was that the ensembles did not validate their expenditure, and that there was no obligation for two large symphony orchestras when professional orchestras already existed at the Kirov and Maly Opera and Ballet Theatres. Mravinsky's contention was the status of classical music was more exalted than ever and that the state must provide for the city's great and flourishing musical traditions.

The Ministry of Culture supported the Philharmonic, which was allowed to give concerts for children to mitigate the petition for money from the education budget. Mravinsky had prepared a solution regarding the Radio Orchestra, and had done so as meticulously as he had done any Philharmonic run through; the officials could not but be in awe of his thoroughness and commitment. Mravinsky was so convincing that ultimately the Party gave its reluctant agreement to the Radio Orchestra being moved under the auspices of the Philharmonic, with its own subscription series and the staff retained, with Rabinovich as conductor. For Mravinsky and the arts community in the city, it was a victory; nevertheless, the director of the Philharmonic (Ponomaryev) warned Mravinsky that the Party would exact its quid pro quo.[1]

The fate of the Leningrad Radio Symphony Orchestra was determined at the Smolny headquarters of the Regional Committee of the Communist Party. The buildings had been in use since 1917, initially as the Bolshevik center, and housed a finishing school for girls of the gentry; nearby, the picturesque ochre-blue Italian renaissance domes of the Smolny Cathedral offered the cityscape a surreal revelation on the square of the Dictatorship of the Proletariat.[2] It was here that on a weekly basis Mravinsky would pull up in his official black limousine and, on submitting his documents to the KGB guard, be met by a small young woman—Inna Mikhailovna Serikova—who would chaperon the conductor up the narrow stairwell to the cultural department's office on the second floor. The vivacious secretary enchanted Mravinsky so much that he would take her flowers, and the pair would spend idle moments chatting in the tiny little anteroom before the formal business meeting. It was the initiation of an unfeigned love affair—at the age of fifty years, Mravinsky was charismatic, strong, and energetic, and the whole world seemed to lay before him. It was at the Smolny that his aunt Alexandra Kollontay had taken part in the congress that pronounced the Great October Socialist Revolution in 1917 and proscribed Mravinsky's caste from power. It was a paradox that here in this building sharing so magniloquent a legacy in sociopolitical and cultural life, Yevgeny Mravinsky made a crucial step in his life.[3]

Yevgeny Alexandrovich Mravinsky's first two wives—Marianna and Olga—had been faithful and met his needs. His supreme attachment, however, was to the orchestra. It is scarcely unexpected that Mravinsky's diaries record a pressing frustration with his personal life; both marriages deteriorated into futile relationships. Mravinsky, having met intense feelings in poetry, music, and the natural world, now found obsession in another human being. Serikova had been *au fait* with the conductor from a distance, admiring his thrilling interpretations of Brahms and Beethoven, of Scriabin and Wagner. Her experience of him was from afar, never intimate, yet they shared the same world. Mravinsky for her was like a god, someone distant yet close in spirit. He was fascinated by her charm and vivaciousness, while Inna was taken by his savoire faire.

The ensuing affair was acknowledged to a tiny coterie of friends. Among the first to know of the liaison was Serikova's former student at the Leningrad Music Institute and her alter ego, Alexandra Vavilina. She advised Inna to get rid of him, as Mravinsky was too difficult, apart from the fact that he was much older and already married. In what became a protracted ménage à trois, Mravinsky's interaction with his wife Olga remained courteous, yet the passion Mravinsky experienced with Inna was something that he could not relinquish. The conductor avowed his gallantry by enlightening his wife and assenting to Olga's rejection of a divorce. Mravinsky abruptly left her and the household shared with his mother, the family servant Klava, and two cats. In the next years, Olga would dutifully attend Mravinsky's concerts, sitting in the conductor's room and discussing the evening's performance with Mravinsky and other musicians there. When guests, such as the London Philharmonic in 1959, arrived on tour, the "official" Madame Mravinsky would regale the visitors with her excellent German. She was there to see off the London Philharmonic's Adrian Boult at the Moscow Station with her husband in 1959, and afterward, as usual, they broke off and went to separate homes.[4]

The liaison was a subject of concern for Mravinsky's aging mother, Yelizaveta Nikolayevna. She realized that the marriage with Olga had long since become unsatisfactory, and she could find forgiveness in that her son's love for Inna was genuine. Yevgeny had always been the focus her affection. All her long life, she had dedicated herself to him; she was his most ardent listener and wrote her own "critique" after each concert. If she had not had the career she had yearned for in tsarist Russia, her search for excellence, beauty, and the deification of art nevertheless was consummated through her progeny.

Yelizaveta Nikolayevna had absolved him in other matters; in the 1920s, an affair with a ballet dancer at the Vaganov Ballet School resulted in a daughter, christened Yelena. Shortly afterward, the mother, Lydia Nikolayevna, hurriedly married a Party member; nevertheless, Mravinsky supported the daughter, who was exiled to Tashkent during the war years.[5] Olga's family was of the former merchant class, and she was constantly at the theater or cinema with friends, playing the role of a famous musician's spouse. For his new life with Inna, Mravinsky set up residence in a small flat near the Taurides Palace on Tverskaya Street. The recognized wife was under public scrutiny at the Philharmonic and would accompany him on tour to the West, all while he was residing with Inna on the other side of the city. It was the most surprising part of his life, one that would go on and on, for four interminable years. Olga supposed this *affaire d'amour* would pass; in spite of everything, she awaited his homecoming. Mravinsky, however, eventually managed to extract a divorce from Olga, after which he quickly married Inna, in January 1960, before taking her on tour with the orchestra shortly afterward.

The new woman in Mravinsky's life—Inna Mikhailovna Serikova—was born in Petrograd on 15 February 1923 and studied at the Conservatoire. Following graduation, she began teaching "Music of the Peoples of the USSR" at the Leningrad Music Institute. Among her pupils was the composer Boris Tischenko, who remembers Serikova as "a wonderful, precious, petite aesthetic woman."[6] In postwar Leningrad, Serikova moved to work at the Radio Symphony Orchestra, and after some years there, she accepted an appointment at the Cultural Department of the Regional Committee of the Communist Party. Regional Secretary Rodionov was an influential patron of the Philharmonic, and Serikova filled her post as dutifully as any other. Inna Mikhailovna was a deeply devout young woman, of medium height and with short dark hair, and she possessed a charisma—when she smiled, she seemed to make the whole room share with her.[7] "Yevgeny Alexandrovich loved her to distraction."[8] Mravinsky's passion was so infectious that he would photograph her in all possible poses and in almost every situation, filling some seventeen massive photo albums with thousands of photographs of her alone.[9]

For Yevgeny Mravinsky, the years with Inna Serikova were the most satisfying of his long life. Climbing the heights of success, however, was unlike the feat of an Olympian; here were the demands of high art coupled with the ever higher demands of the public—one could no sooner immerse oneself in the glory before the adoring acolytes would demand more. With the least mistake, everything could suddenly change. However, for Mravinsky and his orchestra, more awards and accolades would be offered, and the deep reassurance of an intense love at last allowed him to fully release his artistic potential.

The Leningrad Philharmonic now visited Moscow for the first time since the war. Mravinsky and Sanderling gave eight concerts of their standard repertoire by Debussy, Mozart, Prokofiev, Shostakovich, and Tchaikovsky. For the Muscovites, it was as if an orchestra were touring from another planet—here was a distinct level of artistic endowment and a refinement in playing rarely heard in the capital. "How perfectly and compellingly he opens up the ideas and the emotional subject of such multifaceted and challenging work. . . . His style acts as a paradigm for our young conductors."[10]

In 1955, following an interval of nine years, the Leningrad Philharmonic traveled westward, the focal point of the tour being the Prague Spring Festival. One player wrote:

> Prague met us with a blinding May sunshine and unbelievably immaculate streets. The order was so prevalent, one thought akin to a hospital ward, yet there were no rubbish bins anywhere to be seen; to throw on the pavement either a little paper wrapper or a cigarette is as unthinkable as it is to give a round of applause after the end of the first movement of a symphony.
>
> Cigarettes were still not the fashion then; most of us smoked *papirosi*, [and] at once there arose a problem—how to get rid of the buts? I found an easy solution: on one side of the case, I kept some *papirosi*; on the other side under elastic, I kept unused *papirosi*. After a rehearsal, Yevgeny Alexandrovich unexpectedly approached a group of musicians and asked, "Do you have any *papirosi*?" In response, several cigarettes were at once proffered. Yet, one must say that Yevgeny Alexandrovich, as a smoker, always favored cigarettes or *papirosi* of the most down-to-earth or inexpensive kind. I remember there was self-styled "Pamir," in my opinion the cheapest; on the dirty gray cardboard packet is a landscape with a camper walking with a backpack. These cigarettes back home were called by wits of the day—"The miserable in the mountains." This was one of the favorite blends of Yevgeny Alexandrovich. He much preferred them to "Kents," "Dunhill," and "Chesterfields."
>
> Looking at our proffered packets, Yevgeny Alexandrovich enquired, "Don't you at least have 'Belomora'?" With great pride, I took out of my case a packet and presented it to Yevgeny Alexandrovich. Then, what a surprise! On one side of the case, instead of cigarettes were four or five butts; my face instantly changed, becoming the same color of the scarlet chairs of our concert hall. Nonetheless, Yevgeny Alexandrovich with the nobility constantly in his disposition took one scent of the aroma with glee and cheering me, "Don't be so embarrassed. Really, in general, there are no differences between us. Its identical in real life—isn't it so?"[11]

In between the Prague dates (there were eight in all), the respected *Rudé Právo* wrote "there can be no doubt that this magnificent orchestra under the direction of their conductor will be among the highlights of this Prague Spring. Before us is a virtuoso collective of high artistry and rare perfection."[12] The enthusiastic appraisal led to demonstrative receptions in Bratislava and Brno. The Philharmonic returned to Prague, where their two concerts ended in a musical culmination of the tenth postwar festival: "The Leningrad Philharmonic has captivated the hearts of the musical public so much that this jubilee festival could not come to an end otherwise."[13] Mravinsky took tricky touring programs to Czechoslovakia: the Sixth and Tenth Symphonies by Shostakovich, the Fifth Symphony by Prokofiev, Beethoven's Fourth Symphony, and Tchaikovsky's Fifth Symphony. Not all the approval came from Czechoslovak sources; the music correspondent of *The Times* dispatched a report to London proclaiming the Leningrad Philharmonic "may occupy a place among the best world orchestras . . . the members of the Leningrad orchestra may all be portrayed as virtuoso musicians, and their discipline and integral playing is one unified excellence."[14] At last, the curtain was lifting for Mravinsky and his musicians.

Another page in Mravinsky's collaboration with Shostakovich was the Violin Concerto, among the finest works introduced during this decade. The premiere was overdue as much for political reasons as because of the soloist's disinclination to present it. David Oistrakh wrote: "Only now one can understand that this is an awe-inspiring work, and I have fallen in love with it with all my soul."[15] The idea for writing a concerto for violin and orchestra originated from the magnificent series given by Oistrakh in the 1946–1947 season.[16] Shostakovich now believed that he had found a faithful confederate: "the extraordinary musicality of David Fyodorovich, the beauty of his tone, and his magnificent technique cannot naturally pass me by."[17] The themes of the Violin Concerto came to Shostakovich quickly; the sketches were set down at Komarovo, outside Leningrad, in a five-day spell from 21 to 25 July 1947; yet the manuscript would be taken up again, and it would not be completed until 24 March 1948.[18] The work bore a resemblance to a symphony with a leading, solo violin part; as in his finest symphonies and string quartets, the profound, tragic tone was key to the conception. In his own words, the violinist described "the wide-ranging possibilities, first in expressing the most profound feelings, thoughts, and moods."[19] The mode of the concerto and its language and melodies contains those matching qualities, as do all the symphonies bearing a complexity of structure, and Oistrakh unhesitatingly admitted that even for him, the Violin Concerto was not so "trouble-free to play."[20]

The form of the new piece also departed from the traditional concerto in that rather than the usual three-movement framework, there were five-movements—as in his last two symphonies. The tragic theme is heard immediately in the opening "Nocturne,"—in which two soloists play two melodies, similar in rhythmic structure—and the sad foreboding bears a deep element throughout the entire work. The soloist has dialogues with woodwind and French horn. In different sections of the work, solo instruments take the lead, emphasizing the philosophical concept. In the Scherzo, Oistrakh found that it, "makes sense of the slow movement, allowing one to think that there is something in this music that is evil, demonic, and spiky," like barbed wire.[21] Its harmonics at first pose a frightful problem for the soloist, something almost nonexistent in the violin repertoire. The heart of the work is the "Passacaglia," which expresses the innermost funereal tragedy. It evokes comparisons with the great Eighth Symphony and Asaf'yev's words "about the epic song signifying the resistance of a human heart meeting terror head-on."[22] The "Finale—Burlesque" Oistrakh considered among the most effective, festive, and optimistic, following Tchaikovsky's model. The Violin Concerto became one of the most important creations by Shostakovich of the postwar period. It was for these reasons that the work remained under wraps until a time when it could be unveiled before a mature, more aware musical public.

The score had been with Mravinsky for quite some time, and in a letter, Shostakovich asks about the possibilities of a first performance, writing from Komarovo in early August 1954: "We are leaving tomorrow. Moreover, I shall soon be in Moscow for some time. D. F Oistrakh has learned my violin concerto, and I would like to give it a go. On 25 September, Alexander Gauk will play my Tenth Symphony. Will anything happen?"[23] Yet alterations to the work were being slowly introduced by the composer himself, in a letter to Oistrakh, some months later, Shostakovich wrote: "Dear Dodik, I am leaving the old violin score with you, as the new version isn't ready yet. I ask you please, if it's not too demanding, to come and see me tomorrow, on 26 December. I want you to help reveal the two finished movements to Y. A. Mravinsky. The first movement isn't ready yet."[24] These lengthy years allowed some alterations in both the orchestral part and solo. In 1953, there materialized a second edition,[25] and it was this that was given its world premiere on 29 October 1955.

Of the preparations for the premiere, Isaak Glikman remembers that "on 18 October 1955 Shostakovich traveled with David Oistrakh to Leningrad to show the concerto to Mravinsky, who at once determined to prime it with his orchestra, with the scrupulousness and attention customary in the disposition of this eminent conductor. On 25 October, the first rehearsal took place. Dmitry Dmitrevich was in my company at the rehearsals. Oistrakh played beyond reproof, and the impression created was devastating."[26]

Mravinsky's Diary

1956: 3.2—Rehearsal—Reworking of *Oberon*. General Mozart and Shostakovich (Shostakovich told me "The force really catches you"). 4.2—Rehearsals—Shostakovich Violin concerto. First performance in Moscow! 4.5—Rehearsal—Reworking of Mozart B major and the second movement of Shostakovich. Shostakovich was at all the rehearsals. He appeared very contented. 5.5—Rehearsal—Bloody reworking at Shostakovich's concerto with Oistrakh. 6.5—Concert

Mozart—Symphony in B major

Mozart—Violin Concerto in A major
Shostakovich—Violin Concerto (D. Oistrakh)
(Very great success. Shostakovich was there).[27]

Following the premiere, the composer wrote to Mravinsky:

> Now I am busy preparing the score and piano part of the Violin Concerto for
> printing. To this purpose, I have looked over the score and have made some cor-
> rections. I decided to inform you so that you can insert these amendments in
> your own score, for your future performances. In any account, I put it in writing
> for you. They are altogether in the second movement . . . 17 adjustments in all.
> Everything is there. The changes in the solo part I shall introduce when I come
> to Leningrad. Until then I shall live for the Leningrad and Moscow premieres of
> the Violin Concerto.[28]

One unconventional piece introduced by Mravinsky and his musicians on 23
February 1955 was the Violin Concerto by Boris Klyuzner (with the young
Mark Vaiman), which attracted Mravinsky with its out-of-the-ordinary ideas,
professionalism, and most essential for Mravinsky, clarity of form.[29] The
fresh postwar generation of composers, pupils of Shostakovich and students
of the Leningrad Conservatoire for whom Mravinsky and his orchestra gave
premieres, included Arno Babadzhanyan, Janis Ivanovs, Andrey Balanchivadze, Stasis Vainionas, Andrey Shtogarenko, Boris Tchaikovsky,
Valery Galynin, Venyamin Basner, Lucien Prigozhin, Andrey Petrov, Sergey
Slonimsky, and Vladimir Tytovich.

In December 1955, Mravinsky turned his attention to the Ukrainian Boris
Lyatoshinsky's Third Symphony, unveiling the premiere of the modified
work in an impressive triumph. Here the conductor played a conspicuous role
in this "revision." In 1937, his three-movement Second Symphony in B minor was tagged as "formalism," and the Moscow premiere was cancelled.[30] In
1948, the local Composers Union did not miss the opportunity to recall
Lyatoshinsky's former sins and to pronounce him leader of the "formalist"
movement. His next symphony, the four-movement Third in B minor, subti-
tled "Peace will Conquer War," had its Kiev premiere in 1951 under Nathan
Rakhlin and was criticized.[31] The composer determined to petition Mravinsky, who resolved to perform it as soon as possible. The Leningrad conductor invited Lyatoshinsky to his flat and played it through to him on the piano,
having introduced changes in dynamics and tempi. The composer was astonished at the attention paid by Mravinsky to his neglected opus.[32] The critics
paid singular attention to the composer's mastery in handling the work's
evocative "leitmotif"—the momentous variations strike a chord in similar
functional motifs in Liszt, Franck, and Scriabin.[33]

In his rendition, Mravinsky neglected even a hint of *ad libitum*, as marked in the score, and took the main theme at a very austere rhythm, at a constant *fortissimo*, making it sound mechanical and forced. The conductor's portrayal personified some evil, fatalistic power. There is delivered a prolonged mourning theme, as a rejoinder on the cor anglais singing somewhat inhibited yet rhythmically rigid. The restrained development at the entry of the theme in the *Sonata allegro* section is crucial to Mravinsky's careful treatment defining the required balance moving the complete notion. The opening *Andante maestoso* is forceful, with the subsequent *Allegro impetuoso* assuming an invigorating, stormy pace. The tempo is expressed unsurprisingly on the strings, and the measure does not halt for a moment when the calculated theme is engaged by the woodwind. There comes a predictable image of melee with all its associated connotations. The lament in the linking section is without vibrato, arriving at a "white" sound. Mravinsky directs the monumental "theme of the people" without intensifying the tempo, holding back the apotheosis, and stamping out the certainty that the sequence of events has finished.

Mravinsky took on the awe-inspiring "Nocturne" with understated exactness, and at the immense crescendo one has the sense this relates the heartfelt public lament. It is as if one is witnessing a string of grotesque masks, and Mravinsky clearly depicts a diabolic leer in the Scherzo—a hint from Hieronymus Bosch or El Greco. There rises a brilliant waltz motif in the trio with embryonic variations in a folklore character, imparting the sense of a surreal Mephistophelean masquerade.

In the finale, there returns an animated festive march, with intrusion from the woodwind urging some kind of exultant conquest. Every thematic variation is buoyant in affect, reminiscent of some naïve cinematic documentary style. Lyatoshinsky said that Rheingold Glière propped up the superficial and empty "social-realistic" mode.[34] The metamorphosis to shadowy tone colors bears an analogy with Tchaikovsky's Fifth (Mravinsky always contended that the finale is an apotheosis of evil). Kabalevsky believed that "in the finale there is a celebration and joy, but this is of a tortured, oppressed subject matter."[35] Mravinsky unearthed an overstatement in the finale's confidence and intensity; the neurotic brutality expressed in the finale is too bubbly, and it undoubtedly embellished the fusion of mastery in the polyphony revised by Mravinsky to portray satire versus the classic refinement of the preceding three movements.[36] When asked why he performed the Lyatoshinsky symphony, Mravinsky responded "it is adequate to express that I wished to perform it, nothing more can be said. . . ."[37] His recording of the Third Symphony remains the supreme portrayal of writing at the forefront of another symphonic thread in Soviet music.[38]

Mravinsky's zeal for modern-day music was not indeed appreciated; Shebalin nitpicked: "we require enthusiastic performers, above all conductors for the unaffected, dynamic propaganda of Soviet music. Nevertheless, we have hardly any of them. It is impracticable to fault Yevgeny Mravinsky for a lack of passion; he performs with a committed will two or three composers, yet quite fittingly doesn't gladly conduct any others."[39]

During this phase, the Philharmonic arrived at a peak in performing standard, and in popularity:

> I joined the Conservatoire to study with Professor Elenu—a former pupil of Leopold Auer—and of course my first goal was to try to get to the Philharmonic's concerts, and we students would try anything to gain entrance. There was an unparalleled peak in playing during this epoch. One sensed the occasion just walking to the Philharmonic: people would approach one on Nevsky asking if one had a spare ticket; the crowds were so big, special detachments of militia would marshal the eager throng, who would just stand and stare at those lucky enough to have a ticket.[40]

The orchestra's third major tour, in the summer of 1956, covered Austria, the German Democratic Republic (GDR), Switzerland, and West Germany. The Philharmonic arrived by special train at Berlin's Hauptbanhoff station for its pioneer engagements on German soil. It was the opening of a new, exciting vista; here at the old musical centers Mravinsky experienced the same old reservations about performing, even a fear of failure, before audiences who had heard all the great musicians. One of these, the former conductor of the Leipzig Gewandhaus Orchestra, Hermann Abendroth, had often directed Mravinsky's orchestra. "Thanks to its chief conductor, Mravinsky, the orchestra has developed appreciably, attaining exalted musical refinement. One is amazed by the determined endeavor of the orchestra and its capacity to perform."[41] Mravinsky had keenly anticipated meeting Abendroth on his home soil, however the German maestro had passed away in Jena just hours before. Mravinsky received a telegram from Abendroth written just before his death; unknowingly he replied, and only on the following day did he learn of his friend's departure. Mravinsky was invited to conduct the Leipzig orchestra, yet turned the offer down, as he was to decline others in the future.[42] Starting with five concerts in Berlin, Leipzig, and Dresden, "The Leningrad musicians . . . showed what such a magnificent ensemble can do after so many years under such a great conductor."[43] The first night at the Schauspielhaus on Friedrichstrasse included the German premiere of Shostakovich's Violin Concerto, Mravinsky accompanying David Oistrakh, followed by Mozart's overture to *Marriage of Figaro* and Tchaikovsky's *Francesca da Rimini*. Here were the citadels of European culture, in which the magisterial German repertoire was alive with the traditions of Brahms, Liszt, Schumann, and Wagner and held memories of Weingartner and Nikisch, Walter and Furtwängler. Despite the ravaging of these cities in the Second World War and a divided country, adherence to the old values remained constant. Making the short journey westward, the orchestra made its debut in West Berlin's Titania Palast, with its full audience of three thousand. A normally bellicose West Berlin press enthused: "Mravinsky's gestures unified the orchestra in a cogent, disciplined organism, . . . this ensemble is a paradigm for many Western European orchestras."[44] West German artistic centers—Hamburg, Munich, Cologne, and Stuttgart—offered rapturous praise. Under the banner "Light from the East" the Philharmonic continued to receive accolades for playing with "an excitement in its artistic power hardly conceivable in any Western European orchestra—the superlative sound of the orchestra, its discipline, towering technique, inspired execution, and musicality."[45]

Mravinsky and his musicians traveled by continental express to Switzerland for concerts in Geneva and Lausanne, which drew the attention of musicians such as Otto Klemperer, Jascha Heifitz, Nathan Milstein, and Andrés Segovia, all of whom had given concerts with the orchestra before the war. In Geneva, Mravinsky conducted Mozart's overture to *Marriage of Figaro*, Shostakovich's Violin Concerto, and Tchaikovsky's *Pathétique*. The Philharmonic received a telegram from Mravinsky's predecessor, Fritz Steidry, who expressed his regrets that he could not attend their performances and his congratulations on their triumph.[46] This history-making tour ended with their debut at the Mozart Bicentennial in Vienna. At the festival, some of the world's finest musicians appeared, including Böhm, van Beinum, Krips, Karajan, and Walter. Mravinsky offered Mozart's Symphony in B-flat K.319, and Oistrakh performed the Concerto in A major K.219 and the overture to *Marriage of Figaro*. "The Leningrad Philharmonic is an orchestra of the highest class, and we award them the honor of best ensemble; the Leningrad is the most accomplished of all orchestras at the festival. Yevgeny Mravinsky is a great master and trainer of this orchestra."[47] Mravinsky's repertoire included Tchaikovsky's Fifth and Sixth Symphonies and the Shostakovich Violin Concerto.

The orchestra spent some more days at the Grosser Konzerthaussaal taping Tchaikovsky's late symphonies; Kurt Sanderling set down Tchaikovsky's Fourth (he also recorded the Second Symphonies of both Beethoven and Rachmaninov, the latter in Berlin), and Mravinsky recorded the Fifth and Sixth Symphonies. The Fifth was made in three sessions on 26–27 June, while the *Pathétique* was done in a single day using just two periods in seven hours with a break in between. The Deutsche Grammophon (DG) producer and *tonmeister* Heinrich Keilholz and Wolfgang Lohse were in charge of the *Pathétique* session.[48] Rarely has such a famous recording been made so efficiently. Among those present, Professor Schiller exclaimed: "Es war eine Heldentat." These records astonished many for their remarkable quality. Edward Greenfield wrote in *Gramophone* that the records were "a demonstration disc with many collectors."[49] The new long-playing discs brought many more admirers for the Leningrad Philharmonic, which extended its audience, creating a "pre-echo" for their future worldwide tours. For Mravinsky's orchestra, it would be the first of eight visits to the Austrian capital and the beginning of a very special relationship.

Mravinsky's Diary

1956: Went out onto the balcony. The swallows were in the heights and one could hear the shimmer of their wings. On the way down to the water, I met Orlov, who invited me to a celebratory dinner with Zapolotzky. (Close of the Festival). One can do without it. After breakfast, Marta appeared—her reproaches as to why one had not been to visit her. We went to Nina Cherkasova. She was out on the balcony. (On death; about man's merit by the past, yet particular to the future). 4 p.m.—a car arrives. Coffee and cognac with Kapetzky in "Pupe." 6 p.m. at home. Searching for a way out of declining the Prague trip, for which I had given my consent to Kapetzky. Anxiety. High blood pressure. Decide to send a telegram canceling the trip. Spent an evening at "Artists of the Bolshoi Theatre." One was moved by the unexpected charm of the Baturin family.

In 1956, a substantial and authoritative biography by one of Mravinsky's colleagues from his student days, Valerian Bogdanov-Berezovsky, appeared. The young musicologist Leonid Gakkel illustrated the irreplaceable significance of the conductor to the city's cultural ambience during this time: "In the socially accepted precepts, there is nurtured the publicly cherished phenomenon of 'one's artist.' One's performer!"[50] No one epitomized the Leningrad style and the classical heritage of Russian music more than Mravinsky did. The center stage in Leningrad in October 1956 was a concert marking the fiftieth birthday of Dmitry Shostakovich; the program included *Festive Overture* and the Fifth and Sixth Symphonies. Mravinsky believed the symphonies reflected the composer's finest work and bore a common thread in capturing dark Shakespearean tragedy. If Mravinsky empathized with a compatriot's oeuvre, he also paid attention to his long-time friend and colleague Václav Talich, to whom he wrote: "During these long years of service to music, you have generously presented to the people all your boundless talent and the whole of your heart."[51] Talich had suffered as artistic director in Prague, and Mravinsky had much sympathy in Talich's plight. In his "retirement" from the conductorship of the Czech Philharmonic, the Czech had suffered for defiantly promoting his country's music and becoming aware that his work was ostracized in the postwar regime.

In fact, there were fresh troubles in the Philharmonic's internal life. The reasons were as always: political intervention and checks on cultural life, including constraints on the musicians themselves. A system of "collegiality" was set up in which "elected" members of the Communist Party of the Soviet Union (CPSU), Komsomol, and trade unions would exercise a veto on all affairs; in exchange for the "terror" of the Stalinist years, the new legislation enforced the hold of the Communist Party over all facets of life. The Leningrad Philharmonic of the 1950s was at a peak in performance, as the viola player Valentin Stadler verifies: "When we traveled abroad on tour, I listened to other orchestras, and one can say with confidence that no other orchestra I heard came within the range of playing, particularly of the string section."[52]

The new Eleventh Symphony by Shostakovich took shape during the summer of 1957, and he completed it on 4 August.[53] It was ready for performance that autumn, and one of the first to see the score was Khachaturyan, who wrote, "there is always something novel in the dramaturgical conception as well as the purely technical contrivances."[54] The first auditions took place during August 1957 at Komarovo for a select group. Together with the Moscow-based Meyerovich, the composer played it to the Leningrad Board of Composers on 17 September and auditioned it at the Moscow Board a week later.[55] Mravinsky made comments to the media that the Eleventh Symphony was primed for premiere, that the orchestral parts were copied and the Philharmonic could begin sectional rehearsals in the second half of October.

Five world premieres were offered as part of the Festival of Soviet Music in 1957. Mravinsky's orchestra gave concerts of Prokofiev's Sixth Symphony and his *Cantata Alexander Nevsky*, Myaskovsky's Twenty-Seventh Symphony, Khachaturyan's *Rhapsody for Cello and Orchestra*, Sviridov's *In Memory of Sergei Yesenin* song cycle, and the Seventh and Tenth Symphonies by Shostakovich. Center stage was engaged by premieres of Salmanov's *Cantata—The Twelve*, based on Alexander Blok's eponymous poem, and Ustvolskaya's symphonic poem *The Hero's Exploit*. The culmination was Shostakovich's latest symphony. Mravinsky said in an interview that "Shostakovich's own individual language is rather laconic, yet is implicit to his listeners."[56]

Consequent upon the composers' newly attained preeminence, the Eleventh was available at once to several orchestras, with the intention that the symphony be run simultaneously. Therefore, it was the USSR State Symphony Orchestra under Nathan Rakhlin who gave the first performance, on 30 October in the Large Hall of the Moscow Conservatoire. The Leningrad premiere took place shortly afterward, on 3 November, and the symphony was repeated there in following days. Mravinsky twinned the Eleventh Symphony with Haydn's Symphony no. 88 in G minor. Subsequently, the Eleventh was listed with Ustvolskaya's symphonic poem and Klyuzner's Violin Concerto. The performances created an overwhelmingly powerful impression on its audiences. Israel Nestyev christened the new work a "Russian Requiem."[57]

Unlike with past Shostakovich works, innumerable positive reviews of the Eleventh appeared; Lev Lebedinsky praised the use of folk song in the orchestral fabric,[58] while another critic analyzed its rhythmic-intonational idiosyncrasies[59] and Popov discovered parallels with classical Beethoven, Berlioz, and the pictorial invention of the "kuchkists." Relationships with other composers' styles were unearthed: "the broad culmination of the work is offered in Tchaikovsky's typical factura while one can hear the tragic imagery of Musorgsky."[60] Nest'yev evoked Musorgsky, since whom, he wrote, there has "not appeared such force and originality in the depiction of Russian national tragedy."[61] There was a note of irony cast in the use of song in the symphonic genre. Anisimov wrote that the finale expressed "the composer's magisterial approach to tragedy."[62]

The actor Nikolay Cherkasov was in raptures writing in *Pravda*:

I have often heard programmatic music that one can fully understand only with the assistance of notes. On this occasion, I was compelled during one hour of continual sound, by both the virtually vocal expression and visual clarity of musical imagery; one did not for a moment lose one's attention or thread of development. The composer achieved this by an abstract of expressive themes in symphonic music. The idea of awakening revolutionary conscience of the masses and the inseparable power of the people rising in a just struggle for their own freedom and happiness was expressed by the composer with exceptional conviction feasible only through an artist of great talent.[63]

Of course, the events of the three Russian revolutions were close to many—for wholly different reasons—no less so for the Mravinsky family, one of whom was an active participant and left her own reminiscences of the 1905 Revolution. Recalled Alexandra Kollontay, one of the most outstanding women of the Revolution:

Bloody Sunday found me on the streets. I went with the demonstrators to the Winter Palace, and the spectacle of the savage violence meted out to unarmed working people imprinted itself forever on my memory. 9 January was sunny and frosty. From every corner of St. Petersburg, the city's poor wound their way in endless files toward the tsar's palace. The lines of demonstrators crisscrossed the old city like the threads of a spider web. The people crowded close to the palace and waited. They waited patiently for an hour, then another hour: would the tsar not come to them? Who would accept the petition—the workers' petition—to the tsar? However, the tsar did not emerge. The entreaties of the unarmed people were answered by a bugle call. It rang out with unusual resonance and clarity in the frosty air. We could not help glancing at one another. "What's that?" Someone beside me asked. "It's the signal for the troops to straighten ranks," said someone in the crowd reassuringly. Again we waited, tense and with a vague foreboding. Another signal. The troops stirred slightly. Yet, the crowd was still smiling. It was an unarmed crowd, which waited and hoped, shifting from foot to foot from the cold and the frost. There was a third signal, and then an unusual booming sound. "What's that? They're shooting, its nothing." Said a voice, "those are just blanks." Yet people were falling nearby—women, children— the children dropping like wounded sparrows in the snow from the railings of the Alexandrovsky Gardens. "Don't worry, it's an accident." The people could not believe what was happening. But the tsar's mounted police were already galloping to the attack—to attack the people![64]

Mravinsky expressed the symphony's significance:

The Eleventh Symphony is the most epic of all symphonies. Here all the movements have, one could say, an objective content (expressing historical events), but at the same time include organically the artists' inner world, and hence this music sounds as an emotional and personal expression. There is also the link of Shostakovich with the Decembrists, Belinsky, and the artists of the "1860s" being particularly evident). With such an idiosyncratic opening in the finale (Nabat), there is heard the stirring, angry voice of the composer himself in the music. This is an illustration of Shostakovich's development in the mid-1950s in asserting his civil conscience and assuming the more zealous role of an artist entering into the thick of life as an eminent and forceful protagonist for virtue prevailing.[65]

The Eleventh Symphony, in contrast with its predecessors, was met by music critics with unanimous acclaim: "not for a long time, since Musorgsky, has Russian art produced such an immensely powerful musical tragedy having its source in the people."[66] Within a few months, the symphony was heard abroad. "Shostakovich shows its creators' mastery allied with the intensity and fertility of his artistic character."[67] Such was the observation in Paris following the performance of the Eleventh Symphony at the Salle Chaillot. "Such music cannot fail to stir any audience."[68] The exhaustive reviews revealed the growing interest in Shostakovich's music: "There are authentic revolutionary melodies in it, not in 'apt quotations' or 'interpolations' as part of the basic thematic fabric of the symphony; these melodies render a special temperament to the tone of the composition in its total, where everything 'as usual in Shostakovich's work' is fresh and new."[69] Shostakovich himself wrote to a British music critic: "I very much liked André Clutyens's performance of my Eleventh Symphony. Soon they will release Mravinsky's recording of the Eleventh Symphony, which I will send to you. I consider it to be the very best performance."[70]

The first studio recording of the Eleventh created an immense effect as "a performance of extraordinary vehemence. There are pages in the terrifying *scherzo* and in the *finale* that are not so much composed in primary colours as splashed on to a wall in broad strokes of dripping red and black. . . . His brass players yell at the tops of their voices, his percussion threaten to overwhelm the rest of the orchestra, his violins come within an ace of breaking their strings with the sheer scorch of their bows' imprint." Yevgeny Mravinsky, "in a live performance knew how to produce both an electric excitement and a degree of frank emotional histrionics that are arguably at least as valid as reactions to this music as any attempt to water down or mollify its crudity."[71]

The premiere of the new Shostakovich came at an intensely painful period for Mravinsky as Yelizaveta Nikolayevna died suddenly before the New Year. Her death was a grievous wound to Mravinsky, keenly aware of how much she had given through a long and dangerous road together. He took a period of leave from the orchestra, itself prolonged by a long illness caused by bronchial problems. Following his third portrayal of the latest Shostakovich symphony, Mravinsky's next public concert would not be until September 1958, an absence that would result in his missing the Philharmonic's major voyage to Japan, in which he was replaced by Alexander Gauk. Somehow, his absence transformed Mravinsky into an even more enigmatic figure. Mravinsky's disappearance from the podium didn't stop newspapers writing about his exploits:

> In each concert, he unearths something original and added expressive means in opening up orchestral scores. . . . He discovers fresh interesting details revealing his wholly retrospective and creative approach to work. . . . Mravinsky's laconic, severe, and modest gestures at the podium reveal someone quite cold, yet it isn't so in reality, for his altogether expressive, emotional orchestral playing, accurate phrasing, temperamental performance reveal much in the conductor's inner feelings and spirit. . . . Mravinsky in all probability is parallel to a scientist carrying out a new experiment.[72]

Mravinsky took the orchestra to Poland for the opening of the Warsaw Autumn Festival, where they performed works by Soviet composers: Prokofiev's *Romeo and Juliet*, Shostakovich's Eleventh *The Year 1905*, novelties in the Georgian Vano Taktakishvili's Piano Concerto (Yakov Zak as soloist), and Latvian Janis Ivanov's *Lettish* Symphony. There was disapproval at the press conference that no "modern" music was programmed and none of the younger generation was featured.[73] A pair of engagements were given in Lodz and Kraców, and there was a final evening at the Warsaw Palace of Culture—itself an architectural gift from the Soviet Union, in the style of a "wedding-cake." The tour did not attain the success of previous ones, and a disagreeable aftertaste remained following the Polish censure, something that Mravinsky would take to heart.

The Soviet conductor Boris Khaikin described an interesting factor in the evolution of the Philharmonic. In 1929, Khaikhin had conducted the Philharmonic in Camille Saint-Saëns's symphonic poem *Pháeton*; the musicians could not grasp the work, and it was not programmed again until thirty years later, again under Khaikin. On this occasion, "it was a very different performance; the orchestra played it magnificently, with practically no trouble. It was not only that one had matured, but the orchestra had developed immeasurably, acquiring new flair and technique, and in all these years the ensemble had attained superior artistic standards."[74]

Yet another world premiere beckoned: the Concerto for Violoncello in E minor by Shostakovich. The work was completed in July 1959, the composer having announced at the beginning of June that his next major work would be in the traditional three-movement form. The piece had fermented for a number of years—inspiration coming from Prokofiev: "my acquaintance with the *Symphonia-Concertante* interested me and there came a desire to try out my ability in this genre."[75] If the leavening lasted some seven years, the piece's stirring up before a grateful public in the autumn of 1959 presented a new masterpiece for the cello repertoire.

Prior to the concerto's public unveiling, a detailed review appeared proclaiming that "the greatest strength of Shostakovich is attained when he manages to create a sound, in warmth and emotional expression close to the human voice."[76] According to this view, the lyrical passage of the slow movement lies at the core of the work as a whole. As in Prokofiev's work, the *cadenza* acts as an expressive monologue, rich and finely revealing the wealth of virtuoso potential of the cello. Shostakovich rendered integrity in its dynamic development, all four movements unified in one unbroken, almost symphonic canvas. Mravinsky possessed a wonderful instrumentalist in the leader of the horn section in Vitaly Buyanovsky. The composer wrote a beautiful section where the cello "converses" with the horn, drawing some diaphanous musicianship against the exquisite playing of the strings. Once again, the premiere was scheduled for the opening of the Philharmonic season, on 4 October. Programmed together with the Shostakovich piece were Tchaikovsky's *Romeo and Juliet* and Beethoven's Seventh Symphony; the program was repeated within a day, and the Moscow premiere followed five days later under Alexander Gauk.

In 1960, Kurt Sanderling was appointed chief conductor of the Berlin Symphony Orchestra, located in the Russian zone of occupation. The magnificent work of the German conductor since his debut in April 1940 had greatly enriched musical life in the city. Despite having enjoyed prolonged appreciation, the Prussian had a growing son, Thomas, and he wanted to return to Germany now that there was a state in the East where he could work with his own symphony orchestra. Kurt Ignat'yevich Sanderling left behind his own audience in the city, and he was remembered for many years during the Leningrad Philharmonic's ascendancy in the postwar period. His relations with Mravinsky were perhaps naturally delicate in a relationship that saw Mravinsky as *chef d' orchestre* and Sanderling as *kapellmeister*.[77] Sanderling wanted to create a different, "softer" sound color in the woodwind and brass to make it more appropriate for a Western repertoire, however Mravinsky was steadfast to salvage the inimitable "Slavic" sound quality.[78] Highlights of Sanderling's years were his cycles of Rachmaninov symphonies; his scheduling of Sibelius, Brahms, and Prokofiev works, including the Leningrad premiere of Prokofiev's Seventh Symphony; and the opera productions at the Maly, which included a brilliantly triumphant *Fidelio*, *Flying Dutchman*, and all the Mozart da Ponte operas.[79]

In September, when Sanderling was staging his first concerts in Berlin, the Philharmonic's most extensive foreign tour to date was launched, embracing seven European countries and recordings of the last three symphonies of Tchaikovsky for the leading West German record company—owned and controlled by Siemens—Deutsche Grammophon Gesellschaft. In all, the Leningrad Philharmonic Orchestra during a two-month period gave thirty-four concerts in Great Britain, France, Belgium, Holland, Italy, Switzerland, and Austria. For the first time, Gennady Rozhdestvensky shared the duties on the podium. This historic journey began at the Edinburgh International Festival, where the orchestra competed with thirteen other ensembles and earned the highest praise: "The unquestionable superiority of the Russians at the Edinburgh Festival hid something magical; the orchestra stunned Edinburgh like a titanic force. But this force was masterfully directed; they have a secret weapon in their orchestral technique."[80]

Keen attention was directed by the press to the works under Mravinsky's direction: "The surprise packet was Prokofiev's Sixth Symphony, a disturbing . . . and painfully felt three movement work."[81] The same piece elicited a similar opinion from *The Observer's* music critic: "a sustained and deeply moving piece of music. . . . The blend of virtuosity, massive power all show it is beyond question one of the world's great orchestras." While Prokofiev proved a novelty, more familiar repertoire drew great interest: "Occasionally it sacrifices compactness of tone to sheer weight of sound, but its eruptions at climaxes of Tchaikovsky symphonies are prodigiously exciting."[82] The majority of reviews dealt with the Philharmonic's sound qualities, and in a perceptive account, Peter Heyworth wrote:

> Mravinsky's approach is intensely dramatic, his reading has a prodigious force and excitement, and at the *allegro vivo* in the first movement of the *Pathétique* it seemed as though the Usher Hall had been struck by some cataclysm, so huge was the weight of sound and violence the rhythmic force behind it. But the qualities of Mravinsky's performances extend much further than mere dramatic excitement. His ability to weld and phrase its dynamic markings into an organic whole so it seemed to surge forward of its own accord is masterful. His grasp of successive changes of tempo and ability to hold them further in relation to one another which seemed uncertain in Beethoven's Seventh Symphony, is unfaltering in Tchaikovsky, so that the big movement acquires an epic grandeur missing in Western interpretation.[83]

An interval between the Edinburgh concerts and those in London allowed Mravinsky to take the eighty-nine players of the orchestra into Wembley Town Hall to set down Tchaikovsky's Fourth Symphony on 14–15 September. The sessions were observed by *Records and Recording*, who described Mravinsky's work as

> an example of perfectionism at its best: the greater part of the Wednesday afternoon was spent recording merely the coda of the final movement. . . . Carefully Mravinsky took each section of the orchestra through its part separately—even the percussion group was rehearsed alone. Then, when it seemed that the ideal performance had been attained and orchestra members themselves nodded in approval, Mravinsky made a sign of agreement, but added "Nevertheless, the coda again, from its beginning." And yet when the final "take" came, there was the same fantastic virtuosity and spontaneous enthusiasm from the players, not a hint of tiredness or boredom with the music they had played over, and almost dissected, time and again.[84]

This spell before the microphones included Gennady Rozhdestvensky recording Schumann's Cello Concerto and Tchaikovsky's *Rococo Variations* with Rostropovich, and ballet suites by Khachaturyan. The lord mayor of Wembley invited members of the orchestra and Deutsches Grammophon for a reception; as always scorning social events, Mravinsky chose instead to visit the theater in London's West End. There remained four concerts at the Royal Festival Hall, keenly anticipated by the Philharmonic's musicians, as Valentin Stadler recalled: "we had an apprehension because we regarded the English as being cold, lacking in emotion, all from our reading of English literature, particularly John Galsworthy."[85] The principal trumpet Venjamin Margolin, who made a sensation with his playing in the Toccata of Shostakovich's Eighth, recounted: "we enjoyed the opportunity of walking through London's great parks, but we bore an awareness of responsibility for each performance. The auditorium was not full, yet we saw our own Shostakovich sitting in the audience, and this added to the magnitude and conscientiousness of our playing."[86] There was already a keen sense of occasion that a major musical event was to be unveiled: the mono recordings on DG had been on sale, and here was the promise of new Soviet works given their first British performances. The word had circulated that here was a phenomenal orchestra and in its chief conductor a major figure. The writings of the Edinburgh critics had been devoured, and the records were selling like hotcakes. The elite of London musical audiences were all there; present for a performance of his own *Variations on a Theme by Purcell* was Benjamin Britten; so, too, were Yehudi Menuhin and Sir Arthur Bliss. For the first time on British soil, symphonies by Prokofiev and Shostakovich were publicly performed (the Eighth was broadcast by Sir Henry Wood on 13 July 1944 in his last performance)[87], along with works by Glinka, Kabalevsky, Mozart, Rachmaninov, and Tchaikovsky. This was a veritable showcase of the orchestra's repertoire in one of the world's musical centers, where it earned plaudits from every source. Desmond Shawe-Taylor in the *Sunday Times* inspirited on Shostakovich's Fifth Symphony as having "received a glorious performance which must have convinced even the doubters of its great merits. The sustained arguments of the first and third movements were set forth with magnificent breadth and colour."[88] The redoubtable critic of *The Manchester Guardian* Neville Cardus was similarly impressed: "never before has the symphony—one of the most original of all composed in the present century—excited me and so completely bowled me over by its character and genius as in its performance. It transcended music. Khrushchev himself might have been conducting."[89] If the Leningrad musicians had triumphed on British soil, ahead there lay more challenges—the orchestra traveled to Dover for a cross-channel ferry to Calais and further on by coaches to the French capital. As in London, it was Prokofiev's Sixth and Shostakovich's Eighth that captured the Parisian public's attention and all to positive reviews, with no little measure given Yevgeny Mravinsky. Wrote one critic: "Without one unnecessary movement or gesture and standing like a tall monument, he transmits a nerve wave through the orchestra, with one signal indicating the most delicate nuance, freeing or holding tensions; in a word, he conducts not for display or show. True to the smallest whim of the composer, he knows how to be dramatic without being theatrical at the same time."[90]

When the orchestra was on tour in the Netherlands, an article appeared back in Leningrad covering the Anglo-French press reviews.[91] In Switzerland, the Philharmonic revisited Geneva and Lausanne. Following the concert performance in Geneva's Victoria Hall, Ernest Ansermet—who had conducted the Philharmonic in the 1920s—embraced Mravinsky, exclaiming jubilantly: "Joie de vivre!" Returning to the Austrian capital, Mravinsky conducted the Fifth Symphonies of Shostakovich and Tchaikovsky in one program. In Vienna, the orchestra again intoxicated the public with its two engagements, the local press commenting on a performance of Shostakovich's Fifth Symphony in D minor, seldom performed there: "What a work—here one can hear the composer's supremacy, and it is played so by the Leningrad orchestra. The hall felt this, and in excitement, the gushing sweep of applause sounded like a falling waterfall of sound."[92] Tchaikovsky's Fifth Symphony and the *Pathétique* were recorded at the end of the tour in the Grosser Konzerthaussaal of the Musikverein over four days (7–10 November) by the DG engineers Harald Baudie and Helmut Schneider, completing the project begun in London two months before.[93] According to *Gramophone*, the stereo remakes had to be something if they were to displace those made four years before: "The greater intensity of the earlier performance is obvious in the opening bars of the slow introduction. . . . There is spontaneity in the earlier one, which I feel lacking in the new. . . . The strings do not have quite the same miraculous clarity. . . ."[94]

Nevertheless, the recordings were a coup for the West German company—their mono versions of 1956 had already redeemed their investment, accorded the highest acclaim from the media, and earned high sales worldwide. It was an auspicious piece of work as there was a colossal degree of competition between the leading European record companies of EMI, Decca, Philips, Telefunken, and DG. The stereo versions were pronounced by some to be inferior to the mono recordings, regardless of the more refined and highly regarded playing—and the recording is unique in remaining ever present in the company's catalog.[95]

Yevgeny Mravinsky, in a rare essay published in Leningrad, summed up the tour in typically modest fashion, but praised the work and mastery of his musicians to the skies.[96] This unusual diversion to writing for the media carried through into the New Year for Mravinsky, in a revealing feature complaining of the little attention devoted to symphonic music in the press:

> For more than thirty years, I have dedicated myself to symphonic music, and I think that one has the right to express ones' concerns in analyzing the role of symphonic music. In some strange combination of circumstances, symphonic music has been an outcast among the different art forms and in music in general for a long time. Songs are reviewed frequently in the media. Everyone says that our people love the cinema, the theater, and musicals. Symphonic music is neither spoken of in the same manner nor is it related to music in general, yet is least understood, accessible to a select group of listeners; there has even now come to pass a specific phrase—lovers of symphonic music.

Mravinsky complained that while one can find a multitude of articles discussing new plays, films, and literature, little thought is given to reviews on symphonic works. Mravinsky wrote that those at the "top" should do more to safeguard and expand the finest symphony orchestras through enlightening programming.

> My long experience of contact with audiences allows me to state that whether it be the cinema, the theater or at musical performances, concert-goers are searching for genuine art, that distinctive quality of moving their heart with the most sacred music. The people will always remain deaf to modestly articulated and untalented work, however will catch works that are profound in form and content and conceived with true humanity.

Mravinsky continued that it is sufficient to bear in mind Shostakovich's Eighth Symphony winning a special place in the repertoire: "One can understand why! In the final analysis, it is a symphony of song about man of our times, expressed in the most perfect, flexible medium of a modern symphony orchestra." Further, Mravinsky maintained that: "schoolchildren should be taught how to appreciate the beautiful world of music, without words, performed by that ideal musical instrument—a symphony orchestra." Mravinsky described the Philharmonic's initiative to assist the formation of an amateur symphony orchestra in the Vyborg district: "As someone who has devoted all his life to the symphony, I am delighted to see more people being drawn to art of great fervor and profound philosophical conception, something wholly natural for symphonic music." The conductor concluded: "Music is a passionate, compelling language and must be heard and taken into account by everyone!"[97]

In the 1960s, there came an explosion in repertoire for the Leningrad Philharmonic Orchestra, matched with a steady growth in touring. Mravinsky personally collected scores, acquiring them by all conceivable means.[98] Nor was early repertoire forgotten: of importance was the appearance of major vocal cantatas by Vivaldi, Purcell, Corelli, Telemann, and Pergolesi, the Leningrad Chamber Orchestra under Lazar Gozman tackling such works.[99] The Philharmonic made regular tours throughout the Soviet Union, to nearby Riga, Tallinn, and Vyborg. These widened the popularity of the orchestra as well as extending both Soviet and Western classical music to a wider audience, many through the orchestra's gramophone recordings and broadcasts.

Since its founding in 1921, the ensemble had been a "show" orchestra for the government's cultural and education policies. Marking the orchestra's fortieth anniversary, Mravinsky took the Philharmonic on a short visit to the capital. The February 1961 performances, of which three were directed by Mravinsky, embraced the last two Tchaikovsky symphonies, Prokofiev's

Sixth, and the Eighth by Shostakovich, plus a novelty for Moscow audiences, the Second Symphony by Vadim Salmanov. "We shall remember this festival for a long time; each concert evokes deep and strong passions. . . . [O]ne so needs this fine world of music that Yevgeny Mravinsky gives us. Everything is bestowed through his will power and his emotions. It seems to me that the most vital facet in Mravinsky's artistry is in his power of expression."[100] An important critique by the young critic Andrey Zolotov appeared in *Izvestia*.[101]

In April 1961, Mravinsky became the first conductor to receive the coveted Lenin Prize, placing him among an elite group of outstanding figures in Soviet art. Despite his abhorrence for the founder of Soviet power, Mravinsky strangely coveted the colorful and attractive medal, wearing it often in concert.[102] By special invitation from the Ministry of Culture, Mravinsky and the orchestra returned to Moscow for three engagements in April in which the conductor gave two different programs from his treasure trove, including Tchaikovsky's Fifth Symphony, Shostakovich's Fifth Symphony, Beethoven's *Eroica*, and orchestral fragments from Wagner's operas.

This second visit to the capital was a precursor to more foreign touring, this time to Scandinavia. This voyage, involving innumerable changes of transport between trains, coaches, and ferries, became an exhausting, arduous trip. Sharing the conducting responsibilities was Mravinsky's deputy, Arvids Jansons, who gave two of the ten concerts. The orchestra revisited Helsinki and toured the cities of Copenhagen, Göteborg, Stockholm, Bergen, and Türku. At the Bergen International Festival, several concerts were broadcast, and tapes survive of performances of Tchaikovsky's Fifth Symphony, Beethoven's *Eroica*, and Prokofiev's *Romeo and Juliet*. These reveal a rare vivacity and power, showing that Mravinsky spared absolutely nothing when away from his Leningrad home; here are raw, tremendously dynamic expressions of not simply virtuoso playing but also of great artistry and power. "In 1961 the magnificent Leningrad Philharmonic orchestra under Yevgeny Mravinsky were the guests, their Grieg and Tchaikovsky concerts commemorating an old friendship. Grieg called the Russian composer 'a warm friend of any art.'"[103] At the end of the third and final evening in Bergen, the art director, Henryk Jensen, in presenting a bouquet of flowers to Mravinsky, said, "Our city has played host to many great orchestras from all over the world, but never have we heard such a magnificent orchestra as the Leningrad Philharmonic Orchestra."[104] Onward by coach and ferry to Helsinki, and the Philharmonic took part in the Sibelius Week, with Arvids Jansons directing the composer's First Symphony while Mravinsky conducted "The Swan of Tuonela."

Now a freshly written Shostakovich symphony came to fruition at Repino on the Gulf of Finland.

Shostakovich took a great liking to this place; he felt at ease there. At around nine o' clock, he would go to the dining room. He breakfasted quickly, not allowing himself to be distracted, then returned to his writing table. Before lunch, he took a brief break, strolling around the paths of the retreat; he lunched punctually at two, then continued his work unless there were visitors—pupils who had an appointment or friends from Leningrad: Venyamin Basner, Isaak Glikman, Yevgeny Mravinsky, or Nikolay Rabinovich. Sometimes colleagues working in the neighboring cottages would drop by to chat, listen to music, play their latest compositions, or ask counsel.[105]

On 15 August, Shostakovich wrote to Isaak Glikman: "the first movement has succeeded, the second and third almost completely. The fourth, undoubtedly, will not come off. I am writing it with difficulty."[106] All the same, the opus was finished by late August, in time for the new season. Of major significance was that Shostakovich had written a symphonic allegro—a form he had been attempting to accomplish for decades.[107] Within weeks, the Twelfth went into rehearsal at the Leningrad Philharmonic, with Shostakovich sitting in on Mravinsky's sessions.[108] An unusual feature was that access was granted to journalists for Mravinsky's final rehearsals.

Repeatedly, the musicians repeat the same phrase and then a single bar of music. The conductor turns to the brass section, then to the strings, and finally to the percussion, and at last asks them: "All together" correcting, vocalizing and explaining how it should sound. Step by step, level by level, the necessary tempi, dynamics, and color, everything is gradually attained to bring together the symphonic performance. The conductor inquires of the composer sitting in the hall ensconced deep in his score "How does it sound today?" Shostakovich (whose fifty-fifth birthday it is today) nods in approval .The rehearsal moves on. . . .[109]

On 1 October 1961, Shostakovich's Twelfth Symphony in D minor was first heard in the Great Hall of the Leningrad Philharmonic, conducted as always by Mravinsky before TV and radio microphones. The Twelfth was praised, critics noting the folk-music dramatic characteristic of his previous symphony and now describing the Twelfth as being "folk-heroic," claiming musical adherents in Borodin and Musorgsky. Mravinsky found much to admire in the opening movement of the work: "In essence, this is the first satisfactory fulfillment by the composer of a traditional sonata allegro observing all the 'classical' signs of this form. How magnificently he lays this forth in the conscience of the listener, as the culmination is so accurately built and used to fill the contrasts, how skillfully the parts are given, and the thematic material developed! Here the presentation of form is accomplished with high craftsmanship."[110] Until recent years, Mravinsky was the only Soviet conductor to champion the Twelfth.

If the composer really intended to "serialize" his Eleventh and Twelfth symphonies to Soviet themes, Mravinsky discovered important subtextual material, particularly in the Twelfth's third movement, evoking prison and protest songs. The Eleventh Symphony allowed musicologists to suggest that the composer was opening his conscience in the two symphonies, within the musical fabric, as if in sign language to those who grasped how to find it.[111] If the Eleventh was written against the backdrop of the Hungarian revolution, the disillusionment with the failures of the October Revolution could be ascribed to the Twelfth, which was "Dedicated to V. I. Lenin."

There are two themes in the work, A and B they may be called, that appear throughout all four movements in a cyclic form. One may interpret the A motif as depicting the revolution, whereas B is expressing the Lenin theme. There is also a three-part motif—Es-B-C. In the first movement, this comes at bar 407 in the second part and is repeated seven times, given by the strings *pizzicato* unchanging *mp* and then in the interrupted flow of music by the timpani. Practically everything is done to make this sound repressed. In the last bars it is repeated twice, and the motif is divided. In the slow movement, the motif appears at bar 10, is heard five times Dis-Ais-His, again *pizzicato*. Here each time it is heard sharply as if the flow is "before" and "after." The motif does not appear in the third movement. In the finale, against the canvas of sound following the massed introduction of the motif, it is repeated twelve times, beginning from bar 84, then eight times carrying through the brass; the loudness building to *ff*. Each note divides *sf*, and finally the last bars eight times *tutti* is at maximum level of dynamics.

What does this reveal? The veiling is throughout the first movement of the motifs and into the second, and then is taken up by the entire orchestra in the finale. Perhaps there are initials depicting someone or something? In Russian lettering, Es-B-C is transformed into E (or Io.) Ve Es, giving the initials of Iosif Vissarionovich Stalin, fully coinciding with the seventh and eight scenes of *Katerina Izmailova* as the police theme. Also in the first movement and almost lost are lines from a poem by Mandelstam: "We live in the underground" and "Ten steps distant, our speech cannot be heard." In the appearance of the motif throughout the work, one can infer that Stalin is barely present in the Revolution, and becomes more perceptible at the end, where he is dominant.[112] One other theory is that when the main theme appears in the third movement, it takes a darker, more sinister tone.

The Twelfth Symphony did not meet with sustained acclaim, as did its predecessor; together with the composer's enlistment in the Party it led to a partial disenchantment with the composer among the smart set of Soviet life.[113] The Twelfth Symphony tainted Shostakovich's reputation among the so-called *shestidesyatniki* (literally, "men of the 1960s"), that liberal intelligentsia who exerted a strong influence upon the country's spiritual climate between 1956 and 1967–1968. The situation changed a year later with the Thirteenth Symphony.[114]

Following the world premiere of Shostakovich's Twelfth Symphony, Mravinsky made his final studio recording in December 1961 for the locally based Accord studio. The respected producer Alexander Grossman traveled up to the northern capital for the Philharmonic Hall sessions. The recording's subsequent release once again attained the highest praise: "Mravinsky tears into the Twelfth with a near hysterical frenzy that has you forgetting reservation, whether musical or movement."[115]

Mravinsky detested the recording process; the sight of engineers and technicians cutting up his session tapes and sticking them together to produce "a performance" was foreign to his artistic credo. The Philharmonic was paid less than Moscow-based musicians were, and the best facilities were based in the capital; there was prevalent favoritism for Moscow artists and ensembles, which were getting the better tours and recordings offered them. Mravinsky regarded the concert performance as sacred homage to the music and its composer.[116] David Oistrakh was sympathetic with Mravinsky:

> Recording from a concert seems advantageous to me over studio recordings. One can never achieve the artistic level there as one does in concert. And if you disregard technical mistakes and other allowances, such a recording acquires a quality which is difficult to attain in the studio, this live atmosphere of music and real temperament—all born in communicating in a well-built auditorium, the stage lighting and atmosphere of the hall.[117]

Following the departure of Sanderling, a major role fell upon the shoulders of Arvids Jansons.[118] The Latvian conductor shared many of Mravinsky's values: a nobility and clarity in expression matched with thorough preparation and an affinity for the composer's conceptual ideas. Similar to his predecessor, Jansons hailed from the German tradition, proving a masterful interpreter with a wide repertoire. The orchestra regularly invited leading conductors to work with them: Svetlanov, Rozhdestvensky, Guzman, Dalgat, and Kondrashin. Once, when Kirill Kondrashin was rehearsing, there appeared the tall, dark shadow of the Philharmonic's chief conductor against the marble pillars at the side of the hall. Mravinsky was nicknamed "Vasya" by the principal trumpet Venyamin Margolin (something the maestro knew and tolerated); the name seemed to epitomize the conductor's rustic, Russian, down-to-earth personality. At once, the whisper "Vasya is here" shot around the platform, causing a stiffening of the musicians' backs and a qualitative transformation in their playing for the Muscovite conductor. Backstage Kondrashin expressed his thanks to Mravinsky: "for days I have been trying to get these results from them and all thanks to you!"[119]

Shostakovich's latest symphony was not the only premiere that season; a few weeks afterward, Mravinsky conducted the Soviet debut of Arthur Honegger's Third Symphony *Liturgique*, in a program with Bach's Second Suite and Mozart's Concerto for Oboe, Clarinet, Horn, and Bassoon, with soloists drawn from the principals of the Philharmonic: Kirill Nikonchuk on oboe, Vladimir Krasavin on clarinet, Vitaly Buyanovsky on horn, and Dmitry Yeremin on bassoon. Alexey Ratsbaum—principal flute—performed the solo in the Bach. On 16 December, Bartók's Music for Strings, Percussion, and Celesta was given its first hearing in the Soviet Union following long weeks of preparation, Brahms's Fourth Symphony in E minor sharing the bill. At the year's end, Mravinsky took his orchestra on visits to factories in the city, presenting Shostakovich's Twelfth with a variety of short orchestral works by Russian composers. In 1962, Mravinsky's orchestra embarked on two major foreign tours; through January and February they gave seven concerts in Hungary, performing Russian and Soviet works, including Shostakovich's Twelfth Symphony in D minor. The performances were the climax of the Budapest season with greatest praise being given for Tchaikovsky's *Pathétique* and Bartók's Music for Strings, Percussion, and Celesta. The concerts were remembered for years afterward and led to Mravinsky being awarded the Bartók Medal on the occasion of the composer's birth centenary, in 1971.

Following a glorious series of concerts for the "White Nights" in June in which Mravinsky directed works by Beethoven, Bartók, Brahms, Shostakovich, and Wagner, the Philharmonic toured in early July, giving performances on Latvia's Baltic coast of the Fifth Symphonies by Shostakovich and Tchaikovsky and repeating the Bartók and Brahms program of the winter months.

Matching the European concert tours of two years before, and immediately after the opening of the 1962 season in Leningrad, the Philharmonic devoted two months to a demanding tour of the United States and Canada. In the engagements (thirty in twenty-six cities), Mravinsky shared responsibilities with the highly astute Gennady Rozhdestvensky. The orchestra visited New York, Baltimore, Boston, Chicago, Cleveland, Philadelphia, Pittsburgh, Richmond, Rochester, Washington, Montreal, and Toronto. The repertoire included Tchaikovsky's late symphonies; Shostakovich's Fifth, Eighth, and Twelfth Symphonies; Prokofiev's Third and Myaskovsky's Twenty-First Symphonies (both directed by Rozhdestvensky); and works by Glinka, Glazunov, Musorgsky, Lyadov, Mozart, Brahms, Bartók, and Samuel Barber. The New York press was generous: "on 21 October 1962 the Leningrad Philharmonic Orchestra under Yevgeny Mravinsky made its debut in New York; the reception was enthusiastic."[120] Certainly, the famous recordings had played their part in building a reputation for the Leningraders. "Under Mravinsky the Leningrad Philharmonic is so beloved for their recordings of

Tchaikovsky symphonies. Neither he nor the orchestra could be met so heartily."[121] *Time* magazine was enthusiastic: "Accuracy with passion, . . . the Leningraders on their first tour of the US show that they are one of the world's finest orchestras."[122] Mravinsky conducted Bartók's Music for Strings, Percussion, and Celesta in ten of his thirteen concerts, however the maestro admitted his vulnerability. "Mravinsky was a little upset in that at one of the concerts he missed a beat in the second movement and could not find his place for some time. 'But the orchestra carried me through' said the Maestro.'"[123] This lapse may have eluded the usually vigilant and critical press; however it goes without saying the standards of performance were remarkably high. George Szell and Eugene Ormandy expressed their admiration, Szell remarking, "I have never heard the Bartók played so well as tonight."[124] Away from his schedule, Yevgeny Mravinsky took delight in the open vistas available from the panoramic rooftop railway wagons, and took photographs of the unfolding countryside and of his wife Inna. The debut American tour concluded with two engagements in Canada, after which the *Montreal Star* enthusiastically asserted that "this is today one of the greatest world orchestras."[125]

Cultural exchanges and international diplomacy were to the fore of this concert tour, which drew the attention of Secretary-General of the United Nations U Thant, who expressed his wish that his organization "could be so united as this magnificent orchestra."[126] It is astonishing that the visit took place, for it was set against the background of the Cuban missile crisis. All the same, the Philharmonic's music making transfixed all those attending their concerts, allowing everyone to forget about the threat of nuclear war. If the tour to North America was a magnificent triumph for Yevgeny Mravinsky and his orchestra, their return to their home city came under a cloud; for the great conductor, a new crisis was beginning to cause concern for all who were close to him.

NOTES

1. A. M. Vavilina Mravinskaya, author interview, February 2002.

2. Yelizaveta Nikolayevna Mravinskaya studied there as a young girl in the 1890s, learning three foreign languages, taking singing lessons, and learning to play the piano.

3. The Smolny finishing school was established by Catherine II for young fräuleins in the city and as a model institution for the country. Many of the graduates became leading figures in Russian life, among them several musicians. The song "The Wonderful Moment" was inspired by a love affair of Glinka's.

4. Adrian Cedric Boult, *My Own Trumpet* (London: Hamish Hamilton, 1973), 165.

5. Today Yelena Yevgenyevna Mravinskaya lives in Tashkent in the independent republic of Uzbekistan.

6. B. Tischenko, interview with G. N. Enfaldt, June 2002.

7. A. M. Vavilina Mravinskaya, author interview, March 2002.

8. B. Tischenko, interview with G. N. Enfaldt, June 2002.

9. Lia Muradyan, interview, July 2002.

10. A. Khachaturyan, *Sovetskaya Muzika*, no. 3 (1954).

11. A. Sokolov, unpublished memoir made available to author.

12. *Rude Pravo*, 24 May 1955.

13. *Lidova Democrati*, 25 May 1955.

14. *Times* (London), 31 May 1955.

15. David Oistrakh, quoted in Shveyster, "Vospominanii," *Muzikalnaya Akademiya*, no. 4 (1994): 96.

16. S. Khentova, *Shostakovich tridzatiletiya 1945–1975* (Leningrad: Sovetsky Kompositora, 1982), 26.

17. D. D. Shostakovich, "D. F. Oistrakh vospominaniya," in *Statii, Intervyu, Pisma* (Moscow: Muzika, 1978), 11.

18. Khentova, *Shostakovich tridzatiletiya 1945–1975*, 27.

19. D. F. Oistrakh, "Voploscheneniye bolshevo zamysla," 208.

20. Shostakovich, "D.F. Oistrakh vospominaniya," 11.

21. Oistrakh, "Voploscheneniye bolshevo zamysla," 213.

22. B. V. Asaf'yev, *Vosmaya simfoniya Shostakovich* (Moscow: Iskusstvo, Moskovskaya filarmoniya, VTO, 1945), 5.

23. Shostakovich to Mravinsky, *Muzikalnaya Akademiya*, no. 4 (1997): 95.

24. GTsMMK, f.385, e. khr, 494.

25. TcGALI, f. 2048, op. 1, ed. khr, 21.

26. I. D. Glikman, *Pisma k Drugu* (St. Petersburg: DSCH, 1993), 116.

27. Y. A. Mravinsky, "Iz Dnevniki," *Muzikalnaya Akademiya*, no. 4 (1997): 99.

28. D. D. Shostakovich letter, 23 February 1956, *Muzikalnaya Akademiya*, no. 4 (1997): 96–97.

29. A. M. Vavilina Mravinskaya, interview, July 2001.

30. D. Zhitomirsky, "Simfoniya B. Lyatoshinskovo," *Sovetskaya Muzika*, no. 2 (1997).

31. M. Byalik, "Lyatoshinsky, Mravinsky i drugie," *Muzikalnaya Akademiya*, no. 1 (1997): 40.

32. E. Serov, *Dirizher Eduard Serov* (Volgograd: Nizhnevolzhskoye, 1993), 136.

33. G. Rozhdestvensky and M. Kopitza, "A kogda voskresnu-ne znayu," *Muzikalnaya Akademiya*, no. 1 (1996): 29.

34. Byalik, "Lyatoshinsky, Mravinsky i drugie," 43.

35. D. B. Kabalevsky, Plenary SK SSSR, 22 January 1960.

36. Byalik, "Lyatoshinsky, Mravinsky i drugie," 42–43.

37. Byalik, "Lyatoshinsky, Mravinsky i drugie," 41.

38. A. M. Vavilina Mravinskaya, interview, September 2002.

39. V. Shebalin, *Literaturnoye nasledie* (Moscow: Vsesoyusnoye izdat. Sovetsky Kompositor, 1975), 246–47.

40. Liya Muradyan, author interview, July 2002.

41. H. Abendroth, "Nashi zarubezhniye gosti," *Leningradskaya Pravda*, 25 January 1947.

42. A. A. Zolotov, interview, 1983.

43. *Neues Deutscheland*, 26 June 1956.

44. *Bild*, 29 June 1956.

45. *Hamburger Mittag*, 8 June 1956.

46. V. Fomin, *Dirizher Yevgeny Mravinsky* (Leningrad: Muzika, 1983), 69.

47. *Neues Austreicher*, 23 June 1956.

48. Deutsche Grammophon Session Protocol, June 1956.

49. E. Greenfield, *Gramophone* (October 1961): 208.

50. L. Y. Gakkel, "Iz nablyudeniye nad konzertnoy zhiznyu Leningrada 50–60 godov," in *Muzika i Muzikantov Leningrada* (Leningrad: Sovetsky Kompositora, 1972), 124–25.

51. Mravinsky to Václav Talich, 6 June 1957 (Prague: Panton, 1980), 346.

52. Valentin Stadler, interview with the author, July 2002.

53. TsGALI, f. 2048, op. 2, ed. khr, 1.

54. A. I. Khachaturyan, "Poiski sovremmenovo," *Sovetskaya Kultura*, 24 April 1958.

55. Khentova, *Shostakovich tridzatiletiya 1945–1975*, 107.

56. Y. A. Mravinsky, "Odinnadtsatya simfonia Shostakovicha," *Vechernaya Moskva*, 28 September 1957.

57. I. Nestyev, "Simfonia o Russkoi Revolutzii," *Vechernaya Moskva*, 11 November 1957.

58. L. Lebedinsky, "Revolutsionnii folklor v Odinnadtaya simfonii D. Shostakovicha," *Sovetskaya Muzika*, no. 1 (1958).

59. A. N. Dolzhansky, "Kratkiye zamechanii ob Odinnadtsaya simfonii," *Sovetskaya Musika*, no. 1 (1958).

60. I. E. Popov, "Odinnadtzaya simfoniya D. Shostakovicha," *Sovetskaya Kultura*, 31 October 1957.

61. Popov, "Odinnadtzaya simfoniya D. Shostakovicha."

62. A. I. Anisimov, "Novaya simfoniya D. Shostakovicha," *Leningradskaya Pravda*, 12 November 1957.

63. N. K. Cherkasov, "1905 god," *Pravda*, 15 November 1957.

64. A. M. Kollontay, *Proletarskaya Revolutziya*, no. 3 (1921): 1–2.

65. Y. A. Mravinsky, "Tridzat let s muzikoi Shostakovicha," in *D. Shostakovich*, ed. L. V. Danilevich (Moscow: Sovetsky Kompozitor, 1967), 110.

66. Popov, "Odinnadtzaya simfoniya D. Shostakovicha."

67. *L'Humanite*, 30 September 1960.

68. *Le Soir*, 6 October 1960.

69. D. Rabinovich, *Dmitry Shostakovich* (London: Lawrence and Wishart, 1959), 156.

70. Shostakovich to D. G. Stoll, 19 February 1958, GTsMMK, f. 32, ed. khr, 360.

71. Michael Oliver, *Gramophone* (August 1994), 58.

72. A. Anisimov, "Za pultom-dirizher Mravinsky," *Leningradskaya Pravda*, 16 April 1958.

73. Fomin, *Dirizher Yevgeny Mravinsky*, 70.

74. B. Khaikhin, "Artisty vyshevo klassa," *Sovetskaya Kultura*, 16 March 1965.

75. D. D. Shostakovich, "Kontserti dlya violonchello s orkestrom D. Shostakovicha," in *Issledovaniya, statii, ocherki* (Moscow: Sovetsky Kompositor, 1971), 158.

76. M. F. Ber, *Orkestrovka melodicheskiykh golosov v proisvedeniye D. D. Shostakovicha, Cherti stilya D. Shostakovicha* (Moscow: Sovetsky Kompositor, 1962), 225–26.

77. Conversation with Isaak Glikman, July 2002.

78. M. Reznikov, *Vospominanii starovo muzikanta* (West Germany: Overseas Publications, 1984), 177.

79. Kurt Sanderling, "In interview with Alan Blyth," *Gramophone* (April, 1974): 1844.

80. C. Grier, *Scotsman*, 8 September 1960.

81. C. Grier, *Scotsman*.

82. P. Heyworth, *Observer*, 10 September 1960.

83. P. Heyworth, *Observer*, 10 September 1960.

84. *Records and Recording* (October 1960): 8–9.

85. Valentin Stadler, interview with the author, May 2003.

86. Venjamin Margolin, interview with the author, May 2003.

87. A. Jacobs, *Henry J. Wood* (London: Metheun, 1994), 394.

88. D. Shawe-Taylor, *Sunday Times*, 18 September 1960.

89. Neville Cardus, *Manchester Guardian*, 16 September 1960.

90. *L'Humanite*, 30 September 1960.

91. I. Marinina, "Skazochniye orkester," *Leningradskaya Pravda*, 22 September 1960.

92. *Austreiche Neue Zeitung*, 6 November 1960.

93. Deutsches Grammophon session protocol, November 1960.

94. E. Greenfield, *Gramophone* (October 1961): 208.

95. E. Greenfield, *Gramophone* (October 1961).

96. Y. A. Mravinsky, "Eto-Nastoyaschiye," *Leningradskaya Pravda*, 25 December 1960.

97. Y. A. Mravinsky, *Neva*, no. 8 (1961).

98. David Lloyd–Jones, author interview, September 2001.

99. Archives of the St. Petersburg Philharmonia Library.

100. Medvedev, Po bolshomy schetu, *Sovetskaya Kultura*, 16 February 1961.

101. A. A. Zolotov, "Dva pocherka," *Izvestia*, 11 February 1961.

102. A. M. Vavilina Mravinskaya, interview, October 2001.

103. D. Gray Stoll, *Musical Festivals of the World* (London: Pergamon, 1963), 187.

104. V. Fomin, *Stareischie russkiye symphonicheskiye orkester* (Leningrad: Muzika, 1982), 60.

105. S. Khentova, *Udivetelniye Shostakovich* (St. Petersburg: Variant, 1993), 154.

106. I. D. Glikman, *Pisma k Drugu* (St. Petersburg: DSCH, 1993), 167.

107. Sollertinsky constantly joked that Shostakovich couldn't write a true symphonic allegro.

108. S. Khentova, *Shostakovich: zhisn i tvorchestvo*, Vol. 2 (Leningrad: Sovetsky Kompositor, 1986), 370.

109. F. Semyonov, *Vecherny Leningrad*, 25 September 1961.

110. Mravinsky, "Tridzat let s muzikoi Shostakovicha," 112.

111. Leonid Gakkel, interview, July 2002.

112. F. Hitotzuyagnagi, "Novy lik Dvehandtzatoy," *Muzikalnaya Akademiya*, no. 4 (1997): 87.

113. L. Hakobian, *Music of the Soviet Age* (Stockholm: Melos Music Literature, 1998), 230.

114. Among the liberal intelligentsia were poets Okudzhava and Akhmadulina; writers Trifonov, Aitmatov, and Shukshin; theater directors Lyubimov and Efros; and film directors Tarkovsky, Klimov, and Ryazanov.

115. David S. Gutman, *Gramophone* (August 1994): 55.

116. A. A. Zolotov, conversation with the author, October 2001.

117. Y. Soloker, *Oistrakh* (Jerusalem: Tarbut, 1981), 146.

118. Following his winning second prize at the second All-Union Conducting Competition in 1946, Arvids Jansons made his debut and frequently worked with the Philharmonic.

119. Serov, *Dirizher Eduard Serov*, 140.

120. B. Schwartz, *Music and Musical Life in Soviet Russia, 1917–1982* (Bloomington: Indiana University Press, 1983), 358.

121. *New York News*, 25 October 1962.

122. *Time*, 9 November 1962.

123. E. Serov, *Dirizher Eduard Serov*, 140.

124. George Szell, quoted in V. Fomin, *Orkestrom dirizhiruet Mravinsky* (Leningrad: Muzika, 82.

125. *Montreal Star*, 30 November 1962.

126. U Thant, *New York Times*, 26 November 1962.

Chapter Thirteen

The Unfortunate Thirteenth

On the Tsar's head, by those fiendish looks chilled, the Monarch's orb began to tremble, and brutally, not hiding its triumph, the head began laugh-
ing at the tsar!

— Yevtushenko, "The Execution of Stepan Razin"

If there was a resilient and creative friendship between Mravinsky and
Shostakovich, there was an equally fastening relationship between the composer and the Leningrad Philharmonic Orchestra. It was after all this ensemble that had given the premieres, under Malko and Gauk, of Shostakovich's
first three symphonies. It was the virtuoso musicians of the Philharmonic, the
timbre of its woodwind, the color and bloom of its strings, and its magnificent brass dynamics that were present in Shostakovich's imagination. With
the sensation of the Fifth Symphony in D minor under the young Mravinsky
there launched a harmonious collaboration lasting thirty years, and in each
first performance "there was . . . a struggle with the authorities; barriers
would emerge hindering the premiere."[1]

In the early 1960s, the borders of permissibility in the USSR had retreated,
allowing cultural life to grow much more abundant; almost every strand of
cultural life experienced a fresh burst of vigor. However, there were problems. Of course, as many of the executants of Stalin's policies were very
much alive and in power, literature largely treaded the borderline of permissibility. Among the young poets enchanting Soviet youth, Robert
Rozhdestvensky, Andrey Vosnesensky, and Yevgeny Yevtushenko were writing with refreshing liberalism and against the political and social dogmas of
the past. As never before, the cinema and theater were going through a renaissance, allowed to explore the formerly forbidden issues of ethics and the

family unit. Soviet musicians would board this period of renewal through the music of the second Viennese school and avant-garde music. As ever, the Party's conservative faction in Mikhail Suslov and Leonid Brezhnev mounted a fierce and determined battle against fresh artistic ideas, and the "thaw" would reach its greatest challenge.

If the musical language of the avant-garde had touched upon tender nerves, the appearance of a new symphony dealing with anti-Semitism by the country's most lauded composer presented for the authorities a great conundrum because the composer himself was now a member of the ruling Party.[2] To have many of the Party's most inviolate values challenged, and for this to come from the doyen of Soviet music, was wholly unexpected. Following the premiere of the Twelfth Symphony in 1961, it was surprising that Shostakovich would so promptly issue a brand new symphonic piece; yet as so often happens, the composer himself did not plan to write a symphony. In the first months of 1962, the composer had found a new partner in Irina Antonovna Supinskaya, a young literary editor with whom he had worked on his operetta *Cheryomushki* three years before.[3] Supinskaya came from a troubled past; her father had been accused of being an enemy of the people, and she spent her childhood in an orphanage.[4] Shostakovich's resurgent domestic happiness spurred him to begin a piece based on Yevtushenko's verses *Babiy Yar*,[5] which had appeared the previous autumn (and which were suggested to the composer by Glikman)[6]. The opus expanded far beyond the subject's text; four additional poems would eventually become five movements for large orchestra, male choir, and bass-baritone. Dissimilar from anything Shostakovich had written before, the work followed the structure and form of a cantata.

Shostakovich naturally had Mravinsky's orchestra in mind as the principle protagonist for his new symphonic poem, and his choice as soloist was the great Ukrainian singer Boris Gmyrya. Shostakovich knew the vocalist well, for Gmyrya, who possessed a particularly rich, charcoal-black voice, had already premiered his settings of Pushkin. Gmyrya had been singing professionally since winning a vocal competition in 1938 and contracting to the Kiev Opera. The singer had lingered behind when the Nazis occupied Ukraine, and he sang in concerts for the German troops. Upon liberation, Gmyrya was accused of being a collaborator; pleading his naïveté in performing for the Germans, Gmyrya vowed that he would serve the Soviet authorities faithfully. What kept him out of jail was the plain fact that he was too great a singer to waste a prison sentence on. Gmyrya was awarded the title of Peoples Artist of the USSR in 1951 and a Stalin Prize the following year, and he was accordingly expected to sing at all sorts of concerts, parades, and rallies, ordered by the Ukrainian Party and government.[7]

In July 1962, Shostakovich had still not completed his new work when he started making approaches to the Ukrainian singer. At last having copied the final bars, Shostakovich sent Gmyrya a telegram about his imminent arrival in Kiev.[8] Despite the bolt from the blue, Gmyrya reacted favorably, inviting him to his home.[9] Shostakovich emerged from hospital and traveled with Irina by overnight train to Kiev, where Gmyrya and his wife rapturously met them. The two men spent some time going over the work, however the singer could not give his agreement to sing in the Leningrad premiere.[10] Gmyrya told Shostakovich that he would have to ask the Party's cultural department for permission to sing the part. Shostakovich returned to Moscow, unable to believe that the Party would not accede to Gmyrya's participation. The composer confided to Glikman: "I am excited with this poem and would really like to meet Mravinsky in Leningrad, although as he is in Ust-Narva it is hardly likely. I don't want to stay too long, just a couple of days (to see you, to acquaint both you and Mravinsky with the symphony, and to return to Moscow)."[11] The Shostakoviches traveled by the Red Arrow express to the northern capital and stayed at the Yevropeiskaya hotel for one night before making their way out to Mravinsky's dacha eighty miles away in Estonia. As usual, the Mravinskys were dead to the world at Ust-Narva following the White Nights Festival. It was balmy weather, and this fresh meeting between the old friends was uncommon because the composer had never visited Mravinsky's summer retreat—the cause informing the exigency of the moment. Following social banter, Shostakovich and Mravinsky left their wives together and searched for a piano so they could go through the score as in the old days. There was enough time for Shostakovich to play through the entire piece before the Shostakoviches made their way back to Leningrad.[12] Isaak Glikman's brother Gavriil, a painter, was a neighbor of the Mravinskys in the same hamlet. According to Isaak Glikman: "the conductor took the new work without his time-honored acquiescence and conviviality. He neither grasped its form nor identified with its spirit. To satisfy these questions is challenging, but in the subsequent weeks, he did not act in the best manner, being taciturn."[13] Glikman has said that he assumed Mravinsky "did not identify with, in particular, the great opening movement of the symphony based on Yevtushenko's *Babiy Yar*."[14]

Shostakovich left the score with Mravinsky and wrote to Gmyrya: "I have shown the Thirteenth Symphony to Yevgeny Alexandrovich Mravinsky and told him about our conversation. He is interested in the symphony and thinking about preparing it for performance. His plans are that he will be in Ust-Narva until 15 September, returning before 1 October, after which the orchestra will go on tour to the USA through October and November. Then upon his return to Leningrad, he will begin work on my symphony."[15]

Shostakovich, reinforced by his tentative concord with Mravinsky, tried to allay Gmyrya's doubts: "As far as your concern about possible attacks on the Thirteenth Symphony are concerned, based on my own experience, this all falls on the back of the composer. You shouldn't worry about it."[16]

Shostakovich wrote to Gmyrya once more and concluded on a note of anticipation and hope: "If the symphony is against your artistic convictions, then certainly, you should inform me about it; regardless, I shall always be your most hearty admirer."[17] In mid-August, prior to departure for the Edinburgh International Festival,[18] Gmyrya wrote to Shostakovich: "I have been informed that the Ukrainian leadership is categorically against my taking part in Yevtushenko's *Babiy Yar*."[19]

Mravinsky's wife, Inna Mikhailovna, had been ill for some months, and none of the prescribed treatments had brought any upturn. Mravinsky wanted his young wife to recover during this summer period, so as to allow him peace of mind to work on the next season. Despite the wonderful summer of that year, Inna's health did not improve, and it was hoped that some treatment could be sought in America.

The Mravinskys stayed at their dacha longer than planned, not returning until immediately before the first rehearsals. On 30 September, Mravinsky opened the new season with Mozart's Symphony No. 33 in B-flat major, K.319, which was followed after the interval by the mighty Shostakovich Eighth Symphony in C minor. It was a foretaste of the orchestra's major two-month tour to North America opening two weeks later. As always, the composer was present at Mravinsky's performance, and Mravinsky gave an intensely moving performance of this chef-d'oeuvre expressing not only the tragic war years but also the Russian people's burdens in the twentieth century. "I closed my eyes and it seemed to me that I could see a Siberian landscape and thousands, if not tens of thousands, of condemned people walking along a snowy path. I always heard this unmusical connotation in Mravinsky's reading, but that is how Mravinsky's performances were at all times."[20]

Following the concert, Shostakovich went into the conductor's room to express gratitude and ritually autograph his score. Judging all was well, the Shostakoviches returned by Red Arrow to Moscow that night, without broaching the issue of the new symphony. Glikman writes: "On 7 October, Shostakovich phoned from Moscow asking me to find out from Mravinsky if he was preparing the Thirteenth. Yevgeny Alexandrovich was not forthcoming, [an attitude] somewhat unrecognizable in him. He chatted about the prospective tour to America and about affairs in general without saying anything about the music. I was flabbergasted by this turn of events. In this perplexing situation, Dmitry Dmitrevich held himself nobly, with impressive worth, not saying one bad word about Mravinsky."[21] Two days following this phone call, Shostakovich himself phoned the conductor at his home. One witness who listened to the conversation was a confidante of Inna, the flautist Alexandra Vavilina: "Dmitry Dmitrevitch phoned Yevgeny Alexandrovich, asking if he could perform the Thirteenth Symphony before the end of the year. Yevgeny Alexandrovich replied that it would be exceedingly demanding to make it by late December and that it would only be practicable in the New Year."[22] Mravinsky did not turn down the first performance, failing to see the exigency—why could the Thirteenth not wait for another month or two? Shostakovich assumed that Mravinsky's qualms were centered on his unwillingness to work with a male voice choir and bass soloist. Irina Shostakovich believes there was no bitterness by the composer toward Mravinsky (validating Glikman's opinion).[23] This was also the judgment of the composer's son Maxim, related in a discussion with the author.[24]

Shostakovich had found an impressive interpreter for his neglected Fourth Symphony in the Moscow-based conductor Kirill Kondrashin. In December 1961, the artistic director of the Moscow Philharmonic Moshei Grinberg had "arranged" the belated world premiere of the Fourth Symphony, as it were "pulling one over" on the Leningrad Philharmonic. Nevertheless, the chance of performing another Shostakovich work came as a surprise to the Moscow conductor: "I was invited to Shostakovich's flat with Khachaturyan, Wainberg, and others to hear the composer play a run-through of the Thirteenth Symphony on the piano; I was sure that Mravinsky would give the premiere, yet a few days afterward, Shostakovich phoned and asked me if I would prepare the world premiere."[25]

The failure of Mravinsky to conduct the premiere of the Thirteenth Symphony is one of the significant points in the conductor's career. The reasons are disparate and unclear, as the conductor rarely responded as to why he never conducted this work, or indeed any other. However, Mravinsky's primary stimulus in repertoire was an unvarying craving for artistic fulfillment. Politics and culture he held incompatible—more so statecraft hindered the arts—and he withstood any endeavor to bind power battles with the arts.

The Philharmonic did not have its own professional chorus, and several choirs in the city worked in partnership with the orchestra: the Glinka State Choir, the Conservatoire Students Choir, and the Kirov Theatre Chorus. During the 1960s and until the 1970s, there did not exist a first-class professional choir, and frequently ensembles from Latvia, Estonia, or as far away as Armenia would be invited for concert performances of major works; sacred music was banned until the late 1980s, and even a rendering of Mozart's *Requiem* would require permission from the Party cultural department. Nor did Mravinsky enjoy any rapport with the conductors of the city choirs, none of whom aspired to the ethics that he himself savored. The impeccable Glinka

State Choir had reached its all-time low, the Kirov was constrained by the the-ater's schedules, and similar problems hindered the Conservatoire Choir. Ex-cept for a rendition in the previous year, of Borodin's *Polovtsian Dances*, in which the mixed choir from the Glinka State Choir was employed, a full ten years had elapsed since Mravinsky had worked with any choral group. The concerts in October 1952 of Shostakovich's *Song of the Forests* and Tchaikovsky's *1812 Overture* had followed triumphant readings that year of Beethoven's Ninth Symphony and Prokofiev's oratorio *On Guard of Peace*.

There is another explanation why Mravinsky never conducted the Thirteenth, and that lies in its musical form; throughout his career, Mravinsky had been dis-creet about such things, but if there prevailed problems in musical content or form, he would be averse to go back to a work. Several symphonies by Shostakovich, including the First, Fourth, and Fourteenth, he never scheduled. Mravinsky was discriminating in his choice of scores from whatever source, and many choral works were forsaken, including Prokofiev's *Alexander Nevsky* and Berlioz's *Roméo et Juliet*. On one occasion, Vavilina asked Mravinsky why he didn't conduct Beethoven's Ninth Symphony, to which the conductor replied, "What, and work again with soloists and a choir? On no account!"[26] The slight-est imperfection—evident only to Mravinsky—would result in a work being abandoned or conceded to one of his assistants, and this is what happened with Shostakovich's Thirteenth Symphony in B major. The Thirteenth was given over to Igor Blazhkov, who conducted the symphony, using the original texts (now banned),[27] with the Philharmonic, using the Male Voice Choir of the Glinka Choir and a local student choir on 11 December 1966.[28]

The existence of any fear or reluctance in Mravinsky's heart to performing the Thirteenth can be excluded beyond doubt. The conductor had defended Shostakovich's music, so many times paying no heed to bans when his ac-tions could have easily inflicted serious consequences on both his own career and those of his musicians. The grand mystery behind why Mravinsky did not premiere Shostakovich's Thirteenth Symphony in 1962 was in his wife's ter-minal disease. On the very day that Shostakovich phoned the conductor at home, Mravinsky had learned that his wife's illness had been mistakenly di-agnosed and that her medical condition was a rare, incurable bone cancer— *myeloma multiplex*. Just a few months before, the Mravinskys had been on top of the world, with fresh tributes and success, and now a debut tour to America beckoned. The urgent phone call from his long-standing colleague and friend Dmitry Shostakovich on 9 October 1962 had come at the wrong time. Shostakovich's first wife had died from a comparable disorder; nonetheless, Mravinsky could not share with Shostakovich such a private predicament—it was quite beyond so introverted, noble, and deeply private a human being as Yevgeny Mravinsky.

For Inna and Yevgeny Mravinsky, the balance of 1962 rested in two months of concert touring throughout North America. The orchestra had never before had such an extensive touring program; it involved thirty-four concerts, including several premieres of Soviet works. The Philharmonic, with Rozhdestvensky, Rostropovich, and Shostakovich, flew out following the Mravinskys' own departure by train for the seaport of Odessa. Seen off by close friends and musicians at Vitebsky Station, the Mravinskys were outwardly happy, their minds set on the long journey down to the Black Sea port. Onward lay a voyage through the Dardanelles and across the Mediterranean, through the Straits of Gibraltar, and north to the English Channel abroad their Soviet ship—the MS *Maria Yermolova*—before docking at Tilbury. They were met there by the cultural attaché of the Soviet Embassy in London, and after some brief sightseeing, the couple was driven down to Southampton, where they embarked on the Queen Mary for a five-day voyage to New York.[29] The sea crossing allowed them a pause to prepare mentally for the arduous weeks of daily concerts and countless changes of transport and hotels. Evermore, the conductor's concern was for his wife's well being, seeing her decline almost daily; photographs taken on the cruise liner let slip the grim anxiety pinched on the conductor's face.[30]

The very last concert for the Philharmonic's chief conductor in 1962 was on 30 November at Montreal in performances of Shostakovich's Twelfth and Tchaikovsky's Fifth Symphonies. Mravinsky did not take up his baton again for three long months. During the tour, no fresh cures had proved beneficial, Inna's health had declined, and her well-being was now of the greatest concern. Within a fortnight, they were back in Leningrad and Inna was immediately taken to a specialist hospital in Moscow—now in the depths of a Russian winter—where the best medical help available treated her. Recuperation followed more tests, and Mravinsky took her back to Leningrad by overnight train and to the Composers Home of Rest at Repino on the Gulf of Finland. As Yevgeny Mravinsky was taking her to the Leningradsky Station, just a few miles away, Kirill Petrovich Kondrashin was conducting the Thirteenth Symphony in B major, opus 113, *Babiy Yar*, with the Moscow Philharmonic Orchestra, the Male Voice Chorus of the Yurlov State Choir, and the bass Vitaly Gromadsky as third-choice soloist.

Following the American tour, it would not be for another three years that the Leningrad Philharmonic Orchestra would travel outside the Soviet Union, and their concerts inside the country were restricted to short journeys to the Baltic States or to the capital—Moscow. As seldom happens in life, Yevgeny Mravinsky had found in Inna Mikhailovna the ideal companion; they had enjoyed a beautifully romantic affair in the mid-1950s, before their wedding in January 1960. They shared a great chemistry, and in photographs Mravinsky appears to lose ten years in age. Their vacations were spent in the delightfully wild and profuse greenery of the forests and woods on the Karelian peninsula. The years from 1954 to 1962 were years of continuing triumph, every trace of which was shared with Inna Serikova; now the prospect of losing her left the conductor devastated. The creative collaboration between Dmitry Shostakovich and Yevgeny Mravinsky had reached an interregnum, providing a new division in the conductor's life and work. There now lay before Yevgeny Alexandrovich Mravinsky the greatest ordeal in his career.

NOTES

1. Y. A. Mravinsky, "Tridzat let s muzikoi Shostakovicha," in *D. Shostakovich*, ed. L. V. Danilevich (Moscow: Sovetsky Kompozitor, 1967).

2. D. D. Shostakovich joined the CPSU in 1960.

3. Although the couple lived together for a prolonged period, the marriage was not official until the autumn of 1962, following Supinskaya's divorce.

4. I. Glikman, *Pisma k Drugu* (St. Petersburg: DSCH, 1993), 174.

5. Y. Yevtushenko, *Literaturnaya Gazeta*, 19 September 1961.

6. Glikman, *Pisma k Drugu*, 173.

7. *Muzikalnaya Entziklopedia* (Moscow: Sovetskaya Entziklopedia, 1998), 140.

8. S. Khentova, *Udivitelniye Shostakovich* (St. Petersburg: Variant, 1993), 67.

9. Khentova, *Udivitelniye Shostakovich*, 67–69.

10. Khentova, *Udivitelniye Shostakovich*.

11. Glikman, *Pisma k Drugu*, 179–80.

12. Irina Shostakovich, conversation, May 2003.

13. Glikman, *Pisma k Drugu*, 180–81.

14. Glikman, conversation, with the author, July 2002.

15. Glikman, conversation, with the author, July 2002.

16. Glikman, conversation, with the author, July 2002.

17. Khentova, *Udivetelniye Shostakovich*, 67–69.

18. The Edinburgh International Festival in 1962 was dedicated to Shostakovich's music.

19. Khentova, *Udivetelniye Shostakovich*, 67–69.

20. Interview with Boris Tischenko, October 2002.

21. I. Glikman, *Pisma k Drugu*, 180–81.

22. A. M. Vavilina Mravinskaya, author interview, July 2001.

23. Interview with Irina Shostakovich for Leningrad TV, 1989.

24. M. Shostakovich, author interview, September 2002.

25. V. Raznikov, *Kirill Kondrashin rasskazyvaet* (Moscow: Sovetsky Kompozitor, 1989), 184–85.

26. A. M. Vavilina Mravinskaya, author interview, July 2001.

27. Following the first performance, on 18 December 1962, the text in four lines of the first movement was changed by Yevtushenko. It was then performed in its new variation on 20 September 1965. Blazhkov, however, used the "old" text.

28. I. I. Blazhkov, *Shostakovich mezhdu mgnoveniem i vechnostyu* (St. Petersburg: Kompositor, 2000), 897.

29. Alexandra Vavilina Mravinskaya, author interview, July 2001.

30. Alexandra Vavilina Mravinskaya, author interview, July 2001.

Chapter Fourteen

The Years of Crisis

If one could not know and yet hope—each leave-taking would be for people like a fatal hour.

—Y. A. Mravinsky, *Musikalnaya Akademia*

The New Year of 1963 was among the most intense soul-searching periods of Mravinsky's life. If former predicaments had always proved surmountable, now he did not know which way to turn in his dilemma. The Philharmonic arranged entrée to privileged facilities, the conductor pleading only that he be released from supplementary schedules and that engagements be restricted to the monthly subscription series. No stone was left unturned to rebuild Inna's health, yet Mravinsky's solitary solace in life was in prayer. Overseas touring had now led to a denunciation from Madame Furtseva, who had been "informed" that one of the Philharmonic's musicians had been sanctioned for mingling with his long-lost relatives in America.[1] Now in his sixtieth year, Mravinsky discovered in his religion the power to carry on as if music gave him that intimate tranquility.

For listeners at the Philharmonic, there was no perceptible transformation as Mravinsky's storehouse of musical treasures unfolded in the great philosophical and emotionally searing performances as of old. The opening concert Mravinsky gave on 22 February 1963 included Shostakovich's Sixth Symphony and Wagner's overture to *Tannhäuser*, prelude to Act I and the "Liebestod" from *Tristan und Isolde*, "Forest Murmurs" from *Siegfried*, and "The Flight of the Valkyries" from *Die Walküre*. The program was repeated on the following evening, all concerts fully subscribed, young and old standing in the spaces along the massive white marble columns, amazed at the fantastic, spellbinding sound Mravinsky extracted from the Philharmonic.

Mravinsky's audiences had read the reviews of the spectacular American tour of the previous year. As always, he reserved his private thoughts to himself, sheltered from public view; his channel for expressing emotion was through his orchestra.

There now set in train a series of paired concerts at monthly intervals. The March programs comprised Bartók's Music for Strings, Percussion, and Celesta and Brahms's tragic Fourth Symphony in E minor. The theme continued in April, when Mozart's Symphony No. 39 in E-flat and Tchaikovsky's *Pathétique* were scheduled. In May, there was framed an evening of fragments from Wagner, including the prelude to *Die Meistersinger*, "Siegfried's Funeral March" from *Götterdämmerung*, and the preludes to Acts I and III of *Lohengrin*, and a Tchaikovsky night, with the suites from *The Sleeping Beauty* and *The Nutcracker*, the Violin Concerto (with concertmaster Victor Liberman), and *Francesca da Rimini*. To bring the 1963 season to a close, Mravinsky turned to two composers closest to him—Shostakovich and Tchaikovsky—in readings of their Fifth Symphonies: exceptional in that Mravinsky united in concert these two great tragic works, transforming Tchaikovsky's romanticism to contemporaneousness for the musical public.

For Mravinsky, it was a relief to bring to an end this trying and heartbreaking season. Inna was in the hospital, and his visits were restricted to certain days and hours, although he elicited great delight in being able to gain entrée to his wife when this was stringently prohibited. "It was a deep love. When Innochka was in the hospital, he would secretly climb up the fire escape to the floor where she was located and would peek in at her through the window."[2]

It was August 1963, and Yevgeny Alexandrovich's wife Inna Mikhailovna Serikova was mortally ill. Canceling all his touring, Yevgeny Alexandrovich did not leave Leningrad for a single day. The orchestra was based in Kislovodsk for the summer season. Here at the end of August, there rose the necessity to turn up even if for just a week to Kislovodsk and conduct the final concerts there. Strengthening his heart, Yevgeny Alexandrovich traveled to the south and received a firm assurance that every day a telegram would be sent informing him of his wife Inna Mikhailovna's health and well-being. Such was the situation on his departure for Leningrad. He traveled alone, as always in a four-seated compartment; one needs to say that he never made use of his privileges and always traveled in the same carriage as the other musicians. All those who knew what was going on in his family affairs knew that if he did not get the telegram . . . he would be thinking the worst. Yevgeny Alexandrovich almost never left his compartment, eating nothing; in general, his situation was terrible. That was the situation until we arrived at Kharkov. . . . The stop was quite prolonged, and the carriage quickly emptied and everyone went to concern themselves with their own affairs.

Quite by chance, I was standing near the door of the carriage and suddenly the following scene unfolded: along the platform, a group of people led by a tall railway official was heading clearly toward me. He called out, "Is there in this train the Peoples Artist of the USSR (he declared his other titles) Yevgeny Alexandrovich Mravinsky?"—"Yes, he's in this carriage." The leader of this group, with palpable relief, offered the telegram marked "urgent—governmental" to me. "To be passed to Comrade Mravinsky." The group vanished instantaneously. One was left with a sensation of trepidation holding this telegram in my hands, understanding that there might be something terrible inside, but that one cannot but pass it on straight away to Yevgeny Alexandrovich. Seeing me on the entrance of his compartment, he at once grasped what had happened and with trembling hands began to search for his spectacles. Not finding them, he softly requested of me, "you read it."

What could one do? I opened the telegram and by now, it became obvious that nothing had happened and that all was as it should be—the condition of the patient was no worse—everyone was waiting for him. Yevgeny Alexandrovich somehow immediately felt at ease; as if without life his hands slumped and not hiding his emotions, [he] began to weep, the tears flowing, like a child wiping them from his cheeks. Suddenly, one felt that one had no right to observe this, yet he bore no shame at one being there. One even reflected that it was comforting to share this with me.[3]

Mravinsky's vale of sorrows led to friends and relatives arriving at Tverskaya Street to help and rally around him. These well wishers included his former spouses Marianna and Olga, the mother of his child Lydia, and most frequently, Alexandra Vavilina, the alter ego and former student of Serikova. Vavilina took up residence at Tverskaya, overseeing the daily medication and therapy, as well as preparing food and serving as pro tem home help. Vavilina's special experience gave Mravinsky the fair wind indispensable to putting his life in order, and allowed him to bring Inna Mikhailova home again. Vavilina had studied at the Conservatoire and following her triumph at a music competition in 1957 had signed on at the second orchestra and was promoted as principal flute, before joining the Philharmonic in 1962. Alexandra Mikhailovna had lived through a childless marriage, her ex-husband dying in an automobile accident.[4]

There now saw a burgeoning of contemporary and rarely performed repertoire—a whole cycle of premieres unfolded during the 1963–1964 season. The brand new concert year opened on 1 October with Prokofiev's Sixth Symphony in E-flat minor and Beethoven's Fifth Symphony in C minor. The second program contained the Soviet premiere of Sibelius's Third Symphony in C in a bill shared with Tchaikovsky's Violin Concerto (soloist Victor Liberman) and *Francesca da Rimini* on 26 October. Changing to works of the more recent past, on 30 November 1963 Mravinsky unveiled Honegger's

Liturgique (premiere in the USSR) and Debussy's *Nocturnes* and *Prélude à l'après-midi d'un faune* and concluded with Ravel's *Boléro*. The revelations enduring into 1964, in January, Mravinsky conducted Hindemith's *Die Harmonie der Welt* (premiere in the USSR) and Shostakovich's Sixth Symphony. Mravinsky's release from anxiety and constraint at home now allowed him more freedom in studying diverse scores. Further into the series came the world premiere of Boris Klyuzner's Second Symphony—an esoteric piece reminiscent of Mahler and the second Viennese School.[5] Klyuzner's work was coupled with Debussy's *Prélude à l'après-midi d'un faune* and Honegger's *Liturgique*. On 29 March, Richard Strauss's Horn Concerto No. 1 (Buyanovsky as soloist) together with *Ein Alpensinfonie* were unveiled to Leningraders. Yet another first performance, of Vadim Salmanov's Third Symphony, was given on 23 May, and audiences at Philharmonic Hall also listened to an evening of Beethoven, including *Egmont*, the Fourth Piano Concerto (Vasso Devetzy as soloist), and the Fourth Symphony in B-flat. During the captivating White Nights Festival, Shostakovich's Sixth played fellow traveler to Tchaikovsky's Fifth Symphony on 21 June, and the season was completed with another commitment, repeating the March billing, to Richard Strauss.

Mravinsky was scrupulous in ensuring that the appropriate medicine be given Inna at the correct time and constantly chided Vavilina for not adhering to the planned treatment procedure—itself as thorough as any of the conductor's rehearsals. In the face of all this, Inna trusted her friend and threatened her husband that she would go back to the hospital if he did not tolerate Vavilina.[6] These last months had been difficult, again an apparently endless period of transfusions, check-ups, and waiting for news of the analysis. A final curtain on the prolonged anguish was drawn with the death of Inna Serikova Mravinskaya at home on 4 July 1964. It was a moment long foreseen, and for which Mravinsky had inwardly prepared, yet there was no reprieve from the purgatory into which the conductor declined after his wife's burial at Bogoslovsky Cemetery.

Vavilina continued to be a resident at Mravinsky's home. Observing an agreement with Inna that she would not abandon the conductor—Serikova was mindful of her impending end and fearful for Mravinsky's future welfare—Vavilina remained as confrere and housekeeper for the conductor. A week or so following the funeral, on one afternoon Vavilina sensed that the flat had all of a sudden become hushed—a deathly silence reigned through the rooms. Her worst fears were stirred when she entered Mravinsky's study to catch sight of the conductor sitting with an army pistol poised at his temple like Herman from *The Queen of Spades* about to take his own life. Vavilina slumped on her knees before Mravinsky, beseeching him to give up the gun, crying this was a sin against himself and Inna. Uncontrollably weeping, Mravinsky handed the weapon over, hiding his features with his enormous hands, crushed and humiliated, masking his exposed feelings.[7]

> By an uncharted path—on an unknown course
> He goes: ahead silence surrounds him—
> The eternal holy night
> There lie misty roses
> And fall stars without sound—alight
> He goes—on his way without help
> He quietly goes, bent over, he is white
> And a glance falls on the pale image—
> Only tears shine from the ages . . .
> By an uncharted path, on an unknown route
> He goes: ahead silence surrounds him
> And his name—A man.[8]

Vavilina remained with Mravinsky, becoming a quintessential colleague and friend, her precious care and attention lessening the struggle for his concert regime. "The person who resuscitated him was Alexandra Mikhailovna," Boris Tischenko recounted, "a respectable, compassionate woman combining in her character loyalty and bonhomie."[9] Vavilina's experience of music was crucial, and altogether conscious of Mravinsky's idiosyncrasies and inscrutable characteristics, she furnished a refreshing boost to his music making in his last decades at the Philharmonic, permitting him both spiritual refuge and harmony.

During this period, Mravinsky employed several assistant conductors, among whom was the capable Eduard Serov: "I was terribly anxious upon arriving at his small flat at Tverskaya Street. 'Sit down,' he told me, 'you have the same long hands as I have, and as in my own youth, you don't know what to do with them!'"[10] The young student secured Mravinsky's trust, becoming one of his favored protégés. Serov also attended Mravinsky's Conservatoire class, however he discovered that there the maestro was no instinctive lecturer. He attended just three sessions. "When we were working on Glazunov's *Raymonda*, Mravinsky was so taken by the music that he stood up and began to conduct the ballet suite." On the other hand, for Serov, the great piece of providence was in attending the rehearsals: "here were unraveled many secrets of the conducting profession both in technique and psychology."[11] An addendum to studying at Mravinsky's home, these sessions brought extraordinary value in musical analysis.[12]

Mravinsky was present at all of his assistant's own rehearsals. Among Serov's first engagements was Beethoven's Fifth Symphony in C minor;

influenced by Furtwängler's elegiac, philosophical readings, Serov hoped to give his own portrayal more free expression. "Mravinsky was sitting in the loge with his ears pricked up. In the second movement, I heard behind me a metallic voice loud enough for everyone to hear, 'we are accustomed to play without *ritardando* here.'"[13] The young Serov caught on to Mravinsky's feeling of possession over the orchestra. "Mravinsky loved to hold all the beads in his own hands."[14] Nonetheless, Serov only found his admiration mounting, observing that "Mravinsky's work with his orchestra has no equal." Verification of this came when Karajan arrived in the northern capital with the Vienna Philharmonic in March 1962. The Austrian maestro had forbidden anyone to enter his rehearsals, however Mravinsky took Serov with him and entered the Philharmonic Hall. Karajan noticed the Russians and turned around to his players saying, "Gentlemen, I want you to welcome a great conductor of our times!"[15] Mravinsky, regardless of his own quintessence, would find approval for other conductors, although with a trace of sangfroid. Mravinsky and Serov studied Karajan's reading of Dvořák's Eighth Symphony (a work Mravinsky never performed). Karajan vocalized a fragment from the secondary theme in the second movement and asked the musicians to repeat this theme to attain accuracy in this hardly discernible accent; he repeated this a second and, eventually, a fifth time. Subsequent to this, Karajan requested another section to be played, after which he declared the rehearsal closed, and here Mravinsky, the architect of the rehearsal, exclaimed with clear delight, "Now that's how a sitting should be run!" However, the Russian said this with a measure of diplomacy; Serov himself listened to more of Karajan's rehearsal work and found Mravinsky an unparalleled master of the operation.[16]

Among Mravinsky's finest interpretations was Brahms's Fourth Symphony, and on one occasion the Swiss conductor Paul Kletzki directed this symphony with the Philharmonic and caused "a furor both among the Leningrad public and musicians and attracted only disapproval from Mravinsky, who complained that they had forced the sound, losing balance in ensemble."[17] Mravinsky used the score at the piano exclusively in his own preparations, and exceptions to this occurred only when he began to select twentieth-century works.[18]

During 1963, there emerged a controversy around the programming of the young, enterprising conductor Igor Blazhkov. He had studied under Mravinsky and upon graduation was invited to work as his assistant, Mravinsky procuring a flat for him and his wife in the city. Blazhkov had a penchant for the avant-garde; he constantly sought the latest unorthodox compositions and exchanged correspondence with Igor Stravinsky for a long number of years. One of Blazhkov's conspicuous realizations was the restoration of Shostakovich's Second and Third Symphonies, neglected since their first performances. It was after an interval of thirty-eight years that the Second Symphony took place under Blazhkov's direction on 31 October 1965. Shostakovich and Mravinsky both attended the second performance.[19]

If the second Viennese school had "bypassed" Soviet music, nevertheless Mravinsky gave a carte blanche to his assistants in formulating their programs, although discussing composers and styles with them. Mravinsky took up modern pieces and championed Stravinsky's ballets in the 1930s, continuing into the mid-1960s. Mravinsky gave *Apollon* on 20 October 1964 and *Agon* in the following season, on 29 October 1965 (both premieres in the Soviet Union), and he also performed *The Fairy's Kiss* and revived *Petrushka* during this period. The Philharmonic became the pace-setters in new music, and not only in Russian repertoire. In 1964, Blazhkov conducted the Leningrad Philharmonic in an all-American program including William Schuman's Third Symphony (*May Day*), Samuel Barber's Piano Concerto, and Gershwin's *Porgy and Bess* in Bennett's symphonic arrangement.[20]

Igor Blazhkov's promotion of modern music caused disquiet with numerous Soviet authorities, and he ultimately fell into disrepute with the State Committee for the Ministry of Culture. This was encouraged by an anonymous letter complaining about the young musician. The principal objection to Blazhkov was his infatuation with "unfashionable" music that was deemed discordant with "traditional" Soviet art. Vasily Fedosyevich Kucharsky, a musicologist who had occupied a leading position in the Union of Composers since 1948, was appointed a secretary at the Central Committee of the CPSU in 1960, and he now led the campaign to remove Blazhkov. Kucharsky claimed Blazhkov was "ideologically incompatible, not only active from the podium but with his pen, and the platform of the Leningrad Philharmonic is the most prominent in the whole country."[21] In ensuing months, the stigmatizing would continue—all to no avail. Mravinsky unrelentingly supported his protégé, yet relentlessly Kucharsky amassed a disparaging catalogue of opposition. Blazhkov's wife, a musicologist, unable to take the public calumny, tragically took her own life.[22] Galina Mokreyevna (writing under her maiden name) had written a feature article, titled "Letter from Kiev," for a Polish magazine, about Ukrainian composers who wrote in the twelve-note system.[23]

Mravinsky remained a supporter of Blazhkov, and it proved difficult to get rid of the young musician. With Mravinsky's blessing, Blazhkov recorded regularly with the Melodiya label, producing a batch of fine LPs of pieces by Stravinsky, Schoenberg, Shostakovich, Webern, Varese, and Ives. The crusade against Blazhkov came to a head on 21 June 1968 in a meeting of the Ministry of Culture collegiate with the agenda "Shortcomings of the Leningrad Philharmonic's repertoire." The conference condemned Blazhkov's activities in Leningrad for performing "formalistic, decadent" works by Schoenberg, Webern, Ives, Varese, Volkonsky, Silvestrov, and Denisov. Vasily Kucharsky, now first deputy minister of culture, wrote in the journal *Sovetskaya Muzika*, "As a propagandist of dodecaphony, punctualist, and other 'avant-garde' music, the conductor I. Blazhkov . . . is the author of apologetic, sickly sweet, excited annotations for his own 'avant-garde' programs"; and also, "state organs will repulse antagonistic challenges by followers of 'avant-gardism' to mount major concert platforms and acquire a permanent home there."[24] Consequently, Blazhkov was sacked on 1 July from the Philharmonic and lost the right to work in Leningrad.[25] That was not the last admonition; the Leningrad Philharmonic and its chief conductor were severely reprimanded for a reprehensible repertoire policy.

Dmitry Shostakovich wrote to Kucharsky asking for Blazhkov to be reappointed, but to no avail.[26] Shostakovich later wrote to Blazhkov: "they do not listen to me; you have to go yourself and see them. They love it when you go down on your knees and beg."[27] It took another decade before Blazhkov was permitted back to Leningrad; in 1977, at last winning the battle with the Party, Mravinsky invited his prodigal son back to work with the Philharmonic. Until 1988, Blazhkov would present no less than five new programs every year of new and interesting repertoire at the Philharmonic.[28]

The excellence of the Philharmonic was borne out when Mravinsky took his orchestra to Moscow in February 1965. There he directed four concerts of twentieth-century music, all of which had been unveiled in recent years to his Leningrad audiences. The programs included Sibelius's "The Swan of Tuonela" and his Seventh Symphony, Stravinsky's *Apollon*, Hindemith's *Die Harmonie der Welt*, Bartók's Music for Strings, Percussion, and Celesta, Honegger's *Liturgique*, Debussy's *Prélude à l'après-midi d'un faune*, and Shostakovich's Sixth and Tchaikovsky's Fifth Symphonies. The Moscow critic Andrey Zolotov applauded the performances: "we hear these little-known pieces by great masters of the twentieth-century so perfect and alive. We have discovered what real classics are now before us!"[29] Moscow Radio broadcast them live, and they were later released on LP and issued under license to Western record companies. *Gramophone* wrote, "The Sibelius symphony receives a no less highly charged reading. Mravinsky shows a genuine feeling for the epic sweep and majestic power of the work. The string playing has something of the same fervour and intensity."[30] There was a sociopolitical aspect in that it was a means of lending color to the preeminence of Leningrad over the capital. "No other city in the Soviet Union has made any comparable efforts, and in fact no other city can dispute Leningrad's historical leadership in the arts."[31]

It was in the mid-'60s, and my cousin Grigory Sokolov, then just a teenager, was making his first steps in the music world. He was scheduled to play with the second orchestra of the Philharmonic. The day of his concert coincided with that of Mravinsky's rehearsal, which was due to begin at 11 a.m. finishing at 3 p.m., meaning that the second sessions could start no earlier than 4 p.m., leaving little time remaining before their performance; this, of course, was difficult. Grigory's teacher, Lilya Ilyichna Zelichman, was concerned, as he was himself, yet nothing could be done, the hall being booked in advance. On the eve of the rehearsal, I decided to speak to Yevgeny Alexandrovich: "Would it be possible to move tomorrow's rehearsal one hour ahead so as to allow the second orchestra more time to practice?" In response, I heard at once, "There can be no talk of it!" Yevgeny Alexandrovich disappeared with his great strides into the conductors' room. I had already begun to regret my action with such a badly put question, and started to practice. About five minutes before the rehearsal began, the inspector of the orchestra approached me and said, "Yevgeny Alexandrovich wants to see you." Now I thought that I would get it for my indelicate and bold attitude to Yevgeny Alexandrovich.

To my great surprise, Yevgeny Alexandrovich began to explain with great respect why he had to decline my request. He explained that the psychological relations of the rehearsals were extraordinarily important, so that both conductor and musicians adjusted to bioclock; to move at certain times was very hazardous, and this is reflected in their work. A musician used to rehearsing in the morning and during the day will work quite differently at other times; this was not a caprice, but very important. Therefore, I should not be upset. Naturally, one was let down by this course of events a lot more so than [if one had gotten] a rebuke from him. Unusually, Yevgeny Alexandrovich began asking about Grigory's affairs, [remarking] that playing with him in the future would be fascinating, saying he would like to play with him at some point, and the conversation ended on a quite different note.

Following the rehearsal three hours later, when Yevgeny Alexandrovich was already going off stage, the orchestra inspector emerged and proclaimed, "Comrade artists, tomorrow the rehearsal will begin two hours later, at 1 p.m." For all my life, I have tried to resolve what sort of will power, real or imaginary, can one submit one's will to others, while decent human wisdom can lead one to second oneself to age-old human pride.[32]

A major Festival of Leningrad Music was organized in Moscow between 24 November and 2 December 1965, and Mravinsky returned to the capital with his Philharmonic. No fewer than eighty-four concerts were given, and six hundred performers from Leningrad participated, in addition to various Moscow organizations. The Leningrad Philharmonic Orchestra arrived with its five conductors: Mravinsky and Jansons as well as three young assistants in Blazhkov, Serov, and Aliyev. "Nothing was neglected to stress that Leningrad was a leader in cultural affairs, and the lesson was not lost on the

Muscovites."[33] Among works by contemporary Leningrad composers performed at the festival were Salmanov's Third Symphony and his oratorio *The
Twelve* (after A. Blok), the Second Symphony by Yevlyakhov, the Violin Concerto by Arapov, and the *Partita for Piano and Strings* by Bogdanov-
Berezovsky. The Piano Concertos of Ustvolskaya and Tischenko and the
vocal-symphonic *Songs of Freedom* by Slonimsky represented the younger
generation, the symphonic cycle *Songs of Our Days* (based on epigraphs by
Soviet poets) by Andrey Petrov and the oratorio *Poem of Leningrad* (based on
verses by the poet Olga Berggoltz) by young Gennady Belov.[34]

Yevgeny Mravinsky gave just one concert comprising Salmanov's Third
Symphony, Bogdanov-Berezovsky's *Partita for Piano and Strings*, and in the
second half, Shostakovich's redoubtable Fifth Symphony. The consensus
among the Moscow press was that the greatest triumph of all was the portrayal of Shostakovich's Fifth—"as if they were listening a to a completely
new work rather than the one they already knew."[35] In bringing his assistant
conductors, all highly talented young musicians, Mravinsky was unmasking
the finest of the current generation together with the upcoming and mature
Leningrad composers, the wealth of Petersburg-Leningrad tradition—all this
and the finely honed virtuoso orchestra of the Philharmonic.[36] "It is as if the
Leningrad Orchestra knows how to create the most finite sounds with such an
ease and freedom it appears as if everything is natural without the need of the
most painstaking and endless rehearsals . . . as if one is present at music being born."[37] It was an audacious tour de force by maestro Mravinsky.[38]

Following the replacement of the Soviet leader Nikita Khrushchev in October 1964, a freeze in political and cultural life would now sink in that involved exacting consequences for Mravinsky and his orchestra. If he perse-
vered with a delicate alignment with Yekaterina Furtseva at the Ministry of
Culture and Rodionov at the Smolny, this was now checked following the latter's removal to distant Chelyabinsk and the ban on foreign touring. In November 1964, Grigory Romanov was appointed in charge of the Leningrad
Regional Committee of the Communist Party; Romanov was a man oblivious
to the arts and a careerist who regarded the city as a stepping stone to the top
echelons of power.

The Party was keen to avoid a repetition of the embarrassment caused by
the defection of the great dancer Rudolph Nureyev during the Kirov Ballet's
visit to Paris. If this had been a blow to the Soviet Union's prestige, the loss
of its leading conductor would be an even greater blow to the country's image.[39] In the wake of Romanov's appointment, there arrived at the city's cultural department Galina Semyonovna Pakhomova, a woman of cold design
and modest subtlety who now trained her sights on the Philharmonic's chief
conductor.

She began collecting a thick and weighty file, upon which she would mount her endeavor to replace Mravinsky with a younger man who would be subordinate. She made instructions to prepare a special pension for Mravinsky, to which he was now qualified.[40] Romanov, however, at the outset rejected her scheme, conceding that Moscow recognized Mravinsky's value as a cultural icon, and there was no one of similar standing to replace him with; Mravinsky could simply be withdrawn from foreign touring for the time being. For many years, Mravinsky was labeled in party circles, "the unrepentant bourgeois." In an underground vault in the city lay documents going back to the Civil War recording his ancestry, covering every facet of the conductor's life and work, and including dispositions by enemies and informers; mysteriously, the letter of guarantee from Madame Kollontay had somehow vanished.[41]

By the mid-1960s, the liberalization of the arts was dead in the water when the writers Sinyavsky and Daniel were imprisoned and the works of Alexander Solzhenitsyn and other dissidents were prohibited. Throughout their reign of power, the Party had used letters of denunciation against their opponents that would traditionally appear in *Pravda*; leading artists including Oistrakh, Ulanova, Kogan, Gilels, Shostakovich, and Sholokhov would be enlisted to sign such condemnations. In Leningrad, two young officials from the Party's cultural department visited Mravinsky to obtain his signature to a letter of censure. Mravinsky asked how could he sign a letter against Solzhenitsyn when he had never been able to read his works. When the Central Committee of the Party published this denunciation in 1968, Yevgeny Mravinsky was the only major figure in the arts community who refused to sign it; such circumstances were unprecedented, almost a state of *lèse-majesté* for the Party.

How did Yevgeny Mravinsky manage to maintain his position, despite the undisputed power and influence the CPSU enjoyed—if the Party wanted to get rid of him, why didn't they manage this? Cultural life was controlled in each city and region by a Party cultural department that had control over things ranging from the TV programs broadcast to the flowers planted in public parks, yet there were a number of factors that sustained the framework of Soviet existence. It was always a conundrum whether to sack someone if they were valuable in their job and indeed publicly renowned for their service. The commonly held view for many years—from the war years and into the "thaw"—was that the figure of Mravinsky was "canonized," even by the Party press. Here was the almost legendary figure who had directed the venerated Shostakovich war symphonies and who had unveiled the premieres of Shostakovich's symphonies *The Year 1905* and *The Year 1917*. Mravinsky's aunt Alexandra Kollontay was a distinguished minister and diplomat (the only member of Lenin's first cabinet who, apart from Stalin, died a natural death), and Mravinsky was esteemed because he had chosen to remain with his Leningrad musicians when, as a former aristocrat, he could have gone into exile as many others did in the 1920s. Yevgeny Mravinsky together with Richter, Oistrakh, Sofronitsky, and Kozlovsky occupied an almost unassailable position in Soviet cultural life. For many in the ruling Party, "he was like a relic from the past that we couldn't get rid of."[42] Mravinsky was comparable to a "god" who was unapproachable and indeed above criticism.

At the 1948 Union of Composers sessions attack on leading Soviet composers for writing allegedly formalist works, Mravinsky declared at the meeting of the Leningrad branch that, "rather than attacking formalism one should combat dilettantism in music."[43] The maestro's view of politics was analogous to that of the music critic Vladimir Stasov: "He didn't care for politics and used to frown when he spoke about it. He said that it was an outrage that interfered with people's lives and that spoiled their minds and distracted them from worthwhile deeds."[44] Continuous bickering in the Party group in the orchestra was a thorn in Mravinsky's side vis-à-vis repertoire, studio work, staffing, and touring. The Ministry of Culture in Moscow would have been happy to limit his foreign touring, yet his figure was far too valuable to Soviet art. The lengthy voyages to America and Western Europe were major opportunities to earn foreign currency for Goskonzert, as were his recordings released to Western companies under license. Quite simply there was no heir apparent—no other Soviet conductor enjoyed such respect either at home or abroad. Pro tempore, the Leningrad Philharmonic without Yevgeny Mravinsky was not an option for the Ministry of Culture in Moscow.

Following a concert in Leningrad, the conductor Yevgeny Svetlanov approached Mravinsky:

> Sometimes one met Yevgeny Alexandrovich at times when he was very upset and in great distress. This was at the end of the '60s, and it was as if a bolt from the blue had struck him. I could not imagine that this man with steel will power, as it were without nerves, was almost weeping, chatting about the dilemma in his work with the orchestra. . . . But thank God, they found people in Moscow who wouldn't allow this.[45]

During the White Nights Festival of 1966, Dmitry Shostakovich performed at a concert in the Maly Hall, after which he suffered a relapse and was hospitalized at Medvichovo. "Several days later, Mravinsky called on the sick man. He too had matters to talk and reminisce about. There was the premiere of the Fifth Symphony, the collaboration on the Seventh in distant Novosibirsk, and their last meetings with Sollertinsky. There was also Mravinsky's presentation of the Eighth and its dedication, of which the celebrated conductor was no less proud than of the high honors he had been accorded."[46]

Mravinsky took a copy of the new cello concerto by Shostakovich on holiday to Ust-Narva and gave instructions to program the new piece in opening the 1966–1967 season, the highlight of which was to be the celebrations of Shostakovich's sixtieth birthday. "The premiere was arranged for the beginning of September under Mravinsky's direction. During the summer, wanting more time to prepare the program, Mravinsky decided to put the premiere back to October, asking the director Osik Sarkissov to inform Rostropovich about this, however he neglected to tell him. Rostropovich, unaware and not suspecting anything was amiss, arrived in Leningrad five days before the concert to hear the orchestra under rehearsal. He was surprised that no one met him at the station and went to the Yevropeiskaya hotel, opposite the Philharmonic, not seeing even a poster there, [and] affronted and fuming turned to Rabinovich and arranged the premiere with the Students Orchestra at the Conservatoire."[47] The incident led to a clouding of relations between Mravinsky and Rabinovich and not least between the cellist and Mravinsky, although the problem was alleviated in years to come.[48]

Following the U.S. debut—with one exception—Mravinsky was prohibited from traveling to the West until the early seventies. The slighted Mravinsky led many to suppose that he was being prepared for retirement. There were those who were averse to Mravinsky's "dry" manner, and the non-premiere of Shostakovich's Thirteenth was perceived as *lèse-majesté* by Mravinsky when the composer most needed his assistance. The supposed fallout between Shostakovich and his hallowed conductor was believed irreversible, a perception reinforced when Mravinsky failed to give the Second Cello Concerto.

The emergence of the young conductor Maxim Shostakovich, the composer's son, was another element, as some saw him as an alternative to Mravinsky, the irony being that Maxim's inspiration to take up conducting "was in being taken by his mother to a performance of the Eighth Symphony under Mravinsky during the 1950s."[49] Throughout the decade, Kirill Kondrashin and Maxim Shostakovich would get preference for giving Shostakovich's works, a trend encouraged by the establishment. Unwilling to indulge in petty vendettas, the composer showed no ambivalence in his relationship with the old Leningrad maestro, which remained one of respect and courtesy.[50]

Following a concert in Leningrad, Mravinsky and Glikman would often see Shostakovich off at the Moscow Station when he was boarding the Red Arrow overnight express to Moscow. On one occasion, it was raining and Shostakovich waved them to go home and not get drenched, yet the two friends stayed till the train's departure; Glikman glanced across at the conductor who was looking with some adoration at Shostakovich, muttering to himself: "Ah, my little pet, how I love you!"[51] Mravinsky repeated these words quite lost to his surroundings. Mravinsky often used such terms in referring to close friends and colleagues; Glikman was addressed by Mravinsky as "little sugar,"[52] to which Glikman responded by calling him "Yevgeny the Great."[53] Isaak Glikman acted as Shostakovich's confidant through many years and had a keen admiration for the conductor, of whom he was an intimate for thirty-three years, "almost the life-span of Christ, but thank God, they never crucified Mravinsky."[54]

Dmitry Shostakovich was enthusiastic in supporting his own son's career. Kirill Kondrashin writes: "It was in 1966 when I was chairman of the Second Competition of Conductors. Maxim Shostakovich proceeded into the second round easily, but it was clear that he was not good enough to progress any further."[55] This cost Kondrashin many a sleepless night, as he had to speak in favor of certain candidates and consulted with his colleagues. They agreed that Maxim would make a career, anyway, so winning a prize was irrelevant. He would just be taking a more worthy person's place. Despite this, Kondrashin consulted other jury members. The composer Kara Karayev told him,[56] "Kirill Petrovich, you are quite right, but I worship Dmitry Dmitrevich and know that he adores his Maxim and will not vote against him." Maxim got through with the minimum votes. The following day, Kondrashin approached Shostakovich, knowing well that he would be aware of Kondrashin's position. The composer, with anxiety etched across his face, replied:

> Kirill Petrovich, I am very grateful that you have come and said exactly what you think. I appreciate this, but one cannot agree with you; maybe Mansurov is better than Maxim and of all those who are taking part he is a lot stronger. In any case, as an old friend, I would like you to help Maxim.[57]

In 1966, the great thespian Nikolay Cherkasov died following a protracted illness, and the Philharmonic performed in his memory at the Pushkin Drama Theatre. It would have been easy to pass the role to one of his assistants; all the same Mravinsky insisted on conducting for his friend and loyal confidant. In the last months of his life, despite his terminal illness being known, Cherkasov had been sacked from the theater.[58] Mravinsky drew out the finest from his musicians in Tchaikovsky's Introduction to *Swan Lake* and the Entr'acte from Glazunov's *Raymonda*, works that the two artists shared in their years of apprenticeship at the ballet.[59]

In October 1966, Mravinsky was permitted to take his Philharmonic to the West once more. This revival of touring was at the insistence of Emmi Moresko-Erede. The Italian impresario had been seduced by the Philharmonic's concerts in Leningrad and went to Furtseva demanding a tour to Italy, promising the minister whatever she wished, providing she allow Mravinsky's orchestra permission to travel. Presents of every description were bestowed upon Furtseva, who grudgingly relented. A warm friendship developed between the impresario and the Mravinskys that was broken only by the Italian executive's premature death in 1969.[60]

Mravinsky's musicians revisited Vienna and toured northern Italy with a repertoire of Mozart, Lyadov, Honegger, Shostakovich, and Tchaikovsky. If the latter two Russians were familiar, the miniatures of *The Enchanted Lake* and *Baba Yaga* by Anatol Lyadov caused a stir for their impressionistic colors and brilliantly rich orchestration. Nevertheless, it was the Tchaikovsky that left the most lasting impression: "Tchaikovsky's Fifth Symphony was opened up in all its rhythm and color to Romans for the first time. The performance by Mravinsky of this symphony, with its clear and uncanny gamut of feelings and its finale, with stunning mastery achieves the peak of conducting art. We would not be surprised to discover there is something new in this performance of Tchaikovsky's music. Mravinsky's excellence is in his lucid reading, true to the spirit and letter of the score, yet impassioned and moving at the same time—noble and epic."[61]

The next foreign voyage, in May 1967, took them to familiar territory, as they revisited the Prague Spring Festival and played Prokofiev's Sixth and Shostakovich's Fifth Symphonies, Mozart's Symphony No. 33 in B-flat, K.319, his No. 39 in E-flat, K.543, Bartók's Music for Strings, Percussion, and Celesta, and Debussy's *Prélude à l'après-midi d'un faune*. The trip continued with visits to Basel, Geneva, Paris, and Lyons, where the repertoire included Shchedrin's Piano Concerto with the composer performing at the keyboard. Shchedrin described how painstakingly Mravinsky rehearsed his musicians, recalling an evening of Debussy, Bartók, and Honegger. "It was a fantastic concert, and everyone was overjoyed, yet the conductor was concerned, asking his musicians: 'wasn't the 9/8 in Debussy similar to 9/8 in Bartók? It should have been quite different. . . .'"[62] This was the last visit to the West for a full five years to be led by Mravinsky; his outings were later restricted to Eastern Europe.

On 14 January 1967—by the old Julian calendar, New Years Day—Yevgeny Mravinsky married Alexandra Vavilina in a civil ceremony. Alexandra Mikhailovna shared many interests with Mravinsky, one of which was a love of animals. Boris Tischenko recalled that when he was staying at the Composers Union rest home, he saw her trying to save the life of a poor cat that had been chased to the top of a tree by a hostile dog. Having banished the poor hound, she then enlisted the help of some young boys to get a ladder and climb up to rescue the distressed cat—which became another member of the Mravinsky household![63]

During his ban from foreign touring, Mravinsky was contented to spend more time at his dacha at Ust-Narvi, with his friend Nikolay Rabinovich of student years. Rabinovich was a "Westerner," long idolizing the music of Gustav Mahler and having promoted the composer's music extensively since the 1930s. The two confederates would often sit in their garden chatting about music, on a splendid summer's evening, with the sunlight slowly disappearing through the tree branches. Mravinsky would say wistfully how much he yearned to listen to some old romances by Rachmaninov or Tchaikovsky, to which Rabinovich would reply: "I think that I would rather prefer some *lieder* by Hugo Wolf."[64] Mravinsky bought himself a speedboat that he loved to use on his summer vacations to his dacha. Should the weather be fitting, in early morning he would take the boat out, Rabinovich often joining him for a spot of fishing upriver. There they would spend days sharing a primitive, peasant-like existence far away from the moribund threat of civilization. Mravinsky would often leave his flat in Leningrad in the charge of his students, as much to look after the plants as anything.[65]

The composer Boris Tischenko remembers meeting him once at the canteen in the Composers Union rest home at Repino: "We sat with Issay Braudo and Yevgeny Alexandrovich Mravinsky. During our discussion, a wasp flew in and began circling around the room. Having just come from swimming, I thought it would sting someone and used my towel to swat the wasp. Yevgeny Alexandrovich looked at me angrily and said 'What did she ever do to you?' Seeing myself chastened, Issay raised my spirits with a joke. 'He probably prefers to squirt water on them.'"[66]

Before a performance, Yevgeny Mravinsky was so anxious that even his chain smoking would not help him to concentrate. It was even worse on tour, particularly in Germany when he was playing the great German classics. For many years, one of the viola players would tie his bow tie for him, the conductor being incapable of doing this himself. Alexey Ludewig would spend some time with Mravinsky as he tried to calm his nerves, acting naïvely sensitive in these private moments. "Why did they choose me of all people to play the Beethoven symphonies? I know naught about them!"[67] Ludewig would try to restore the confidence of the conductor, who was incredibly vulnerable in these minutes; Ludewig was keenly aware that this was a ritual that Mravinsky found crucial before going on stage. Just seconds after seeing Mravinsky on the brink of despair, Ludewig would see Mravinsky come into view, as if he had donned a mask—completely without emotion—and walk resolutely to the rostrum.[68]

There were other moments when the conductor would lower his guard. On one summer's evening following drinks with friends, Mravinsky and his wife walked into the little square of Ust-Narvi. As in many Soviet towns, here there stood a monument to Lenin, the founder of Soviet power. Astonishingly, Mravinsky began to shout at full voice at the statue before him: "You bloody murderer, you bastard, you shot the tsar's family!" Alexandra Mikhailovna attempted to restrain her husband, yet the conductor went on: "What sort of swine are you, not even sparing little children, you. . . ."[69] Fortunately, this scene took place late on an August night, and few saw or heard the spectacle. At breakfast on the following morning, Mravinsky confided to the composer Sergey Slonimsky, "Of course, you won't bear in mind what I said last night, will you?" He flashed a meaningful smile, trusting that his friend would keep his silence.

During a break in rehearsals at the Philharmonic, three officers of the Leningrad KGB visited Mravinsky in his room, asking for an audience in strict privacy. They presented a list of accusations against one of the cellists, who had been caught in flagrante performing a homosexual act. The conductor was somewhat surprised by this turn of events and asked what they could possibly want him to do about this matter. Mravinsky was charged to sign a letter that this musician was in negligence of his duties and was dismissed, and that they could arrest him. Mravinsky replied that he could not accede to this, as the man was a first-class cellist, and he asked them to leave so he could proceed with the day's business. Taken aback by this rebuttal, the security men made tracks, and Mravinsky returned to his rostrum, giving one of his deathly stares at the poor distraught cellist, as if to say, "pull yourself together and let us continue our work."[70] The musician continued to play at the Philharmonic until his retirement.

From Kishinev to Tomsk, Vyborg to Novosibirsk, the Philharmonic's concerts would sell out many weeks in advance. In 1969, for Mravinsky and veterans of the Philharmonic, a nostalgic and memorable event was the return visit in May and June to Siberia. The touring that Mravinsky's orchestra experienced in 1969 was de rigueur; in spite of that he reveled in it, selecting all the programs himself, with an accent on Russian repertoire: Glazunov, Lyadov, Prokofiev, Shostakovich, and Tchaikovsky.

The journey was well organized, although there were still special ration cards in force and "privileged dinners" were hosted. In Chelyabinsk, the Secretary of the Regional Committee Rodionov warned that huge crowds were outside. "Yevgeny Alexandrovich advised to let them in as best they could. These people had been waiting for weeks, why disappoint anyone?"[71] There as on other nights, disregarding fire regulations, young and old alike occupied every part of the theater, many sitting on the steps and passageways, enraptured by the orchestra's brilliantly radiant music making.

The orchestra also visited the Siberian towns of Krasnoyarsk, Novosibirsk, Barnaul, Omsk, and Tomsk. Reviving memories of the orchestra's performances during wartimes, the concerts reflected a quarter century of peace. A huge number of articles and reviews chronicle the packed halls, with vast crowds waiting to see and meet Mravinsky and his musicians outside. "There has never been such an ovation in this hall," wrote *Vecherniye Chelyabinsk*, "the round of applause would not end as long as the musicians remained on stage."[72] These festive nights were repeated elsewhere: "It is impossible to relate all the beauties and transports of delight bewitching this evening' reported *Novosibirsk Vecherniye*; the public was enthusiastic in its feelings. Orchestra and conductor were wonderful in portraying the superlative, compelling power in these great works."[73]

The crowning glory of the Philharmonic during this period was the strings. The concertmaster Viktor Liberman had worked in the Philharmonic since winning a prize at the First Tchaikovsky Violin Competition in 1958. Liberman was a musician of extraordinary culture and great erudition, noted Boris Tischenko, "the first to play some of my works (several are dedicated to him), including the highly regarded Concerto, which has been performed on tour by the Philharmonic."[74] At his peak, Liberman was often in demand as a soloist, ensemble musician, teacher, and consultant, his paradigm reflected in the Philharmonic of the 1960s and 1970s. Liberman's deputy in Georgy Kneller was a magnificent soloist, and during Liberman's leadership the string section was renowned as its strongest element.

Valentin Stadler, a viola player since 1960, attended other orchestra's concerts on tour and reinforces the view: "During the thirty-year period up to the 1980s, our string section was the finest of any world orchestra that I heard."[75] Among the first and second chairs were numerous prize winners of prestigious music competitions, virtuosi of international caliber. Ensemble integrality was complemented with the viola group, led by Malkin and his deputy Ludewig (the first to play Britten's *Lacrimae* in the country and a founder of the Chamber Orchestra). The beauty of sound and tone color were characteristics of the cello section, led by Alexander Nikitin, a merited artist of the Russian Federation: "This capable musician knows how to combine both his performing artistry and leadership of the whole section with the flow of orchestral play."[76] According to a professor of the Cello Faculty at the Conservatoire, "this is a gifted musician able to unite both his individual mastery and the ensemble virtuosity as an orchestral musician."[77]

If the heart of the orchestra of the 1930s were the woodwinds, the latest generation, all disciples of the prewar group, was no less brilliant. The timbre perpetuated with little difference. The principal oboe was Vladimir Kurlin, who had won competitions in Prague in 1953 and Vienna in 1959. He created a rare nobility of sound and expressive phrasing with a wealth of dynamic range. Valery Bezruchenko, a master of his instrument, a loyal artist of the Philharmonic, and a brilliant musician, worked from 1960 into the 1990s and led the clarinet group. The principal bassoon was Oleg Talypin, whose mastery would often be noted in press reviews, and his pupil Lev Pechersky effected the most sublime playing in his thirty years service in Mravinsky's orchestra.

The masters of the brass were led by Vitaly Buyanovsky, son of the distinguished bass player of the 1930s and without doubt the finest player in the country. Venjamin Margolin served as trumpet from 1948 and was an intimate of Mravinsky, sharing his love of poetry and writing several verses in honor of the conductor. Small and compact, he displayed a ribald humor that often transformed the character of a rehearsal when it had reached the depths and everyone, including Mravinsky, was depressed. Margolin was audacious enough to call Mravinsky "Vasya," the Russian equivalent of Joshua—a man of the soil. Akim Kozlov, who led the trombones, was a veteran of the prewar orchestra and portrayed through four decades a superb brightness in color and timbre.

The single most important factor in the Philharmonic's excellence was the uninterrupted tradition, and it was hardly surprising that the qualities evolved through years of rehearsal in the Leningrad "piano" timbre of the Leningrad "brass" and indeed the Leningrad "Shostakovich" sound. As Rozhdestvensky detected, "how marvelous it is based on constant practice and creating their own style in making music."[78] There was a nobility and simplicity, matched with a reserve in emotions, combined with distinct taste and an extraordinary artistic caliber—the Leningrad Philharmonic demonstrated academicism in the best meaning of the word.

In 1969, the Berlin Philharmonic Orchestra under their chief conductor Herbert von Karajan visited Leningrad. Mravinsky's assistant director Galina Retrovskaya remembers Karajan's spellbinding performance of Russian music, and that the Austrian had to wrap himself in a fur coat afterward to revive himself.[79] In listening to Karajan's interpretations of the Beethoven symphonies (the 1962 set), Mravinsky valued them for their beauty, in spite of believing that they lacked a "depth of vision."[80] For all that, Mravinsky approached the podium after the performance, and they embraced as if old friends. Herbert von Karajan was reverential toward Mravinsky, calling him his *alter bruder*.[81]

Another jubilee arrived on 22 April 1970—marking Lenin's birth centenary. Mravinsky conducted Shostakovich's Twelfth and Tchaikovsky's Fifth Symphony at the Philharmonic Hall, a program that was taken a few days later to Ulyanovsk—birthplace of the revolutionary—on the river Volga and visiting venues encompassed in Koussevitsky's famous provincial tours of the 1910s. In Ulyanovsk, the large modern hall was full to the rafters, with young and old taking up every free space, all ensconced in the awesome, revelatory music making of the Philharmonic. "The symphony was celebrated, euphoric applause amid a long standing ovation."[82]

Entering a new decade, Mravinsky renewed his symphonic repertoire, including Glazunov's Fourth and Fifth, Bruckner's Seventh, Prokofiev's Sixth, Brahms's Fourth, and Beethoven's mature symphonies: *Eroica*, Fourth, Fifth, and Sixth. The latter were preparation for the Beethoven Bicentennial and the tour to the GDR later that season. Revisiting once again the venues of its debut German visit of 1956, the orchestra gave additional concerts in Magdeburg, Erfurt, Jena, and Gera. Closing the tour in Berlin's splendid old Schauspielhaus, Mravinsky programmed Beethoven's Fourth and Fifth symphonies. The reaction from the press revealed that Mravinsky should not have been so circumspect about his portrayals of the great masters: "this orchestra is one of the finest, perhaps even the best, in the world. Leading this orchestra for thirty-two years, Yevgeny Mravinsky is one of the great conductors of modern times. This orchestra arriving from the musical city of Leningrad has brought us a gift in its Beethoven."[83] At the age of sixty-seven, Mravinsky had suffered intractable troubles and dilemma; now he had emerged triumphant, defying his adversaries and affirming his artistic credo.

NOTES

1. A. M. Vavilina Mravinsky, author interview, September 2002.
2. Lia Muradyan, author interview, July 2002.
3. A. Sokolov, unpublished memoir made available to the author.
4. A. M. Vavilina Mravinskaya, author interview, September 2002.
5. Sergey Slonimsky, author interview, May 2003.
6. A. M. Vavilina Mravinskaya, author interview, October 2001.
7. A. M. Vavilina Mravinskaya, author interview, July 2001.
8. Y. A. Mravinsky archive, 18 February 1925.
9. B. Tischenko, author interview, May 2002.
10. E. Serov, *Dirizher Eduard Serov* (Volgograd: Nizhnevolzhskoye, 1993), 132.
11. Serov, *Dirizher Eduard Serov*, 133.
12. Serov, *Dirizher Eduard Serov*, 133.
13. Serov, *Dirizher Eduard Serov*, 134.
14. Serov, *Dirizher Eduard Serov*, 134.
15. Serov, *Dirizher Eduard Serov*, 136.
16. Serov, *Dirizher Eduard Serov*, 148–49.
17. Serov, *Dirizher Eduard Serov*, 137–38.
18. Serov, *Dirizher Eduard Serov*, 146.
19. I. I. Blazhkov, *Mezhdu mgnoveniyiem i vechnosti—Shostakovich* (St. Petersburg: Kompozitor, 2000), 491.
20. B. Schwartz, *Music and Musical Life in Soviet Russia 1917–1982* (Bloomington: Indiana University Press, 1983), 443.
21. V. F. Kucharsky, *Sovetskaya Muzika*, no. 10 (1968): 7.

22. L. Mikheyeva, *Zhisn Dmitriya Shostakovicha* (Moscow: Terra Terra, 1997).

23. G. Mokreyeva, *Ruch Muzyczny*, 1 May 1962.

24. V. F. Kucharsky, *Sovetskaya Muzika*, no. 10 (1968): 7.

25. I. I. Blazhkov, *Mezhdu mgnoveniyiem i vechnosti—Shostakovich*, 499.

26. Shostakovich to V. F. Kucharsky, 9 June 1969, GTsMMK, f. 32, ed. Khr, 2048.

27. *Zerkalo Nedeli* (Kiev), 5 October 96.

28. Blazhkov to the author, September 2002.

29. A. A. Zolotov, "Klassika nashikh dnei," *Izvestia*, 17 March 1965.

30. R. Layton, *Gramophone* (July 1972): 192.

31. Schwartz, *Music and Musical Life in Soviet Russia 1917–1982*, 465.

32. A. Sokolov, unpublished memoir.

33. Schwartz, *Music and Musical Life in Soviet Russia 1917–1982*, 465.

34. Schwartz, *Music and Musical Life in Soviet Russia 1917–1982*, 464–65.

35. A. A. Zolotov, "Klassika nashich dnei."

36. Leningrad fights to maintain its preeminence. The Moscow Festival of Leningrad Musical Art was one such effort; similar festivals had been held previously in Saratov (1964) and Yaroslavl (1965).

37. K. Sakva, *Sovetskaya Kultura*, 4 December 1965.

38. Schwartz, *Music and Musical Life in Soviet Russia 1917–1982*, 464–65.

39. Valentin Stadler, author interview, September 2002.

40. V. Lopatnikov, author interview, July 2002.

41. A. M. Vavilina Mravinskaya, author interview, July 2001.

42. V. Lopatnikov, conversation with the author, July 2002.

43. Y. A. Mravinsky archives.

44. M. Gorki, "O Stasove," in *Vladimir Vasilyevitch Stasov. 1824–1906. K 125-letii so dnya rozhdeniye. Sbornik statei i vospominanii* (Moscow, 1949), 10.

45. Y. E. Svetlanov, interview made available to author by A. M. Vavilina Mravinskaya.

46. I. Glikman, *Pisma k Drugu* (St. Petersburg: DSCH, 1993), 179.

47. Serov, *Dirizher Eduard Serov*, 165.

48. Serov, *Dirizher Eduard Serov*, 166.

49. Maxim Shostakovich, author interview, September 2002.

50. Irina Shostakovich and Dmitry Rozhdestvensky, interview, 1989.

51. Glikman, *Pisma k Drugu*, 286.

52. I. Glikman, author interview, July 2002.

53. I. Glikman, speech at the Philharmonia Library, 1989.

54. I. Glikman, speech in Mravinsky's memory at Library of Leningrad Philharmonic, 1989.

55. V. Razhnikov, *Kirill Kondrashin rasskasyvaet* (Moscow: Sovetsky Kompozitor, 1989), 195.

56. Kara Karayev, a composer and disciple of Shostakovich.

57. Razhnikov, *Kirill Kondrashin rasskasyvaet*, 195.

58. E. Nikitina, "Byl tsarem i dvornikom," *Kultura*, no. 30 (August 2003): 1–7.

59. Serov, *Dirizher Eduard Serov*, 147.

60. A. M. Vavilina Mravinskaya, author interview, October 2001.

61. *L Unita*, 8 November 1966.

62. R. Shchedrin, "Leningradskaya ordena Trudovovo Znameni filarmonia," in *Stati, vospominanii, materialii*, ed. V. Fomina (Leningrad: Muzika, 1971), 303.

63. B. Tischenko, author interview, May 2002.

64. Serov, *Dirizher Eduard Serov*, 166.

65. Serov, *Dirizher Eduard Serov*, 167.

66. B. Tischenko, author interview, May 2002.

67. A. Ludewig, author interview, July 2002.

68. A. Ludewig, author interview, July 2002.

69. G. Envaldt, author interview, May 2002.

70. A. M. Vavilina Mravinskaya, author interview, September 2002.

71. A. M. Vavilina, "Obruchennii Muzikoy," in *Muzikalnaya Akademiya*, no. 4 (1997): 91.

72. G. Kuzmin, "Svidaniye s volshebnikami," *Vecherniye Chelyabinsk*, 1 May 1969.

73. Y. Fain, "Poema o krasote ducha chelovecheskovo," *Vecherniye Novosibirsk*, 31 May 1969.

74. B. Tischenko, *Orkestrom dirizhiruet Mravinskim* (Leningrad: Muzika, 1976), 116–17.

75. V. Stadler, author interview, July 2002.

76. A. Dmitryev, *Vecherny Leningrad*, 12 March 1975.

77. A. Dmitryev, *Vecherny Leningrad*, 12 March 1975.

78. G. Rozhdestvensky, *Rodnoy i zhelanniye dom* (Leningrad: Leningradskaya filarmonia, 1972), 289–90.

79. G. Retrovskaya, author interview, October 2001.

80. Serov, *Dirizher Eduard Serov*, 148.

81. I. A. Shostakovich and D. D. Rozhdestvensky, interview, 1989.

82. Vavilina, "Obruchennii Muzikoy," 91.

83. *Volksstimme*, 18 December 1970.

Chapter Fifteen

The Patriarch

> And light up the candle in the conductor's study, where we find the hero
> of this book in the most comfortable attire, piano and tobacco at hand, and
> drinks not too far off, preparing his next concert. He is bent to that effect
> over his book of books—Law, Prophets and gospel to him—the full score,
> or orchestral score.
>
> —Frederick Goldbeck, *The Perfect Conductor*

It was well known that Mravinsky was fond of going down to the little café
in his apartment block, where he would sit reading a favorite volume, away
from the pressure of his work. Established comfortably there on one tranquil
morning, Mravinsky was approached by a young man who joined him at his
table. A dialogue developed between the two and reached the point where the
normally reticent Mravinsky was asked what his livelihood was. Following
through, the taciturn conductor in the end let drop that he worked at the Philharmonic. The man feigned disbelief and requested proof, and Mravinsky
proffered his passport, declaring, "Here, look, it's still a Soviet one!" The
conductor's anonymous "friend" (in fact, a policeman) accordingly reported
the faux pas, and Mravinsky was summoned to the Smolny headquarters.[1]
Once again, political troubles emerged in an affair insidiously set up in the
most repulsive cloak-and-dagger style.

Meetings were convened for musicians to give dispositions for or against
their chief conductor. Upon leaving his individual cross-examination, one of
his assistant conductors deliberately gave Mravinsky a wide berth when he
met him; Mravinsky surmised his motivation and addressing his bête noire,
said, "young man, you should know my grandmother lived until she was
eighty, so I am going to be here for a very long time!"[2] The deliberations led

to Mravinsky being excluded from another international tour, the consequences of which gave some alarm to Alexandra Vavilina: "My appeal to release me from the tour was refused under threat of dismissal. There then arose the need to go into hiding Y. A. in Siddamyae with some charitable people." While the Philharmonic was on tour, the conductor lived until late autumn in a hotel on Vabudze Street adjacent to a factory on the Baltic coastline. Mravinsky took his meals with the workers in a partly heated little canteen there and acquired a multitude of new acquaintances in his wife's absence.[3]

If the conductor's contempt for Soviet power was one cause for concern, a bitter cup for the Party was the emigration of Jews to Israel. Mravinsky's unfettered will was so renowned that a story disseminated in which Romanov chided Mravinsky as to why so many Jews were quitting the Philharmonic, to which Mravinsky responded, "Oh, but it is you they are leaving—not me!"[4] In the growing exodus, twenty of Mravinsky's orchestra emigrated, including the concertmaster Viktor Liberman. Mravinsky cherished most of all the moral issue in the satisfaction of a desire to live in the Holy Land. Upon Liberman's departure, the Party clique demanded that a violinist of "Russian" extraction be selected for his position. However, Mravinsky asserted that Jews were recruited to leading positions in the orchestra, and when Liberman left, Georgy Gertzovitch Kneller, a violinist of Jewish origin, replaced him.[5]

In November 1971, the Leningrad Philharmonic celebrated its fiftieth anniversary as a state orchestra and apportioned several honorary concerts in addition to its subscription series. The Melodiya record company released a set of recordings from the 1965 Moscow tour, including works by Bartók, Honneger, Hindemith, Mozart, Stravinsky, and Sibelius. The booklet notes were written by one of Mravinsky's younger colleagues—Gennady Rozhdestvensky: "I recollect how many times in rehearsal Yevgeny Alexandrovich returns to the opening of the famous Toccata in Shostakovich's Eighth Symphony. It would look as if everything is played absolutely correct in orchestral ensemble, dynamics, and tempo. All the same, the conductor goes over the opening bars time after time. Then ultimately one hears a unique touch in the music—beating the exact note!" Rozhdestvensky described Mravinsky "as making no compromises and burning still with the sacred fire of allegiance to his ideal."[6]

The culmination of celebrations were the Moscow concerts in January 1972; this coincided with the governmental award of Honored Ensemble of the Republic to the orchestra. On 26 January, Mravinsky played an evening of Brahms's Third Symphony coupled with fragments from Wagner: the Bacchanale from *Tannhäuser*, "Dawn and Siegfried's Rhine Journey" and "Funeral March" from *Götterdämmerung*, and the "Flight of the Valkyries" from *Die Walküre*. This was followed on the next night by Russian works in

Shostakovich's Sixth Symphony, Stravinsky's *Apollon*, and Tchaikovsky's *Francesca da Rimini*. Two days later, and a Beethoven concert consisted of Symphonies 4 in B major and 5 in C minor. The final concert of the short visit brought together those erstwhile favorites in Mravinsky's programming in Prokofiev's *Romeo and Juliet* and Tchaikovsky's Fifth Symphony in E minor. "These are all familiar works, yet one feels a sensation of freshness as if hearing them for the first time," wrote Andrey Zolotov. "Suddenly, the inner world of this music opens up."[7] The acclaim surrounding Mravinsky's performances was echoed by the State Symphony's chief conductor, Yevgeny Svetlanov. "The renowned hallmark in this orchestra's character is in their conductor," he added, "there is always an aspiration to the highest level of performance and artistic perfection."[8] All the concerts were broadcast and subsequently issued by Melodiya.

Mravinsky and his musicians now had an opportunity to rekindle the lifelong association with Shostakovich, for after a gap of eleven years, the doyen of Soviet music had composed a purely orchestral symphony. If the opening night did not go to Mravinsky, the world premiere was very much calculated as Shostakovich's "gift" to his son.[9] Mravinsky had attended the Leningrad premiere of the Fourteenth Symphony given by the Moscow Chamber Orchestra under Barshay, sitting in the box at the Capella Hall with Dmitry Shostakovich, Boris Tischenko, and their wives. In the last year, the two had reestablished their friendship; the conductor had sought out Shostakovich's assistance on a private affair, and ever since found a mutual ground in their relationship.[10]

As always, the climate and atmosphere in the Leningrad countryside seemed to create the ideal conditions for Shostakovich, as Mravinsky recalled:

In the autumn of 1971, one had the fortunate opportunity to live at Repino in the Composers Home of Rest when Dmitry Dmitrevich was staying there. He was completing the Fifteenth Symphony and worked a tremendously long time each day. I shall never forget the evening hour when I passed by his little cottage. It was setting dusk, and in the window, the light from the green lamp fell upon the head, shoulders, and hands of Dmitry Dmitrevich, who was constantly turning to left and right with his marker as he was working on the score.

One had the impression that he was trying to use every single second available. This was his work, and he was somewhat absent to everything around him. Time did not seem to exist for him—the scene in the gathering twilight with his familiar face at the window lost in his score—one shall never forget it. It was encapsulated in just a few seconds of time.[11]

The issue of not giving another world premiere by Shostakovich was never of great consequence: "It's not so important who plays it before one. One doesn't have to be first." After all these years, it would appear that the right to give the first performance was insignificant: "I didn't premiere the Fifteenth Symphony of Shostakovich, Maxim played it; neither did I premiere the Eleventh—the number one was Rakhlin, what of it?"[12] The satisfaction at revitalizing the partnership was mutual, as Glikman wrote: "Mravinsky's work brought him great pleasure; in his own words, 'there was a profound and astonishing attention to detail.'"[13] Alexandra Vavilina, principal flautist, recounts the first rehearsal: "Dmitry Dmitrevich, Irina Antonovna, and Boris Tischenko sat in the tenth row of an empty hall; there was a tense atmosphere on stage, everyone was so emotionally stimulated! In the interval, Yevgeny Alexandrovich asked Dmitry Dmitrevich if everything was appropriate, if there were corrections to be made, or perhaps change the tempi. Shostakovich replied: 'No, no, everything is perfect, like in a dream.'"

On the second day of the sessions, Shostakovich agreed to a proposal by Mravinsky in altering a nuance in the double basses, to play at *mezzo forte* instead of *piano*. "You're quite right, quite right—it's better that way." To every detail, the composer duly marked his own score.[14] Mravinsky himself recalled that, "we met directly at the rehearsals and usually had such a system, he would make notes and let us play on. I would open his score during the break and make remarks to the composer; we would change what he wanted and slowly but surely eliminate the flaws."[15]

Mravinsky found material in the Fifteenth that proves surprising in terms not only of our understanding of Shostakovich's late work but also of the entire Shostakovich canon. The new symphony was assimilated by Mravinsky as with all the great tragic symphonic pieces, permitting one to consider the Fifteenth as among Shostakovich's most anguished, uncovering music that mysteriously divulged dissimilar themes. "To make a way into the music, one must slowly remove layer after layer and discover new and different subtexts underneath."[16] The Leningrad premiere on 5 May 1972 was a scintillating salutation, unveiling a deeply profound canvass by a composer now widely regarded as the greatest living symphonist. "The Fifteenth Symphony is a work that I admire enormously. . . . [T]he music is so simple: some laconic notes approach aestheticism. . . ."[17]

With a lifting of restrictions, in the autumn of 1972 Mravinsky traveled with the Leningrad Philharmonic on a tour in which they gave thirty-three concerts in Austria, Germany, and Italy. This grand undertaking opened in Hamburg with familiar stock in trade in Shostakovich's Sixth and Tchaikovsky's Fifth Symphonies; further engagements saw Mravinsky directing Mozart's Symphony No. 33 in B-flat, K.319, Glinka's *Ruslan and Lyudmila*, and Prokofiev's *Romeo and Juliet*. On 14 October in Munich, Mravinsky played wholly German music, conducting Beethoven and

Brahms's symphonies: "Mravinsky does not permit himself any superfluous gestures, nor does he lose control in the great concentrated moments. Everything is achieved in the rehearsals, which set such breathtaking results yet must be a sign of extraordinarily colossal work."[18] One of the reviewers commented that this was "a lesson for all Germans."[19] The headlines from the Viennese press proclaimed the Philharmonic's arrival ("The Festival brought from Leningrad"), and other writers were finding it difficult to find the fitting terminology ("Searching for the first thoughts"), however they could still despair of making any apt association ("Is there another orchestra of comparable sound?"). Ultimately, some differentiation in style was noted: "The Leningrad Philharmonic plays with the perfection of American orchestras and with the musicianship and sound of the best European ensembles."[20] One of Mravinsky's assistants—Alexander Dmitr'yev—recounted the impression made on local musicians by Mravinsky's reading of Beethoven's Fourth Symphony. "People who had heard all the great conductors conducting this symphony at the Musikverein could not believe the quality of sound achieved by Mravinsky."[21] In Italy, where the traveling musicians gave their finale, one of the analysts compared the performances of the La Scala Milan orchestra under Claudio Abbado with those of Mravinsky's Philharmonic and favored the Russians.[22] It was something not lost on the Italian maestro, who took into account the stimulus of Mravinsky on his work.[23]

Mravinsky's Diary

23 March 1973, Repino: The Shostakoviches arrived. After breakfast in the forest, we went to visit him. It was a sunless day, but bright, blinding white light. During the night, much snow had fallen, and there were soft powdery chains through the forest. Neither were there any footprints; walking was difficult due to the snow and my difficult breathing. . . . I walk slowly, so as to breathe better, I amble along. Shostakovich welcomed us warmly, and it was comfortable in his cottage. Irina was full of concern and offered us coffee and whiskey. Shostakovich was concerned about his deteriorating legs and hands, and for the first time in his life such a long break in his composing: "For two years I haven't written a note . . . one can't drink—I just lie in hospitals. One wants to drink again. Here, lets share a drink with you."[24]

After two or three days, Irina Antonovna told me, "Dmitry Dmitrevich is writing"—"What is he writing?"

"A string quartet; the first movement is already complete." I was the fortunate witness to the birth of two new compositions.[25]

In April, Mravinsky made the first of a series of music films with the Moscow musicologist Andrey Zolotov. The making of the films was extraordinary in that the conductor had long abandoned studio recordings, believing the concert performance to be paramount. Zolotov and the conductor were acquainted when the Muscovite began writing for *Izvestia*; the expressive nature of Zolotov's writing and his knowledge and aesthetics impressed Mravinsky.

By the late 1960s, Zolotov was working on Soviet TV, presenting short reviews on culture on the nightly *Vremya* news program. His chats drew a large audience, one of whom was Leonid Brezhnev, who took umbrage at the presenter's beard and posted orders that Zolotov be clean shaven if he was to continue on TV. This was a phase when many intellectuals wore beards as almost a sign of defiance, a display of dissidence and rebelliousness.

Zolotov was called into the Communist Party headquarters, situated in the wooded, secluded Old Square, to meet the éminence grise, Vasily Kucharsky. Ushered into one of the reception rooms, Zolotov was told straightforwardly that he would have to shave off his facial growth—this was not the type of model for young people. Looking around the wood-paneled interiors, Zolotov observed the large, bewhiskered portraits of Karl Marx, Friedrich Engels, and Vladimir Lenin. Zolotov looked askance at Kucharsky and glanced again at their surroundings. All rooms were wired; all the same, Zolotov responded by saying that he would like to fulfill his request but his work proved no hindrance to Soviet arts policy and—gazing around at the pictures in the room—that his beard only followed in the traditions of the founders of scientific socialism. Kucharsky, following his eyes, picked up his innuendo, and Zolotov commented that he would much prefer to keep his appearance as it was. Meeting with such a riposte, Kucharsky could find nothing more to say, but he passed on Zolotov's comments to his superiors. Within a fortnight, Zolotov was promoted to head of classical music at Soviet TV.[26]

Andrey Zolotov began putting into motion plans to make documentaries about the great musicians of the day: Richter, Oistrakh, Shostakovich, and Mravinsky. However, the Leningrad conductor's aversion to recording led to an initial rebuff; nonetheless, the Moscow journalist persisted and obliquely approached Alexandra Mikhailovna, who persuaded her husband to participate. Upon Zolotov's next phone call, Mravinsky suggested that he bring his TV crew, although Mravinsky still wouldn't give his final approval—he would see how it unfolded before allowing him to film.

Zolotov duly brought a full team of film engineers and technicians and began to observe Mravinsky's running through of Beethoven's Fourth Symphony. Before the sessions started, the conductor made Zolotov swear by his young daughter Olga that he would withdraw his crew if the test filming disturbed him. Zolotov obediently agreed to Mravinsky's demands, instructing his crew to sit there quietly with cameras turned off; thus there was no way that they would get in the way. After a break, Mravinsky asked Zolotov if it is always so quiet when they were filming. Suitably pleased, the Leningrad maestro gave his permission for the crew to tape the sessions and, later that week, a live performance of Brahms's Second Symphony.[27]

Andrey Zolotov gathered some of the finest cinematographers and technicians for his project. His chief cameraman was Grigory Rehrberg, who had worked on Andrey Tarkovsky's art house films of the 1960s and 1970s—*Andrey Rublev*, *Solaris*, and *Zerkalo*. His camera work was deeply poetic and artistically truthful, capturing the beauty, history, and tradition of the Grand Hall of the Philharmonic. The noble architecture of the interiors, the shades of the light falling upon the faces of the captivated listeners, children and adults—here was an unraveling of wonders visual and aural. His sound engineers were the best that Melodiya possessed in Gerhard Tses and Semyon Shugal, both of whom were well aware of the auditorium's acoustics. Zolotov's "fly-on-the-wall" treatment revealed this pious conducting figure as a distinctive personality, making the immovable, statuesque sentinel into a warm, sensitive, and deeply intense musician with his quintessential aristocratic aloofness.

One of Zolotov's films featured Shostakovich's Fifth Symphony, and this was duly broadcast following the opening concert of Shostakovich's Fifteenth Symphony on 16 September 1973. Zolotov sat down next to Shostakovich in the parterre and told him that his film would be broadcast, suggesting that if he were to stay over, they could watch his film together. However, the composer answered that they were booked on the Red Arrow that evening and would watch Zolotov's film in Moscow. On the subsequent evening, Zolotov was sitting with Mravinsky, and as the film ended, the phone rang and Zolotov forecast "That will be Shostakovich!" Mravinsky picked up the receiver and stood for a long time over the phone and little by little, tears began to flow down Mravinsky's face. In due course, he replaced the handset and went into the adjoining room to collect his thoughts.[28] Afterward, Mravinsky told Zolotov that Shostakovich had confessed that "he was grateful for everything, thanking me for all that I had prepared for him."[29]

As Andrey Zolotov pictured a cycle of documentaries, he would exchange ideas for future films with Mravinsky. A major assignment, *Thoughts on Mravinsky*, reflected on the conductor's career, marking his seventieth birthday; among those interviewed were Galina Ulanova, whose association with Mravinsky went back to the 1920s; choreographer Yuri Grigorovich, who recalled his deep veneration for Mravinsky's plasticity and expressiveness, of his artistry and firmness, musicality and friendship; and the conductors Claudio Abbado, Igor Markevitch, and Lorin Maazel, who discussed Mravinsky's portrayals of Russian and Western music and his rehearsal methodology. The film effectively enshrined the "canonization" of a legendary figure in Soviet life—a remarkable achievement in an atheist state.

Mravinsky's seventieth birthday was marked with yet another honor from the Soviet government—the Order of Socialist Labor and a second Order of Lenin. On this very day, the conductor was on tour in Japan with his orchestra. Mravinsky underscored in an interview his appreciation to his homeland and looked upon this as reward not for his own labors, "but as an acknowledgment of the Soviet symphonic school in general."[30] Back in Moscow for the presentation, the Minister for Culture Yekaterina Furtseva considered that "the enormous success of foreign touring is obliged to Mravinsky's leading role in forming and perfecting the mastery of the orchestra."[31]

Among the more gracious and heartfelt accolades was that penned by Vadim Salmanov, which overflowed with the enthusiasm of a creative artist who felt himself fully in harmony with the conductor.[32] Viktor Liberman spoke of the conductor's "ability to extract the maximum from his players and raise the level again by setting the goals even higher."[33] Mravinsky was as demanding of others as he was of himself—a "thinker" among conductors, erudite, widely educated and with a firm grasp of the international repertoire. Boris Schwartz acknowledged that "for decades [Mravinsky] was the only Soviet Russian conductor of world stature."[34] The American musicologist continued: "He earned the highest critical praise not only for his interpretations but also for the quality of the orchestra, which he had shaped since 1938."[35]

Against this backdrop, Mravinsky's first Japanese tour in May 1973 took place with exceptional success and acclaim. The country's music lovers were drawn to Mravinsky's phenomenon like few others, the degree of adulation approaching hero worship. Mravinsky's recordings had been best-sellers in the classical market and his nonappearance on the 1958 tour had transformed him into an even more elusive figure. All the same, Mravinsky personified the Philharmonic Orchestra: "They are a national treasure for Russia and leave one with an impression all one's life."[36] The greatest triumphs were in performances of Schubert's *Unfinished* Symphony, Brahms's Second Symphony, and the complete second act from Tchaikovsky's *Nutcracker*, an old favorite of the conductor harking back to his days at the Mariinsky. The records issued under license by Shinshekai had become popular with collectors, and Mravinsky's concerts were broadcast on NHK Radio and TV.[37] The maestro also won the friendship of his interpreter Midori Kawashima. The young Japanese woman, sharing Mravinsky's love of animals and nature, spent her free time in taking Mravinsky to the zoo and to public gardens.

Kawashima had worked with a number of Russian artists visiting the Japanese islands, notably Richter, and was somewhat intimidated by Mravinsky, because of his strict and disciplined approach. However, after a few days, her fear melted away as she discovered in the Leningrad maestro a down-to-earth human being.[38] "Everyone admired and respected Mravinsky, everyone in Japan knew him,"[39] she said. Mravinsky's popularity developed to the extent that a Japanese Mravinsky Society was established to promote the conductor's life. Mravinsky took particular delight in Japanese customs and traditions, adoring its countryside and the people's love of poetry and music. The wayfaring straddled both the main islands, and there necessitated a prolonged journey by ferry during which everyone except Mravinsky was upset by sea sickness, as Valery Bezruchenko recalled: "it seemed to give him a particular joy that he alone was fit and strong while everyone lay in bed sick, mischievously chuckling to himself about it!"[40]

After opening the 1974 season on 8 September with readings of Prokofiev's Sixth Symphony and Beethoven's Fifth Symphony, the Philharmonic left for a visit to Austria, Czechoslovakia, and West Germany. In the course of the Beethoven Festival in September 1974, the critic Gerhard Schumann described the Leningrad orchestra as "a perfect instrument."[41] *General Anzeiger* continued the chorus of praise: "The Bonn public was so taken by such a modern performance of Beethoven: stormy applause transmitted through the concert hall as a mark of gratitude."[42] In Vienna, *Die Presse* was enthusiastic in making comparisons: "as the legendary Chicago musicians, the Leningrad musicians performed Beethoven. Moreover, the diversity was in that the sound was quite different! So European and correct, as Mravinsky wanted it be. What a feeling of happiness when all this was possessed by another audience."[43] At the Wien Festwoche, Mravinsky's "perfect instrument" took part in a series featuring the world's finest conductors and orchestras, including Claudio Abbado, Karl Böhm, and Leonard Bernstein. Mravinsky's orchestra was called "the basso profundo among the top world orchestras, with a sound dominated by dark colors—velvety yet with a firm metallic base. Mravinsky wants everything—except to be conspicuous."[44] On the program that evening were Prokofiev's Sixth Symphony and Beethoven's glorious Fifth. The music writer in another Viennese broadsheet had to acknowledge that he "had never heard the pianissimo transition from the Scherzo to the Finale in the Beethoven played with such sculptured tenderness."[45]

In November, David Oistrakh died of a heart attack. There had been many fine collaborations between Mravinsky and Oistrakh since the 1930s, and Mravinsky was once asked to facilitate the instrumentalist in study of the conducting art, to which Mravinsky responded: "How could I possibly give you a lesson in anything!"[46] Even so, the Leningrad conductor magnanimously encouraged Oistrakh to sit in on his rehearsals:

> I have learned so much from the Leningrad musicians. There is always something to pick up from them. They surprise one with their great consistency, quality of play, and high-class musicality, all with a beautiful manner of performance.

The Leningrad Philharmonic Orchestra can always be recognized for its unique sound, integrity in ensemble, and polished detail. In this ensemble, there continue the finest traditions of Russian culture of many decades. First, there reigns the spirit of Music. To convince one of this, it is sufficient to see the orchestra just once to observe the concentration each musician prepares in his work. Following rehearsals, they do not scamper off anywhere (as in most other orchestras). On the contrary, they rehearse in groups and only reluctantly part to go home. They arrive some time before the beginning of work, gather together—particularly the trumpets, the trombones—separately to repeat parts of the score.[47]

Oistrakh's death was as unexpected as the suicide of the Minister of Culture a few days later.[48] The golden-haired Furtseva was a charismatic, beautiful, enchanting woman, almost a Soviet sex symbol—chic and always immaculately coiffured. All the same, she was a solitary figure occupying a tremendously influential position in Soviet society.[49] She experienced as many setbacks as conquests and would have risen to a higher position if she had not been perceived as a defender of Khrushchev and been removed from the Presidium. Unable to formulate policy on the arts—still the preserve of the CPSU Central Committee—Furtseva was able to guide it in a way few others had managed to do. Furtseva walked a fine line between what could and could not be done in Soviet life.[50]

With the sudden passing of the Moscow minister, the regional offices at the Smolny now resuscitated their plans to get rid of Mravinsky, and the leader of the pack was the secretary of the Cultural Department. She epitomized a generation that had come to power in the 1960s–1970s and who imposed their authority over each and every one.

Pakhomova was a cultured woman, dressed almost as a femme fatale among the elite. Even Romanov noted her taste in fashion. In the 1970s, there existed a House of Fashion in the Petrogradsky area, which lured all of Leningrad's fashionable women. In advance of her own arrival, Pakhomova's secretary would notify the manager of her impending appointment. There everyone took in this woman, sanctioned to conduct herself in such a manner, and for her to pose rather risqué without a bra—a Party official—before the crème de la crème of Leningrad society.[51]

Pakhomova's appearances at the Philharmonic, presenting her own aura and entourage, heralded the entry of her master in Romanov.

She appeared at the Philharmonic, sitting in the loge, attired in a low-cut dress, and at the interval, there appeared Romanov with his suite of assistants and bodyguards. All were in gray, functional suits, yet the Party boss was distinctive in his dark-blue suit. Of short height, his "Napoleonic" high-pitched voice, manner, and pose. His entire party gave the impression that all this was of no consequence to them, as nothing but a frittering away of time, each looking at his or her watch. While Romanov makes his speech, one tries to bear in mind a Chekhov idiom, "if you have no time, then do nothing!" Romanov administers the awards with his authoritative Party hand, glaring into ones' eyes as if to say, "I concede you are a decent artist, but you could do so much better"[52]

Galina Pakhomova ratcheted up her efforts to retire the chief conductor now that she had discovered an alternative in the dark, handsome, and young Yuri Temirkanov, a student of Ilya Musin who matched his hatred of Mravinsky with his own forceful ambition. Temirkanov had won the Third All-Union Conducting Competition, and he was perceived as a conductor of potential. Among his admirers was Pakhomova, who kicked off a crusade with Temirkanov's appointment to the conductorship of the Philharmonic's second orchestra, and later the music directorship at the Kirov Opera and Ballet Theatre.

Pakhomova's right-hand man, Viktor Lopatnikov, was instructed to ring up Mravinsky (the chore being undeserving of her) and induce him to retire; however, when Lopatnikov phoned the Mravinsky flat, Alexandra Vavilina enlightened the party functionary that Mravinsky was not available, but that if he had anything useful to say, then the two of them could meet on the street outside. Alexandra notified her husband that she was just going out to get a loaf of bread and then descended in the lift from the fifth floor to meet Lopatnikov by the memorial house of Peter I nearby. There the Party man proclaimed to Vavilina that Mravinsky was too old and there was "much disquiet in the city"; the veteran was blocking the way for the younger generation. Vavilina responded that this was ridiculous; the Ministry in Moscow was inundated by invitations from impresarios inviting Mravinsky and his orchestra— she would phone them to inform what they were trying to do to Mravinsky. Lopatnikov constrained her, "No, no, don't do that, but bear in mind we can offer Yevgeny Alexandrovich a fantastic pension."[53] There ensued another four similar encounters outside Mravinsky's house before the Party came clean that they had been humbled. Lopatnikov confessed that ultimately the Party attempted to avoid conflict between the two contenders for Mravinsky's position.[54]

Scorning political intrigues of the state, Yevgeny Mravinsky looked at revitalizing his stock in trade in this phase; the most significant of the revivals were the Bruckner Seventh and Ninth Symphonies, Brahms's Third Symphony, Richard Strauss's *Ein Alpensinfonie*, Wagner overtures, Prokofiev's Sixth Symphony, and Scriabin's *Le poème de l'extase*. In May 1975, the orchestra under its chief conductor visited Japan, taking in twenty-one concerts in sixteen cities, ten of the concerts directed by Mravinsky, as many by his assistant Dmitr'yev, and one by Serov. Mravinsky's repertoire on this occasion was drawn from Beethoven's Fifth Symphony, Mozart's Symphony No. 39 in E-flat, Prokofiev's Sixth Symphony in B-flat, Shostakovich's Fifth Symphony in D minor, and Tchaikovsky's *Pathétique*. Japan continued to be the most favored of those countries visited by Mravinsky. Kenzo Amoh considered his influence: "his music penetrated one's body and soul more naturally than any other performers. His tempo, rhythm, and contrast of *fortissimo* and *pianissimo*—all seem to be in perfect accord. If one could define Mravinsky's music in three words, I should characterize him as majestic, rational, and elegant."[55] Mravinsky's portrayal of Tchaikovsky's Fifth evoked rapture: "I was shattered by what clear life force I experienced in Tchaikovsky."[56] The atmosphere and positive reception for art gave Mravinsky many happy and contented hours in Japan and encouraged his wanderlust further. For many years, Mravinsky subscribed to a popular magazine called *Vokrug Sveta*, full of colorful travelogues recounting picturesque lands and natural features of exotic destinations, almost all an illusion for the ordinary Soviet reader. (*Vokrug Sveta* is most equivalent with *National Geographic*.)

The triumphant tour of Japan was extended for virtually a month, until mid-June, and back home the Mravinskys went to their refuge in Estonia, where they recuperated for the new season: "It was a rainy, autumn day; we went down to the sea past Rabinovich's dacha, where the sculptor and artist Gavriil Davidovich Glikman lived at the time. He cut across our path with the terrible news 'Dmitry Dmitrevich has died.' Shattered, we returned home by taxi, traveling across an empty Leningrad."[57]

Nothing could have prepared Mravinsky for the unexpected death of Shostakovich on 9 August 1975. The Mravinskys traveled by the Red Arrow overnight express to Moscow. They were met there by the stepson of the composer and visited Irina at their dacha. On the day of the funeral together with Zolotov, the Mravinskys went directly to the Large Hall of the Conservatoire already in mourning drapes.[58] Rather than stand in the guard of honor immediately beside the coffin, Mravinsky sat quietly near his friend's widow, keeping his own thoughts and memories to himself, listening to the official speeches by Khrennikov, Kucharsky, Kabalevsky, Shchedrin, and others. Mravinsky noticed the bird-like features of the composer's nose and how his hands were crossed as if ready to meet his maker. Slowly, the coffin and mourners went out into the warm August sunlight to make their way out to the Novodevichy cemetery near the Moscow River. Together, the Mravinskys and Zolotov traveled in an old Lada motorcar loaned by a friend for the occasion. It was one of the saddest days in the composer's life; he hardly spoke a word all day to anyone, completely lost in his own meditations.

By the time that the cortege reached the southern precincts of the cemetery, the weather had worsened, a light, warm drizzle descended over the final bur-

ial ceremony, and the out-of-tune playing by a military band left a disconcerting impression. This and the overlooking wedding-cake architecture of
Moscow University left mourners feeling as if Shostakovich had not left at all.

> A man cannot be silent and content if there is common evil in the world; this in-
> iquity must be destroyed! For one this is the primary concept in Shostakovich's
> art. Great civil duty, humanity, and honor are the paramount qualities of this
> artist. They are part of the noble traditions of Russian social thinking, from the
> Decembrists and Belinsky to the Russian writers of the 1860s, in Tolstoy,
> Nekrasov, Dostoyevsky, and many other writers, and of Russian music. . . . [59]

Mravinsky announced that the 1975–1976 season would be in memoriam to
Dmitry Shostakovich. Following Mravinsky's silence on the day of the funeral, all his feelings and emotions were expressed in full force in his performances of that year. The first concert, on 24 October, was of
Tchaikovsky's *Pathétique* and Shostakovich's Fifth Symphony. The staggering interpretation left an unforgettable effect on its audience; regular concert-
goers had never experienced such an atmospheric, emotional musical offering. The affinity in the countenance of these two symphonies—in
Mravinsky's reading—was rather an expression of their immortality than re-
quiems for the dead.

> As I listened to Tchaikovsky's final symphony, it seemed to me that I understood
> and had come to terms with Mravinsky's conception. He brings Shostakovich
> together with world art, elevating him to the most unattainable heights and all
> of a sudden, this cosmos opens up to us. The range of this universe as shown by
> Mravinsky is impracticable to measure. One can only attempt to speculate his
> idea (I repeat attempt), and it looks to me that it is somewhat straightforward:
> music characterizes God and such figures, as Tchaikovsky and Shostakovich
> materialize to awaken this music in us. When their mission on earth comes to an
> end, nothing can be done; God takes them to himself. In actuality, these geniuses
> are united in spirit. [60]

Shostakovich's symphonies were the focal point of Mravinsky's programming, with the Sixth, Eighth, Tenth, and Fifteenth Symphonies all performed
from January to April 1976. Mravinsky's readings were momentous in that
they were not only technically superbly played but also imparted a classicism
to what was modern music—they became classics of today. Viktor Liberman
gave idiosyncratic readings of the First Violin Concerto, revealing "a fresh,
unique, and symphonic concept to this work." [61] In an interview with Boris
Schwartz, Shostakovich's son Maxim confessed that "Mravinsky is the closest to my father's thoughts." [62] Mravinsky never hid his feelings and belief in
Shostakovich.

I shared with Dmitry Dmitrevich Shostakovich many years together; in using the word *together* I have in mind that we shared the one earth, country, and time. Shostakovich was a chronicler of his epoch, and all that he created in his symphonies and other works is so close to me. I find that one shared his world of music. Of course, Shostakovich is a genius of a composer. I perform his work as best as one can. The proximity of the subject matter and the focus of his reflections have always facilitated my work, and I do not find the unambiguous complications in performing his music that one discovers in works by other composers. There opens up before me something that one was conscious of for a long time. Consequently, it is only required for me to marshal my forces (and it seems to me they are always inadequate) to recreate what he has written. All that he composed and has shown me is as a reflection of life around us.[63]

One of Mravinsky's ideas was to encourage composers to write works in Shostakovich's memory, among which was a commission for Boris Tischenko to write a twenty-minute orchestral piece for performance by the Philharmonic. However, the scope grew to a symphony of fifty minutes that was ultimately given its premiere by Kondrashin in Moscow.[64]

On 25 September 1976, observing Shostakovich's seventieth birthday, the Philharmonic programmed the Fifth and Sixth Symphonies before a most important tour to Austria, the GDR, Switzerland, and West Germany encompassing thirty-one concerts. Mravinsky's assistant on this occasion was a brilliant young protégé, Yuri Simonov. The repertoire was extensive: Musorgsky's *Night on a Bare Mountain*, Stravinsky's Piano Concerto, Sibelius's Seventh Symphony, Tchaikovsky's *Manfred*, Prokofiev's Third Symphony, along with works by Mozart, Beethoven, Shostakovich, and Boris Tischenko.

A major musical exchange with the German Democratic Republic took place in which innumerable Soviet cultural ensembles toured the towns and cities of East Germany, performing some two hundred concerts under the heading "Days of Soviet Musical Culture in the GDR," of which those featuring the Leningrad Philharmonic were the focal point. "Berlin gave the Leningrad Philharmonic under Yevgeny Mravinsky a rousing welcome."[65] The city council of Leipzig awarded Mravinsky the Arthur Nikisch Medal in recognition of his achievements in underpinning cultural associations between the Soviet Union and the German Democratic Republic. It was a major honor for Mravinsky, as previous musicians who received this prize included Franz Konwitschny, Kurt Masur, and Karl Böhm, the Leningrad conductor being the first non-German to receive the medal.

At the end of January 1977, Mravinsky conducted the world premiere of Salmanov's Fourth Symphony, programmed with fragments from Wagner: the prelude to *Die Meistersingers*, the prelude to Act I of *Lohengrin*, the overture to *Tannhäuser*, and "Flight of the Valkyries" from *Die Walküre*.

Salmanov dedicated his Fourth to Mravinsky and the Philharmonic—together they had shared common ideas in music and completed a remarkable cycle of works motivated by Nature. Mravinsky's February program included Weber's *Oberon*, Schubert's *Unfinished* Symphony, and fragments from *The Nutcracker*. The choreographer Yuri Grigorovich, a long-time friend, proposed to Mravinsky when he was producing *The Nutcracker* for the Vienna State Ballet that he should conduct it there—an offer Mravinsky approved with delight, although the plan unfortunately never came to fruition due to a conflict of touring schedules.[66]

The Philharmonic sustained its tradition of inviting guest artists; in the late '70s a familiar figure returned in the veteran Kurt Sanderling. Also, the mark made on the orchestra by the young Bulgarian Emil Chakirov was so powerful that he was considered by Mravinsky as a successor.[67] His deeply compelling debut with *Eroica* made an impact on everyone in the musical community in the city, but what promised to be a long and rich relationship with the Philharmonic ended with Chakirov's early death.[68]

An amusing episode unfolded on one occasion when the Leningrad actor Oleg Borisov found himself in the conductor's room following a concert. During a break in the conversation, Mravinsky began to look intently at Borisov with a questioning stare, and the thespian felt compelled to say something. "I thought the performance so powerful tonight that I will not attend the ballet in the theater again." It looked as if Mravinsky appreciated this praise. He whispered something to a cello player and, contented, slumped his arms to his sides, "Ah, so, very good." Buoyed by this, Borisov added, "Yevgeny Alexandrovich, you know that in Shakespeare's *King Lear* there is a scene where the King is asleep and music is playing quietly. . . ." Borisov could not finish, having noticed that Mravinsky's face had suddenly changed complexion, his eyebrows raised in anger, as if the play actor had played a false note in his orchestra. Mravinsky began to preach in a measured tone. "In my opinion, there can be no comparison with Shakespeare. No, not in any case. . . . Tchaikovsky in the *Nutcracker*—this is something quite, quite different," shaking his head gravely. Borisov understood that he had made a faux pas and caused discomfiture. Everyone looked down at their shoes while Mravinsky continued to smoke, and Borisov now contemplated how he could quickly disappear. People began to depart; Yevgeny Alexandrovich rose and shook hands with everyone and warned Borisov, "your comparison would be more appropriate with Shostakovich. He has his own music to *King Lear*. It is superb! On the other hand, Tchaikovsky, no, it is not appropriate. But in any case, thank you for your kind-hearted words!" As if they were meeting each other again soon, Mravinsky slapped his hand so strongly on Borisov's shoulder that he long felt the strength of the action.

Later that evening, Zolotov phoned Oleg Borisov and told him, barely disguising his amusement, that Mravinsky had mistaken the actor for someone else. When everyone had left the dressing room, Mravinsky told Zolotov "'You see, Andrey Andreyevich, what a KGB man I have with me now? Isn't he so sophisticated?' On that very day, a new security man was due to introduce himself to the conductor before a tour to Austria, and Mravinsky had mistaken Borisov for him. Yevgeny Alexandrovich sent his apologies, commenting that the KGB officer Borisov played on TV looked quite dissimilar."[69]

Yet another major tour covering Austria, Italy, and Germany beckoned. The concert in Florence marked his seventy-fifth birthday. On the same day, the Presidium of the Supreme Soviet awarded the Order of Friendship of the Peoples to Mravinsky; upon announcement to the audience, a stormy ovation erupted in the hall. "The performance of this famous Soviet orchestra in the Communalle," *La Natione* declared, "again awoke that unfathomable wave of great emotion that one comes into contact with before one of the most perfect creations."[70] On their foreign traveling, the conductor attained as elevated a standard as normal: "I am deeply convinced that tours do not require any special preparations. The main criteria are the constantly high level of daily concerts. Abroad we should simply play no worse than at home. One should prepare not for a number of programs but for the quality, the least the better."[71] However, it was the very standard of their playing that so impressed audiences and critics: "The storm of applause and adulation," wrote *La Natione*, "is for one of the most astonishing and stunning musical performances, it is difficult to find words to describe it. . . ."[72]

At the beginning of the tour in Milan, where the Leningrad musicians performed in the famous La Scala, Mravinsky was filmed in Toscanini's famous dressing room under the portraits of the many great conductors who had worked there. It was here almost one hundred years ago the great soprano had Mravina arrived at the very beginning of her career. The triumph of her nephew's visit was sensational; as one of the Milan papers described, the audience was dumbfounded by the orchestra's brilliant playing, and applauded and called for Mravinsky to return. "The Philharmonic is one of the four or five greatest world orchestras," wrote *Tempo*.[73] After La Scala in Milan, there followed concerts in Venice, Bologna, and Florence. Accompanying the Philharmonic was Andrey Zolotov. After Mravinsky gave Schubert's *Unfinished* at the beautiful Teatro La Venezia, the two colleagues went for a stroll. Upon seeing two coffins sailing by on a gondola, Mravinsky became quite upset and confided to his friend that his parents had once vacationed here in Venice and that his mother had conceived here; and now this vision seemed to remind him of his long-departed mother and father.[74]

The grand finale of the whole tour came in Austria, where the conductor's special triumph fell on the back of the Viennese concerts of the Philharmonic. "One of the culminating points of the Wien Festwoche," noted the local press, "was the performance by the Leningrad Philharmonic Orchestra, an ensemble, which in precision, brilliant technique, and rhythm does not have any equal."[75] Mravinsky's performances were broadcast live by Austrian State Radio, and from these tapes, recordings were issued of Brahms, Schubert, Shostakovich, and Tchaikovsky. The Austrian musicologist Rudolph Hanisegh described the Leningrad conductor's work with his orchestra as reminiscent of that of a surgeon or psychiatrist—"he could instantly diagnose and resolve the fault."[76]

Following the prestigious title received from the old musical city of Leipzig, another beckoned with the award to Mravinsky of the honorary membership of the Vienna Friends of Music, whose recipients included Beethoven, Weber, and Schubert. It was a supreme honor for the former Russian aristocrat, and it rekindled memories of the long-standing associations between Vienna and St. Petersburg. The letter from the Society declared that this is "in recognition of your great artistic activities," wrote General Secretary Mozer, "by your musical merit, in being associated with Austrian composers, and not in the least that you and your magnificent orchestra have become friends of our city, your concerts have been outstanding events in Viennese musical life."[77] Mravinsky was only the fourth conductor to be awarded this distinction, others being Karl Böhm, Carlo Maria Giulini, and Herbert von Karajan. The award ceremony took place on 14 June, when Mravinsky was presented with a facsimile of Schubert's *Unfinished* Symphony. He was an august company, and Mravinsky spoke in fluent German about his first visit to Vienna twenty years before, when he met Bruno Walter—Mravinsky remembered how he had with trepidation awaited his first rehearsal following a matinee concert by Walter and his apprehension at working in such a famous and venerable hall for the first time.[78]

A member of the audience at one of the performances in Vienna was the great ballet dancer Rudolph Nureyev. As a dancer at the Kirov, he had attended Mravinsky's concerts in Leningrad. After this concert, Nureyev approached Alexandra Vavilina and asked if it would be possible to meet Mravinsky. At the appointed hour, Nureyev arrived at Mravinsky's hotel and spent some pleasant, nostalgic hours with the Mravinskys talking about the past. Upon his leaving, Nureyev bowed low to the maestro, kissing his hand in gratitude at getting together.[79] It was a unique association between a man who sought refuge abroad and one who had defied all yet had managed success at home and abroad—both great artists and patriots.

If there existed gaps in Mravinsky's schedule that allowed him to sit in on other concerts, regrettably these only blighted his hopes with the sentimental and light-hearted readings of Shostakovich symphonies by Leonard Bernstein with the Vienna Philharmonic.[80]

Mravinsky bought a new superfast motor for his fishing boat that he would use during his summer vacation at Ust-Narva. With this Japanese motor, he could travel much faster than the militia boats out on the Gulf of Finland. Of course, Mravinsky's dacha was situated near territorial waters, and eventually the river police were so exasperated by the old conductor outpacing them in local rivers that they asked him to replace it with the old Soviet-made version. It was only a matter of time before his orchestral players heard about it, and soon Mravinsky was to be heard before the beginning of rehearsals asking his musicians if anyone wanted a motor, whispering: "Is anyone looking for a speedboat motor?"[81]

Due to the extensive international touring commitments of the orchestra, Mravinsky would be absent from the city for several months every season; there was too the cost of his years to his ability to study and work with the Philharmonic. The absence of his name from the subscription series gave Mravinsky's own appearances there a certain ambience—they were special events and almost impossible to gain admittance to. Mravinsky concerts would be announced just a few weeks beforehand; following the initial notice, the rehearsal process would begin, posters would go up outside the Philharmonic, and as soon as the box offices opened, regardless of weather conditions, the tickets would be gone within a few hours.

Health problems did not hinder another Japanese tour in 1979; of the sixteen concerts, seven were taken by Mravinsky and another member of the Jansons family with Arvids sharing the remainder. As always, the classics drew his audience's attention, as Kenzo Amoh describes: "It was in 1979 in Tokyo—his last visit to Japan—that I finally attended his concert. The main work of the program was Beethoven's *Pastoral*, about which Alexandra Vavilina told me recently that the conductor had confided after the concert: 'I did my best *Pastoral* in Tokyo.' That evening was unforgettable. His conducting gesture was powerful and elegant, just like the music he created."[82] Mravinsky's new revival on this visit was Glazunov's Fifth Symphony in B major—a major discovery for Japanese audiences (and the conducting of which was a long-standing act of loyalty to his rector at the Conservatoire). Mravinsky was one of few Russian conductors to program Glazunov's symphonies and ballets consistently throughout his career.

From 21 September to 31 October 1980, Mravinsky visited familiar territory: Austria, West Germany, and Switzerland. Even so, for the first time Mravinsky conducted Bruckner's Ninth Symphony, as the central piece in his programs, and his remaining repertoire included just two composers in Tchaikovsky and Glazunov. The work of the second conductor, Mariss Jansons, included Tchaikovsky, Rachmaninov, Shostakovich, Brahms, Beethoven, Berlioz, Schumann, and Prokofiev. The spiritual core and intellectual power of the Bruckner symphonies were central to Mravinsky's ethic as a musician: the power of religion and nature. Mravinsky used different versions, making his own performing editions in facilitating the timbre of Russian brass and woodwind. In reverence, Vienna christened Mravinsky "Herr Bruckner," and the Swiss press wrote of his Bruckner as being "not so much a version of the romantic as the expression of a tortured soul."[83] Other broadsheets discovered fresh and redeeming qualities: "The performance of Bruckner's Ninth Symphony was a magnificent demonstration of orchestral mastery, of conducting talent revealing the composer's greatness." The *Die Welt* correspondent continued: "the conductor sat before the score without a baton with such assurance and discarding any ostentatious glitter . . . approaching the essence of the music with greater affinity than more famous masters. After directing the orchestra for so many years, he doesn't need ecstasy of the hands any longer—the musicians react to his gesture as to their great master's life-long teaching—and what musicians they are!"[84]

NOTES

1. A. Petrov, author interview, May 2002.

2. G. Retrovskaya, author interview, July 2002.

3. A. M. Vavilina, "Iz dnevnikov," *Muzikalnaya Akademiya*, no. 4–5 (1995): 13.

4. A. A. Zolotov, author interview, July 2001.

5. A. M. Vavilina Mravinskaya, author interview, July 2001.

6. G. Rozhdestvensky, "Yevgeny Mravinsky," *Sovetskaya Muzika*, no. 7 (1963).

7. A. Zolotov, "Dirizher i muzika: Moskovskie gastroli," *Pravda*, 8 February 1972.

8. Y. Svetlanov, "Mravinsky," *Sovetskaya Rossia*, 29 January 1972.

9. Maxim Shostakovich, author interview, September 2002.

10. Irina Shostakovich, author interview, May 2003.

11. Y. A. Mravinsky, "Iz besed," *Muzikalnaya Akademiya*, no. 4 (1997): 102; Y. A. Mravinsky, interview with A. A. Zolotov, March 1983, *Vosmaya Shostakovicha*, Ekran TV.

12. Boris Tischenko, conversation with the author, May 2002.

13. I. Glikman, *Pisma k Drugu* (St. Petersburg, DSCH, 1993), 287.

14. A. M. Vavilina Mravinskaya, "Obruchyonniye muzikoy," *Muzikalnaya Akademiya*, no. 4 (1997): 91.

15. Y. A. Mravinsky, interview with A. A. Zolotov, *Shostakovich Pyataya Simphony*, Ekran TV, 1973.

16. Mravinsky, "Iz besed," 102.

17. Y. A. Mravinsky, "Iz besed," *Muzikalnaya Akademiya*, no. 4 (1997): 91.

18. *Die Welt*, 5 October 1972.

19. *Kurier*, 30 October 1972.

20. *Kurier*, 30 October 1972.

21. A. Dmitr'yev, author interview, July 2002.

22. *Tempo*, 15 November 1972.

23. Y. A. Mravinsky, interview with A. A. Zolotov, *Myshlenie o Mravinskovo*, Ekran TV, 1978.

24. Y. A. Mravinsky archive.

25. Y. A. Mravinsky archive.

26. A. Zolotov, author interview, October 2001.

27. A. Zolotov, author interview, July 2001.

28. A. Zolotov, author interview, July 2001.

29. A. Zolotov, author interview, July 2001.

30. *Moscow Radio*, 4 June 1973.

31. V. Fomin, *Dirizher Yevgeny Mravinsky* (Leningrad: Muzika, 1983), 75.

32. V. Salmanov, "Khudozhnik. Myslitel," *Sovetskaya Muzika*, no. 6 (1973): 53–54.

33. V. Liberman, "Rukovoditel, pedagog, vospitatel," *Sovetskaya Muzika*, no. 6 (1973): 54–55.

34. B. Schwartz, *Music and Musical Life in Soviet Russia 1917–1982* (Bloomington: Indiana University Press, 1983), 548.

35. Schwartz, *Music and Musical Life in Soviet Russia 1917–1982*, 547.

36. *Sankey Simbun*, 28 May 1973.

37. Kenzo Amoh, author interview, November 2002.

38. Kenzo Amoh, author interview, November 2002.

39. Midori Kawashima, author interview, October 2001.

40. Valery Bezruchenko, author interview, May 2003.

41. *Die Welt*, September 1974.

42. *General Anzeiger*, 26 September 1974.

43. *Die Presse*, 7 October 1974.

44. *Die Vienna Presse*, 7 October 1974.

45. Karl Lobl, *Kurier*, 8 October 1974.

46. A. M. Vavilina Mravinskaya, author interview, September 2002.

47. D. Oistrakh, *U vas est chemu pouchitsya* (Leningrad: Leningradskaya filarmonia, 1972), 283–84.

48. S. Aleshin, "Teatr vremeni—Iosifa, Nikity I Leni," *Ogonyek*, no. 28 (May 2001), 53–54.

49. A. A. Zolotov, author interview, October 2001.

50. S. Aleshin, "Teatr vremeni—Iosifa, Nikity I Leni."

51. O. Borisov, *Bez znakov prepinaniya, dnevnik 1974–1994* (Moscow: Artist-Rezhisser-Teatr, 1999), 86.

52. Borisov, *Bez znakov prepinaniya, dnevnik 1974–1994*, 87.

53. A. M Vavilina Mravinskaya, author interview, July 2002.

54. A. M Vavilina Mravinskaya, author interview, July 2002.

55. Kenzo Amoh, author interview, November 2002.

56. *Mainiti Simbun*, 21 May 1975.

57. Vavilina Mravinskaya, "Obruchyonniye muzikoy," 91.

58. A. Zolotov, author interview, July 2001.

59. Y. A. Mravinsky, *Sovetskaya Muzika*, no. 9 (1966): 7.

60. Borisov, *Bez znakov prepinaniya dnevnik 1974–1994*, 45.

61. Era-Sophia Barutcheva, author interview, December 2001.

62. Schwartz, *Music and Musical Life in Soviet Russia 1917–1982*, 646.

63. Y. A. Mravinsky, interview with A. A. Zolotov, *Shostakovich Pyataya Simphony*, Ekran TV, September 1973.

64. B. Tischenko, author interview, September 2002.

65. B. Schwartz, *Music and Musical Life in Soviet Russia 1917–1982*, 589.

66. Y. Grigorovitch, interview for St. Petersburg TV.

67. A. M. Vavilina Mravinskaya, author interview, July 2001.

68. Chakirov died in 1988 in Paris. Others of his interpretations in Leningrad included Mahler's Fifth Symphony, Brahms's *Deutsches Requiem*, and Bruckner's Fourth, *Romantic*, Symphony.

69. Borisov, *Bez znakov prepinaniya dnevnik 1974–1994*, 75–76.

70. *La Natione*, 5 June 1978.

71. Valentin Stadler, author interview, July 2002.

72. *La Natione*, 7 June 1978.

73. *Tempo*, 1 June 1978.

74. A. A. Zolotov, author interview, May 2003.

75. *Volksstimme*, 15 June 1978.

76. E. Serov, *Dirizher Eduard Serov* (Volgograd: Nizhnevolzhskoye), 135.

77. Letter of award of the Society of Friends of Music, 1978.

78. Documentary film, June 1978, private sources.

79. A. M. Vavilina Mravinskaya, author interview, September 2002.

80. A. M. Vavilina Mravinskaya, author interview, September 2002.

81. O. Borisov, *Bez znakov prepinaniya dnevnik 1974–1994*, 317.

82. Kenzo Amoh, author interview, November 2002.

83. *Die Tagesanzeiger*, 9 October 1980.

84. *Die Welt*, 21 October 1980.

Chapter Sixteen

The Last Concerts

Even if you know that conducting is very difficult,
one needs to be seventy years old,
To discover how hard it really is. . . .

—R. Strauss, *Tempo*

A concert by Yevgeny Mravinsky was always an event, a happening, and a phenomenon for anyone fortunate to be present. However, on 31 December 1981, there took place a unique experience for listeners at the Large Hall of the Philharmonic. This was a festive program comprising ballet pieces in the Second Suite from *Romeo and Juliet* by Prokofiev and Mravinsky's own arrangement of Tchaikovsky's *Nutcracker*. If both were among his favorites, on this evening nevertheless a special atmosphere reigned in the auditorium. The musicologist Sofia Barutcheva recalled: "the level of sound produced in the great *Adagio* quite stunned everyone both by the degree of power and the sheer range of rich tone of the orchestra's playing. We could feel the great chandeliers shudder and shake as no one else could achieve at the Philharmonic."[1]

Following the end of the concert, the conductor acknowledged the ovation from his exultant audience. Quite unexpectedly, after the musicians had long since left the stage, Yevgeny Mravinsky turned to his public, for once directing his attention to them, instantly stopping the applause with a sudden movement of his arm, and for the first time in all his many years addressed his listeners. Few had ever heard his voice, and now his patriarchal, dry baritone was speaking to them. Beginning slowly, Mravinsky greeted everyone in the hall on the forthcoming New Year, and without pausing, began talking about his orchestra. Recalling that he had listened to the Philharmonic as a child, he

246

preserved a deep gratitude to his musicians after six decades and picked out individual players in the Philharmonic. He recalled such conductors as Walter and Steidry from the 1930s. Everyone felt a shared experience with the conductor, and the audience left with a unique sense of parting with the old and starting anew—it was an unforgettable event.[2]

There was already a long-standing tradition to open the season with Shostakovich, and the 1981–1982 series was no different. On the composer's birthday, Mravinsky played the Fifth and Sixth Symphonies as never before, attaining a new degree of power and intensity. In November, Mravinsky played Salmanov's Second Symphony, combining it with Tchaikovsky's Fifth. If in his seventy-ninth year Mravinsky constrained his repertoire, he would not tire of reviving long-abandoned scores. In January 1982, he programmed Beethoven's First Symphony (for the first time in thirty years!), billing it with fragments from Wagner: the prelude to *Die Meistersinger von Nürnberg*, the prelude to *Lohengrin*, the overture to *Tannhäuser*, and the "Flight of the Valkyries" from *Die Walküre*. Through ensuing months, there followed trusted pieces from his treasure chest in Prokofiev's Sixth Symphony with Shostakovich's Eighth, Mozart's Symphonies No. 33 in B-flat K.319 and No. 39 in E-flat K.543, and as always, Tchaikovsky's *Pathétique* and the symphonic fantasia *Francesca da Rimini*.

In March 1982, the penultimate film was set down for Andrey Zolotov's Moscow TV crew, and it was to be a special project. This was the Eighth Symphony in C minor by Dmitry Shostakovich. The screening included a long interview in which Mravinsky spoke of his relationship with Shostakovich, the Fifteenth Symphony, and interesting subtextual material. Unlike the other films made by Zolotov, the shooting included detailed close-ups of soloists (without an audience at the Philharmonic Hall) and lent a grainy, tightly drawn tension to the production. The project at once attained a higher degree of artistic success for Zolotov; here was unveiled the intimate art of Mravinsky's music making from his words on its creation—their moral and social import—the artistic processes in rehearsal, and finally, a complete performance. The documentary film made a unique impression; the interview was never broadcast in full in the Soviet Union, although its text was published fifteen years later.[3]

In the summer of 1982, Mravinsky took his orchestra on its thirty-third foreign tour, visiting Austria, the GDR, Spain, and Switzerland. Everywhere, the orchestra's musicians were met by standing ovations and endless applause. Their success particularly exceeded all expectations in Spain. Mravinsky's concerts in Madrid and Grenada became events that audiences, as one newspaper wrote, "will long remember and talk about."[4] The Spanish reviews were the most ecstatic and impressive among the hundreds of newspaper reviews written about the orchestra: "The concert of Yevgeny Mravinsky was not only unusual. . . . With Yevgeny Mravinsky the Leningrad orchestra actually appears as a virtuoso instrument as an extension of his body, his hands. There is no pomposity, no particular tension. Without a baton, sitting on a stool, as if touching the score with his left hand, the 79-year-old maestro hardly with a movement of his hands or even a hint of it leads the orchestra, and the music flows, perfect and profound. This is the fruit not of one rehearsal and one's artistic career, but one's whole life."[5]

On several consecutive evenings, Tchaikovsky's Fifth Symphony was scheduled, and having already performed the work in Barcelona, two days later, on 17 June, Mravinsky was to conduct Prokofiev's *Romeo and Juliet* and the Fifth Symphony. The violinist Liya Muradyan recounts that after Mravinsky's sightseeing on the afternoon of an evening concert, "he was totally devastated by seeing the Goyas and Titians at the Prado Museum, and this stimulated his reading of Tchaikovsky's Fifth Symphony—it was wholly different from that given elsewhere on that tour."[6]

In the Philharmonic subscription concerts, music lovers were still finding exceptional results hearing works that many believed they already knew. The actor Oleg Borisov described a Tchaikovsky concert: "*The Nutcracker* stunned me—so tragic and quite unlike ballet music! How he conducted the battle of the mice! . . . On this occasion, there was no coughing among the audience—there reigned complete silence in the hall. He sat on a high stool and placed his right foot on it nonchalantly as if tonight's program was easier for him. He moved his spectacles, and there began the famous *Adagio*."[7]

Mravinsky's opening concert of the 1982–1983 season was with two Viennese classics in Beethoven's Haydnesque First Symphony in C and his *Pastoral*. Zolotov's last film was one of his finest—consisting of a complete performance solely for TV cameras of Tchaikovsky's Fifth Symphony. Tchaikovsky's Fifth was filmed live ten years before; this was among the last readings before microphones, and it was a grim tragic canvas that was unveiled before television audiences. Following past practice, Zolotov's film was shot before a performance at the Philharmonic. TV audiences were shown Mravinsky in his room talking to Zolotov. Mravinsky described the great Waltz as "an interlude," a grotesque dance masking a terrible fate. It is quite false to call this work romantic; there is an oppressive theme of destiny in the final pages of the symphony. Mravinsky spoke about his interpretations as each being different—they cannot be the same—every performance must be distinct, dependent on mood, acoustics, and other circumstances. There can be discerned a reluctance and slight unease before the cameras, yet the tension slowly melts, as he drinks tea and habitually smokes, his hand shaking nervously. This as it happens was the last occasion that Mravinsky was interviewed on camera.

To live within oneself more wise—
There is a whole world in your spirit
Of secret, magical thoughts....[8]

The local filmmaker Dmitry Rozhdestvensky continued Zolotov's mission, albeit restricted to conventional filming of engagements in Leningrad, Moscow, and Minsk. As many works were taped, however, the compassionately artistic style that Zolotov had attained throughout the 1970s was absent. Rozhdestvensky's Leningrad TV crew filmed the gems of this late period. Shostakovich's Fifth and Twelfth Symphonies, Schubert's *Unfinished Symphony*, Salmanov's *Second Symphony*, Tchaikovsky's *Francesca da Rimini*, and Musorgsky's prelude to *Khovanschina*, "Dawn on the Moscow River."

Mravinsky's Philharmonic embarked on a three-concert visit to Moscow. In the concert on 18 November 1982, there was an incredible atmosphere outside the Large Hall of the Conservatoire; a huge crowd was gathering, several thousand strong, some with tickets and many without, and special police were marshaling the growing multitudes. "Throughout the afternoon the people began waiting in queues; everyone knew that this was an extraordinary concert." Among the violin section that evening, Liya Muradyan recalled that she saw Mravinsky come out on stage following the announcer Anna Chekhova: "as soon as Mravinsky appeared, the huge audience rose as one in respect to this veteran. As he moved to the rostrum, I noticed in his eyes a tear; he realized that this storm of affection was for him, yet he bowed stiffly, turned around to his players, and immediately began to conduct, and the hall went quiet as a mouse."[9]

This concert featured the Fifth Symphonies of Shostakovich and Tchaikovsky. During the finale of the Shostakovich, almost all the lights in the hall were extinguished: "it was an unreal situation, yet the orchestra did not stop; we just continued playing, we knew the music inside out, we knew his reading, a sign of how good this orchestra was at the time."[10] These were a commemorative series in Moscow's Grand Hall of the Conservatoire. The centenary of the orchestra was celebrated in 1982—one hundred years since its founding by Nikolay Rimsky-Korsakov as the Imperial Court Orchestra. Following tradition, Mravinsky unveiled a showcase of music before the Moscow intelligentsia, directing long-standing favorites: Shostakovich's Fifth Symphony, Beethoven's First and Sixth Symphonies, Tchaikovsky's Fifth Symphony, Prokofiev's Second Suite to *Romeo and Juliet*, and fragments from *The Nutcracker*. Sitting on a tall stool, without baton and under TV lights, the gaunt, elderly figure of Mravinsky transfixed the audience with his magical music making. "For a long time we have not seen the public overfilling the Great Hall of the Conservatoire moving with one gesture of deep respect and sincere expectation."[11]

The final concert of the series was on 24 November and comprised Prokofiev's *Romeo and Juliet* and fragments from the *Nutcracker*. During the intense development at the transition to the *Adagio*: "At one moment Mravinsky rose from his stool, reaching to his full enormous height, raising his left clenched fist over the orchestra, giving his brass players a look of terror—and how they played for him! One wanted only to weep that evening. Everyone was so familiar with his strictly restrained gestures, the barely discernable glances at his musicians, a cold half smile and a slight movement of the eyebrows. All of this was as it were collected in a precise scheme, and suddenly such a blazing outburst in the culmination! For some this was the end of the dream, of the vision and for the listener no less than the end of the world."[12]

Leningrad marked the anniversary only in spring of the next year, with a brace of concerts. In the wake of Brezhnev's passing, Romanov had attained his promotion, and his replacement, Vladimir Soloviov, had overbearing priorities. The event was another ordeal for the aging maestro, for he intensely disliked official social ceremonies and insisted on abstaining, but this was one that he could not duck out of as it was covered by local TV.[13] The second concert on 8 April 1983 comprised first Glinka's overture to *Ruslan and Lyudmila*. For the TV audiences watching at home, the three figures sitting in the loge beyond the conductor seemed so disenchanted and gloomy listening to Glinka's bright, dynamic, and effervescent overture. However, this trio were leaders of the Regional Committee of the Party: Vladimir Soloviov, Politburo member; Galina Pakhomova, cultural secretary; and assistant Viktor Lopatnikov. The lack of concord so clearly expressed by them suggested that the conductor at the podium represented defiance to their power. Here at the Philharmonic, Yevgeny Mravinsky offered his public a retreat of riches and forbidden fruits, of dreams and fantasy that could allow them, albeit for a few short hours, a sanctuary from tyranny and oppression.

At the end of April 1983, the Leningrad Philharmonic revisited Barcelona, Madrid, and Seville, on this visit playing fragments from Wagner, Brahms's Fourth Symphony, and familiar favorites in Tchaikovsky and Shostakovich. Upon his return in late May, Mravinsky went out to spend some months of rest at his own sanctuary of Ust-Narva. In a home movie Mravinsky is caught on camera walking along the beach, looking out westward, as if reflecting on a long career, wistful at what could have been. It was a poignant scene.[14] Here he had found so many days of freedom and peace, away from the stress and ordeals of the city; close friends and colleagues would come out and spend some days with him. One of those was a journalist from the small-circulation *Literary Russia* who interviewed Mravinsky on his eightieth birthday. In this last published interview, the old maestro recorded his memories of the 1930s, the war years, and his acquaintance with Prokofiev and Shostakovich. He summoned up recollections about his players and their loyal service to the Philharmonic through four long decades. Asked at last if he had found happiness, Mravinsky responded in the affirmative for he was fulfilling "a mission to bring good to people."[15]

There appeared to be a leave-taking in Mravinsky's selecting "final" symphonies. The opening curtain on 21 October 1983 unveiled Schubert's *Unfinished* Symphony and Shostakovich's Fifteenth Symphony. This was repeated when he took the Philharmonic on tour to Minsk in the following month, an event that was televised. A solitary camera at the back of the stage recorded the power and intensity of the conductor still at a peak of performance. In the auditorium beyond Mravinsky, no less compelling was the visual effect of this music upon his audience.

This was the last full season for the maestro, as his health now began to decline significantly. Further engagements in this period included Mozart's Symphony No. 33 in B-flat, Tchaikovsky's *Pathétique*, Salmanov's Second Symphony, Shostakovich's Twelfth Symphony in G, and Tchaikovsky's Fifth Symphony in E minor. Several of these were televised, notably the Salmanov and Shostakovich, revealing his magical artistry in arcane twentieth-century pieces. Following his last performance in April 1983, Mravinsky spent some time in clinics being treated for bronchial ailments. Not helped by his continual smoking and the harsh Leningrad climate, he was hospitalized with pneumonia as many as four times a year. The strenuous work regime he pursued all his life was now too much for his weakening body; the immense strength for each concert required more time for recovery and replenishment.[16]

However, there were engagements that he refused to cancel, and these included the opening of the Shostakovich Festival held in the city of Duisburg. Mravinsky opened on 16 September 1984 with the Fifth Symphony in D minor and two days later gave Schubert's *Unfinished* and Shostakovich's Fifteenth Symphonies. He directed the latter in a quite revelatory manner, the magnitude of which so affected the public that after the final bars there was total silence; the audience did not know how to respond, whether they should applaud or just to go away into the night. In the auditorium was the composer's son Maxim: "It was a quite fantastic, astonishing concert, one of the greatest performances that I have ever attended."[17]

Yevgeny Alexandrovich's character was complex, and another sign of this came at one of the engagements on tour in West Germany. The program consisted of German works by Beethoven and Brahms, and the burgomaster was present with the Soviet ambassador, Valentin Falin. The latter approached Mravinsky during the interval and suggested that if he was to give an encore that it should be a German piece. Yevgeny Alexandrovich responded saying he had actually been thinking of Musorgsky's prelude, "Dawn on the Moscow

River." Falin rather indelicately persisted, pointing out that the local dignitary was a music lover and had a very talented young son who was studying music and this would be a friendly gesture. Having quietly heard the diplomat out, Mravinsky responded that this was a reasonable idea. Of course, at the end of the concert, the orchestra played as an encore the Musorgsky.[18]

Mravinsky was never interested in material things. Alexandra Mikhailovna earned three times as much as did her husband—she taught at the Conservatoire and was principal flute. For most of his last thirty years, Mravinsky spent most of his salary in alimony payments to his previous spouses.[19] His flat was full of ancient, unfashionable furniture, much of the space taken by books and scores, his sole possession being the grand piano—the center of his world and his music. Following a concert, he would often return home, descend to the off-license downstairs, and spend time discussing world affairs with the shop assistant. The summers spent at Ust-Narvi in communion with nature brought him his greatest joys; wrote Serov: "like the hero from Hermann Hesse's *Steppenwolf*, Mravinsky could never imagine that his reflection split into dozens of pieces revealed his image as that of a master spirit."[20]

Mravinsky would also spend much of his time at the Composers' Union rest home, socializing with musicians and friends there. Tischenko recalls that when he was recuperating from a fractured limb, "I arrived at Yevgeny Alexandrovich's home. I had broken my leg and had to use a walking stick, and when Mravinsky saw me, he exclaimed sympathetically, 'Borenka with a walking stick!' This touched him to the heart, because Shostakovich employed a stick after he broke his leg. 'Now well, lets have dinner together.' He was such a touching man, and there was something in him quite childlike, lacking any of the malevolence or frostiness attributed to him. He was a warm and sensitive person with everything reserved within him. He was not sentimental, although once I saw tears in his eyes."[21]

If there was a significant decline in concerts in the mid-'80s, nevertheless it is amazing that Yevgeny Mravinsky confided to the Leningrad composer Andrey Petrov "that his dream was not to go on stage but to sit in a studio and make recordings without a public."[22] Mravinsky gave just two performances in 1984, a solitary concert in 1985, three performances in 1986, and the final night in 1987. Yevgeny Alexandrovich Mravinsky's penultimate concert was of fragments from Wagner's operas, including the "Forest Murmurs" from *Siegfried*, "Wotan's Farewell" (soloist Gleb Nikolsky) and the "Magic Fire Music" from *Die Walküre*, and "Siegfried's Funeral March" from *Götterdämmerung*. Forty years had passed since Mravinsky last directed "Wotan's Farewell," and this was an incredibly deep and tragic portrayal.

> Farewell, you bold, wonderful child
> You, my heart's holiest pride!

Farewell, farewell, farewell!
If I must reject you
And may not lovingly
Greet you again with my greeting[23]

The final concert, on 6 March 1987, was of Schubert's *Unfinished* Symphony in B Minor and Brahms's Symphony No. 4 in E minor. For many minutes afterward, Mravinsky returned to the platform to take his bows from the hundreds of music lovers; there it was from the rear of the hall (after the orchestra had long since left the stage) that the last photograph was taken of him before the adoring and standing listeners—a lonely figure.[24]

In his last years, Mravinsky would delve into familiar scores, searching for subtext and fresh material. Serov found him sitting over Tchaikovsky's Fifth Symphony with a magnifying glass, explaining "I am looking for more detail."[25] If he found more time at home, an unusual pastime was in Mravinsky's addiction to watching ice hockey on TV, together with his wife and some close friends, not allowing anything to interrupt his enjoyment of this intrinsic Russian winter sport. For Mravinsky, there was something engaging and curiously artistic in the balletic movements of the hockey players moving at great speed, without someone pulling the strings, their movements combined as if to a preordained script.[26] That was something that was more a distraction from the pressures of his profession than a source of fulfillment in his last years of declining health.

He would sit for long hours at the piano in the large spacious front room of his fifth-floor flat before the house in which Peter I lived when he founded the city. Overlooking the wide expanse of the Neva River, he could see opposite the Summer Gardens beloved of Pushkin's *Yevgeny Onegin* and depicted in the *Queen of Spades*—the venue of his first Philharmonic concert. Looking at this vista through the massive windows out onto the Neva, there was an eternal calm reigning, the flat landscape, the Hermitage and St. Isaacs far in the distance—this panorama had been his world for so many years, and it seemed somehow timeless.

In November 1987, the Leningrad Philharmonic Orchestra and its Chief Conductor Yevgeny Mravinsky were to mark the fiftieth anniversary of Shostakovich's Fifth Symphony—the concert that changed everything both for Shostakovich and for himself as a conductor. Despite every attempt to be in good fettle, Yevgeny Alexandrovich suffered a mild heart attack, which prompted the Philharmonic to take extraordinary measures to get him the best medical care. Following diplomacy at a high level, a special aircraft flew the Mravinskys for treatment to a clinic specializing in heart problems in Vienna. Nevertheless, the Austrian doctors could do little. The condition of "diffuse bronchitis" had affected his kidney, which in turn incurably weakened his

heart. Although Mravinsky enjoyed robust health over many years, the doctors concluded that they could only make his last months as comfortable as
possible.[27]

The flight back to Leningrad on 7 January 1988 brought the dying conductor back to his home on the Petrovsky Embankment. Unwilling to relinquish his old habits, Mravinsky continued to study scores for his next concert
of the French masters Debussy and Ravel. He delved into Shostakovich's
Fifth, claiming to find still new subtexts there, and he also looked at Mahler's
Fifth Symphony.[28] As always, friends and colleagues visited; however, a
week following his return, the director of the orchestra Shishmanov came to
see him on a question that considerably upset the conductor. Following this
rendezvous, the old maestro fell into an extremely depressed mood. On Tues-
day 19 January, at three o'clock in the afternoon, Yevgeny Alexandrovich began feeling very poorly, and a doctor was summoned who immediately called
the heart reanimation team. Alas, there was little that could now be done for
he had suffered another heart attack; nevertheless, for several hours, they attempted to prolong his life. Mravinsky sat in an armchair facing his bedroom
window, still alert to what was going on around him, and his eyes took a pal-
lid, glazed appearance. The doctors asked continually for him to clench his
right hand; slowly he dropped off into an unconscious state, and between 7:20
and 7:30 that evening he passed away. His last words were that he wanted to
be aware of passing from one world into the next. Mravinsky departed this
life looking onto the snow-covered trees of the icy city street.[29]

Among the first to hear of his passing was Liya Muradyan, a friend of the
family. She had finished her rehearsal that evening, and as she was leaving
through the stage door, the janitor whispered to her, "Please don't tell anyone,
Yevgeny Alexandrovich has died. Alexandra Mikhailovna asks you to come
as soon as possible."[30]

A funeral service was given in his memory, as is the custom in the Russian
Orthodox Church, on the eve of his burial on 21 January at the Preobrazhensky Cathedral, before the coffin was taken to the Philharmonic. At the Hall of
the Nobility, the people who had been enraptured by his art came to honor the
memory of Yevgeny Alexandrovich Mravinsky. Many thousands paid their
last respects throughout the day. Above the organ gallery, there hung a portrait, and his musical public looked in veneration at the figure who had built
their city's orchestra into one of the finest in the world, at the face who had
lit both fear and joy in his musicians for five decades. Alexandra Mikhailovna
insisted that no speeches be made at the funeral meeting at the Philharmonic,
asking that his music be heard as the public's last memory of him. Present
were the Politburo member Soloviov, City Council members, local dignitaries
and representatives of the Ministry of Culture from Moscow, and leading mu-

sicians, conductors, and composers from all over the Soviet Union. The greatest number were his own musicians who had played for him in past years. Throughout the time in which he lay in state, loudspeakers in the auditorium played music from his recordings, of Beethoven, Brahms, Prokofiev, Shostakovich, Tchaikovsky, and Wagner. The music was relayed outside, where tens of thousands of his devoted public stood in the freezing cold Leningrad, filling the Square of Art and Brodsky Street and spilling out onto Nevsky Prospekt.

To the strains of "Siegfried's Funeral March," Yevgeny Alexandrovich Mravinsky left the Philharmonic for the last time as the coffin was brought out to a hushed crowd. The cortege passed the locations associated with Mravinsky's life—the Nikolsky Cathedral, the State Conservatoire, and the Mariinsky Theatre—and moved through the streets and past the beautiful canals and squares of an icy and frozen Petersburg-Leningrad. As they had on so many nights at the Philharmonic, lines of police and soldiers on this day now paid reverence for the maestro. The final journey of a few miles through the city center was one of great emotion and memories for all who lined the route; the traffic halted as seldom had happened in recent times. Now, for one who had brought music to the world, a deep mourning stillness reigned for him.

In the falling dusk, Yevgeny Alexandrovich Mravinsky was buried beside his third wife, Inna Serikova, at the Bogoslovsky Cemetery on the eastern precincts of the city. Among the still living trees and growing vegetation of the cemetery, the birds and animals would be his final partners in the world he so adored and revered all his life.

NOTES

1. Era-Sofia Barutcheva, author interview, December 2001.
2. Era-Sofia Barutcheva, author interview, December 2001.
3. This interview is provided in appendix A.
4. *Le Pais*, 19 June 1982.
5. *Le Pais*, 19 June 1982.
6. Liya Lilik-Muradyan, author interview, July 2002.
7. O. Borisov, *Bez znakov prepinaniya, dnevnik 1974–1994* (Moscow: Moskovskaya Novosti, 1999), 73.
8. Fyodor Tyutchev, *Sochineniya F. F. Tyutcheva* (St. Petersburg: Komarov, 1888).
9. Liya Lilik-Muradyan, author interview, July 2002.
10. Vladimir Ovcharek, author interview, May 2003.
11. Y. Ratzner, "Poslusheny vole dirizhera: Vystupleniye E. Mravinskovo v Moskve," *Sovetskaya Kultura*, 23 November 1982.

12. Borisov, *Bez znakov prepinaniya*, 74.

13. L. Volkhova, author interview, February 2002.

14. A. Petrov, author interview, May 2002.

15. Y. A. Mravinsky, interview with Konstantin Panferov, "Chitayu sebya schaslivym," *Literaturnaya Rossia*, 3 June 1983, 9.

16. A. M. Vavilina Mravinskaya, author interview, July 2001.

17. Maxim Shostakovich, author interview, September 2002.

18. V. M. Falin, interview for Leningrad TV, 1989.

19. A. M. Vavilina Mravinskaya, author interview, March 2002.

20. E. Serov, *Dirizher Eduard Serov* (Volgograd: Nizhnevolzhskoye, 1993), 150.

21. B. Tischenko, author interview, September 2002.

22. A. Petrov, interview with G. N. Enfaldt, May 2002.

23. Richard Wagner, "Wotan's Farewell," Act Three, *Die Walküre*.

24. Galina Retrovskaya, author interview, July 2002.

25. Serov, *Dirizher Eduard Serov*, 145.

26. M. Jansons, author interview, September 2001.

27. A. M. Vavilina Mravinskaya, author interview, October 2001.

28. Era-Sofia Barutcheva, author interview, December 2001.

29. A. M. Vavilina Mravinskaya, author interview, October 2002.

30. Liya Lilik-Muradyan, author interview, July 2002.

Andrey Zolotov Interview
of Yevgeny Mravinsky

AZ: Our discussion will preface the performance of the Eighth Symphony for a huge television audience. What would you like to say to those people who are about to listen to this overwhelmingly tragic music?

YM: This is a difficult question of course, what should they experience in the first bars? All three symphonies—the Fifth, the Sixth, and the Eighth—begin quite emphatically with such an almighty thesis expressed on the strings, and extraordinary as it may sound, bearing a powerful statement and an enigma. Following the expressed idea, there enters a consciousness of hollowness, of a freedom that is rather serene and compassionate. The first movement of the Eighth Symphony brings one at the closing stages to this barren, tenuous material that gradually develops, conveying a tragic culmination that one could only express as a barrier to human aspiration for something. . . . This is an inspired revelation by the composer. Beginning with such somber material and ending at such a pinnacle, the whole thing can be poised upon this interrelated culmination. It's breathtaking! I find it difficult to name another piece of music containing such an idea.

That is so much for the first movement.

The fifth movement, and finale of the symphony, is very interesting—it also begins quietly, on the solo bassoon; it slowly builds, transforming itself into quite irreconcilable material; one can feel it is cataclysmic, and it doesn't last, and the symphony concludes in peace and tranquility. This represents a very positive creative departure. It is fascinating that this is among the few pieces written by Shostakovich in a pastoral disposition. When the fifth movement starts, there is a complete sense of entering into an almost idyllic world. But there enters quite different music, and it fosters, assimilates, resists, and I would say that it all descends not to a closure—a tranquility and a distance as in the beginning—but to enlightenment, to affection and eleva-tion. It rises, rises, and disappears. . . .

For me, the second, third, and fourth movements appear to be a trio of two extremes to the central movements. The second movement is difficult to char-acterize in words, there is so much grotesque, all sorts of intensity—bitter and unpleasant. In spite of which, it has a secondary nature. The third movement is a so-called toccata. I would have said that it may be "an unstoppable hap-pening"; it's terrible propulsive force attains its own zenith and subsides into the fourth movement. The fourth is nothing short of a miracle. Precisely as Asaf'yev wrote about this symphony: "there is a human heart beating in the secret depths." . . . It is magnificent, prolonged, and is heard quite abruptly because it so engages the listener, one forgets everything. I remember very well hearing this music for the first time played on the piano in his home, I experienced a feeling as if it were being born within me, harmonious in a veiled tranquility, distanced from reality and in this liberation from something terrible. Taking the fourth movement musically—it is a slow movement. It is surprising because it is for chamber forces . . . for 106 musicians—for over a hundred persons, the most fragile chamber piece—a passacaglia.

AZ: It is well known that the Eighth Symphony is dedicated to you personally, and that the first performance was in Moscow in 1943. You came especially from Novosibirsk for this. How did this dedication happen?

YM: I was summoned to Moscow on two occasions from Novosibirsk to par-ticipate in very important events: the fiftieth anniversary of Tchaikovsky's death and for the premiere of Shostakovich's Eighth Symphony. It was sched-uled with the USSR State Symphony Orchestra. The living conditions in Moscow were not so pleasant at the time. Of course, when we began work, the orchestra did not expect such a difficult piece would be in store for them. One must confess that few of us got any comfort from the first rehearsal. Nev-ertheless, one did have youth and strength in one's favor. We labored a great deal—for a whole two weeks in rehearsal. On one occasion, in the finale, when the bassoon plays a high note (the most difficult passage) not every-thing happened as it should. We took a break. I descended into the body of the hall and began to stroll around the stalls. Dmitry Dmitrevich—the poor soul was also walking back and forth—and like two trains on the same line, we bumped into one another. Suddenly, he stopped and asked me: "I want to ded-icate this symphony to you." Of course, one can't remember what was said in response, however this symbolized the ultimate happiness of my life. At once, he wrote in the score: "dedicated to Yevgeny Alexandrovich Mravinsky." It was later that one would mark all my performances and there next to it would be the signature of the composer.

AZ: Was this for all the performances?

YM: Yes, practically all of them. For Dmitry Dmitrevich, this was a work acutely important to him. Actually, he did not miss either a Moscow, Leningrad, or performance abroad. At each one, he signed the score, with the exception of the last two occasions. Once after his death, and on the thirty-first performance, on 17 November 1967 (in brackets it reads: "Shostakovich broke his leg and is just learning to walk again"). This is a dreadful score, it is printed poorly, annotated throughout, and is falling apart, but I always use it and continue to conduct with it until it quite falls apart or I give up. . . .

Together with Dmitry Dmitrevich, we shared many decades of life. We both lived for and breathed for music. Shostakovich is the greatest composer of our time; he was and remains a true chronicler of our day. I have also lived many years and familiar with this same entity and hence all that is created by him is sacred to me, all that he has written is reflected in his symphonies and his entire canon. The difficulties that one experienced with other composers' music were never encountered in his works. It is as if I knew his music within me and it was only for me to muster my forces as best I could to realize them. It seemed that one did not always fulfill all that was written.

In my article written for the composer's sixtieth birthday, I wrote about this and pointed out that the Fifth Symphony, like no other, has sustained trans-formations, visibly changed, and has made in my opinion, its own qualitative development. Why has this happened? First, I was young as was Dmitry Dmitrevich youthful. He had to search for a metronome; we both looked for one and somewhere managed to get hold of one. A metronome is a tricky con-traption. At the beginning we had a problem following it. Now nothing matches the timings of the first performance, hence at each and every per-formance, different timings would be set down for different sections—not only in tempi, but in the entire conception. This relates to the beginning of the first movement, the tempi of the second movement, and to the finale. Perhaps least of all changes are reflected in the slow movement, although it is ac-cepted that one has greater freedom here. But this freedom certainly is a re-sult of a conscious, deliberate process. As a consequence, the Fifth Symphony of 1937 and that of today are quite different from each other.

One must say that one did not recognize the greatness and magnitude of the responsibility that had fallen upon my shoulders. If one was conscious of it, then perhaps I would not have accepted the task. . . . If I were to foresee the whole perspective of this astonishing figure and of this personality in Shostakovich. . . .

Certainly youth always assists one. . . .

Together with Dmitry Dmitrevich, we only expressed a few words about music, except for the Fifth Symphony. . . . All the other symphonies were not subject to such discussion. Both the methodology that I utilized for the Fifth to get him to open up—"What do you want here?" "What would you like here?" I abandoned for good. I simply *immersed* myself in the score and played as well as I could. When we sat together at the piano, I read on his face whether it was spot on or not. The slightest "not wholly true" meant for Dmitry Dmitrevich the greatest despair. He didn't express what he had in mind, but I understood why. . . .

I have great admiration for the Fifteenth Symphony and upon each opportunity attempt to open up new and fresh subtexts. It is difficult to discover these subtexts as the material is actually written simply, sometimes with laconicism or aesthetically. When I performed the Fifteenth, we met at the rehearsals. We usually had such an arrangement in which the composer would sit in on the rehearsals, during which he would make his own notes on his score. Then during the break or afterward preferably (during the interval there was never adequate time), I would open up his score and make my corrections based on his annotations. During the next run-through (we musicians in the orchestra call such—run-throughs), we would make those changes considered necessary by the composer and gradually eliminate those blemishes that in our opinion existed.

The Fifteenth Symphony is the most complex, most profound, and difficult work. To grasp its music, one must slowly remove layer after layer and hence find new and fresh subtexts. The first movement is multithematic, and all the themes are intertwined like figures in an opera. Someone mentioned that this is like a toy-shop—this is nonsense! There is the theme from *William Tell*, although formally it expresses a jolly old sage. In tangible fact it is the theme of fate: throughout there is a periodic appearance of this form of ostentatious musical fabric impeding life. One may say that there are not four movements, but a first, second, and fourth. The third is a scherzo-interlude where the composer appears in some kind of masquerade . . . and the work concludes with a delicate question and a tortuous departure into immortality.

Appendix B

Selected Discography

It is difficult to offer an accurate discography of Mravinsky's recordings, as there are constant reissues of old recordings and issues of formerly unreleased materials. It is true that almost all his recorded legacy is of interest, however I have selected the recordings that represent his finest interpretations, both from the studio and concert hall. Thankfully, Mravinsky's finest recordings have a habit of being reissued and can usually be accessed through one source or another. These, then, are those selected CDs that are available at time of writing.

Bartok Music for Strings, Percussion, and Celesta, CD: 1965, ZYX/Melodiya MEL 46070-2 (1994)
Beethoven Symphonies 5 and 7, CD: Elatus 09274 67192 (2003)
Beethoven Symphony No. 4, 1973, CD: ZYX/Melodiya MEL 46033-2 (1994)
Beethoven Symphony No. 6, CD: Erato 2292-45761-2 (1992)
Brahms Piano Concerto No. 2, 1961, CD: Russian Disc RDCD 11158 (1993)
Brahms Symphony No. 2, 1978, CD: BMG 74321-25190-2 (1995)
Brahms Symphony No. 4, 1973, CD: BMG 74321-29401-2 (1996)
Bruckner Symphony No. 7, 1967, CD: EMI/IMG 7243 575953 (2003)
Bruckner Symphony No. 8, CD: BMG 74321-29402-2 (1996)
Bruckner Symphony No. 9, 1980, CD: ZYX/Melodiya MEL 46011-2 (1993)
Debussy *Prélude à l'après-midi d'un faune*, 1965, CD: BMG 74321-25197-2 (1995)
Glazunov *Raymonda*, CD: Erato 2292-45757-2 (1992)
Glazunov Symphony No. 5, 1969, CD: EMI/IMG 7243 575953 (2003)
Glinka *Ruslan and Lyudmila* overture, 1983, CD: Russian Disc RDCD 10912 (1996)

Lyatoshinsky Symphony No. 3, 1955, CD: Russian Disc RDCD 10902 (1994)

Mozart *Don Giovanni* overture, CD: EMI/IMG 7243 575953 (2003)

Mozart Symphony No. 39, 1972, CD: Erato 2292-45758-2 (1992)

Musorgsky "Dawn on the Moscow River," 1983, CD: Erato 2292-45757-2 (1992)

Prokofiev Symphony No. 6, 1967, CD: Praga PR 256004 (1998)

Prokofiev *Romeo and Juliet* Second Suite, 1982, CD: Philips 420483-2PH (1988)

Rimsky-Korsakov *Legend of Kitezh* prelude, CD: BMG 74321-29408-2 (1996)

Schubert Symphony No. 8, 1978, CD: BMG 74321-25190-2 (1995)

Scriabin *Poem of Ecstasy*, 1978, CD: Russian Disc RDCD 10900 (1994)

Shostakovich Symphony No. 5, 1966, CD: Russian Disc RDCD 11023 (1993); 1978, CD: Praga PR 250085 (1994)

Shostakovich Symphony No. 6, 1972, CD: Praga PR 254017 (1994)

Shostakovich Symphony No. 8, 1960, CD: BBC Legends BBCL 4002-2 (1998)

Shostakovich Symphony No. 10, 1976, CD: BMG 74321-25198-2 (1995)

Shostakovich Violin Concerto No. 1, CD: Praga PR 250052 (1994)

Sibelius "The Swan of Tuonela," 1965, CD: BMG 74321-25191-2 (1995)

Sibelius Symphony No. 7, 1965, CD: Olympia OCD 223 (1988)

Stravinsky *Apollon Musagete*, 1965, CD: BMG 74321-25197-2 (1995)

Tchaikovsky Serenade for Strings, CD: Revelation RV 10055 (1996)

Tchaikovsky *Francesca da Rimini*, 1983, CD: EMI/IMG 7243 575923 (2003)

Tchaikovsky *Nutcracker Suite*, 1981, CD: Philips 420483-2PH (1988)

Tchaikovsky Symphony No. 5, 1956, CD: DG 447423-2GOR2 (1995), 2 disc set; 1982, CD: Revelation RV 10077 (1995)

Tchaikovsky Symphony No. 6, 1956, CD: DG 447423-2GOR2 (1995), 2 disc set; 1960, CD: DG 419747-2 in 419745-2GH2, 2 disc set

Wagner "Ride of the Valkyries," 1978, CD: Erato 2292-45762-2 (1992)

Wagner *Lohengrin* prelude to Act 3, CD: Olympia OCD 224 (1988)

Weber *Oberon* overture, CD: BMG 74321-25190-2 (1995)

Bibliography

Abendroth, Hermann. "Nashi zarubezhniye gosti." *Leningradskaya Pravda*, 25 January 1947.

Akhmatova, Anna. *Stikhitvoreniye*. Moscow, 1961.

Akhmatova, Anna. "Requiem." *Anna Akhmatova works Vol. 2*. Munich: Inter-Language Literary Associates, 1965.

Aleshin, Sergey. "Teatr vremeni—Iosifa, Nikity i Leni." *Ogonyek*, no. 28 (May 2001).

Andronikov, Irakli. *K Muziki*. Moscow: Sovetsky Kompositor, 1975.

Anisimov, A. I. "Novaya simfoniya D. Shostakovicha." *Leningradskaya Pravda*, 12 November 1957.

Anisimov, A. "Za pultom-dirizher Mravinsky." *Leningradskaya Pravda*, 16 April 1958.

Asaf'yev, Boris N. "Cherez proshloye k Buduyuschemu." *Sovetskaya Muzika* (1943).

Asaf'yev, Boris N. "Vosmaya simfoniya Shostakovicha." *Moskovskaya Filarmonia*. Moscow: Iskusstvo, 1945.

Asaf'yev, Boris V. *Akademik B. V. Asaf'yev Isbranniye Trudi, Vols. 2 and 5*. Moscow: Akademiya Nauk SSSR, 1952.

Asaf'yev, Boris N. *Kriticheskiye statyi ocherkii, retzensti*. Moscow: Muzika, 1967.

Asaf'yev, Boris N. *Na baleta*. Moscow: Muzika, 1974.

Avakumov, senior ed. *Leningrad v Velikiye otchestvenniye voine—Dokumenti i Materiali, Vol. 2*. Leningrad, 1947.

Belyakayeva-Kazanskaya, Lyudmila V. *Silueti Musikalnye Piterburg*. St. Petersburg: Lenizdat, 2001.

Ber, M. F. *Orkestrovka melodicheskiykh golosov v proisvedeniye D. D. Shostakovicha, Cherti stilya D. Shostakovicha*. Moscow: Sovetsky Kompositor, 1962.

Berggolts, Olga. *Dnevnye Zvezdy*. Leningrad, 1960.

Berggolts, Olga. *Dni Mechti. Izbranniye Vols. 1 and 2*. Leningrad: Lenizdat, 1967.

Beria, Sergey. *Beria, My Father*. London: Duckworth, 2001.

Bibergan, V. "Udarniye instrumenty v proizvedeniye D. D. Shostakovicha 60–70 godov." In *D. D. Shostakovich v gody Velikoi Otechestvenniye voini*, edited by Sophia M. Khentova. Leningrad: Musika. 1979.

Blazhkov, Igor I. *Shostakovich mezhdu mgnoveniem i vechnostyu*. St. Petersburg: Sovetsky Kompositor, 2000.

Bloch, J-R. "V strane musyki." *Literatura i Iskusstvo*, 7 November 1943.

Bogdanov-Berezovsky, V. M. *Sovetsky Dirizher*. Muzika, 1956.

Bogdanov-Berezovsky, V. M. *Dorogi Iskusstvo, Vol. 1*. Leningrad: Muzika, 1971.

Borisov, Oleg. *Bez znakov prepinaniya, dnevnik 1974–1994*. Moscow: Artist-Rezhisser-Teatr, 1999.

Boult, Adrian C. *My Own Trumpet*. London: Hamish Hamilton, 1973.

Braudo, Yevgeny. "Pyataya simfoniya Shostakovicha." *Rabochaya Moskva*, 1 February 1938.

Bronfin, Evgeny. *Muzikalnaya Kultura Petrograda pervovo poslerevolutsionnovo pyatiletiya 1917–1922*. Leningrad: Sovetsky Kompositor, 1984.

Byalik, Mikhail. "Lyatoshinsky, Mravinsky i drugie." *Sovetskaya Muzika*, no. 1 (1996).

Cardus, Neville. *Manchester Guardian*, 16 September 1960.

Cherkasov, Nikolay K. "1905 god." *Pravda*, 15 November 1957.

Cherkasov, Nikolay K. *Notes of a Soviet Actor*. Moscow: Foreign Languages Publishing House, 1960.

Cherkasova, Nina. *Ryadom s Cherkasovym*. Leningrad: Lenizdat, 1978.

Chulaki, Mikhail. "Vydayuschashisya proizvedeniye." *Smena*, 23 December 1937.

Chulaki, Mikhail. *Izkusstvo i Zhizhn*, 2–3 March 1948.

Chuyev, Felix, *Molotov. Poluderzhavny vlastitel*. Moscow: OLMA, 1999.

Danilevich, Leonid V. "Posle decady." *Sovetskaya Muzika*, no. 12 (1939).

Danilevich, Leonid V. *Sovetskaya Muzika*, nos. 8–9 (1946).

Davydov, R. O. "Devyatoy simfoniya Shostakovicha: perviye vpechatleniya." *Trud*, 16 September 1945.

Dimitriadi, Odissey A. "Dni Yunosti." In *Leningradskaya Konservatoriya v vospominaniyakh 1862–1962*. Leningrad: Gozudarstvenniye Muzikalniye Izdatelstvo, 1962.

Dmitr'yev, Andrey N. *Vospominanii o B. V. Asaf'yeve*. Leningrad: Leninizdat, 1974.

Dolzhansky, A. N. "Kratkiye zamechanii ob Odinnadtsaya simfonii." *Sovetskaya Muzika*, no. 1 (1958).

Dranishnikov, Vladimir A. *B. V. Asaf'yev i evo baletnaya muzika*. Moscow: Izdanie Gozmuz Teatra im Nemirovicha-Danchenko, 1936.

Druskin, Mikhail. "Prekrasni konzert." *Smena*, 20 October 1938.

Entelis, Leonid. "Y A Mravinsky." *Rabochi i Teatr*, no. 36 (1933).

Fadeyev, Andrey A. *Subjectivniye noti, Tridzat letiya*. Moscow: Sovetskiye pisatel, 1957.

Fain, Y. "Poema o krasote ducha chelovecheskovo." *Vecherniye Novosibirsk*, 31 May 1969.

Fomin, Vitaly. *Orkestrom dirizhiruet Mravinsky*. Leningrad: Muzika, 1976.

Fomin, Vitaly. *Stareischey Russki simfonicheski Orkester*. Leningrad: Muzika, 1982.

Fomin, Vitaly. *Dirizher Yevgeny Mravinsky*. Leningrad: Muzika, 1983.

Farnsworth, Beatrice. *Aleksandra Kollontai*. Stanford, CA: Stanford University Press, 1980.

Fried, Oskar. *Pariser Nachrichten*, 21 January 1935.

Furtwängler, Wilhelm. *Tagliche Rundschau*, 25 December 1946.

Gakkel, Leonid E. "Iz nablyudeniye nad konzertnoy zhiznyu Leningrada 50–60 godov." In *Muzika i Muzikantov Leningrada*. Leningrad: Sovetsky Kompositor, 1972.

Gakkel, Leonid E. "Yevgeny Mravinsky—Patritzii za pultom." *Delo*, 2 October 2000.

Gauk, Alexander V. *Memoiri, izbranniye stati, vospominanii sovremminikov*. Moscow: Muzika, 1975.

Gayevsky, V. M. *Dom Petipa*. Moscow: Rezhisser-Teatr, 2000.

Geroicheskaya oborona Petropavlovsk-Kamchatsovo v 1854. Kamchatka: Dalnevostochnoe knizhnoe izdatelstvo, 1979.

Ginzburg, Leonid. "Dva Konzerta." *Izvestia*, 23 May 1940.

Glikman, Izaak D. *Pisma K Drugu*. St. Petersburg: DSCH, 1993.

Glumov, Alexander. *Nestertiye Stroki*. Moscow: Vserossiskiye Teatralnoye Obshestvo, 1977.

Goldbeck, Frederick. *The Perfect Conductor*. London: Dennis Dobson, 1950.

Goldstein, Mikhail. *Zapiski Starogo Muzikanta*. Frankfurt: Posser-Verlag, 1970.

Gorki, Maxim. "O Stasove." In *Vladimir Vasilyevitch Stasov. 1824–1906. K 125-letii so dnya rozhdeniye. Sbornik statei i vospominanii*. Moscow, 1949.

Gozenpud, Abraam. *Russkiye Operniye Teatr mezhdu Dvuch Revolutsiye 1905–1917*. Leningrad: Muzika, 1975.

Gray, Stoll Dennis. *Musical Festivals of the World*. London: Pergamon, 1963.

Grigoryeva, A. P. *Mravina*. Moscow: Sovetsky Kompositor, 1977.

Grikurov, Eduard. "Gody minuvshiye." In *Leningradskaya Konservatoriya v vospominaniyakh 1862–1962*. Leningrad: Gozudarstvenniye Muzikalniye Izdatelstvo, 1962.

Grinberg, M. "Y A Mravinsky." *Sovetskoye Izkusstvo*, 4 October 1938.

Gusev, Pavel. "Drug Baleta." In *Vospominanii o B. V. Asafyeva*. Leningrad: Lenizdat, 1974.

Hakobian, Leonid. *Music of the Soviet Age*. Stockholm: Melos Music Literature, 1998.

Heyworth, Peter. *Observer*, 10 September 1960.

Heyworth, Peter. *Otto Klemperer: His Life and Times Vol. 1*. Cambridge: Cambridge University Press, 1983.

Hitotzuyagnagi, F. "Novy lik Dvehandtzatoy." *Muzikalnaya Akademiya*, no. 4, (1997).

Informatsionii sbornik SSK SSSR, Moscow, no. 7–8 (1945).

Jacobs, Arthur. *Henry J. Wood*. London: Metheun, 1994.

Josefivich, Viktor. "Razgovori s Igorem Oistrakhem." *David Oistrakh*. Moscow: Muzika, 1978.

Kabalevsky, Dmitry M. *Sovetskaya Muzika*, no. 5 (1954).

Karayev, Kara. *Statyi, Pismo, Vospominanii*. Moscow: Sovetsky Kompositor, 1978.

Karsavina, Tamara. *Theatre Street*. London: Constable and Company, 1930.

Khachaturyan, Aram I. "Desyataya simfoniya Shostakovicha." *Sovetskaya Muzika*, no. 3 (1954).

Khachaturyan, Aram I. "Poiski sovremmenovo." *Sovetskaya Kultura*, 24 April 1958.

Khachaturyan, Aram I. *Stranitsi zhisni i tvorchestvo*. Moscow: Sovetsky Kompositor, 1982.

Khaikhin, Boris. "Artisty vyshevo klassa." *Sovetskaya Kultura*, 16 March 1965.

Khentova, Sophia M. *D. D. Shostakovich v gody Velikoi Otechestvenniye voini*. Leningrad: Muzika, 1979.

Khentova, Sophia M. *Molodiye gody Shostakovicha*, Vol. 2. Leningrad: Sovetsky Kompositor, 1980.

Khentova, Sophia M. *Shostakovich—Tridzatiletiye 1945–1975*. Leningrad: Sovetsky Kompositor, 1982.

Khentova, Sophia M. *Udivitelniye Shostakovich*. St. Petersburg: Variant, 1993.

Khubov, Georgy I. "Pyataya simfonia Shostakovicha." *Sovetskaya Muzika*, no. 3 (1938).

Klemperer, Otto. *Izvestia*, 1 January 1925.

Klemperer, Otto. *New York Times*, 5 May 1935.

Kirov, Sergey M., and A. M. Kollontay. "Beseda s Segeyem Mironovichem Kirovym." In *Diplomaticheskiye dnevniki 1922–1940, Vol. 2*. Moscow: Akademiya, 2002.

Kollontay, Alexandra M. "Vospominanii." *Proletarskoi Revolutsie*, no. 3.

Kollontay, Alexandra M. *Den forsta ëtappen*. Stockholm: Bonniers, 1945.

Kollontay, Alexandra M. *Iz Moyei Zhisni i Raboti*. Moscow: Sovetskaya Rossia, 1974.

Kollontay, Alexandra M. *Diplomaticheskiye dnevniki 1922–1940 Vol. 2*. Moscow: Akademiya Izdatelstvo, 2002.

Kolomytseva, V. *Novaya Rus*, no. 16 (1910).

Kondrashin, Kirill P. *Mir Dirizhera*. Moscow: Muzika, 1976.

Kondrashin, Kirill P. "Moy vstrechi s Shostakovichem." In *Dmitry Shostakovich—stati i materiali*, edited by Grigory M Shneerson. Moscow: Sovetsky Kompozitor, 1976.

Koussevitsky, Serge. "O Sedmoy simfonii Shostakovicha." *Pravda*, 3 August 1942.

Kremlyov, Yuri. *Sovetskaya Muzika*, no. 5 (1954).

Kucharsky, Vladislav F. *Sovetskaya Muzika*, no. 10 (1968).

Kuzmin, G. "Svidaniye s volshebnikami." *Vecherniye Chelyabinsk*, 1 May 1969.

Layton, Robert. *Gramophone*, July 1972.

Lebedinsky, Lev. "Revolutsionnii folklor v Odinnadtaya simfonii D. Shostakovicha," *Sovetskaya Muzika*, no. 1 (1958).

Leichtentrit, H. *Serge Koussevitsky, the Boston Symphony Orchestra, and the New American Music*. Cambridge: Cambridge University Press, 1946.

Leonov, Leonid. "Pervie vpechatlenie." *Literatura i iskusstvo*, 7 November 1943.

Leningrad Branch of Union of Composers of the USSR minutes. LGALI F. 9709 OP. 1 C. 37.

"Leningradskaya Philharmonia vosvratilas v rodnoy gorod." *Leningradskaya Pravda*, 8 August 1944.

Levik, S. I. *Chetvert Veka v Opery.* Moscow: Izkusstvo, 1970.

Liberman, Viktor. *Leningradskaya Pravda*, 6 June 1973.

Liberman, Viktor. "Rukovoditel, pedagog, vospitatel." *Sovetskaya Muzika*, no. 6 (1973).

Lunacharsky, Anatoly. "Otvet Komsomolstii Konservatorii." *V Mire Muziki.* Moscow, 1926.

McNeal, R. H., ed. *Na filmax Velikova Zhiznya: Resolutions and Decisions of the CPSU.* Toronto, 1974.

Malko, Nikolay A. *Vospominaniya-Statii-Pisma.* Leningrad: Muzika, 1972.

Makarov, Y. *Muzikalnaya Akademiya*, no. 1 (1993).

Marinina, Irina. "Skazochniye orkester." *Leningradskaya Pravda*, 22 September 1960.

Medvedev. "Po bolshomy schetu." *Sovetskaya Kultura*, 16 February 1961.

Melik-Pashayev, Alexander. *Sovetskaya Muzika*, no. 9 (1963).

Merkuryev, P. "Istoriya odnovo portreta." *Sovetskaya Muzika*, no.10 (1990).

Meyerbeer, Giocomo. "Musical World." In *Notes on Conductors and Conducting*, by T. R. Croger. London: Willam Reeves, 1907.

"Mikhail Alexeyevich Domontovich." *Voennaia Entsiklopedia St Piterburg.* 1912.

Mokreyeva, Galina. *Ruch Muzyczny*, 1 May 1962.

Mikheyeva, Lyudmilla. *II Sollertinsky: zhisn i naslediye.* Leningrad: Sovetsky Kompositor, 1988.

Mikheyeva, Lyudmilla. *Zhisn Dmitriya Shostakovicha.* Moscow: Terra-Terra, 1997.

Mravinsky, Yevgeny A. "Proizvedenie potryasayuschie sili." *Smena*, 28 December 1937.

Mravinsky, Yevgeny A. "Blizhaishi zadachi." *Izvestia*, 17 October 1938.

Mravinsky, Yevgeny A. "Za novi pobedy sovetskovo iskusstva!" *Leningradskaya Pravda*, 18 October 1938.

Mravinsky, Yevgeny A. "Tri Goda v Sibiri." *Sovetsky Sibir*, 16 June 1944.

Mravinsky, Yevgeny A. "Devyataya simfoniya Shostakovicha." *Vechernaya Moskva*, 11 September 1945.

Mravinsky, Yevgeny A. "Odinnadtsatya simfonia Shostakovicha." *Vechernaya Moskva*, 28 September 1957.

Mravinsky, Yevgeny A. "Eto-Nastoyaschiye." *Leningradskaya Pravda*, 25 December 1960.

Mravinsky, Yevgeny A. *Neva*, no. 8 (1961).

Mravinsky, Yevgeny A. "Schastliva pora." In *Leningradskaya Konservatoria v vospominaniyax 1862–1962.* Leningrad: Gozudarstvenniye Muzikalniye Izdatelstvo, 1962.

Mravinsky, Yevgeny A. "Stranichka memuarov." *Sovetskaya Muzika*, no. 4 (1964).

Mravinsky, Yevgeny A. "Tridzat let s muzikoi Shostakovicha." In *D. Shostakovich*, edited by L. V. Danilevich. Moscow: Sovetsky Kompozitor, 1967.

Mravinsky, Yevgeny A. Interview with Konstantin Panferov, "Chitayu sebya schastlivym." *Literaturnaya Rossia*, 3 June 1983.

Mravinsky, Yevgeny A. "S Yevgeniyem Aleksandrovichem Mravinskovovo." In *V Mire Shostakovicha.* Moscow: Kompositor. 1996.

Mravinsky, Yevgeny A. "Iz besed." *Muzikalnaya Akademiya*, no. 4 (1997).

Mravinsky, Yevgeny A. "Iz Dnevniki." *Muzikalnaya Akademiya*, no. 4 (1997).

Napravnik Eduard A. E. F. *Napravnik—avtobiograficheskiye, tvorchesckiye materialii, dokumentii, pisma*. Leningrad: Muzika, 1959.

"Nashi zarubezhni gosti." *Leningradskaya Pravda*, 25 January 1947.

"Nashi zarubezhni gosti." *Leningradskaya Pravda*, 18 June 1947.

Nestyev, Izrael. "Shestaya simfoniya Prokofieva." *Sovetskoye Iskusstvo*, 18 October 1947.

Nestyev, Izrael. *S. S. Prokofyev*. Leningrad: Gozudarstvenniye Muzikalniye Izdatelstvo, 1957.

Nestyev, Izrael, "Simfonia o Russkoi Revolutzii." *Vechernaya Moskva*, 11 November 1957.

Neuhaus, Heinrich H. "Pyataya simfonia." *Vechernaya Moskva*, 31 January 1938.

Neuhaus, Heinrich H. "Yevgeny Mravinsky." *Sovetskoye Iskusstvo*, 18 October 1938.

Nikitina, E. "Byl tsarem i dvornikom." *Kultura*, no. 30 (August 2003).

Novikov, Andrey P. "Zametki-Razmyshleniya." From manuscript in the archive of A. A. Asinovskaya, Novosibirsk.

Oistrakh, David F. *U vas est chemu pouchitsya*. Leningrad: Leningradskaya filarmonia, 1974.

Oleinik, M. "Kutaisskiye vechera (pamyati Evgeniya Mikeladze)." *Muzikalnaya Zhizh*, no. 24 (1988).

Orlova, E., and A. Kryukov. *Akademik Boris Vladimirovich Asaf'yev—monografiya*. Leningrad: Sovetsky Kompositor, 1984.

Popov, I. E. "Odinnadtzaya simfoniya D. Shostakovicha." *Sovetskaya Kultura*, 31 October 1957.

Popova, Nina. *Krepostnaya Aktrisa*. St. Petersburg: Avrora, 2001.

Prokofiev, Sergey S. *Dnevniki*. 17 May 1933. London: sprkiv, 2003.

Rabinovich, David. *Sovetskoye Iskusstvo*, 4 October 1938.

Rabinovich, David. "Dirizher i Orkester." *Leningradskaya Pravda*, 24 May 1940.

Rabinovich, David. *Dmitry Shostakovich*. London: Lawrence and Wishart, 1959.

Radlov, Sergey. *Rabochii i Teatr*, no. 23 (10 September 1931).

Ratzner, Yevgeny. "Poslusheny vole dirizhera: Vystupleniye E. Mravinskovo v Moskve." *Sovetskaya Kultura*, 23 November 1982.

Razhnikov, Vladimir. *Kirill Kondrashin rasskazyvaet*. Moscow: Sovetsky Kompositor, 1989.

Reznikov, Mikhail. *Vospominanii starovo muzikanta*. West Germany: Overseas Publications, 1984.

Rozhdestvensky, Gennady N. *Rodnoy i zhelanniye dom*. Leningrad: Leningradskaya filarmonia, 1972.

Rozhdestvensky, Gennady N., and M. Kopitza. "A kogda voskresnu-ne znayu," *Sovetskaya Muzika*, no. 1 (1996).

Salmanov, Vadim. "Khudozhnik. Myslitel." *Sovetskaya Muzika*, no. 6 (1973).

Sarkisov, Osik, and V. Fomin. *Zasluzhenniye kollektiv RSFSR akademicheskiye simfonicheskiye orkestr filarmonii*. Leningrad: Leningradskaya Philharmonia, Lenizdat, 1972.

Semyonov, F. *Vecherny Leningrad*, 25 May 1961.

Schwartz, Boris. *Music and Musical Life in Soviet Russia 1917–1982*. Bloomington: Indiana University Press, 1983.

Serov, Eduard. *Dirizher Eduard Serov*. Volgograd: Nizhnevolzhskoye, 1993.

Severyanin, Igor. *Tost Otvetny*, Moscow: Respublika, 1999.

Shafran, Daniil B. *Daniil Shafran—Violoncello solo*. Moscow: ACT, 2001.

Shawe-Taylor, Desmond. *Sunday Times*, 18 September 1960.

Shaporin, Yuri. "Diskussionaya zametki o simfonisme." *Sovetskaya Muzika*, no. 5 (1955).

Shchedrin, Rodion. "Leningradskaya ordena Trudovovo Znameni filarmonia." In *stati, vospominanii, materialii*, edited by V. Fomina. Leningrad: Muzika, 1971.

Shebalin, Vissarion M. "Zabytaya simfoniya Glinki." In *Shebalin: Literaturnoye Naslediye*. Moscow: Sovetsky Kompositor, 1975.

Shebalina, Allisya M. "S Alisoy Maksimovnoy Shebalinoy." In *V Mire Shostakovicha*, edited by Sophia M. Khentova. Moscow: Kompositor, 1996.

Shlifstein, Sergey. "Konzerti E. Mravinskovo." *Sovetskoye Iskusstvo*, 24 April 1940.

Shneerson, Grigory. "Zhisn musiki Shostakovicha za rubezhom." *Sovetskaya Muzika*, no. 2 (1948).

Shostakovich, Dmitry D. *New York Times*, 20 December 1931.

Shostakovich, Dmitry D. "Moy tvorchesky otvet." *Vechernaya Moskva*, 23 January 1938.

Shostakovich, Dmitry D. "Yarkii talent." *Smena*, 18 October 1938.

Shostakovich, Dmitry D. "Novy Raboty D. Shostakovicha." *Leningradskaya Pravda*, 28 August 1939.

Shostakovich, Dmitry D. "Zamechatelniye orkester." *Literatura i Iskusstvo*, 1 August 1942.

Shostakovich, Dmitry D. "U Shostakovicha." *Uchitelskaya Gazeta*, 10 September 1942.

Shostakovich, Dmitry D. "Vydayuchy konzert." *Leningradskaya Pravda*, 13 February 1947.

Shostakovich, Dmitry D. "O Desyatoy simfoniya." *Sovetskaya Muzika*, no. 6 (1954).

Shostakovich, Dmitry D. "Kontserti dlya violoncello s orkestrom D. Shostakovicha." In *Isledovaniya, statii, ocherki*. Moscow: Sovetsky Kompositor, 1971.

Shostakovich, Dmitry D. "Sovetskaya muzika v dni voiny." *Sovetskaya Muzika*, no 11 (1975).

Shostakovich, Dmitry D. "D. F. Oistrakh vospominaniya." In *Statii, Intervyu, Pisma*. Moscow: Muzika, 1978.

Sokolsky, M. M. "Zrelost i masterstvo." *Sovetskaya Kultura*, 23 February 1954.

Sollertinsky, Dmitry, and Lyudmilla Sollertinsky. *Pages from the Life of D. Shostakovich*. London: Hale, 1981.

Sollertinsky, Ivan I. "Lebedinoye ozero." *Rabochi i Teatr*, no. 12 (1933).

Sollertinsky, Ivan I. *Rabochi i Teatr*, no. 15 (1933).

Sollertinsky, Ivan I. "Tselunchik." *Rabochi i Teatr*, no. 4 (1934).

Sollertinsky, Ivan I. "Vpered k Noverru." *Rabochi i Teatr*, no. 29 (1934).

Sollertinsky, Ivan I. *Sovetsky Sibir*, 24 June 1942.

Sollertinsky, Ivan I. "Sedmaya simfoniya Shostakovicha." *Sovetskaya Sibir*, 16 July 1942.

Soroker, Y. *David Oistrakh*. Jerusalem, Tarbut, 1981.

Stark, Edward. *Peterburg Operniye masteri 1890–1910*. Leningrad: Iskusstvo, 1940.

Stark, Edward. P. I. *Tchaikovsky on Stage of the Kirov Opera and Ballet*. Leningrad: Kirov Theatre, 1941.

Strauss, Richard. *Tempo*, no. 12 (1938).

Sudoplatov, Pavel A. *Spetzoperatsia—1930–1950*. Moscow, OLMA, 1997.

Svetlanov, Yevgeny F. "Mravinsky." *Sovetskaya Rossia*, 29 January 1972.

Tavastverna, Erik. "Vstrechi s Shostakovichem." In *D. Shostakovich—stati i materiali*, edited by G. M. Shneerson. Moscow: Sovetsky Kompozitor, 1976.

Tolstoy, Alexey. "Pyataya simfoniya Shostakovicha." *Izvestiya*, 28 December 1937.

Toradze, Grigory. *Gruzinskaya Muzika 1917–1941—Istoriya Gruzinskoi Muzika*. Tbilisi: Tbilisi Gosudarstvennaya Konservatoriya imeni Saradzhishvili, 1998.

Tyrkova, Vilionis. *Na putakh k svobodu*. New York: Chekhova, 1952.

Unger, Heinz. *Hammer, Sickle and Baton*, London: Cresset, 1939.

Utesov, Leonid. "Do samovo serdtsa." *Sovetskaya Sibir*, 16 July 1942.

Vainkop, Yuri. "Leningrad kompozitori za raboty." *Sovetskaya Muzika*, no. 8 (1940).

Vainkop, Yuri. "Festival sovetskoi muziki." *Vechernaya Leningrad*, 25 December 1947.

Vavilina, A. M. "Obruchennii Muzikoy." *Muzikalnaya Akademiya*, no. 4 (1997).

Veresayev, Vladimir V. *Sobraniye sochineniye, Vol. 5*. Moscow: Pravda, 1961.

Vieru, Anatole. "Neskolko mysley o Shostakoviche." In *Dmitry Shostakovich*. Moscow, 1977.

Volkhov, N. "Obnovleniya Spektakli." *Sovetskoye Iskusstvo*, 29 June 1935.

Volkhov, Solomon. *Strasti po Tchaikovskomu: razgovori s Georgem Balanchinem*. New York: Slovo Word, 1999.

Volkhov, Solomon. *Istoriya Kulturii Sankt-Piterburga*. Moscow: Nezavisimaya, 2001.

Volkonsky, Sergey M. *Moya vospominaniyi*. Berlin, 1923–1924.

Walter, Bruno. *Of Music and Music-Making*. London: Faber and Faber, 1961.

Werth, Alexander. *Musical Uproar in Moscow*. London: Turnstile, 1949.

Yarustovsky, Boris. *Na Shostakovicha desyataya simfoniya, Sovetskaya Simfonicheskaya Muzika*. Moscow: Muzika.

Yastrebtsova, V. V. *Nikolay Rimsky Korsakov, Vospominanii. Vol. 1, 1886–1897*. Leningrad: Muzgiz, 1959.

Yelagin, Yuri. *Ukroshchenie iskusstv*. New York: Chekhov, 1952.

Yevtushenko, Yevgeny. *Literaturnaya Gazeta*, 19 September 1961.

Yevtushenko, Yevgeny. "The Execution of Stepan Razin." *Bratskaya GES, Yunost*, no. 4 (1965).

Yudin, Gavriil Y. *Za gran yu proshlihk dnei*. Moscow, Muzikalnoe Nasledtsvo-Muzika, 1966.

Yudin, Gavriil Y. "Razroznenniye stranitsii iz vospominaniye o DD Shostakoviche." In *D. Shostakovich, Tridzatiletiye 1945–1975*, edited by L. V. Danilevich. Leningrad: Sovetsky Kompozitor, 1982.

Yudina, Maria. *Luchi Bozhestvenniye Lyubvi.* St. Petersburg: Universitetskaya Kniga, 1999.

Yur'yev, Yuri Y. "Eto ispytivaeyet kazhdy sovetsky grazhdanin." *Sovetsky Sibir*, 16 July 1942.

Zagursky, I. "Moy Konservatorskiye gody." In *Leningradskaya Konservatoriya v vospominaniyakh 1862–1962.* Leningrad: Gozudarsvenniye Muzikalniye Izdatelstvo, 1962.

Zak, Yakov I. "Posle Konkurs Dirizherov." *Sovetskaya Muzika*, no. 4 (1972).

Zhilyaev, Nikolay. *K novym beregam.* Moscow, January 1923.

Zhitomirsky, Dmitry. "Simfoniya B. Lyatoshinskovo." *Sovetskaya Muzika*, no. 2 (1937).

Zhitomirsky, Dmitry. "Noviye proisvedeniye sovetskikh kompositorov." *Informatsionniye sbornik SSK SSSR*, no. 5–6 (1944).

Zolotnitsky, A. *Sergei Radlov: The Shakespearian Fate of a Soviet Director.* Luxembourg: Harwood Academic, 1995.

Zolotov, Andrey A. "Dva pocherka." *Izvestia*, 11 February 1961.

Zolotov, Andrey A. "Klassika nashikh dnei." *Izvestia*, 17 March 1965.

ARCHIVES

Archive of Yalta Region Museum.

Archive of Mravinsky Y. A.

Archives of Novosibirsk Oblast, GANO, f. 1376, op. 1, d. 42.

St. Petersburg Philharmonia Library Archive.

Index

Abbado, Claudio, 229, 231, 233
Abbaza, Julia, 5
Abendroth, Hermann, 60–61, 83, 171
Achkasova-Brandt, Olga, 17
Adam, Adolphe, 43
Akhmatova, Anna, 87, 137–38
Albeniz, Isaac, 49
Alexander 1, Tsar, 1
Alexander 2, Tsar, 1, 4
Alexander 3, Tsar, 4, 5, 7, 10
Amoh, Kenzo, 236, 242
Amosov, Georgy, 59
Anderson, Marian, 61
Andronikov, Irakli, 43
Anosov, Nikolay, 61
Ansermet, Ernest, 60–61, 133–35, 182
Arapov, Boris, 85, 212
Arensky, Anton, 8, 11, 119
Aruntunyan, Alexander, 141
Asafyev, Boris, 28–29, 31, 42, 44, 46–50, 53, 58, 66, 68, 73, 84, 87, 100, 115, 128, 168, 258
Auer, Leopold, 49, 171

Babadzhanyan, Arno, 141, 169
Babel, Isaac, 87
Bach, J. S., 60, 77, 115, 162
Balakirev, Mily, 1, 144
Balanchivadze, Andrey, 56, 169
Balanchivadze, Georgy (Balanchine, George), 17
Barber, Samuel, 209
Barinova, Galina, 132
Barshai, Rudolf, 227
Bartók, Bela, 204, 210, 217
Barutcheva, Era-Sofia, 246
Basner, Venyamin, 169, 185

Baudie, Harald, 182
Beethoven, Ludwig van, 30, 35, 52, 54, 56, 60, 61, 82, 89, 108, 115, 126, 128, 188, 199, 205–7, 218, 228, 241, 247
Beethoven Quartet, 114, 144, 151
Beinum, Eduard van, 172
Belov, Gennady, 212
Berdayev, Nikolay, 80–81
Berggolts, Olga, 87, 97, 106, 125, 212
Beria, Lavrenti, 37–38
Berlioz, Hector, 32, 118, 128, 139–40, 143, 175, 199
Bernstein, Leonard, 133, 233, 242
Berton, Henri, 46
Bezruchenko, Valery, 220, 233
Bizet, Georges, 36, 55, 61, 119–20, 131
Blazhkov, Igor, 199, 208–11
Blech, Leo, 60, 81, 91
Bliss, Sir Arthur, 181
Boccherini, Luigi, 141
Bogdanov-Berezovsky, Valerian, 32, 71, 73, 100, 135, 173, 212
Bogoslovsky, Nikita, 65
Bolshoy Theatre, orchestra of, 56, 65, 79, 114
Bonaparte, Napoleon, 1
Borisov, Oleg, 239–40, 248
Borodin, Alexander, 1, 59, 65, 73, 119–20, 132, 144, 185, 188, 199
Bosch, Heironymous, 170
Boult, Sir Adrian, 133, 164
Brahms, Johannes, 16, 28, 38, 55, 89, 102, 118, 127–28, 132, 140, 143, 151, 178–79, 188, 204, 208, 220, 226, 228, 231, 247, 253
Braudo, Issay, 218
Brezhnev, Leonid, 195, 250
Brik Ilya, 53, 57–58, 79, 126
Britten, Sir Benjamin, 181, 220

Bruckner, Anton, 28, 82–83, 90–91, 119–20, 128, 143, 220, 242–43
Bunin, Revol, 136
Busch, Fritz, 81
Buyanovsky, Vitaly, 59, 178, 206, 221
Böhm, Karl, 172, 233, 238, 241

Cardus, Sir Neville, 181
Casadeseus, Robert, 61
Celibidache, Sergiu, 109
Chabrier, Emmanuel, 119
Chabukiani, Vasso, 41
Chakirov, Emil, 239
Chekhov, Anton, 112, 160
Cherepnin, Nikolay, 11, 32, 119
Cherkasov, Nikolay, 19–24, 54, 64–65, 89, 92, 97, 99–101, 119, 175, 216
Cherkassova, Nina, 101
Chernov, Prof., 27–28
Cherubini, Luigi, 46
Clutyens, Andre, 81
Coates, Albert, 15–16, 23, 42
Cooper, Emil, 23, 42, 52–53, 80–81
Corelli, Arcangelo, 183
Cùi, César, 1
Czech Philharmonic Orchestra, 133–35

Danilevich, Lev, 117
Dargomyszhky, Alexander, 8, 20
Davidenko, Alexander, 30
De Rezke, the brothers, 9
Debussy, Claude, 30, 60, 118–19, 131, 165, 206, 210, 217
Delibes, Leo, 119
Denisov, Edison, 210
Deshevov, Vladimir, 142
Désormière, Roger, 73
Devetzy, Vasso, 206
Dmitrev, Alexander, 229, 236
Dmitrev, Vladimir, 42, 44, 48
Dobrowen, Issay, 109
Dolukhanova, Zara, 139
Domontovich, Konstantin, 5
Domontovich, Mikhail, 2, 3, 4, 5
Dorliak, Nina, 139
Dostoyevsky, Fyodor, 2, 30, 52, 112
Downes, Olwin, 109
Dranishnikov, Vladimir, 28, 42, 49, 61, 66
Drigo Riccardo, 44, 119
Druskin, Mikhail, 58, 78, 80
Dudinskaya, Natalia, 24, 41, 43
Dunayevsky, Isaak, 66, 72, 77, 85
Dvořák, Antonin, 126, 141, 208

Eisenstein, Sergey, 64, 138
El Greco, 170
Elenu, Prof., 171
Eliasberg, Karl, 61, 79, 89, 91, 100, 125, 162

Eliot, T. S., 138
Enesco, Georges, 61

Fadeyev, Alexander, 71, 138
Fayer, Yuri, 114
Figner, Nikolay and Medea, 9
Filkova, Yelizaveta, 14, 18
Fitelberg, Gregorz, 80
Fournier, Pierre, 61,
Franck, Cesar, 55, 169
Fried, Oscar, 29–30, 61, 77
Furtseva, Yekaterina, 203, 208, 212–13, 216–17, 232, 234
Furtwangler, Wilhelm, 109, 172, 208

Gakkel, Leonid, 156–57, 173
Gaklin, David, 150–51
Galsworthy, John, 180
Galynin, Valery, 169
Gauk, Alexander, 32–33, 36–38, 52, 59, 61, 71, 77, 80, 129, 131, 151, 152–53, 168, 173, 177–78, 194
Genshaft, Yakov, 35
Gensler, Vladimir, 59, 89, 108
Gerdt, Elizaveta, 23, 97
Gershwin, George, 209
Gilels, Emil, 73, 77, 213, 229
Giulini, Carlo Maria, 241
Glazounov, Alexander, 9, 11, 17, 20, 27–28, 30, 41–42, 53, 119–20, 144, 188, 207, 216, 219–20, 242
neglect of, 58–59
Glazounov Quartet, 108
Glière, Reinhold, 30, 41
Glikman, Gavriil, 196, 286
Glikman, Izaak, 43, 71, 85, 113, 115, 168, 185, 195–96, 198–99, 215–16, 228, 100, 252, 253, 254, 256
Glinka, Mikhail, 1, 8, 9, 11, 20, 58–59, 65, 115, 119–20, 128, 132, 143–44, 188, 228, 250
discovery of music by, 33
Glinka State Choir, 91–92, 198–99
Glumov, Alexander, 56, 69–70
Gmyrya, Boris, 195–97
Gnessin, Mikhail, 68
Gogol, Nikolay, 8, 52, 126
Goldenweiser, Alexandr, 77, 129
Goldstein, Boris, 60, 73
Goldstein, Mark, 143
Golovanov, Nikolay, 53, 61, 114, 145
Golubev, Yevgeny, 85
Gossêc, F.-J. 46
Gounod, Charles, 6, 7, 32, 35
Goya, 248
Granados, Enrique, 49
Grechaninov, Alexander, 11
Greenfield, Edward, 173
Grétry, A.-E.-M., 46

Grieg, Edvard, 57–58, 119
Grigorovitch, Yuri, 231, 239
Grikurov, Eduard, 31
Grossman, Alexander, 187
Gusev, Pavel, 48
Gvozdev, Alexey, 42

Hanisegh, Rudolf, 241
Haydn, Joseph, 119, 129, 141
Heifitz, Jascha, 61, 172
Heyworth, Peter, 180
Hindemith, Paul, 28, 206, 210
Honneger, Arthur, 119, 205, 210, 217

Ivanov, Konstantin, 78, 151
Ivanovs, Janis, 169, 177
Ives, Charles, 209–10

Janacék, Leos, 135
Jansons, Arvids, 143–44, 150, 184, 187, 211, 242
Jansons, Mariss, 243
Jena, 171, 222

Kabalevsky, Dmitry, 30, 33, 77, 104, 142, 158–59, 170
Kalinnikov, Vassily, 11, 140–41, 144
Karajan, Herbert von, 160, 172, 208, 221, 241
Karayev, Kara, 153, 216
Karpinsky, Prof., 54
Karpova, Olga, 92, 99, 110, 133, 163–65, 205
Kawashima, Midori, 232–233
Keilholz, Heinrich, 172
Khachaturyan, Aram, 30, 33, 41, 61, 68, 79–80, 85, 87, 104, 129, 135, 136, 138, 158–59, 174, 188
Khaikhin, Boris, 61, 91, 178
Khodasevich, Valentina, 42, 46
Khrapchenko, Vladimir, 111
Khrennikov, Tikhon, 158, 236
Khruschev, Nikita, 181, 212, 234
Kirov Theatre, 48, 66, 79–80, 83, 90–91, 97, 120, 163, 212, 235
Kirov, Sergey, 42–43, 48
  assassination of, 77
Kleiber, Erich, 60
Klemperer, Otto, 29, 33, 38, 42, 47, 60, 83, 172
Kletzki, Paul, 208
Klyuzner, Boris, 143, 169, 175, 206
Knabbertsbusch, Otto, 60
Kneller, Georgy, 142, 220, 226
Knussevitsky, Svyatoslav, 91
Kochurov, Mark, 85
Kodaly, Zoltan, 134
Kogan, Leonid, 141, 213
Kollontay, Alexandra:
  7th symphony, 109
  at debut of YAM, 43

description of 1905, 175–76
  influenced by, 36
  reminscences about Mravina, 27, 36, 109, 145, 163, 175, 213
  support by, 27
  visit to Italy, 5, 6, 9
Kompanietz, Zinovy, 85
Kondrashin, Kirill, 61, 78–79, 81, 98, 114, 151, 153, 187, 198, 200, 215–16, 238
Konwitschny, Franz, 238
Kotlayevsky, Arseny, 142
Koussevitsky, Serge, 80, 91, 109, 133, 221
Koval, Maryan, 31, 116, 158
Kozlov, Akim, 59
Kozlovsky, Ivan, 214
Krauss, Clemens, 83
Krips, Josef, 134, 172
Kukharsky, Vasily, 158, 209–10, 230
Kurlin, Vladimir, 220
Kushnarev, Prof., 28

Lemeshev, Sergey, 114
Lenin, Vladimir, 27–28, 28–29, 85, 108, 186, 213, 219, 221, 229
Leningrad Drama Theatre, 101
Leningrad Jazz Orchestra, 101
Leningrad Philharmonic Orchestra, 79
  anniversary celebrations, 226–27, 249–50
  debut, 52
  formation and state support, 52–53
  sound of, 57–58, 125–26, 134, 174, 212, 221, 233–34
Leningrad Radio Orchestra, 65, 79, 125, 162–63, 165
Leséuer, J.-F., 46
Leskov, Nikolay, 112
Levitin, Yuri, 131, 135, 139, 141
Liberman, Viktor, 204–5, 220, 226, 232, 237
Lisitsian Pavel, 49, 132
Liszt, Franz, 35, 81, 119, 144, 165, 172, 188
Lohse, Wolfgang, 172
Lokhin, Alexandr, 118
Lopatnikov, Viktor, 235, 250
Lopukhov, Fedor, 42
Ludewig Alexey, 127, 218, 220
Lunacharsky, Anatole, 18–19, 27
Lyadov, Anatole, 119, 217, 219
Lyapounov, Sergey, 144
Lyatoshinsky, Boris, 169–70
Lyuk, Ekaterina, 23

Maazel, Lorin, 231
Macharavani, Alexey, 142
Mahler, Gustav, 29, 83, 102, 108, 120, 129, 218, 254
  cult of, 58
Mainardi, Enrico, 61
Maksakova, Mariya, 114

Malko, Nikolay, 32, 72, 80, 194
Maréchal, Maurice, 61
Margolin, Venjamin, 180, 187, 221
Mariinsky Theatre, 6, 41, 255
Markevitch, Igor, 231
Massalin, Alexander, 2, 3, 4
Massalina, Alexandra, 2, 3, 4, 5, 11
Massenet, Jules, 7, 119
Matsov, Roman, 144
Mayboroda, Vladimir, 16
Méhul, Etienne, 46
Melik-Pashayev, Alexander, 32, 33, 36–7, 52, 78–79, 92, 114, 151
Melodiya, 209, 226–27, 231
Menuhin, Yehudi, 133, 181
Meyerbeer, Giacomino, 9, 80
Meyerhold, Vsevolod, 87
Mikeladze, Yevgeny, 32–33, 37–38, 56–57
Mikhailov, Mikhail, 114
Miklashevsky, Iosif, 92
Milstein, Nathan, 172
Mitropoulos, Dmitros, 159
Mokreyeva, Galina, 209
Molotov, Vyacheslav, 77
Moresko-Erede, Emmi, 216–17
Moscow Chamber Orchestra, 227
Moscow Philharmonic, 65, 79, 89, 198, 200
Moscow Radio Orchestra, 65, 79, 131, 145, 152
Mosolov, Alexander, 30, 88,
Mozart, Wolfgang Amadeus, 78–79, 102, 126, 129, 156, 170–71, 179, 217, 228, 247
Mravina, Jenny:
    early years, 2, 4, 5, 41, 240
    first singing reminiscences, 7–10
    retirement and death in Yalta, 11
    visit to Italy, 6
Mravinskaya, Adèle
    birth and marriage of, 2, 5
    death of son, 36
Mravinskaya (Filkova), Yelizaveta, 14, 21–22, 26–27, 64, 92, 99, 102, 177
    death of, 177
Mravinsky, Alexander, 2, 14–15, 18
Mravinsky, Yevgeny:
    1965 Moscow tour, 212–17
    1st symphony, 247–48
    2nd symphony, 231–32
    3rd symphony, 205, 210
    3rd symphony, 226, 235
    4th symphony, 56, 167, 204, 220, 229–30, 253
    5th symphony, 59–60, 151–52, 206, 210, 217, 220, 227, 242, 247–48, 253
    5th symphony, attitude toward, 218, 233, 236, 220
    6th symphony, 60, 204, 217, 220, 236, 238, 239
    7th symphony, 220, 235

    9th symphony, 235, 242–43
    50th birthday, 152
    70th birthday, 231–32
    75th birthday, 240
    80th birthday, 250
    acquintance with Mravina, 11
    appointment to Philharmonic, 79
    article by, 73, 176, 182–83
    articles, 73, 130, 182–83, 237–38, 240
    attempted sacking, 214, 235
    attitude to Israel, 226
    attitude to Lenin, 219
    attitude to nature, 112, 156, 162, 218, 230
    Bártok, 188–89, 204, 210, 217, 226. *See also* Bártok
    Beethoven bicentenary, 222
    Beethoven, 35, 82–83, 126, 128, 167, 218, 205, 184, 205–6, 233, 243, 247, 255. *See also* Beethoven
    Berlioz, 118, 139–40, 143, 243. *See also* Berlioz
    birth of 14
    Borodin, 59, 188, 204. *See also* Borodin
    Brahms, 118, 128, 140, 243, 255. *See also* Brahms
    Bruckner, 82–83, 90, 124, 143, 128, 220, 243. *See also* Bruckner
    call to Moscow, 111
    childhood 15,
    compositions, 30
    conducting competition, 77–78
    Corelli, 83
    daughter Lena, 164
    Debussy, 165, 118, 131, 205, 217, 254. *See also* Debussy
    debut at Leningrad Ballet Theatre, 43
    debut at Philharmonic, 52
    debut in Moscow, 48
    defence of Shostakovich in 1948, 138
    diary entries, 127–28, 145, 150, 154–55, 168, 173, 228
    early working life, 34
    emotional life, 206–7, 214, 217, 240, 249
    entry to Conservatoire, 29
    first attraction to music 15–16
    first rejection at Conservatoire, 26–27
    Glazunov, 144, 207, 219, 243. *See also* Glazunov
    Handel, 82–83
    Haydn, 82, 175. *See also* Haydn
    Hindemith, 206, 210, 226. *See also* Hindemith
    Honegger, 118, 187, 205, 210, 217, 226. *See also* Honneger
    Japan Mravinsky Society, 233
    Khachaturyan, 68, 79, 133. *See also* Khachaturyan
    letter to Stalin, 151–52

lifestyle and friendships, 19–24, 36–7, 43,
    64–5, 67, 87–88, 99–100, 133, 137,
    152–53, 162, 164, 166, 173, 194, 196,
    204, 213–14, 216, 230, 252–53
Liszt, 35, 60, 152. *See also* Liszt
Lyadov, 217, 219. *See also* Lyadov
Mahler, 82, 254. *See also* Mahler
meetings with Shostakovich, 34, 66–67, 214
memorial concerts for and appreciation of
    Shostakovich, 66–67, 214–16, 227, 229,
    237, 255, 257
Mici, F., 143
morals, first studies 18, 19
Mozart, 35, 78–79, 83, 103, 165, 168–69,
    197, 171–72, 177–78, 204, 217, 226,
    236, 238, 249, 251. *See also* Mozart
naming as "Vasya," 221, 187
The Nutcracker, 239, 248, 250
outbreak of war, 97–98
performances of Bach, 60, 77–78, 82–83,
    188. *See also* Bach
performing style, 54, 57, 67–68, 81–82, 89,
    107, 139–40, 145, 165–66, 169–70,
    177–78, 189, 236, 243, 246, 248, 250
popularity in Japan, 232
premiere of Shostakovich's 10th symphony,
    153–57, 167, 237
premiere of Shostakovich's 11th symphony,
    174–76
premiere of Shostakovich's 12th symphony,
    185–87, 195
premiere of Shostakovich's 13th symphony,
    194–200, 215
premiere of Shostakovich's 15th symphony,
    227–28, 247, 251, 260
premiere of Shostakovich's 5th symphony,
    61, 65–74, 257, 259–60
premiere of Shostakovich's 6th symphony,
    85–87, 127, 167, 203, 257
premiere of Shostakovich's 7th symphony,
    108–13, 125–26, 144–45
premiere of Shostakovich's 8th symphony,
    112, 125–26, 197, 226, 237, 247,
    257–59,
premiere of Shostakovich's 9th symphony,
    129–31
premiere of Shostakovich's cello concerto 1,
    178
premiere of Shostakovich's violin concerto,
    168–69, 171
Prokofiev memorial concert, 153
Prokofiev, 84, 104, 118, 165, 167, 133, 135,
    141, 167, 205, 227, 233, 235–36, 238,
    246, 249, 179, 184, 205, 243, 250. *See
    also* Prokofiev
Ravel, 128, 131, 254
recording of Shostakovich's 12th symphony,
    187

recording of Shostakovish's 11th symphony,
    177
recording of Shostakovish's 7th symphony,
    150–51
recordings, 145, 150–51, 172–73, 182, 187,
    241, 252, 255
rehearsal routine, 113–14, 131–32, 135–36,
    155–56, 168, 180, 185, 208, 211, 226
remaining in Russia, 34
reminscences, 238, 246–47, 250–51
removal from touring, 225–26, 225
restoration of relations with Shostakovich,
    227–29
return to Leningrad, 121–22, 125–26
reviews of Moscow performances, 89–90,
    140, 165, 226–27
Rimsky-Korsakov, 58–59, 188. *See also*
    Rimsky-Korsakov
Schubert's 8th symphony, 126, 232, 239,
    251, 253. *See also* Schubert
Schumann, 243
Scriabin, 59, 83–84, 235. *See also* Scriabin
Shcerbachyov, 90
Shostakovich, 34, 104, 134, 165, 167, 172,
    204–5, 214–15, 217, 221, 227, 236–37,
    243, 249. *See also* Shostakovich
Sibelius, 184, 210, 226, 238. *See also*
    Sibelius
Strauss, Richard, 44–45, 206, 235, 246
Stravinsky, 58–59, 131, 208–10, 226–27.
    See also Stravinsky
study of other conductors, 16, 20, 22–23,
    55–56, 60–61, 81, 135
Tchaikovsky, 35, 43, 49, 58, 60, 77–78, 84,
    90, 131, 199, 208, 228, 243, 246, 249,
    255. *See also* Tchaikovsky
teaching, 64, 207
tour to Prague Festival, 133–34, 165, 173, 217
TV documentary, 229–32, 247–51, 257
Violin Concerto, 58, 167–69, 172, 204
Wagner, 60, 80, 83, 203–4, 226, 247. *See
    also* Wagner
Weber, 168, 239
work on Lyatoshinsky, 169–70
Mrovinsky, Konstantin, early career, marriage,
    and assasination affair, 2–5
Munch, Charles, 133–35
Muradeli, Vano, 71, 118, 137
Muradyan, Liya, 248–49, 254
Musin, Ilya, 32, 38, 61
Musorgsky, Modeste, 1, 19–21, 52, 65, 73, 79,
    119, 109, 128, 132, 175, 185, 188, 238, 249,
    251–52
Mussolini, Benito, 77
Myaskovsky, Nikolay, 30–31, 68, 71, 77, 104,
    116, 127, 138, 159, 174, 188
    appraisal of music, 142
    death of, 142

Napravnik, Eduard, 8–9, 42
Nelepp, Georgy, 49
Nemirovich-Danchenko, Vladimir, 89
Nestyev Israel, 71, 130, 175
Neuhaus, Heinrich, 72, 77–78, 129
Nevéu, Ginette, 61
Nevsky, Alexander, 3, 64, 100, 104, 118, 138, 174, 199
Nikisch, Arthur, 29, 32–33, 68, 172
Nikitin, Alexander, 220
Nikolay II, Tsar, 10, 14
Nikolayev, Leonid, 43
Nikolayeva, Lydia, 164, 205
Nikolsky Gleb, 252
Noverre, 46
Novikov, Alexey, 120,
Nureyev, Rudolf, 212, 241

Oborin, Lev, 61, 68, 73, 77, 79, 85, 92, 139, 151, 133
Odnoposov, Riccardo, 133
Oistrakh, David, 57, 73, 77, 128, 133, 159, 167–68, 187, 213–14, 229–30, 233–34
Orakhvelashvili Ketevan, 37, 56
Orbeli, Isaak, 54
Orlov, Alexander, 61
Ormandy, Eugene, 189
Ossovsky, Alexander, 28, 53
Ovsyaniko-Kulikovsky, Nikolay 143

Paganini, Nicolo, 90
Paisin, Abraam 85
Pakhomova, Galina, 212, 234–35, 250
Paliashvili, Zakhari, 56
Pasovsky, Ariy, 48–49, 77, 114
Paverman, Mark, 79, 120
Pechersky, Lev, 221
Pergolesi, Giovanni, 183
Peter the 1st, 1, 86, 235, 253
Petipa, Maurice, 48
Petrov, Andrey, 169, 212, 252
Piotrovsky, Adrian, 42
Polyakin, Miron, 82
Ponomarenko, Pantelion, 157–58
Popov, Gavriil, 30, 116
Preobrazhenskaya, Sophia, 49
Prigozhin, Sergey, 169
Prishvin, Ivan, 112
Prokofiev, Sergey, 30, 37–38, 41, 57, 84, 104, 116, 118, 129, 133, 135, 136–37, 142, 159, 165, 174, 188, 199, 205, 220, 249
Pryanishnikov, Ippolit, 5, 6, 7
Purcell, Henry, 183
Pushkin Theatre, 27, 54, 98–99, 101, 103, 119
Pushkin, Alexander, 5, 52, 85, 108, 195, 253

Rabinovich, Dmitry, 78, 116–17, 159

Rabinovich, Nikolay, 32, 61, 64, 89, 91, 100, 103, 120, 185, 215, 218
Rachmaninov, Sergey, 30, 33, 42, 59–60, 80, 119, 132, 179, 188, 218, 243, 33
appointment to Mavrinsky, 42–44
resignation, 49–50
Rakhlin, Nathan, 78, 111, 169, 174, 228
Ratsbaum, Albert, 187
Ravel, Maurice, 108, 126, 128, 131
Rehrberg, Grigory, 231
Reizen, Mark, 49
Retrovskaya, Galina, 221
Richter, Svyatoslav, 128–29, 139, 144, 151–53, 157, 214, 230, 232
Rimsky-Korsakov, Nikolay, 1, 8, 21, 41, 53, 58–59, 65, 80, 84, 119, 132, 249
letter to from Mravina, 20
Rodionov, Nikolay, 212, 219
Rodzinsky, Arthur, 81, 118
Romanov, Grigory, 212–13, 218, 226, 234–35
Rossini, Giacomo, 10, 119, 132
Rostropovich, Mstislav, 139, 180, 200, 215
Rozhdestvensky, Dmitry, 249
Rozhdestvensky, Gennady, 179–80, 187, 200, 221, 226
Rozhdestvensky, Robert, 194
Rubinstein, Anton, 1, 35, 56, 102
Ryazanov, Prof., 28

Safonov, Vassily, 33, 87
Saint-Saëns, Camille, 60, 119–20, 132, 178
appreciation of Mravina, 7
Salmanov, Vadim, 142, 156, 206, 212, 232, 238–39, 247, 249, 251
Samosud, Samuil, 61, 77, 107, 114, 129
Sanderling, Kurt, 58, 77, 91, 165, 106, 120–21, 187, 131, 140, 150, 172–73, 239
Sanderling, Thomas, 103, 179
Saradzhayev, Konstantin, 53, 61
Sarkissov, Osik, 215
Scherbachyov, Vladimir, 28, 66, 86–87, 118, 141, 144
Scherchen, Hermann, 60
Schiller, Professor, 173
Schnabel, Arthur, 61
Schneider, Helmut, 182
Schoenberg, Arnold, 209–10
Schubert, Franz, 56, 119, 126, 232, 239, 241, 249, 253
Schuman, William, 209
Schumann, Gerhard, 233
Schumann, Robert, 91, 129, 141, 172, 243,
Schwalk, Marianna, 26, 163, 205
Schwartz, Boris, 160, 232
Scriabin, Alexander, 30, 59, 77, 83–84, 91, 119, 169, 235
neglect of 59, 83–84
Sebastyan Georges, 77, 83

Segovia, Andrés, 172
Serebryakov, Pavel, 55, 59
Sergeyev, Konstantin:
  meeting with YAM, 23–24
  at theater, 41–42, 162
Serikova, Inna, 163–65
  death of, 206–7
  illness of, 197, 199–201, 203–4, 255
  teaching by, 165
Serov, Alexander, 8, 20–21
Serov, Eduard, 8, 142, 207–8, 211, 235, 252–53
Shafran, Boris, 58, 90, 120, 169
Shafran, Daniil, 60, 73, 77, 141
Shakespeare, William, 64, 87, 116, 239
Shalyapin, Fedor, 19–21, 162
Shaporin, Yuri, 43, 129, 158
Shaw-Taylor, Desmond, 181
Shchedrin, Rodion, 217, 236
Shebalin, Vissarion, 30–31, 58, 70, 86–87, 102, 107, 118, 138, 144, 153, 171
Sherman, Issay, 32
Shishmarev, Vladimir, 68
Shkolnikov, Mark, 32
Shkolnikov, Nikolay, 103
Shlifstein, Sergey, 84, 89, 109, 111
Shneiderman, David, 142
Sholokhov, Mikhail, 213
Shostakovich, Dmitry, 30, 34, 41, 43, 53, 138, 213–14
  1st symphony, 199
  2nd and 3rd symphonies, 208–9
  4th symphony, 198
  5th symphony, 61, 66–74, 85–87, 120–21, 134, 156, 195, 212, 214–15, 231, 238, 249, 253
  6th symphony, 85–87, 203, 206, 227, 237–38
  7th symphony, 106–25, 108, 150, 104, 106 150–51, 214
  8th symphony, 125–26, 134–36, 197, 214, 226, 237
  9th symphony, 129–30
  10th symphony, 153–60, 158–59, 237
  11th symphony, 213, 228
  12th symphony, 195, 213, 221, 249, 251
  13th, "Babi Yar, " 195–200
  14th symphony, 227
  15th symphony, 227, 231, 251
  death of, 236–37
  cello concerto no. 2, 215
  socialization with, 214, 227
  Song of the Forests, 199
  violin concerto, 167–68
Shostakovich, Irina (Supinskaya), 195, 228
Shostakovich, Maxim, 215–16, 218, 237
Shpilberg, Ilya, 58, 86, 90, 108
Shteiman, Mikhail, 61

Shteinberg, Lev, 61, 77
Shteinberg, Prof., 28, 90
Shtogarenko, Andrey, 169
Sibelius, Jan, 132, 179, 184, 210
Silvestrov, Valentin, 210
Simonov, Konstantin, 61, 118
Simonov, Yuri, 238
Slonimsky, Sergey, 141, 169, 212, 219
Smetana, Bedrich, 119, 135
Sofronitsky, Vladimir, 43, 84, 139, 145, 214
Sokolov, Grigory, 211
Sollertinsky, Ivan, 35, 42, 44–45, 54, 58, 71, 79, 91–92, 98, 100–102, 108, 111–12, 102–3, 107, 116
Solzhenitsyn, Alexander, 213
  death of, 120–21, 136
Spendiarov, Alexander, 11
Stadler, Vadim, 180, 220
Stalin, Iosif, 60, 87–88, 101, 151–52, 186, 194–95, 213
Stanislavsky, Konstantin, 89
Stasevich, Abraam, 120
Stasov, Vladimir, 8, 214
State Symphony Orchestra, USSR, 60, 77, 79, 86, 111–12, 115, 118, 130, 140–42, 151–53, 157, 174, 258
Steidry, Fritz, 43, 53–55, 58–59, 61, 67, 80–81, 83, 172, 247
Steinberg, William, 83
Stokowski, Leopold, 73
Strauss, Johann the younger, 119
Strauss, Richard, 30, 44–45, 91, 206, 235, 246
Stravinsky, Fedor, colloboration with Mravina, 7
Stravinsky, Igor, 17, 21, 28, 102, 108, 131, 135, 188, 208–9, 238
  neglect of, 58
Strem, Valentina Augustova, 15
Suk, Vyacheslav, 54, 61
Suslov, Mikhail, 195
Svetlanov, Yevgeny, 187, 214, 227
Sviridov, Georgy, 60, 68, 107, 174
Szell, George, 189
Széngar, Eugene, 81, 83
Szigéti, Josef, 59

Talich, Vaclav, 61, 83, 135, 173
Taktakishvili, Otari, 56, 177
Taneyev, Sergey, 119
Tarkovsky, Andrey, 231
Tavastverna, Erik, 134
Tchaikovsky, Boris, 169
Tchaikovsky, Piotr, 1, 5, 8, 15–17, 20, 21, 35, 41, 49, 52–54, 57, 60, 68, 73, 77–78, 80, 90–91, 93, 151, 165, 170, 188, 204, 210, 216–17, 239, 253
  comparisons of Shostakovich premiere with *Pathetique*, 68

Mravinsky's debut, 30
  taste in, 84, 170
Telemann, Georg, 183
Temirkanov, Yuri, 212
Teplitzky, Mark, 85
Thompson, Virgil, 109
Tischenko, Boris, 165, 207, 212, 217–18, 220,
  227–28, 238, 252
Tolstoy, Alexey, 70
Tolstoy, Lev, 2, 84
Tomars, Prof., 31
Tomilin, Viktor, 68, 85
Toscanini, Arturo, 109, 113, 151, 240
Trisno, Boris, 59
Tsaritsa Mariya, 10
Tsaritsa Yevdokiya, 139
Tses, Gerhard, 231
Tsvetaeva, Marina, 87
Tytovich, Andrey, 169
Tyulin, Prof., 28

Ulanova, Galina, 24, 41, 45, 47–48, 90, 213,
  231
Unger, Elga, 54
Unger, Heinz, 33, 65, 83
Ustvolskaya, Galina, 142, 169, 174, 192, 212
Utesov, Leonid, 107

Vaganova, Agrippina, 23, 42
Vaiman, Mark, 142, 169
Vainonen, Vasily, 42, 45
Vainonis, Stasis, 169
Varese, Edgar, 209–10
Vasilyev, Alexander, 59, 81, 90, 108
Vavilina, Alexandra, 164, 198–99, 205–7, 217,
  228, 235–36, 241–42, 252
  marriage to, 217
  protection of YAM, 219, 226, 235
Vavilov, Sergey, 151
Vecheslova, Tatyana, 34
Vecheslova-Snetkova, 23
Verdi, Guiseppe, 9, 35
Vishnevsky, Prof., 27
Vivaldi, Antonio, 91

Volkonsky, Andrey, 209
Volovnik, Iosif, 84
Voznesensky, Andrey, 194

Wagner, Richard, 16, 23, 30, 55, 60, 80,
  90–91, 93, 119, 140, 143, 203–4, 226, 238,
  252
Wainberg, Mozhey, 154
Walter, Bruno, 32, 43, 54, 60, 81, 83, 172, 241,
  247
Weber, Carl von Maria, 119–20, 132, 239, 241
Webern, Anton, 209–10
Weingartner, Felix von, 60, 172
Weisberg, Juliya, 68
Werth, Alexander, 137
Wolf, Hugo, 218
Wood, Sir Henry, 181

Yakobson, Leonid, 45
Yakunina, Yevgeniya, 110
Yegorov, Prof., 26
Yershov, Ivan, 16, 21, 28, 35, 53, 28, 70, 89
Yevlyakhov, Orest, 87, 212
Yevtushenko, Yevgeny, 194
Yudin, Gavriil, 61, 131
Yudina, Mariya, 43, 82, 139, 145
Yurlov State Choir, 200
Yuryev, Yuri, 43, 82, 88, 107, 119

Zak, Yakov, 73, 132
Zakharov, Leonid, 47–48
Zavetnovsky, Viktor, 58, 81, 87, 126
Zelichman, Iya, 211
Zemlinsky, Alexander von, 83
Zhelobinsky, Valery, 68, 86
Zhemchugova, Praskovya, 6
Zhilyaev, Nikolay, 87
Zhivotov, Alexey, 27, 57, 60, 90, 131, 135
Zhukov, Georgy, Marshal, 247
Zhukov, Mikhail, 79
Zolotov, Andrey, 184, 210, 227, 229–31, 236,
  240, 247
Zolotova, Olga, 230
Zoschenko, Mikhail, 137

About the Author

Gregor Tassie was born in Bristol, England, in 1953. He was educated in Glasgow, Scotland, where he studied Russian, music, and engineering and was awarded degrees from Glasgow University. He worked in the Soviet Union between 1977 and 1986, in 1991 organized the Prokofiev Centenary Festival, and subsequently acted as a concert agent. He has written numerous articles on music and performance in magazines such as *The Gramophone*, *Musical Opinion*, and *Classical Record Collector*, has worked on research projects for the BBC and documentary films, and has contributed notes for CD programs. Mr. Tassie presently teaches in Glasgow.